ITALY 1943-1945

THE POLITICS OF LIBERATION SERIES

General Editors: Geoffrey Warner and David W. Ellwood

David W. Ellwood

ITALY 1943-1945

Holmes & Meier
New York

First published in the United States of America 1985 by
Holmes & Meier Publishers, Inc.
30 Irving Place
New York, NY 10003

Designed by Douglas Martin
Phototypeset by Alan Sutton Publishing Limited, Gloucester
Printed in Great Britain by The Pitman Press, Bath

The publication of this book has been assisted by a grant from the
Twenty-Seven Foundation

Library of Congress Cataloging in Publication Data

Ellwood, David W.
Italy, 1943–1945
(The Politics of Liberation Series)
Bibliography: P.
Includes Index.
1. World War, 1939–1945—Italy.   2. Italy—
History—Allied Occupation, 1943–1947.   3. Italy
—Politics and Government—1943–1947. 4. Re-
construction (1939–1945)—Italy.   I. Title.
II. Series
D763.18E38 1985   940.53'45   85-859

ISBN 0-8419-0987-3

Contents

Illustrations

Editors' foreword

EARLY IN 1945, Josef Stalin enunciated the following proposition to a visiting delegation of Yugoslav Communists: 'This war is not as in the past; whoever occupies a territory imposes on it his own social system. Everyone imposes his own system as far as his army has power to do so. It cannot be otherwise.' (Milovan Djilas, *Conversations with Stalin.*) The purpose of the volumes in the Politics of Liberation series is to examine the liberation of Europe at the end of the Second World War in the light of this statement, which involves taking a new look at the link between international and national politics in both western and eastern Europe from the moment when the defeat of the Axis became apparent to that when the boundaries of the post-war political, economic and social systems were definitively established. The act of liberation from German occupation is seen as the focal point of this period, and the series sets out to examine the way in which the perceived national interests of the liberating powers – Britain, America and Russia – were translated into policies in the liberated countries, and the extent to which these policies were modified to take account of local forces and situations. In particular, while it has long been recognized that a key factor in the communization of eastern Europe was its liberation by the Red Army, the role played by Anglo-American forces in influencing developments in western Europe has received much less attention, and the series will aim to redress this balance.

Of necessity, each country is the subject of a separate volume in the series, but a common framework of enquiry unites them all. A number of areas have been defined as being of particular importance in each investigation: the nature of the country's political, economic and social system prior to enemy occupation during the Second World War and the impact of the occupation on this system; the nature, strength and long-term objectives of the Resistance movement in the country, its relationship to political forces from the pre-war era and to outside influences during the conflict; and the composition, strength and objectives of a government in exile or a well-defined alternative leadership abroad, if any, and the relationship of such a leadership with the host government. Examination has also to be made of the plans of the liberating power or powers with regard to the country, their attitudes towards the interests and activities of each other in the country, and the contrasts, if any, between their short-term and long-term objectives. The form of the liberation process itself, its speed and duration, the machinery used to regulate relations inside the country and the degree of intervention by the liberating powers in the country's process of reconstruction at its earliest stage all must be considered. Finally, the duration or otherwise of the political, economic and social arrangements which emerged at the time of liberation and the traces of the conflicts of that time remaining to the present day are critically examined.

Within this common approach, individual authors have nevertheless been left considerable scope to draw out specific features of each national situation; practical comparison is left to the reader. It is hoped that in this way questions will emerge which will take the comparative politics of the Second World War in Europe beyond the venerable problems of the 'origins of the Cold War', the 'development of European unity', or the 'rebirth of European democracy' round which they have revolved for so long. Much of the writing on resistance and liberation in the Anglo-Saxon world has so far tended to concentrate on the military as opposed to the political and economic aspects of the subject and while no one would want to deny the value of this kind of history it is clearly incomplete.

The sources for a series as envisaged are now plentiful. The German archives for the Second World War, which go into considerable detail concerning the politics, economics, etc. of occupied Europe have been available for research for some years. More recently, extensive British and American archives have been opened to scholarship. Nearly every European country has an institute for the study of its wartime resistance movement in which are to be found collections of primary documents, clandestine newspapers, oral testimony and other sources. While Russian archives are not of course open to unauthorized researchers from the West, the amount of Russian literature dealing with the role of the U.S.S.R. in liberating eastern Europe and based upon these archives is now voluminous. Individual East European governments and communist parties have also published collections of documents and official histories of the subject. In addition, all the contributors to the series are familiar with the local historiography of the countries they treat and are thus able to take into consideration the influence of debates and analyses not normally accessible to the English-speaking reader.

It is proposed that the series cover as many European countries as possible. Initially, however, four countries will be considered: Belgium, France, Italy and Poland. The choice reflects the interests of the editors, the availability of the authors and the desirability of including an east European country at the earliest possible stage. Students of the individual countries, of the Second World War in Europe, of contemporary international history and comparative European politics will all, we hope, find useful, new and stimulating material in the volumes of this series.

G.W./D.W.E.

Preface

AS THE SHELVES continue to fill up with books on the Second World War, so the gaps become clearer. We now know a good deal about what happened in the Balkans, a great deal less about what happened in Russia, much about the British military and their operations, relatively little about British foreign policy, and still less of Whitehall's (or anyone else's) overseas economic operations. When this work was begun Italy was clearly the major European battleground neglected by English-speaking historians of the Second World War. In the intervening years this situation, surprisingly, has not changed and it is therefore with particular interest, and some apprehension, that we await the reaction to the work offered here of the public, the professionals and those who were there.

Essentially this book deals with 'the politics of war' in Italy, but it attempts to do so in a way which includes economic realities as an essential part of the overall picture. In addition to the usual mass of official papers (British, American and Italian) have been added where possible the comments of the press, in the belief that policy-makers did not act in a vacuum of opinion, not even when the press was extremely fragmented, as in Italy, or where public interest in the Italian situation was relatively low, as in Britain during the war. In this context, as in the decision-making process itself, the opportunity to confront British and American approaches to the same problems turned out to be richly rewarding, sometimes curious, often full of unintended irony; it is a method probably worth applying to other events in recent international history.

This material first appeared in the shape of a Ph.D. thesis, discussed in the University of Reading in 1977. However, the genesis of that project took place in the Bologna Center of the John Hopkins University, School of Advanced International Studies, in 1971, under the auspices of the director, the late Professor C. Grove Haines, and Professor E. Krippendorff. Grants by the Ministero degli Affari esteri, Rome, and Scuola normale superiore, Pisa, the University of Reading and the Istituto universitario di Studi europei, Turin, enabled the basic research to be undertaken and I remain extremely grateful to those institutions for their support. The Ph.D. thesis appeared in a somewhat shorter form as a book, *L'alleato nemico. La politica dell'occupazione anglo-americana in Italia 1943–1946* (Milan, 1977), published under the auspices of the Istituto nazionale per la Storia del Movimento di

Liberazione in Italia. The present work has been substantially modified as a result of criticisms made of that volume. It is much shorter – while containing sections on the Resistance movement and the Trieste question not present in the earlier text – and incorporates the result of recent research by others in this area.

For their continuing interest and encouragement I should like to thank Gianni Perona and the Istituto storico della Resistenza in Piemonte, Turin (without whom the original project might never have been completed), Professors Guido Quazza, Turin, and Enzo Collotti, Milan, and the staffs of the network of institutes for the history of the Resistance movement, which continue to be indispensable reference points for anyone working in the field of contemporary history in Italy. Friends and fellow researchers Ennio Di Nolfo, Elena Aga-Rossi, John L. Harper and above all James Miller have always been supportive while the staff of Leicester University Press, in particular Peter Boulton, also deserve sincere thanks. Most deserving of recognition, however, is my fellow-editor, Geoffrey Warner, who has read and analysed each succeeding version with extraordinary patience and professionalism. For the content of the pages that follow, however, the author as usual bears sole responsibility.

Bologna, March 1984

'EVEN PEOPLE who were not there remembered vividly exactly what happened next'

Joseph Heller, *Catch-22* (1982 edition, 359)

Introduction

THIS BOOK deals with the liberation of Italy on two distinct but related levels. On one level we have the story of the Italian Question in international politics after the surrender of September 1943, of Italy's fate as the first grand test of cooperation between the Big Three of the anti-Hitler coalition, and scene – some would say victim – of their first efforts to invent policies for liberated Europe. On the second level there is the Allied presence inside the country. Here the key elements are the immensely destructive and painful war campaign, the installation of a military government destined to be present at every level of Italian life and very similar to a regime of occupation, and finally the laborious attempts to demonstrate to Italians a way forward for their future, both politically and economically, after the fall of Fascism and the subsequent collapse of the State. During the course of the prolonged war effort challenges to the Allied view of the Italian situation emerged in the form of the renascent political forces of liberated Italy, finally in the 'wind from the North' of the Resistance movement: they fit into the picture at all those points where Allied, essentially Anglo-American, intentions and local aspirations confronted each other.

For much of the time the international and internal dimensions tended to develop separately, each following its own logic. But at the two most crucial moments of the story they came together: in September 1943, when the armistice was signed, and in April 1945 at the time of the final liberation of the country. The liberation of Italy was a very confused and disorderly affair of which no one on the Allied side was particularly proud in the end, but at no point was it more so than after the surrender of Mussolini's successor, Marshal Pietro Badoglio. Our opening chapters attempt to piece together and make sense of this story in the light of the established facts and the documentation now available. However, the point to be made here is that the documents eventually signed were largely of British origin, and it is British policy and British men who dominate much of what we have to recount, in spite of the fact that the liberation was nominally a joint Anglo-American affair. Since the British had urged the Mediterranean campaign and the invasion of Italy on their American comrades-in-arms, and wished to be 'senior partner' in the whole business, since the British had detailed plans, as we shall see, to make Italy pay for her role in the war, so it was the British who triumphed over the armistice, which turned out to be extremely punitive and provided for a full-scale military occupation of the country. The local commanders and their political advisers soon discovered that many elements of Italian life – ex-Fascists, non-Fascists, anti-Fascists – wished Italy to become a kind of ally and that they needed Italian help to keep life going behind the lines and to fight the campaign. The result was the idea of 'co-belligerency,' 'which means treating the Italians as friends and foes at the same time', as the Foreign Office said disparagingly. But as long as the armistice held, and as long as the British insisted on its application, Italy was frozen into the position of being a country without sovereignty or its own voice, defeated and in effect occupied.

This was the first decisive moment in the history of the Italian liberation, and it reveals how the international and internal dimensions were to interact. Eighteen months afterwards, the final liberation of the North took place with great speed and drama and in an atmosphere many saw as pre-revolutionary. The Resistance had by now become a mass movement with its own dynamic in the factories and towns, as well as in the mountains and plains. Although its fighting potential was very largely the product of Communist Party organization and manpower, as a whole – and it was remarkably united all things considered – the movement represented a quite new factor on the political scene, explicitly demanding a break with the past and a radical reform of the State and of Italian political development. Moreover governments supposedly under the banner of anti-Fascism had been meeting in Rome for nearly a year. The Italians in other words had acquired a political voice of their own and a whole range of views on their future.

Other factors too had changed the balance of debit and credit: the participation of Italian military forces in the Allied war effort, the Italian material resources devoted to it, the willingness of the population as a whole to accept the consequences of the Fascist defeat, and the enthusiasm for the Anglo-American armies of liberation. How would all this be taken into account now that the final reckoning was at hand? Would the Italians get a rapid and favourable peace treaty, and help to enable them to recover and take their place with the United Nations? Or would they still be victims of the vindictiveness or confusion of the Big Three?

By the summer of 1945, of course, the situation at this level had changed dramatically. A gulf of suspicion separated the British and Americans from the Russians, who although excluded from the Allied management of post-Fascist Italy were presumed to have a potent bridgehead there in the shape of the Italian Communist Party (PCI). Between the British and Americans, who had tried to maintain a united front in Italy, things were hardly less difficult. The Americans by now had progressive plans for the country (if not the means to put them into effect), and wished to bring their power in the situation into line with their commitment of men, material and money. The British in contrast continued to insist on maintaining the essentials of the armistice in order to get the peace they thought appropriate, that is a punitive one. Yet at the same time they feared American withdrawal, feared the rise of communism, and feared social collapse and disorder in the chaos of the post-liberation months.

The result was that the Italians paid again for their war experience and for the contradictions in the Big Three coalition and for the world-shaking power struggle going on within it at that time. The Resistance movement's eventual neutralization, the continuation of the armistice regime up to 1946, governments in Rome without power or authority, long delays in starting free political processes and elections, confusion and waste in long-promised economic aid programmes, all reflected to some degree the lack of commitment by the United Nations, or by any of the Allies, to a genuine, constructive interest in Italy's future in 1945. Later, when the Cold War really got under way, the indifference would disappear and the country would be regarded as a prime battleground. In 1945 there were men in Washington and Rome who had become involved in Italy's problems, knew how serious the situation was and who fought bureaucratic (but not political) battles to unblock it. But they had little success: no one at the top had sufficient time or interest in those days. The Italians' new post-Fascist voice was largely ignored.

The Italians of course recovered from it all and carried out a far more robust and faster reconstruction – especially of their economic life – than anyone would have given them credit for in the war years. As we shall see, few elements in Italian life took a positive attitude to the Allied presence, which was rarely up to the expectations the British and Americans helped to generate with their massive propaganda efforts. Grateful for the liberation from Nazi-Fascism, thankful for the food and supplies, anxious to restart their peacetime activities, most Italians seem to have hoped above all that the entire experience would end as quickly as possible and that 'gli anglo-americani' and all their paraphernalia would then go home.

Allied commanders concerned with 'civil affairs' – as all the realities behind the lines were called – must have often felt the same. Their training, attitudes and inclinations ill-fitted them to deal with the intricacies of local politics, or the chaos which arises when a State administration breaks down in wartime, not to mention all the demands of economic life, from the supply of water to the control of inflation. Inevitably the resources were inadequate to the gravity of the human and physical situation on the ground; so were the pre-liberation plans, often too complex, too inflexible and too abstract compared with reality. So although there is much which comes under criticism in this book in terms of attitudes and policy decisions, there was also a great deal of hardship and suffering which simply could not be avoided as long as the country was a battleground.

IT SHOULD NEVER be forgotten that the liberation of Italy took far longer than anyone expected. When Sicily was invaded and Mussolini fell in July 1943, Rome in the autumn seemed a realistic possibility. When the autumn came and with it the surrender, no one doubted that the Eternal City could be gained within weeks. Then of course came the remarkably swift, efficient and massive German response, flooding the entire area north of Rome with ten new divisions. Naples was entered by the Allies only in October, then winter descended and they were taken aback by its severity. Only in January 1944 could a fresh assault be envisaged and after the bitter battles of Anzio came Monte Cassino, the infamous fortified monastery on the road to Rome which held up the advance from February to May. Rome fell only in June 1944, in the same days as the Normandy landings. The Americans at this point had their way, withdrawing seven of their eleven divisions in Italy to implement their own plans in France, but the British were optimistic nevertheless. If the rhythm of the summer advance could be maintained, then the North might be freed and even central Europe penetrated by late autumn, said the military planners at Allied Force Headquarters (AFHQ). Again the Germans surprised everyone, falling back on a massive, purpose-built fortification spanning the country from Massa Carrara to Pesaro, known as the Gothic Line. A new autumn campaign was mounted by the Allied armies in Italy and the end was confidently predicted for November or December. They were beaten off, and in the worst winter in living memory the armies remained deadlocked 15 miles south of Bologna for over five months. Only in March–April 1945 did the final push at last turn out to be what it promised. The effects of all this on the politics and economics of the war in Italy are apparent wherever one looks at the story.

When military progress stopped for months on end, the Anglo-American allies lost prestige, especially the British who were always the keenest supporters of the Italian campaign and provided its supreme commanders after December 1943. The British line on any subject became harder to fight for *vis-à-vis* the Russians and Americans at the top level; in Italy itself local politicians became more troublesome; and in related areas which the British considered important to them, such as the Balkans, their influence declined. In those days, as the Foreign Office was all too aware, the currency of power was military success and without it the fight to hold one's own in the jockeying for stakes in liberated Europe became very much more difficult.

As for action inside the boundaries of free Italy, the more the Anglo-American presence and assumption of power was prolonged, the more the confusion and half-heartedness of 'civil affairs' planning became obvious. Within the command machinery interminable arguments broke out over the extent of Allied responsibilities, over the armistice and its enforcement, over relations with Italian institutions and political life. By the end of 1943 the key Americans present had become convinced that the British were trying to dominate the Italian situation for their own ends, and the passage of time only exacerbated the resentments which sprang up, often involving London and Washington directly. The machinery of the Allied presence proved far too cumbersome to deal with local conditions, while demands on it actually increased in the extended absence of local administration. Yet it proved practically unreformable and embarrassment over its effects grew as the self-confidence of Italian political forces returned and the challenges of the future came closer.

The economic costs of the war obviously mushroomed the longer it went on. This meant not just increased outlays for the fighting armies, but vast problems of feeding, clothing and sheltering the direct victims of war and the indirect victims of total economic dislocation. Aid programmes were improvised and put into action as fast as the machinery at home would allow, but by the spring of 1945 this constant use of first aid methods just to prevent 'disease and unrest' (the military formula of the time) was clearly inadequate. Decisions were required on aid for long-term rehabilitation and reconstruction, on what the British and Americans would do separately for the country, if anything, and on how the Italians could be helped to help themselves. Here again a substantial difference of interest and vision had sprung up between the Americans and the British, since the Americans had supplied far more aid in terms of finance and supplies than the British, took a more expansive, benevolent view of their responsibilities in this area and were ready to contemplate long-term reform of the Italian economy. To the Americans' considerable resentment, their allies were neither able nor willing to take such an interest in Italy's economic future in 1945, although both shared the view that the solutions to many of Italy's political problems, in particular the rise of a powerful Communist Party, were economic in nature.

Thus there often spread in high quarters a feeling that the Italian situation was 'bogged down', that the questions which arose, especially the political and economic ones, were intractable, confused and messy, without any clear-cut, easily accessible solutions. Overall objectives were easy to state: as Roosevelt and Churchill said in September 1944 when announcing the first real package of aid and political support to Italy since the armistice:

> We all wish to speed the day when the last vestiges of Fascism in Italy will have been wiped out, when the last German will have left Italian soil, and when there will be no need of any Allied troops to remain – the day when free elections can be held throughout Italy and when Italy can earn her proper place in the great family of free nations.

But it proved difficult to gain anything like the necessary degree of control of the situation on the ground or even the attention of the controllers of supplies, of propaganda, of military government, of the Allied soldiery itself, for long enough to give substance to these auguries. Part of the Resistance began to see ulterior motives behind the 'snail-like' pace of the Allied advance and even in the centre and south of the country there was by the end of 1944 gloomy surprise that so potent and vast a war machine should produce so much confusion and so little progress either against the Germans or in favour of the Italians. Rich material for novelists and film-makers was to come from all this.

LEAVING ASIDE for a moment the objective evolution of the war in Italy, how were decisions made about the policies and their execution? Who were the key men involved and what was the machinery they created and ran?

On the spot all power inevitably lay in the hands of the huge, multinational Allied armies, where it was embodied in the person of the Supreme Allied Commander Mediterranean (SACMED). Even now the scale and complexity of the military machine strikes the imagination. In the early phases there were headquarters in north Africa, in Sicily and Brindisi; there were American armies and British armies and corresponding fleets and air forces, which, constantly in motion, transformed and united the whole Mediterranean 'theater'. The memoirs of those present at the top give an impression of intense movement and glamour, of hard work in exciting surroundings, of brilliant personages thoroughly involved in their war while conscious that the worst was probably over and victory could only be a matter of time. Visitors from London or Washington noted how the key men moved 'with their courts', and reflected ironically on the scale and grandeur of the military headquarters, especially after AFHQ had become installed in the vast Bourbon palace at Caserta, near Naples.

Three supreme commanders ruled over the campaign in succession. The invasion of Italy was launched and some of the hardest strategic choices were faced by Eisenhower, under whose auspices a number of significant American military men came to the fore: Bedell Smith, Patton and Mark Clark among them. It was Eisenhower who did most to strike a balance between the British and Americans in the management of the surrender crisis, and who insisted that military, not political, priorities should decide the nature of the Allied presence in the first liberated country in Europe. Eisenhower was unable to mitigate the agony of the armistice, but he did his best to abbreviate it and to encourage a positive attitude to post-Fascist Italy's immediate problems.

Eisenhower's successor, the bluff, soldierly figure of H. M. 'Jumbo' Wilson, reigned from the end of 1943 to December 1944. A classical product of the British imperial experience – South Africa, the North-West Frontier of India, Egypt – Wilson left much of the running of the campaign, at least after Anzio, to the commander of the Allied Armies in Italy (their formal title from February 1944), Harold Alexander, his own attention being much taken up by events in the Balkans and elsewhere. Although he generally showed scant interest in Italian internal affairs, Wilson began urging on Washington and London the need for positive political concessions to Italy from early 1944, when he realized how late the full liberation might be. But his own attitude to his responsibilities was rarely creative and he has left little trace in the political history of the war.

Harold Alexander presents an interesting contrast. This tough but unassuming and cultured soldier was destined to plough a thankless furrow after so much of his army was taken away to southern France in the summer of 1944, and there has been endless debate about his subsequent campaign strategy. But Alexander was also a general capable of looking political problems in the face and formulating a point of view on them. On the armistice Alexander opposed a strictly punitive attitude, and even insisted that when it came to the peace, Italy should keep her empire as an outlet for exports and emigration. It was Alexander who first told the Foreign Office that they must get used to the idea of the United States 'taking the lead' in Italy, and that it was in fact in the British interest to get them 'well-embedded' there. By the end of the war Alexander was worrying over how to rebuild Italy as a 'second-class' power able to withstand the presumed threats from the Communist Party inside the country and the Soviets to the East. Concluding his campaign as the third Supreme Allied Commander, Alexander played an important role in the months during and after the liberation.

Beyond the military men, who formally took their orders from the Combined Chiefs of Staff Committee (CCS) seated in Washington, we find the decisive influence on Italian policy wielded by Roosevelt and Churchill, assisted by a small group of ministers and functionaries, with the key dividing line drawn between the British and American sides.

In Washington the major decisions were invariably taken by Roosevelt, sometimes aided by Hopkins, but almost never by people outside the White House. At one point the president even telegraphed to the British prime minister telling him that if only the two of them could run 'the Italian business' all would be well; 'we would not need anyone else'. If it was difficult to interest Roosevelt on any single subject for more than a few moments, then Italy was certainly not one of them. The fragmentary references he made were full of praise for the fighting men and the democratic values they bore, but evasive on America's long-term intentions. For many months Roosevelt preferred to postpone consideration of political questions on Italy – as on all else – until the end of hostilities, and in the early phases at least he seems to have been inclined to let the British take over entirely. This attitude began to change when the president realized how important the Italian-American vote would be in his 1944 re-election campaign, but by then a more aware attitude to the problems of liberated Europe was developing in many other parts of Washington. This was particularly the case in the State Department, which had shown itself adept at drawing up detailed plans for the reconstruction of every country it knew of, but weak at influencing key policies or even their day-to-day management. Prodded by a vigilant press with influential observers in Italy, energized by a new secretary, Edward R. Stettinius, from late autumn 1944, the Department began to draw up specific policy options and recommendations in time for the Yalta conference.

American faces tended to come and go much more frequently at AFHQ than British ones, and there were far fewer who were significant figures in their own right. In the early phases the rule was established that the supreme commander should be flanked by a British and an American political adviser (called a Resident Minister in the British case to increase his prestige), and the first American to hold the position was the well-known diplomat Robert Murphy. His British counterpart was Harold Macmillan, and the two, said Murphy, 'got along famously together', or as Macmillan put it: 'There is no man with whom I had a more pleasant relationship, often in difficult and baffling circumstances, and whose character I grew so quickly both to appreciate and to admire'.

However, Murphy left with Eisenhower, to be succeeded by an almost unknown figure, the career diplomat Alexander Kirk. Kirk was a curious remnant from the early days of modern American diplomacy, when the profession was occasionally chosen by wealthy individualists, and he is movingly described in this light by one of his most illustrious pupils, George Kennan. He was scorned by the British for his low profile and his awkward moralizing about what the Allies ought to be doing for the country, but Kirk was a shrewd reader of the Italian situation – and British policy towards it – even if his views apparently had little impact in Washington (a partial cause of his eventual resignation in 1946).

A more weighty American presence was that of Myron P. Taylor, the former head of U.S. Steel, who was Roosevelt's personal ambassador to Pope Pius XII. A gentleman extremely conscious of his dignity, Taylor took care to have almost all of his communications recorded for posterity, and they have by now been published and analysed in detail (see bibliography). They reveal the efforts of one intent on becoming the sole go-between linking the Vatican and the White House, mediating particular situations in Italy in which American interests appeared to him to be involved, and later transmitting the pope's message of anti-communism and of the need for a continued American presence in Italy after the war. One of Taylor's recurrent themes in his personal letters to Roosevelt concerned the alleged evil-doing of the British on the scene, whom Taylor accused in the autumn of 1944 of arrogance and intolerance in their conduct of the Italian occupation/liberation. As we shall see, it was a common complaint among Americans returning to Washington from a tour of duty in Italy.

Right or wrong, it was in fact the British who for most of the time provided the senior men and much of the soldiery in Italy concerned with 'civil affairs', who sent over a stream of important figures either to observe or to participate in the running of the country and whose prime minister showed the keenest interest in what went on. Policy was made by a small group of people at the top, largely unhindered by the normal impact of public opinion. In the last analysis only four people really counted during the war period: Churchill and Eden in London, and Alexander, the military commander, and Harold Macmillan, the British resident minister, at AFHQ. There was of course considerable tension between them and each had his own view of the situation, although those on the spot were almost invariably more favourably disposed towards the possibilities of the Italian situation than those at home.

Churchill vacillated. He could be cruel or kind according to his own mood or according to political opportunity. He came to Rome in August 1944 and was angry and belligerent, wanting only to be tough: 'Italy had done us great damage and must be punished and ground down', he told a Foreign Office representative present. He left to cheering crowds and was clearly impressed; he even told Stalin so at Moscow in December. For Italy as a power he had no use whatsoever, but for her as a battleground, a field of display for British arms, he could not have been more enthusiastic. Alexander was known to be his favourite general and he liked to see British armies fighting. In common with everyone else concerned with Italy, Churchill too became seriously worried by the rise of the Communist Party in the country after the spring of 1944, but unlike others the prime minister maintained a particular flexibility of attitude and his own brand of hard realism.

Eden was violently anti-Italian. His unpleasant, even humiliating experiences at Mussolini's hands had obviously left very bad memories. To these were added the almost racist scorn for the Italian – not Fascist – war effort which he shared with the popular press. Eden was convinced that Italians were Fascists to a man and had only changed sides when they were obviously losing. On a despatch from the leading British diplomatic representative in Rome advocating a more forward-looking policy Eden thundered: 'This is the worst despatch – because the most remote from reality – that I have ever read from one of our Ambassadors abroad. I suppose . . . Sir Noel Charles has forgotten which country was our ally and which our enemy in the war that is not yet won. But the British people haven't forgotten nor have I'. This was July 1944. A year later things had not improved and Alexander told the Americans in Italy that Eden would block any opening towards the ex-enemy. He was considered 'irrational, even psychopathic' on Italy even by his own functionaries in the Foreign Office, according to Alexander.

If this were true they never said as much on paper. The Foreign Office and Eden worked extremely well together and made up a formidable, united hierarchy. As it was from here that much of the day-to-day running of British policy was carried out, the six or seven functionaries below Eden had considerable power. Their outlook was not substantially different from that of their minister, though they used a different tone. To the suggestion that Italy receive a reconstruction loan from Britain at the end of the war, one of them remarked that it would be considered 'outrageous by us individually as well as by the public', and the issue went no further. The Foreign Office was not above using the cheapest stereotypes, denouncing the faintly ridiculous Italian declaration of war on Japan of July 1945 as 'yet another stab in the back . . . [but] it is, after all, in their nature so to do'. And in the face of direct evidence to the contrary, the men of the Foreign Office insisted that the average British soldier thought the Italian people 'a pretty feckless crew – which, in the South at least, they are'.

The one person willing and able to challenge this kind of outburst was Harold Macmillan. 'We are playing our hand very foolishly with regard to Italy,' he writes in April 1945, 'there seems to be a kind of childish animosity towards the Italians which does not do us or them any good. Can [we] not exorcize this spirit from Whitehall?' Until he leaves the theatre in May 1945 – after 'liberating' Modena in a jeep – Macmillan is the crucial figure in Allied – not just British – action towards Italy, advising, predicting, suggesting and acting, very often on his own account. 'Macmillan's power at the time, however temporary, was colossal,' says his first biographer, Anthony Sampson, 'perhaps more absolute than it ever would be again.' Macmillan's reputation is to some extent in eclipse at the moment: too glib, too egoistic and superficial is the accusation. But for sheer political intelligence he towered above all others at the time, certainly at that crowded military court at Caserta.

It was Macmillan who finally cut short the surrender drama, who contributed more than anyone to the manœuvres which kept the Russians out of the Italian occupation, who reorganized the sickly military government machinery in 1944. It was Macmillan who first insisted that a strictly punitive line by the British would be counter-productive, that economic power would eventually determine who was to supervise the Italian reconstruction, and that the Americans would and should take over in the end. His master-stroke was the agreement with the northern Resistance command, the Committee of National Liberation of Upper Italy (CLNAI), in December 1944. By clever psychological and political manœuvring Macmillan succeeded in gaining a stranglehold over the Resistance movement from which it never recovered, at least in political terms. The dispersion and disorientation of the Resistance after April 1945 were in a sense Macmillan's 'victory', if such it can be called in view of the lasting rancour it produced. Although he did not oppose it as far as we know, Macmillan never used the language of British hegemony for Italy, unlike so many others, but then he was a politician, not a diplomat, and he could see quite clearly in whose favour the wind was blowing.

After the war ended there was of course a period of upheaval and the four dominating wartime figures all dispersed, to be replaced by Labour politicians with very little knowledge of or interest in southern Europe. Macmillan was not replaced at all, and in terms of personalities the only link with the past was the chief British diplomat Sir Noel Charles, a career diplomat previously in Brazil, who soldiered on until the Peace Treaty was signed at the end of 1947. Sir Noel had long been a supporter of dominant British influence in Italy and it is interesting to trace the downward curve of his rhetoric on this subject as the months passed after the end of hostilities. It was Sir Noel too who was in the best position to chronicle the rise of American influence, in particular after Alexander Kirk was replaced in 1946 by the formidable and energetic James Clement Dunn, formerly head of the State Department's Office of European Affairs. Since the wishes and sensibilities of the Americans were the principal outside factor conditioning British policy towards Italy – in 1946 even more so than in 1943 – the arrival of this important figure from the State Department hierarchy signified that Churchill, Macmillan and Alexander could count on one satisfaction: the Americans were on the way to being 'well-embedded' in Italy.

FINALLY, a word on the nature of the country and the society which surrendered to the Allies in September 1943, six weeks after the end of Fascism's 20-year reign. All observers agree on the confusion, resentment and passivity which dominated the atmosphere during that historic summer. The end of Fascism and its war was initially greeted with relief and joy, but fear of the Germans and the prospect of a full-scale clash between Allied and German armies on their soil soon took away from the Italians and their rulers any hope of better times to come in the future: no one knew what to do or what would happen.

The country had in fact been on a war footing to a constantly growing degree ever since the Abyssinian adventure and the regime's economic revolution of 1935–6. At that time economic self-sufficiency was elevated to the level of a system called 'autarky': these were Mussolini's responses to the world economic crisis. From then on, through the Spanish Civil War to the invasion of France in 1940 there was an unceasing effort mobilizing people, resources and industries to play the role of a Great Power locked into the Pact of Steel with Hitler. Although production did increase and armies were raised and battles fought, there was nothing like the total mobilization of all sections of society visible in Germany and Britain, and the social costs of autarky and war together were such that the experience of conflict, far from uniting people and government as elsewhere (or even in Italy itself during the early part of the First World War), gradually split them further and further apart. Eventually came the point in 1943 when even the social groups who had been Fascism's promoters and supporters, the semi-feudal large landowners, the owners of heavy industry, the officer class, the petit bourgeoisie of rentiers and smallholders, lost faith and saw that the game was up.

For while Fascism had been many things to many men, it was also a state of mind in its believers which sought tranquillity, not conflict or adventure, order instead of change, respect for authority rather than open battle over claims and choices. When in the post-First World War chaos which culminated in the occupation of the factories in Turin, an organization emerged ready to use violence to do what the State seemed incapable of doing – namely crush the Reds and instil a proper respect for established authority and traditional interests – then the *squadristi* had their day and Mussolini, the supreme political operator of his time, rode the wave and steered it all the way to supreme power. But Fascism's paymasters never asked any more of it than this, and if Fascism stayed in power for 20 years and was able to gain a mass base among the petit bourgeoisie, parts of the peasantry and working class, the white-collar workers, it was because the threats in those chaotic interwar years seemed as vivid as ever, especially with the consolidation and expansion of Bolshevik Russia. The Concordat between the Fascist State and the Vatican in 1929 was the regime's greatest victory from this point of view, producing an all-encompassing vision of order based on the two greatest sources of authority in the country. By this time all the system's political opponents had been either liquidated (very few), imprisoned or sent into exile (rather more, the majority Communists), or simply rendered impotent and irrelevant. Not a strike or demonstration was to be seen.

The other side of the medal was the relative superficiality of Fascist control, far removed from the total penetration of every aspect of life promised by the duce. Large areas of Italian society remained relatively untouched by it; these included the armed services, much of industry, the aristocracy and crown, and the landowners. Geographically the depth of Fascist influence was extremely uneven. Some areas, such as Emilia Romagna, were known as Fascist strongholds, while others, such as Piedmont, were only superficially involved. There was nothing like the systematic restructuring of social life seen in Germany, while the Fascist Party itself and the imposing 'corporations' which substituted for trade unions were by 1940 little more than empty shells. In reality the regime had simply struck up various forms of cohabitation with traditional institutions; in this way appearances were maintained and some of the regime's needs met, but the autonomy of the partners was not seriously compromised. From the crown and the Vatican to Fiat, from the army to the film industry, this was the situation, with all sorts of contradictions and incongruities visible by the time the war came.

Economically the country was hardly more industrialized when the war began than when the Fascist regime had begun, in spite of the duce's incessant modernizing rhetoric. Then some 55 per cent of the active population worked in agriculture; by the late 1930s the figure was just under 50 per cent with the greatest growth in the service sector, particularly in State employment, the one area Fascism did expand notably with its innumerable agencies, corporations and surveillance organizations. Above all Fascism had been able to do nothing about, in fact had aggravated, the fundamental socio-economic contradiction of the country first discovered after national unification in the 1860s and still present to this day: the gulf between the modern North and the 'underdeveloped' South. To be more precise, the contrast lay between on the one hand an industrial 'triangle' based on Genoa, Milan and Turin where large oligopolies in the engineering, textile, chemical and electrical sectors ruled surrounded by hundreds of tiny workshops which fed them and lived on them, and on the other hand a rural economy in the South, the Po valley and the eastern margins based on large, feudal land-holdings, an age-old labyrinth of patronage centring on the State, and finally on emigration and its returns. In the middle stood Rome, a time-worn metropolis entirely unproductive and dependent on the inadequate taxes which supported the monarchy, the ministries and the Vatican.

Neither Fascism nor the traditional State apparatus on to which it was fastened were in the slightest degree capable of or interested in changing the disequilibrium between North and South: if agrarians supported Fascism alongside industrialists it was in order to keep industrial capitalism and its dynamism away from the countryside, to maintain the traditional balance between town and country and ensure that the working class remained a relatively isolated, numerical minority (little more than a quarter of the active population in 1936). When the crisis of Fascism's war came in 1942–3, this industrial/rural contradiction showed up again. The northern working class openly expressed protest and discontent, above all in a great strike wave during March 1943; the South, even its large cities such as Naples, Bari, Palermo, though restless, remained passive and resigned to fate.

Even more than the disastrous military situation, it was in fact the March strikes which sounded the death-knell of Fascism. The protest wave was almost entirely spontaneous, the result of physical conditions – Allied bombing, shortages of food and fuel, inflation, large-scale deportation of workers to Germany – and the knowledge of the way the war was evolving after Stalingrad and the loss of the north African colonies. Following these strikes the major industrialists began to change sides once and for all, seeking contacts in Britain and America, preparing for an end to war production. But Mussolini's fall was brought about neither by the industrialists nor by the workers. It was instead a palace coup, designed by the aged and taciturn King Victor Emmanuel III to take control of power back into traditional hands, with the least possible inconvenience to himself and the least possible public knowledge. Ideally the next step would be to withdraw Italy quietly from the war and freeze the status quo as of that moment, and it was with these purposes in mind that Marshal Pietro Badoglio, the veteran 'hero' of Abyssinia, was called to power after the duce's approval. But Hitler immediately blocked off this escape route, leaving the tiny group around the king and Badoglio to bluff ever more desperately, trying to convince first the

Germans that Italy would fight on, then the British and Americans that Italy would fight with all her weight on their side. The gambit failed miserably: while the German armies occupied the country as fast as possible, the Allies imposed unconditional surrender (over-riding their own impulse to make things easier for this not very serious enemy).

Even the main object of the operation, the survival of Victor Emmanuel as undisturbed monarch of the realm, would in the end be denied, since immediately after these events armed Resistance to the Nazi-Fascist occupiers would start, a movement soon dominated by objectives which looked beyond the war, to the renewal of the State and the removal of the monarchy as its precondition.

Thus with the fall of Fascism the day of reckoning came too for Mussolini's enemies, the anti-Fascists in exile abroad, in island prisons or in hiding. They were not prepared for it, neither was the Italian people prepared for them. A Socialist leader said at the time: 'In shop queues and in the workshops you hear pleas for help to everyone – Badoglio, the Church, God, Russia – but not to us.' As the summer wore on with a new round of strikes taking place in August, organization began to impose itself, partly from below, partly from newly returned political prisoners and exiles. Anti-Fascist committees sprang up independently in the major cities of the centre and north of the country, and immediately faced repression, as did every strike and demonstration. The Badoglio government did not hesitate to use Fascism's laws (and often its functionaries in the key administrative posts) to apply the severest measures, and crowds were fired on or violently dispersed on many occasions.

Nevertheless, by the end of the summer only a handful of groups had established a semblance of national organization, and had developed an identity and a minimum of contact with popular sentiment. These were the five political currents which had best survived both morally and intellectually the rigours of Fascist exile and prison, and 'the long, interminable discussions on politics and liberty' which went on therein, according to survivors. These five formations were, to use a scheme developed by the historian Federico Chabod:

(1) *the Communists*: the only group to maintain a serious clandestine organization, even with many of its leaders imprisoned, through the application of leninist quasi-military principles. Hence the only group ready to act politically when Fascism fell. Its leader was Palmiro Togliatti, then in Moscow, one of the Third International's most imposing, politically acute figures and one of the few to survive the late 1930s purges.

(2) *the Catholics*: heirs to a political tradition stemming from the Partito popolare of the years 1919–21, founded by the Sicilian priest Don Sturzo (in America in 1943). With men of those years present in many

cities, their most distinguished representative was Alcide De Gasperi, resident in Rome and closely connected to the Vatican, which had offered him work and refuge in the preceding years. The future organizational strength of the Catholics would be based on the lay Catholic Action organization, hastily mobilized and re-energized by the Vatican during the summer of 1943. Present throughout the country, this body provided the Church with direct channels to many sectors of society and gave it a large-scale voluntary dimension. The new 'Christian Democrat' Party would make ample use of this resource.

(3) *the Socialists*: the formation with the longest tradition of organized activity, stretching back to the end of the nineteenth century. With most of its leaders in exile in 1943 this group would spend much of the summer reconstituting itself as a party and would never dispose of anything like the organizational capacities of the Communists or the Catholics. Divided as ever between maximalist tendencies (centred on Milan) and reformism of various hues (concentrated on Rome), the bridging function fell to the experienced Pietro Nenni, a political animal through and through who had shared a number of the experiences of early socialism with Mussolini, including prison. Like the Communists, much stronger potentially in the North than in the South.

(4) *the Liberals*: a small elite group lent prestige by the presence of the supreme Italian philosopher of his times, Benedetto Croce, as well as by a number of ex-ministers and by the noted economist Luigi Einaudi, the future first president of the post-war republic. Conservatives in the classical nineteenth-century meaning of liberalism, they were the only anti-Fascists allowed contact with the king, a crucial advantage in the intrigues of 1943. Like the Christian Democrats, their aim was to go back to the situation of 1921, and eliminate the Fascist encumbrances from an otherwise healthy body.

(5) *the Actionists*: members of the Action Party founded in 1942 as heirs to the 'Justice and Liberty' group, the most active anti-Fascist and exiles organization, led until his murder in France by the Florentine democratic socialist Carlo Rosselli. More a movement than a party, the Actionist tendency was the only new element in the political spectrum and although heterogeneous, its various components all demanded a reformed liberal democracy, based on renewed parliamentary and State institutions. Widely regarded as a head without a body, the Actionist formation would have a largely intellectual leadership, which although active in the Resistance would eventually prove itself incapable of planting roots in mass society.

Between the leading elements of these embryonic parties and the consti-tuted authority of the king and Badoglio, only one man proved able to keep contact in 1943, a pre-Fascist prime minister named Ivanoe Bonomi. In earlier days a reformist socialist, this unprepossessing, 72-year-old figure represented many of the other amorphous currents whose impulse at this time was to make as swift a return as possible to conditions as they were when 'interrupted' by Fascism. It was a widely based, spontaneous form of conservatism and the wily Bonomi was able to use it to emerge as a key mediator between the king and the 'opposition' (calling itself the 'United Freedom Front') until the German takeover of Rome. At that point he went underground, to emerge nine months later as the first 'Prime Minister' of the liberated capital, at the head of a 'Committee of National Liberation' consisting of the five parties just mentioned together with his own 'Labour Democrats', a shadowy formation present – if at all – only in the South. The committee claimed to be the new government and Bonomi, an aged wire-puller of conservative mentality and monarchist sympathies, its leader. Such was the ambiguous figure who represented reborn, anti-Fascist poli-tics for most of the time the Allies were in command in Italy.

What the Allies knew of these political currents and of conditions general-ly in the country on their arrival is not hard to define: they knew next to nothing. So complete was Fascism's isolation of the country, so marginal the anti-Fascist opposition – and so poorly organized when abroad – that neither the armies, the intelligence services nor the diplomats of Britain and America were able to furnish anything like a complete picture of what they might expect to the invading forces. Prominent exiles in America such as the Liberal aristocrat and ex-minister Count Sforza, and the Socialist intellectual Gaetano Salvemini, based in Harvard, were able to bring public and even State Depart-ment attention to Italy's plight on occasion in the war years, but most Italo-Americans had been enthusiastic admirers of the duce and in any case there was no certainty of what America's interest in fighting a war in Italy might be. In Britain, once the home of Mussolini's most outspoken foreign supporters – Winston Churchill himself had often spoken in praise of the great Italian 'lawgiver' – public feeling was now violently anti-Italian ever since Mussolini had chosen Hitler's side and British and Italian armies had clashed in north Africa. In this atmosphere there was almost no room for organized anti-Fascism and although Radio Londra of the BBC did its bit, and émigré figures on occasion passed through London and attempted official contacts, they found little encouragement in public opinion at large. Even the inform-ation they had to offer was treated with scepticism, an attitude which, how-ever justifiable politically, did nothing to counter the remarkable paucity of facts and figures on a major enemy power in Europe which was characteristic of the British and American war machines in the summer of 1943. When the Allied commanders and their political advisers landed they had to learn from scratch, but as it turned out, they were destined to learn quickly.

PART ONE 1943

1 The Italian surrender and the wartime Alliance

As THE TIDE of war turned from the beginning of 1943 onwards, the major Allied participants began to think more concretely about the relationship between the conduct of the war and their concerns, present and future, in southern Europe and the Mediterranean basin. For the British many facts of history and power contributed to make the area a theatre of supreme interest. As Robert Murphy, the American political adviser to the Supreme Allied Command, noted: 'To the British, the Mediterranean was an essential link in their imperial system, and they were gravely concerned about what would happen in this area after the war as well as during the war.'[1] Before the war, the British chiefs of staff had made it clear to their political masters that a hostile Mediterranean power could easily and disastrously upset the delicate balance of imperial defence between Europe and the Far East and had urged all possible accommodation with potential enemies. This sort of pressure did not come from military men alone. According to Lord Hankey, secretary of the Committee of Imperial Defence, everyone in 1937 except Eden and his 'clique' at the Foreign Office, 'saw that the reduction of Britain's enemies might best be achieved by detaching Italy, whose interests in a free and open Mediterranean, Red Sea, and an independent Austria were so similar to our own . . .'[2] from the strategic clamp of the Axis.

At stake was more than the prospective control by Italy of what E. H. Carr termed in 1937 'the most important sea-channel in the world'.[3] Should that waterway be blocked, said Carr, Britain and the empire would suffer serious material inconvenience, certainly, but much worse would be the blow to prestige (which meant 'the recognition by other people of your strength'). From the end of the nineteenth century onwards, 'Great Britain was not merely a Mediterranean Power. She was *the* Mediterranean Power. This position was unchallenged right down to 1935'.[4] Now, in Carr's view, if Italy obtained command of the Mediterranean she could predictably succeed Britain in the dominant position in Egypt and 'call the tune in the conduct of the affairs of Palestine'. To the North, the entry to the Mediterranean offered to Soviet Russia by the Treaty of Montreaux of July 1936 assumed new and ominous significance depending on how, and in whose interest, the Russians decided to use their opportunity. In the West, there was the massive Italian intervention in the Spanish Civil War with its ultimate objective, Carr felt, of neutralizing the predominant position of Gibraltar, 'the basis of British power in Mediterranean waters'.[5] Britain had been unable to respond to these challenges, had shown herself too weak to defend a foreign policy which 'has brought us too many powerful enemies'. The only alternative left, in Carr's opinion, was that of neutralizing those in Europe to deal with the more dangerous menace in the Far East. In effect this meant coming to terms with Italy, even recognizing Italy's claim to leadership in the Mediterranean, if by so doing Britain could better withstand German claims.[6]

In spite of the gradual shift of much public and government opinion towards similar positions in the course of 1936 and 1937, the prospect of open conflict did not diminish, partly perhaps because such a war seemed a far from formidable undertaking. But the army and navy staffs thought otherwise. 'A hostile Italy is a real menace to our Imperial communications and defence system. We have relied on practically abandoning the Mediterranean if we send the Fleet East,' wrote the chairman of the chiefs of staff after the Abyssinian crisis, suggesting at the same time that even the costs of defeating Italy conclusively were unsustainable. By June 1937 the chiefs of staff had come out openly against sanctions and for a return to 'a state of friendly relations with Italy',[7] and it was with this latter aim in mind that the Chamberlain government signed the agreement with Italy of April 1938 from which the prime minister expected so much.[8] Yet in 1939 as in 1937 the heads of the armed services were still urging that a hard but inescapable choice had still to be made between defending the British stake in the Mediterranean and that in the Far East, and most favoured the latter.[9]

With the fall of Singapore in February 1942 went the keystone of the British empire in the Far East, that spot which pre-war British generals and admirals had insisted be surrendered last of all before the United Kingdom itself. Yet British planners and politicians of 1943 argued as though the ways and means – and obligations – of imperial defence deriving from the maintenance of positions in the Far East, in India, in the Arab world, had not substantially changed. India appeared to remain as a central pillar of the empire, as did much of the Middle East, where Churchill himself had played a significant part in the construction of British imperial interests after the First World War.[10]

All these areas now entered into British strategic ideas on the relationship of the Mediterranean to the war. As Michael Howard has explained:

> The fall of France and the belligerence of Italy eliminated the traditional role of the Suez Canal itself as a lifeline of the British Empire; but Egypt was still the theatre where forces could be most easily concentrated from all parts of the Commonwealth with the exception of Canada. Troops from India, Australia, New Zealand, Southern Africa and the United Kingdom could be brought into action, if not against

Germany, then at least against her vulnerable ally, who could thus be turned into a liability rather than an asset to the Axis. It was an area where British and Commonwealth forces could fight on the scale to which they were accustomed, and perhaps do damage out of all proportion to their size. The defeat of Italy might influence the attitude of the French authorities in Syria, Lebanon and French North Africa. It would be taken into account in Madrid, where General Franco had it in his power to close the Mediterranean to British shipping altogether. And it would have important repercussions in the Balkan peninsula.[11]

The Americans on the other hand found themselves in the Mediterranean largely but not wholly as a result of war. The U.S. had a commercial interest in the area and U.S.-Mediterranean trade, though moderate in absolute terms, had almost tripled in some parts of the region in the 1930s and had shown a healthy and growing balance in favour of the United States.[12] A Senate inspection team of 1943 called for 'a clear statement of American rights and interests in the Mediterranean', adding that 'the U.S. may be in serious danger of being entirely eliminated from world trade in the area'.[13] American oil companies reportedly 'looked forward to vast expansion' from links with British companies, and by 1943 the U.S. Joint Chiefs of Staff [JCS] had decided that America had a strong strategic interest in Middle East oil.[14]

The immediate demands of war planning at the beginning of 1943 were of course only partially connected with all this. American reluctance to share in British enthusiasm for defeating Germany from the Mediterranean is well known; U.S. Secretary of War Stimson later called the Italian campaign, 'another diversion in the interests of the British empire and contrary to our American instincts', and was said to have been appalled at the weakness of Roosevelt in face of the barrage of British insistence.[15]

The crucial confrontations on these issues had taken place at the Casablanca and 'Trident' conferences of January and May 1943, where American suspicions had revolved round the well-founded impression that the British wished to make 'Overlord' – the cross-Channel invasion planned for 1944 – conditional on successes in Italy, and beyond that to regain permanent control of the Mediterranean.

It was at the Casablanca meeting that the JCS decided to ask the British whether they seriously believed that the European war could be won from the Mediterranean and if they had a complete step-by-step plan by which this could be achieved. JCS chairman Admiral Leahy seemed to express a widespread sense of frustration when he said then that the joint chiefs had 'never been able to get out of the British how they expect to win the war'.[16]

Whether the Russians thought consciously in terms of using the war to build up a Mediterranean position is of course not known. Churchill and Eden seemed to share the well-known view of Stalin as a 'Greater Russian', who would pursue the historical power interests of his nation as far as international strategic relationships might allow him. This meant coming to terms with the Soviet leader in explicit ways, making sure that Stalin understood what he might gain from openly acknowledging the objective interests of the other powers. 'Britain must be the leading Mediterranean Power', Churchill informed Stalin at their Kremlin meeting in October 1944, and he 'hoped Marshal Stalin would let him have the first say in Greece in the same way as Marshal Stalin about Rumania'. The prime minister went on to assure Stalin that it was by no means British policy to grudge the Soviets access to warm-water ports and oceans of the world; Britain's only interest was to assist the Soviet Union in any way possible.[17]

In the days of the Casablanca and 'Trident' conferences, Anglo-American planners could not afford to take such an exclusively political view of things. Some, such as Harry Hopkins, worried that Stalin had twice refused invitations from Roosevelt to meet with himself and Churchill, and that whatever happened in Casablanca, the next major strategic move absolutely could not be made without consulting him.[18] There was at this point, 'no question whatever of "forestalling" the Russians, or conducting a strategy based on political foresight,' Michael Howard claims, 'The attention of all, soldiers and statesmen alike, was riveted on helping the Russians and winning the war; and there was, in 1943, no other theatre where this could be done'.[19] To what extent the minds of soldiers and statesmen were concentrated on the problem of aiding Russia by the fear, active in their ranks at this time, that the Soviets might make a separate peace, remains to be seen.[20]

YET IT WAS at Casablanca that the first major political decision concerning the aftermath of the war was taken: that nothing less than the 'unconditional surrender' of the enemy would satisfy the victors and end the war.

Although the formula was Roosevelt's, it had been discussed before Casablanca by the JCS and others, and it was in those earlier discussions of the summer and autumn of 1942 that the possibility of treating Italy in a different manner from the other enemy powers first appeared in American thought. Then a subcommittee of the State Department's Advisory Committee on Post-War Foreign Policy (an institution apparently unique to the Americans at this time) had agreed that, 'as between a negotiated cessation of hostilities or armistice on one hand and an imposed unconditional surrender on the other . . ., nothing short of unconditional surrender by the principal enemies, Germany and Japan, could be accepted, though negotiation might be possible in the case of Italy'.[21] Secretary of State Hull wrote later:

> President Roosevelt and I believed almost from the time of Mussolini's declaration of war against the United States, four days after Pearl Harbour, that we should draw a distinction between the Italians on the one hand and the Germans and Japanese on the other. [They concluded that] . . . it might be possible to withdraw Italy from the war before the surrender of Germany and Japan, and that this

withdrawal would in fact hasten that surrender. Italy's retirement, we felt, would be accelerated if we were to adopt an attitude towards the Italians different from that toward the Germans and Japanese.[22]

The latter powers would be judged according to the severest terms, Hull explained elsewhere, while for the Axis satellites, Romania, Hungary, Bulgaria and Finland, and Italy, 'preliminary informal conversations could be envisaged' which would 'result in substantial adjustments away from the terms of unconditional surrender'.[23]

The domestic factors which pushed the Roosevelt administration in a more lenient direction and in favour of attempts to detach Italy from the Axis by means of a separate peace will be explained later in the context of internal American politics. Beyond these, there was also, between the British and the Americans, the crucial difference of war experience: as the British were to repeat interminably to the U.S. in succeeding years, the British empire had had to fight Italians and had beaten them on the battlefield and at sea. This left the victors with the absolute right to define the losers as 'nation', 'power', 'people' or 'dictatorship', according to their own interests or sentiments, a right which the British exercised ruthlessly in the years from 1943 to 1947. The immediate British reactions to the possibility of not applying 'unconditional surrender' to Italy foreshadowed much of what was to come. Churchill wrote to the War Cabinet from Casablanca explaining that a final communiqué might emerge affirming the intention of the Allies to fight on until the unconditional surrender of Germany and Japan took place, but omitting Italy. 'The omission of Italy would be to encourage a break-up there', Churchill telegraphed. Attlee and Eden replied on behalf of the War Cabinet two days later:

> The Cabinet was unanimously of the opinion that balance of advantage lay against excluding Italy, because of misgivings which would inevitably be caused in Turkey, in the Balkans and elsewhere. Nor are we convinced that effect on Italians would be good. Knowledge of all rough stuff coming to them is surely more likely to have desired effect on Italian morale.[24]

Churchill personally maintained a different view and wrote in his memoirs:

> It will be seen that the opinion of the Cabinet was not against the policy of unconditional surrender. They only disapproved of it not being applied to Italy as well. I did not want this because I hoped – and hope has not been unfulfilled – that Italy, free from Mussolini's dictatorship, might fight on our side, which she did for several years of the war with lasting beneficial results to the state of Europe.[25]

It was soon after Casablanca that the British began to insist on being 'senior partner' in Mediterranean operations, at least as far as the occupation and running of enemy territories were concerned. Eisenhower suggested in February that parity should be the rule, with joint management, while London eventually approved a proposal by Harold Macmillan in favour of joint planning, but for a British-run administration, 'north Africa reversed'. Here too there were ample sources of conflict between the two Allies; Sir John Dill, head of the British Military Mission in Washington, told General George Marshall, Chief of Staff of the U.S. Army, that: 'Since the Mediterranean represents a vital British interest now and in the future, it is logical for us to be pre-eminent in the administration of an area which overlooks the Straits [of Malta].' But the American joint chiefs refused, insisting on equality.

These arguments need to be seen first of all in the context of discussions going on both in London and Washington on plans for the post-war security of Europe and the world. The most vital aspect of the Italian surrender indeed was this: that it forced the Great Powers of the anti-Hitler Alliance to begin to choose how they would set about reconstructing the international system after hostilities had ended. The surrender settled accounts between them for a while, not only obliging the British and the Americans to take a first position on the future role of Soviet power but also bringing some very cool calculations of interest on the Anglo-American Alliance itself. As it turned out the results of all the jockeying were not encouraging to any of the Big Three, but they were encouraging least of all to the Russians, who were to find themselves effectively excluded from the Italian settlement in spite of the general recognition that it constituted 'a test case which [would] determine their future attitude towards collaboration', as the War Cabinet told Churchill.[26] We must now consider how and why this happened.

With one eye on the past, the supposed conditions which had produced German and Italian aggression, and one on the future, the question of Soviet power and Britain's relation to it, Churchill and the Foreign Office in their musings on post-war Europe had elaborated a large-scale hierarchical system for maintaining international law and order. This was based on treating the Continent as one unit, capable of incorporating the Soviets and somehow containing them at the same time. Churchill's personal inclinations were for a subsidiary Council of Europe which would supervise a number of regional confederations: in Scandinavia, the Danube area, the Balkans, and so on. The Foreign Office also thought in terms of confederations; one built round central Europe, the other on its southern and eastern flanks.[27]

When Anthony Eden went to Washington in March 1943 he found the State Department thinking along similar lines, but on a global scale. The three major powers plus China were to assume the entire responsibility for evolving and imposing a new system of world law on all formal relations between states. The Americans wished to legitimize these arrangements through institutional devices: a World Council with regional members supplemented by a general assembly of all nations. They tended to be suspicious of Churchill's plans, not on account of their intrinsic defects but because internal political pressures obliged them to distinguish between sharing in the general 'policing of the world' and direct involvement in European politics. The administration believed that the strong isolationist currents in public opinion would be more easily convinced of a supranational, and therefore more abstract type of responsibility, rather than the precise commitment to European stabilization in a well-defined context which the British sought.[28]

In the Washington meetings of March both sides were agreed that the immediate need was for machinery to ensure civilian control of the political side of military operations in Europe.[29] The State Department had seen its capacity to handle foreign policy dwindle visibly during the war years, partly through the traditional American doctrine of delegating as much operational responsibility as possible to the military man on the spot (though without granting him real functional autonomy in the British army sense), partly as a result of Roosevelt's conviction that the Department was a centre of gravity of Republicanism and opposition to the New Deal.[30] Stalemate and hostility had been the only results of attempts to coordinate policy between the State and War Departments, and civilians were even excluded, for security reasons, from the meetings of the JCS. It was a situation that at times gave London the impression that 'military autocracy is running full blast in the U.S. machine today'.[31]

But here, in planning political arrangements for liberated Europe, was an area where vital ground could and must be regained: 'political problems can't be left to the military', Under-Secretary of State Sumner Welles insisted to a member of Eden's delegation, echoing similar if less deeply felt sentiments in the Foreign Office.[32] Specifically, if anything dramatic did happen in Italy there would have to be a proper surrender policy.

With Italy in mind, Hull and the State Department were thinking at this time of a powerful joint Anglo-American civilian body sitting in London which could supervise the application in Italy of the occcupation system already tried out in North Africa. But in a top-level meeting with the president and Hull, the British again brought up the troublesome request first heard after Casablanca: to be 'senior partners' in the Italian enterprise. Roosevelt refused, saying there were to be no 'senior partners': all were to be equal. The British were dissatisfied but did nothing; in private they concluded there was no coherent American position on these problems, only personal opinions based on fear of the military and distrust of themselves.[33]

EVENTS soon forced these fairly abstract discussions into more concrete channels. By the spring it was clear Fascism was on the verge of collapse in Italy and that Italy's days as an Axis partner might be numbered. A prodigious array of questions immediately presented themselves, hardly touched by the single powers in their own planning machinery, let alone on a coalition basis. Besides the issue of the form and content of the armistice, and to what extent it signified an end to hostilities or the surrender of the entire country, decisions were required on machinery for its enforcement, on the nature and duration of a provisional Allied regime, on the status of Italy's assets as a power – colonies, armies, fleet – and on the responsibilities which might have to be assumed for the welfare of the Italian people in the event of a total social and political collapse: vast and momentous problems whose emergence in Italy implied unmistakably that the post-war era was already opening.

However, reduced to their essentials, the areas of discussion could be roughly divided into two: those defining the international status of the defeated or 'liberated' nation, and those dealing with arrangements inside its borders.

The paper, entitled 'Armistices and Related Problems' which was presented by Eden to the War Cabinet on 25 May 1943 was the first major product of British efforts to think out post-hostilities arrangements, and the first Allied document to offer detailed blueprints for cooperation in the formulation of armistices and in armistice regimes. Distinguishing from the first between military and non-military terms, Eden's paper proposed that all armistices should eventually be controlled by a 'United Nations Committee for Europe', which would be composed of 'high-ranking *political* [sic] representatives of the United Kingdom, the United States of America and the U.S.S.R., of France and the other minor European Allies and, if so desired, of any Dominion prepared to contribute to the policing of Europe'. Full responsibility for the maintenance of law and order in each area was specifically assigned to the commander-in-chief.[34]

This plan, presented to the Americans and Russians at the beginning of July, was an intermediary design, intended to bridge the gap between the end of hostilities and the emergence of the new world security structures. Although it was aimed at Germany more than anywhere else, its overall purpose was Europe-wide. The official historian explains:

> Mr. Eden thought an agreement on these lines necessary if we were to avoid the signature by the Soviet Union of a separate armistice and the organisation of a separate Russian system in Eastern Europe.[35]

The State Department's move came at the Anglo-American Quebec Conference in August and was at the same time more grandiose and more ambiguous than anything planned up to then by the British. It consisted of a draft declaration, to be signed by the three major Allies together with China, which would announce a plan of common action on all problems connected with enemy surrenders and the occupation of ex-enemy territory. Its most important clause proclaimed the establishment of a new world security organization. Its most tendentious one declared that:

> Those of [the Allies] at war with a common enemy will act together in all matters relating to the surrender of that enemy, and to any occupation of enemy territory and of territory of other states held by that enemy.[36]

In line with the American suggestions of March, this formula could be read to imply that in surrender situations military problems would be separated from political ones and the latter postponed, that only the armies doing the fighting would manage the occupations and that powers not directly involved would be cut out. But this exclusiveness was fully consistent with a July policy paper on occupation problems drawn up by the State Department's International Security Division with special reference to Italy. While paying lip service to United Nations participation, the conclusion was that:

> Occupation by American and British forces would in all probability constitute a recognition of actual conditions at the time of the Italian surrender. It would simplify problems of command, division of functions, and cooperation between the occupying forces, and would facilitate the orientation of Italy to the Anglo-Saxon orbit.[37]

The Foreign Office, already thinking in detail of Eden's all-powerful U.N. Commission for Europe, which it hoped would be set up in London, was profoundly dismayed at the discovery of this trend in American thought. The British delegation in Washington was told at the beginning of September that such views had serious implications: 'it is very important that [we] should not (repeat not) give the impression that we favour the idea of separate geographical spheres of interest in Europe'.[38]

But by then Stalin had already seized the initiative. In reaction to the chain of private Anglo-American discussions culminating in the conference of Quebec – which produced among other things detailed armistice terms for Italy – Stalin took up the concepts of Eden's July paper and flung them back at his allies:

> I believe that the time is ripe to organize the military-political commission of representatives of the three countries, Great Britain, the U.S.S.R., and the United States with the purpose of considering the questions concerning the negotiations with the different governments dissociating themselves from Germany. Until now the matter stood as follows: Great Britain and the United States made agreements but the Soviet Union, just as a passive third observer, received information about the results of the agreements between the two countries. I have to tell you that it is impossible any longer to tolerate such a situation. I propose to establish this commission and to assign Sicily at the beginning as its place of residence.[39]

Although they were shocked, this thrust should have come as no surprise to the British or the Americans. When rumours of armistice negotiations began to seem more and more consistent at the end of July, the Soviet chargé d'affaires in London had asked Eden directly why there could be no inter-Allied discussion of armistice terms, especially since the Russians attached great importance to unconditional surrender. Eden's reply was not likely to calm Soviet suspicions; the stumbling block, he said, was Eisenhower whose views had to be taken into consideration.[40] But with CCS approval, Eisenhower had broadcast to the Italians on 29 July – four days after Mussolini's fall – apparently offering them an honourable capitulation.[41] This had 'most handsomely contributed' to Soviet anxieties, the British ambassador to Moscow telegraphed to London. The Soviets, continued the ambassador, were worried over British and American exclusiveness on the Italian problem, and insisted that their having defeated Italian armies on the Russian front and taken prisoners of war gave them as much right as any other Ally to participate in the surrender. The Soviets justified their protests not on procedural but on political grounds: 'Soviet Government much fear', Sir Archibald Clark Kerr's telegram went on, 'that we are going to compound with Badoglio and are asking themselves whether, when the time comes and Hitler expires, we shall compound with Goering'.[42]

On 1 August nevertheless the Soviets approved a British draft of surrender terms which included the concept, though not the details, of *a separate commission, to enforce the armistice on the spot.*[43] A few days later the Americans told the Russians of Eisenhower's instructions: that he was to deal with problems on military lines, thinking of the security of his troops and of creating a basis for future operations. 'The point of this was of course,' James Clement Dunn, the State Department's Adviser on European Affairs, explained privately, 'to establish a precedent for the future case of Germany'.[44]

IN THE British and American camps in August arguments on the nature of the armistice went on at the same time as arguments on how to enforce it. No one doubted that these were separate issues implying separate machinery for the international and the internal aspects of the settlement. Broadly speaking, the British at this stage favoured comprehensive treatment of Italy, covering all the United Nations at war with the country, and with execution to be in the hands of an inter-Allied, not Anglo-American, control commission situated on the spot. This line, laid down by the War Cabinet, dominated British discussions during these weeks.[45]

But the Americans, led by Eisenhower, continued to insist on the sovereignty of the supreme Allied commander, to the extent of wishing to make him directly responsible for execution of the armistice, under the supervision of the CCS, and possibly without even the aid of a subsidiary control commission.[46] Such a scheme, said the Post-Hostilities Planning Staff in London, would serve only to arouse Russian and other Allied suspicion; they 'may think that an effort is being made to perpetuate a sort of Anglo-American, or possibly simply an American form of military dictatorship, which would not take their interests into account'.[47] But more concrete at that point were American suspicions of any form of supranational committee. Hull was eventually to declare himself in favour of on-going negotiation through diplomatic channels as the means of settling the international difficulties arising from surrenders. Eisenhower's attitude, it seems, was dictated in part by the difficulties of the military situation (the

Salerno landings took place on 8 September), but also by the strong desire of the War Department and the American sections of AFHQ to arrange matters as far as possible on tactical lines, thereby reducing the weight of the political questions to be dealt with, but also circumscribing the political influence of the British (and in particular that of Harold Macmillan, the energetic British political adviser at AFHQ).[48]

By proposing the immediate creation of a new, supreme military and political executive on the spot in the Mediterranean, the Russians challenged the British and Americans to settle their differences and commit themselves. The attractions of Eden's July scheme for tripartite control were obvious. As Geoffrey Warner has written:

> If this regime had been applied to Italy, the Soviet Union would have enjoyed complete equality with Britain and the U.S. in implementing whatever armistice arrangement was reached. She would, moreover, have possessed a right of veto over British and American policy, thanks to the unanimity rule in the proposed 'steering committee' of the United Nations Commission for Europe. Whether reciprocal rights for Britain and the U.S. in, say, Rumania, would have been welcomed or not is another matter, but this was not the issue in the summer of 1943, when Anglo-American forces were already in Sicily while the Germans were still deep inside the Soviet Union.[49]

Like many political and institutional failures in history, the significance of the Mediterranean or the Political-Military Commission (as it came to be called) has been largely ignored by later observers and critics. Yet at the time it seemed to its chief supporters, the British and the Russians, that the strategic and diplomatic possibilities of such an organization, set up in such circumstances, were immense: the future evolution of international relations in Europe might depend on it. A high London official wrote that: 'it would mean that we and the Americans would have the day-to-day possibility of cross-examining the Russians on their intentions towards the Allied countries [and] Eastern Europe generally'. The Russians would have the same possibility in the West, but this after all would only be a logical development of our theory that Europe should be treated as a whole; but there will be great reluctance on the part of our own and the American military authorities to allow the Russians any real say in the actual organisation of civil affairs within the Anglo-American theatres'.[50]

When the smoke and confusion of the armistice crisis of September eventually cleared away (analysed in the following chapter), two facts were indeed clear: firstly, that the Soviet Union was not told of the definitive surrender of Italy, signified by the signing of the so-called 'long' document on 29 September, until it was over. Secondly, the terms had been presented to the Italians by Eisenhower, and the centre of gravity of negotiations and immediate post-surrender planning had been AFHQ, not London or Washington, in spite of all the misgivings about political delegation felt in those capitals ever since the Darlan affair in North Africa.[51] Such a reality gave substance to the insistence of the Americans that the majority of problems were in the first instance military, not diplomatic; that the U.S. and the U.K. exercised primary control on behalf of the United Nations via the military; and that no authority should intervene between the supreme Allied commander and the combined organizations in Washington.[52]

By the beginning of September Churchill was arguing that 'we cannot be put in a position where our armies are doing all the fighting but Russians have a veto and must be consulted', and Eden told the State Department at the beginning of October: 'In the view of the Prime Minister and myself nothing must derogate from the authority of the Commander-in-Chief.' Eden went on to suggest that the Political-Military Commission should limit its work to advising the Allied governments on Italian problems; as for the Russian demand for participation, that could be satisfied by offering the Soviets a position on the subsidiary Armistice Control Commission.[53] Meanwhile the American military remained adamant: the supreme commander could not serve two masters, the CCS and the Political-Military Commission.[54]

This then was the key point: the political autonomy or otherwise of the military. When in September (and again in October, after co-belligerency), the Russians insisted that the Political-Military Commission would have sufficient power to handle all problems of control, they were challenging the supremacy of the CCS as directors of the Allied war effort in the Mediterranean, and they were doing so because the most fundamental questions of how the war was to be ended were now on the table. The issue of the Commission, as we shall see, was eventually resolved at the Moscow conference of foreign ministers.[55] But by this time the British and the Americans had Italy's surrender, partial occupation and change to co-belligerent status already behind them, and were firmly dug in with their own military government regime and military mission to Badoglio in Brindisi. The Russians were left standing.

2   The armistice struggle

IF WE NOW turn to look at the armistice crisis itself, the drama and confusion of this crucial moment can only be fully appreciated by bearing in mind all the contingent factors: the rush of events, the physical separation and lack of coordination of the key actors in London, Washington, Algiers and Rome, the simultaneous large-scale landings at Salerno, the surprise discovery that the Germans intended to hold as much of Italy as possible, the desperate impulse of the king and his circle to change sides at minimum cost to themselves and to Italian sovereignty even with their country invaded by two warring armies. But for its effect on Italy's fate in the war, the most significant aspect of the whole process was the difference in outlook and intention it revealed between the Anglo-Saxon Allies on the subject of Italy's future development as a people and as a nation.

Looking back, almost 18 months later, on the course of Anglo-American relations with Italy since September 1943, James Clement Dunn, by now assistant secretary of state, offered his own conclusions on the relative contributions of the British and the Americans:

> The British, in the last analysis, consider the Italian Government and people as a defeated nation which surrendered unconditionally. In the last analysis, they would always fall back on the sweeping conditions of the surrender instrument and refer to Italy as 'a defeated enemy or an ex-Axis power'. We, on our side, had taken Italy's cobelligerency status seriously. When we agreed to accept the Italians as a cobelligerent in the war against Germany if they would declare war on that country, we immediately began putting into practice the policy which would permit Italy to regain her self-respect and political and economic independence in order that she might (1) cooperate effectively in the war against Germany and (2) become a stable and constructive element in post-war Europe.

But this plan, Dunn implied, had been sabotaged from the beginning by British vindictiveness:

> We never wanted to sign the long armistice terms and only did so after considerable British insistence. They were not necessary (the short military terms of September 3 being quite adequate) and by the time they were signed they were in many instances already obsolete. By that time, September 29, 1943, we already had Badoglio's assurances that Italy would go to war against Germany and the unconditional terms of the surrender instrument were obviously inappropriate to apply to a cobelligerent.

Dunn's review, in a letter to a colleague at AFHQ, covers with such precision the basic formal positions of the two powers from the armistice onwards that it has the air of being created for the record.[1]

Both British and Americans began to cast around for clues as to the possible content of a policy for liberated Italy towards the end of 1942. The Americans sought contacts and intelligence through the Vatican and through their embassies in Berne, Lisbon and Madrid, and as we shall see later, received some curious replies. For electoral reasons they also paid a good deal of attention to exile groups and the opinions of the Italo-American community in the United States, which though confused all demanded maximum American liberality.[2] As late as May 1943 the British confessed that they had little information on internal developments in Italy, although His Majesty's Ambassador to the Vatican, Sir D'Arcy Osborne, continued to send despatches, supplementing a trickle of news from exiles in various parts of Europe.[3]

It was on these foundations that the Allies had formed their policy for propaganda to Italy and to Italian groups in other parts of the world, propaganda which might have been expected to reflect, among other things, the outline of their intentions for the armistice and its aftermath. In reality the British and the Americans were not able to agree on a coordinated propaganda line because their views and interest in an Italian surrender differed too widely.[4] The British took up the cudgels late in November 1942, to insist in a note to the State Department that

> there is nothing to be gained at this stage by making any direct or indirect appeal to both sentiment or history or holding out any inducement to the Italian people or armed forces to overthrow [the] Fascist regime and abandon [the] Germans. A policy of appeals and promises could only be really effective when there was a question of building up some dissident movement or leader which could challenge established government. At present there is no such leader or movement in Italy nor are there any potential leaders outside Italy of sufficient calibre.[5]

The State Department, in its private comments on this attitude, insisted that anti-Fascist groups were operating in Italy, and disagreed on not holding out any inducements to the Italian people, or even the slightest encouragement to passive resistance on the part of anti-Fascist forces. Adolf Berle, assistant secretary of state, added that, 'to omit even the most fragmentary suggestion that the essential nationhood of Italy is expected to remain, and to give no intimation that there is any kindly feeling towards the Italian people, strikes me as short-sighted'.[6]

On the other hand, Nelson Rockefeller, in charge of 'plans for Hemisphere support of the Italian campaign' (i.e. propaganda to the 8 million Italian emigrants in Latin America) felt that 'care must be taken not to denounce the "corporative state" *per se* [sic] in order to avoid offence in those countries of Latin America, together with Spain and Portugal, where Fascist theories had aroused enthusiasm. Amid much pseudo-psychological and racial theorizing ('We should not recommend that they go back to music when the tone of our voice indicates we really think of them as organ-grinders . . . The modern Italian resents being classed as merely an entertainer. Any invitation on our part for his return to his guitar, his paint-brush and his chisel will antagonize him rather than please him . . .'), Rockefeller, who claimed that his plans had been cleared by the State Department and the Office of War Information, came to the conclusion that Mussolini and the Fascist Party should take the brunt of the blame for Italy's downfall. America for her part would appear prominent in generous pledges to the Italian people.[7]

In the earlier stages of the war, the Labour minister of information in Britain, Hugh Dalton, had also complained of 'the stupid doctrinaire prejudices against fascism as such' of his Italian propaganda section,[8] but by the end of 1942 the British had gone on to develop at the highest level the line reflected in their note to the Americans. Few people were in a position to criticize this line, but among them was Gaetano Salvemini who fastened initially on the famous occasion in 1940 when Churchill had declared that 'one man and one man alone, against the Crown and Royal Family of Italy, against the Pope and all the authority of the Vatican, against the wishes of the Italian people' had forced Italy into war against the British empire.

> By saddling Mussolini, and not the entire Fascist regime, with the whole responsibil-
> ity for Italy's war against England [Salvemini commented], and by urging the Italian
> people to get rid of 'one man and one man alone', Mr. Churchill was telling the great
> majority of Italians, who never have had, and never will have, any use for Fascism,
> that what they should do is, merely, to substitute Fascism without Mussolini for
> Fascism with Mussolini and everything will be fine.[9]

Had Salvemini known of Rockefeller's or Dalton's attitude, he might have been less surprised by the recognition by both the United States and Great Britain of Victor Emmanuel III's birthday in November 1942, just as if, Salvemini snapped, 'the Declaration of War on England had not been approved and signed by the King himself'.[10] Salvemini had little difficulty in documenting the enthusiasm for Fascism which permeated certain elevated circles in Britain and America, as well as the favourable impression which Admiral Darlan's switch had made in the Fascist hierarchy.[11] Salvemini concluded that what was at stake was not the democratic as opposed to the Fascist idea, the 'salvation of peoples' against dictatorship by State regimes, but tactical expediency and geopolitical power in the classical sense.[12]

BEFORE the invasion of Italy had even been contemplated, in November 1942 Churchill had held out the hope that the pressure of war and defeat could separate the Italian people – including leading men of the Fascist hierarchy such as Dino Grandi – from the person of Mussolini, provoking a collapse of the Fascist regime and an acceptable offer of surrender.[13] In February the State Department thought too that the time had come 'to attempt to detach the Italians from the Fascist regime', and to 'encourage passive resistance and sabotage of the Italian war effort'.[14] But when the drama of Mussolini's removal on 25 July became clear there was confusion: 'unconditional surrender' or 'honourable capitulation'?[15] Roosevelt wished to come 'as close as possible to unconditional surrender', while Churchill concentrated on the vast territorial and military gains which the collapse seemed to promise. On 26 July the president mentioned 'good treatment of the Italian populace', the prime minister the 'new, liberated, anti-Fascist Italy', and the support to the anti-German resistance that the new Italy would surely offer. But once the enthusiasm had cooled other sentiments began to assert themselves and the practical considerations behind armistice and occupation then appeared quite detached, both in past and future terms, from these nobler impulses of the first instant.[16]

Confident of Roosevelt's support, Churchill spoke to the House of Commons on 27 July and warned the Italians that they must 'stew in their own juice a bit'. Yet more pressure was promised to speed up the process of breakdown. But the most significant aspect of this speech is the extent to which it anticipated so many of the problems of the Allies as liberators and occupiers, as victors seeking 'maximum returns with minimum responsibilities' as the American official history puts it. For this reason it is worth quoting at some length:

> I must utter a word of caution [Churchill concluded]. We do not know what is going to happen in Italy, and now that Mussolini has gone, and once the Fascist power is certainly and irretrievably broken, we should be foolish to deprive ourselves of any means of coming to general conclusions with the Italian nation. It would be a grave mistake when Italian affairs are in this flexible, fluid, formative condition, for the Rescuing Powers, Britain and the United States, so to act as to break down the whole structure and expression of the Italian State.
>
> We certainly do not seek to reduce Italian life to a condition of chaos and anarchy and to find ourselves without any authorities with whom to deal. By so doing we should lay upon our Armies and upon our war effort the burden of occupying, mile by mile the entire country and of forcing the individual surrender of every armed or coherent force in every district into which our troops may enter. An immense task of garrisoning, policing and administering will be thrown upon us, involving a grievous expenditure, and still more of time.
>
> We must be careful not to get ourselves into the kind of position into which the Germans have blundered in so many countries, namely, of having to hold down and administer, from day to day, by a system of gauleiters, the entire life of very large populations, thereby becoming responsible under the hard conditions of this present period for the whole of their upkeep and well-being. Such a course might well, in practice, turn the sense of liberation which it may soon be in our power to bestow upon the Italian people, into a sullen, discontent against us and all our works. The rescuers might soon, indeed, be regarded as tyrants; they might even be hated by the Italian people as much or almost as much as their German allies. I certainly do not wish in the case of Italy, to tread a path which might lead to execution squads and concentration camps and above all to having to carry on our shoulders a lot of people who ought to be made to carry themselves.[17]

In this discourse the themes which would determine the nature of Italy's liberation are brought out one by one: the contrast between liberation and occupation, the balance of military benefits against administrative costs and responsibilities, the risk of suspended sovereignty becoming open-ended liability; above all there is the role of the State as guarantor of the fundamental structure of the nation and as indispensable and legitimate reference point for the 'rescuing powers'. Churchill insisted, and would repeat in his memoirs, that Mussolini's dictatorship had been absolute and for the collapse of Italy as a power no blame could be cast on the monarchy, parliamentary institutions, the Fascist Party or the general staff; 'All fell on him'.[18] But what role could then be assigned to the Italian people, what response expected of them in the new situation, what blame attached for the declaration of war on Britain and France, what relationship assumed between the masses and Badoglio's new post-Fascist government?[19]

Churchill took his interpretation of the new realities directly from Count Ciano's former *chef de cabinet*, the Marquis d'Ajeta, who on his arrival in Lisbon on 4 August had reported that,

> Fascism in Italy is dead, every trace of it has been swept away. Italy has turned red overnight. In Turin and Milan communist demonstrations had to be put down by the police. Twenty years of Fascism have eliminated the middle class. There remains nothing between the King and the patriots around him and who have control of the situation, and rampant Bolshevism.

Endorsing this description for Roosevelt's benefit, Churchill declared that from the first word to the last, d'Ajeta had never once mentioned an armistice, and his entire exposition was 'no more than a plea that we should save Italy from the Germans as well as from herself, and do it as quickly as possible'.[20] But whatever scorn felt by the prime minister for the motives behind the plea, its image of bloody anarchy and revolution held fast.

The Vatican served as a key transmission station in that period for news of Italian developments and reactions. The British ambassador, Sir D'Arcy Osborne, wrote:

> I fear that our appeals to the Italian people can do no good. They have neither the democratic instinct nor the democratic machinery for asserting themselves. Their only method would be revolutionary strikes which might invite German repression.[21]

A papal assistant secretary of state visiting Madrid told the U.S. embassy there that Marshal Badoglio was 'undoubtedly the man in popular esteem', but warned that all possible Italian leaders then available were tarred with the brush of Fascism, while popular hatred of the king and Crown Prince Umberto had actually overtaken that felt for Mussolini.[22]

In Parliament the Labour M.P. Ivor Thomas asked what rights the Italian people would have to decide their own government after surrender. Eden refused to comment and the Foreign Office cited a Churchill directive discouraging discussion of this question. Emanuel Shinwell, another prominent Labour member, asked if the government would refuse to deal with a new, Left-wing administration in Italy. The Foreign Office said 'no' but all demands would be maintained and no limitations accepted on Allied liberty of action.[23] Lord Hankey worried that 'scurvy treatment' now would be counter-productive, costing the Allies the support 'of a country from which we had much to gain by kindness and consideration'.[24] But from America Roosevelt transmitted his resentment of press criticism mounting against likely Allied combinations with the House of Savoy and Badoglio, and insisted on disarmament and assurance against chaos first, political concessions allowing the new government some international and internal credibility later.[25]

This was a particularly notable concession to Churchill since it cut across the much-vaunted idea of self-determination, common in American propaganda to Italy and insisted on by White House advisers such as Sherwood on this occasion.[26] As the Darlan affair had demonstrated, the critics of the Roosevelt administration could prove effective and embarrassing when military expediency and political morality seemed too flagrantly entangled, and much of the press kept up a steady barrage of criticism against the House of Savoy and Badoglio in the period before their surrender. Although the *Washington Post* was convinced of Badoglio's anti-Fascist and anti-German leanings, the New York papers – the *Herald Tribune* and the *New York Times* – took the opposite line, the *Times* describing the new government as no more than a military dictatorship which had substituted a Fascist one and owed its legitimacy to a 'puppet king'. Even the propaganda material put out by the Office of War Information and the analyses provided by the military intelligence services saw the new government in terms of military dictatorship in the phase immediately following Mussolini's downfall.[27]

Such factors, together with those of Italo-American electoral politics, the generous-sounding statements from 'Ike', and Roosevelt's constant refusal of precise political commitments limited the administration's freedom of political manoeuvre in a way which the British neither shared nor – at this stage – cared to comprehend. This is the key to understanding the tortuous political and military tug-of-war between the British and the Americans over the immediate content and significance of the armistice: should it be brief and practical, enabling Eisenhower to declare hostilities immediately ended – and thus also Italy's role as an Axis partner – or should it attempt to deliver total control of the Italian nation and people, defining every aspect of their external and internal condition, yet without formally ending the war with Italy? On the outcome of this conflict, with its crucial implications for the future treatment of Italy as a power and the Italians as a 'liberated' people, hung much of the nature and course of the Allied occupation of Italy over the subsequent three years.

'IN OUR VIEW unconditional surrender means both civil and military', the Foreign Office wrote to Harold Macmillan in Algiers at the end of July. But the Americans it seemed wished two stages, first a suspension of hostilities, then a civil agreement.[28]

When the British had begun planning in the spring they had taken as the central variable the existence or non-existence of an Italian authority with whom to deal. The legal and logistical problems posed by the absence of an Italian administration capable of signing a surrender document seemed overwhelming: as Churchill said in the Commons, to guarantee their position the Allies would have to occupy and administer every inch of Italian territory. They would have to use force at every moment, whether to change Italian laws, use Italian labour or conscript the armed forces. The inescapable conclusion was that 'an acceptable Italian administration' should be identified if not actually created as soon as possible. By 16 June the British had presented to the CCS a draft full-scale civil and military surrender document based on this premise.[29]

The Americans were aware of this dilemma but to many of them the use of any Italian government seemed to spell negotiation with the defeated army, and hence to remove some of the force of unconditional surrender, besides conferring on King Victor Emmanuel III and his lieutenants a definite and indispensable status. Although Eisenhower was clear on the need to deal with a central government from the beginning – at least on a temporary basis – sentiment in Washington was confused, with the Joint Intelligence Committee of the military taking for granted the continuity of the State while others, even in the War Department, seemed to be in favour of direct military government of the entire country.[30]

'Your ideas are all new to us', European adviser Dunn told the Foreign Office at the end of July.[31] While the State Department came round ponderously to the Whitehall view on comprehensive economic and political treatment for Italy via the armistice, Eisenhower and Roosevelt pressed decisively for a shorter military instrument for instant application, even at the risk of some vagueness on the absolute rights of the victors. Churchill was sympathetic to these approaches, even suggesting to Eden that 'harping on "unconditional surrender" with no prospect of mercy held out even as an act of grace may well lead to no surrender at all'.[32] By the end of July a purely military surrender document had been drafted in Algiers, and as modified by Churchill and the War Cabinet to increase the supreme commander's powers and encourage Italian resistance against the Germans, was approved for immediate use if necessary. These so-called 'Short Terms' insisted only on a cessation of hostilities and were limited in scope, stating that appropriate political, territorial and economic conditions would arrive later.[33]

The decisive Italian approach of 15 August found Roosevelt and Churchill together in Quebec and there a series of instructions were transmitted to

Eisenhower authorizing him to 'bring about the surrender of Italy but not to negotiate'. The main weapon would be the Short Terms, but they were to be applied in such a way as to encourage Italian collaboration in the approaching Salerno landings, and generally convince the Italians that in this way they might begin 'working their passage home' in the prime minister's phrase, to full Allied benediction. Beyond this there was also the need, says the official Foreign Office historian, 'to avoid the danger of the Germans setting up a "quisling" administration in Rome or of a drift into anarchy'.[34]

But this arrangement still left open the precise nature of a full armistice: what would its contents and direction be? Here only the British had a plan, and while the Italian emissaries attempted to haggle and hedge over the Short Terms with the AFHQ representatives in Lisbon, Churchill and Eden in Quebec took care to get their 'Long Terms' approved by the Americans. The process took a week and was only completed on 27 August when the 'highest levels' instructed Eisenhower that he must henceforth use this surrender document alone, with its 44 clauses, since it also included military terms based on 'unconditional surrender.'

> General Eisenhower thus received several difficult assignments as a result of the [Quebec] conference [write the official American military historians]. With limited forces and resources . . . he was to invade the Italian mainland in two places – across the Strait of Messina and on the shores of the Gulf of Salerno. From the latter landing, he was to sweep rapidly to Rome, 140 miles to the north. Without revealing his hand, he was to bluff Badoglio into surrender to make possible the Allied invasion. In accordance with instructions to use the long terms – an extraordinary complication because negotiations with Badoglio were already under way on the basis of the Short Terms . . . – Eisenhower was to insist on unconditional surrender. By this time, AFHQ intelligence, too, had obtained a clearer picture of German strength in Italy. The estimates . . . were radically wrong. German strength had been grossly underestimated.[35]

Not surprisingly the supreme commander improvised. The 'Short' armistice was eventually signed – but not announced – on 3 September, the day of Montgomery's landing across the Straits of Messina. But this was only after Eisenhower, in the name of inducing a surrender before the Salerno landing at all costs, had explicitly laid aside the full terms and declared their contents of only relative importance.[36] The dismay of London at this apparent reprieve for the Italians was greatly reinforced when on 8 September, the day before Salerno, Badoglio, finally seeing that he would have to defend Rome alone, attempted to evade the armistice and withdrew promised military support on the pretext of German pressure. As soon as Eisenhower called this bluff by announcing that Italy was surrendering unconditionally, the last remnants of effective authority crumbled in Rome, and the king, Badoglio and their circle fled in a tiny cortège for the Adriatic coast. The king took ship off Pescara, while Badoglio continued on south, finally coming to rest in a hotel in Brindisi.[37]

The full political significance of this drama did not strike home immediately in Whitehall. What stood out was the attempted treachery blocked by Eisenhower, and on this ground the Foreign Office, with Stalin's support, pressed for an Italian signature on the full terms as soon as possible. After further hesitations by Roosevelt and with a formal promise from Eisenhower of rewards in return for good behaviour, this was finally delivered in Malta on 29 September.[38]

'By signing the "short" armistice', Katherine Duff has written succinctly, 'the Italians had already, as it were, signed a blank cheque on which the "long" armistice filled in the figures'.[39] The shorter document, besides demanding the cessation of hostilities and the surrender of all Italian territory, included a blanket clause allowing the Allied commander any measure he might prefer in the name of military interest, and bound the Italian government to act under the commander's orders. 'In particular it was laid down that the Commander-in-Chief would establish Allied Military Government over such parts of Italian territory as he might deem necessary in the military interests of the Allied Nations' [explains an official historian], 'and he reserved to himself the full right to impose measures of disarmament, demobilisation and demilitarisation.'[40]

The 'Long' armistice had three official purposes:

> to give the Allies complete control over the Italian armed forces and all the facilities and material resources at their disposal; to ensure the maximum exploitation, consistent with international law, of the resources of the country for the Allied war effort, both as a base of operations and as a source of consumable conditions and services; and to effect the final destruction of Fascism.[41]

What the double surrender amounted to was 'full control and . . . complete capitulation by Italy', as Eisenhower told the CCS immediately afterwards. Wherever their armies held control the Allies would 'exercise all the rights of an occupying power', according to Article 20 of the Long Terms, with local law, public servants and finances at their complete disposition. As a first attempt at armistice design the Long Terms were immediately seen on the spot as far too detailed, inflexible and unilateral to be useful in practice, since they bore little relation to the real needs of the Allies imposing them, which were largely military, economic and utilitarian. Instead the military at AFHQ were now expected to begin destroying Fascism and supervising in detail the transition to peacetime of the defeated enemy. And for these purposes the installation of an armistice control commission was promised as soon as possible, along the lines of an idea long favoured by the British and long doubted by the Americans.

Such was the scope of the many other clauses in the 'Long' document, from the representation of Italy's interests abroad to the regulation of production, from the control of currency to the direction of business and trade, that it was immediately clear that if the Allies so wished this commission would loom large in the life of Italy from that time on until the signing of an eventual peace treaty.

The 'Long' armistice 'imposed the harshest kind of peace on Italy', Robert Murphy wrote afterwards: 'Allied instructions also forbade making the "Long Term" documents public under any circumstances. Eisenhower was not happy about this. He grumbled that it was a "crooked deal", and said that these secret documents would not be published even ten years after the war'.[42] The victorious powers had little doubt that the terms were cruel – there was even mention of 'reparation and payment of the costs of occupation'(Art.33) – and took steps to insulate themselves from criticism in Italy and at home. Not even the directives for the occupation of Sicily – designed as they were for 'enemy territory' and thus closest to a practical translation of the armistice terms – were published, since (among other reasons) the War Office felt that 'their publication would give the enemy an excellent propaganda opportunity and would provide material for ill-intentioned journalists both here and in America'.[43] The terms themselves were not published until after the liberation and for a long time the only individuals in Italy who knew them were the original signers, Badoglio and the king. Not until late 1944 did the members of successive governments, who were required to declare their recognition of the armistice on taking office, come to know of its contents.[44]

In the House of Commons afterwards Nye Bevan declared that the armistice should have been signed with the striking workers and peasants of Milan, a notion dismissed with jocular ease by the majority of members present, men like Harold Nicholson who had no difficulty in seeing that what counted was the loyalty of the army and the navy to the new pact (although by this time the Italian army had almost entirely disintegrated, while the navy had come into Allied hands on 11 September).[45]

Churchill's explanations in Parliament held out little clear hope. By 21 September the king and Badoglio had become the lawful government round whom 'we are endeavouring to rally the strongest forces in Italy to make head against the Germans and the Mussolini–Quisling–Fascist combination'.[46] Yet there remained the weight of 1940, of past corruption and its awful lesson, that 'nations which allow their rights and liberties to be subverted by tyrants must suffer heavy penalties for those tyrants' crimes'.[47] To the anti-Fascist forces struggling to assemble in Italy this was the bleak message of the armistice and unconditional surrender, and the most prescient, including Don Sturzo in New York and the Christian Democrat leader De Gasperi, took pains at this stage to place as much political distance as possible between themselves and the signers of that document.[48]

The endorsement of the two 'mediocre and super-annuated ex-guardians of Fascism' – Badoglio and the king described in the words of the American historian Charles Delzell – came with the declaration of co-belligerency on

13 October. Henceforth they were elevated to the status of symbols of constitutional and non-Fascist unity, for international and internal purposes. Although the 'short' armistice had emphatically not envisaged active Italian participation in the war effort, within days of the military surrender Churchill had single-handedly begun planning for Italy's conversion to the role of co-belligerent and for the necessary adjustment of public opinion: 'I was sure that King Victor Emmanuel and Badoglio would be able to do more for what had now become the common cause than any Italian government formed from the exiles or opponents of the Fascist regime. The surrender of the Italian Fleet was solid proof of their authority', wrote the prime minister later.[49] While still in America after Quebec, Churchill had presented to a high-level conference in the White House a detailed memorandum on 'the conversion of Italy into an active agent against Germany'. Together with plans for the fleet were specific military proposals, based on the use of 'at least a dozen Italian divisions' in the front line when Allied divisions began to move away in November in preparation for 'Overlord', the cross-Channel attack. '[Our] State policy should be adapted to procure this end', the prime minister declared.[50]

The result was a joint message from Churchill and Roosevelt to Badoglio on 10 September urging him 'to restore to the Italian people their peace and liberty and recover for Italy an honourable place among the civilized nations of Europe.'[51]

At this point the running on Badoglio's behalf was taken up by AFHQ, which on 13 September sent a military mission to Brindisi headed by the former governor of Gibraltar, Lt Gen. Sir Noel Mason-MacFarlane. The mission was soon convinced that the aged marshal was working under insuperable difficulties:

Badoglio has made repeated references to the spirit of the message from the President and the Prime Minister [Eisenhower told the Combined Chiefs of Staff in the middle of September] He points out to us that his administration is conscientiously and loyally carrying out the terms of the [short] Armistice and has surrendered the Italian fleet. The Italian people and the armed forces naturally regard an armistice as connoting a cessation of hostilities. His administration, however, stands for war against the Germans. How will the Italian people and the army, Badoglio asks, understand that this is their duty unless a status of at least co-belligerency can be given to Italy.[52]

For Eisenhower the importance of the Badoglio administration was 'its unchallenged claim to legality', so that only two alternatives were available: either 'to sweep this government aside [and] set up an Allied Military Government of occupied Italy', or

to accept and strengthen the legal government of Italy under the King and Badoglio; to regard this government and the Italian people as co-belligerents but with their military activity subject to my direction under terms of armistice, and I, of course, making such military, political and administrative conditions as I find necessary from time to time.[53]

Acting on this belief, Eisenhower and his political advisers, Macmillan and Murphy, decided within days that the king should be given some territory to reign over and consequently 'military government' was not proclaimed in the Apulian provinces around Brindisi. In the same spirit Churchill told Roosevelt on 21 September that it was 'vital to build up the authority of the King and the Brindisi administration and have unity of command throughout Italy.' The result was a new Churchill–Roosevelt directive for Eisenhower (on 23 September), demanding an Italian declaration of war, insisting on the future free choice of the Italian people in their form of government and explicitly holding out to Badoglio the promise of co-belligerency.[54]

But in the Foreign Office the whole concept of the co-belligerency relationship, especially as contemplated without the full armistice signature, was spurious. Commenting on the suggestions from Algiers, a high official wrote that Badoglio and his handful of followers had practically nothing to offer in exchange for 'quasi-Allied status'. In London they had 'always foreseen' that Badoglio would try this manoeuvre, but it should be repulsed. If the Italians were helping at all, then the armistice regime could be softened. To do otherwise would simply lead to 'undefined military commitments. We should place ourselves under a moral obligation to free Italy from the Germans up to the Alps and should be under constant pressure from our new Allies to do so.' In contrast to the base and exclusively selfish motives attributed to Badoglio, stood the competing claims of Greeks, Yugoslavs and Frenchmen, Allies whose populations were, it was said, being actively encouraged to fight the enemy. As for the Russians, the effect of recognition could only be to 'arouse every sort of suspicion', especially if the announcement were made regardless of their demands for the Political-Military Commission. In the absence of overwhelming military considerations, concluded the Foreign Office, political criteria – 'which are practical and real' – should be the deciding ones.[55]

It was an extraordinary analysis, chilling, disdainful and quite different in spirit to Churchill's approach. There was an immediate impact on the conduct of negotiations with Badoglio. The message of the 23rd, drafted by Roosevelt, had declared the 'long' terms laid aside without a signature and Churchill, over-riding his colleagues, had concurred. By the 29th, the Foreign Office and the War Cabinet, backed by an intervention from Stalin on the 26th, had obliged Badoglio to place his name on the same 'long' terms armistice, thereby putting Eisenhower in the embarrassing situation of being obliged to declare simultaneously that the *application* of the terms would be as lenient as possible. Two more weeks were consumed before Badoglio and the king finally signed their declaration of war on Germany; at the same time the Allies formally announced 'co-belligerency' (a word reinvented for the occasion by Harold Macmillan), also indicating that Badoglio would be expected to broaden the base of his government by including anti-Fascist elements, and promising a free political choice in Italy at the war's end.[56]

The usefulness of the co-belligerency concept lay in its imprecision. While guaranteeing some form of assistance to the Allied war effort, the term marked the fact, as British legal experts pointed out, that Italy had *not* acquired Allied status. In fact, while seeming to bestow on the prostrate remnants of Brindisi a new lease of moral and political authority, it acknowledged little more than Italy's objective status as an invaded country and a victim of Nazi aggression. The declaration contained no commitment to practical support of any war effort Italians might make, nor did it guarantee the personal positions of Badoglio or Victor Emmanuel.[57] With the parallel application of a punitive armistice, the declaration had as its most serious long-term consequence the institutionalization of radically different approaches to the Italian internal situation on the British and American sides. '[The] British position, due to Churchill's dynamism, had definition,' writes F.P. King; 'By comparison the Americans groped.'[58]

Recriminations broke out almost immediately. While Churchill was already warming to the task of promoting Victor Emmanuel and Badoglio as long-term retainers in Italy, anxiety was mounting in Washington over the commitment now apparently being made to them. Stimson, the secretary of war, was convinced of the utility of co-belligerency and of the historical respectability of the House of Savoy, but Harry Hopkins was not, and tried to dissuade Roosevelt from any type of recognition of former Fascist collaborators.[59]

Such scruples related more to the administration's sensitivity on the controversial issue of self-determination than to Italy's status as a power seeking self-redemption at Churchill's behest. But Hopkins's anxieties can hardly have been lessened by rumours of a growing special relationship between Badoglio and the British at AFHQ, which began to spread from the beginning of October onwards. Although Robert Murphy claimed that in the later stages the armistice negotiations had been 'taken over and to an important extent directed by American representatives here', he felt bound to report that 'the British have undertaken the lead in the formulation of Allied policy in Italy. The Prime Minister and the Foreign Office have shown a daily interest in the Italian problem, making suggestions to Macmillan, keeping him fully advised of their current thought, definitely supporting the retention of the Italian Monarchy . . . from the very beginning.'[60]

ON 19 OCTOBER, less than a week after the co-belligerency announcement, the opening meeting took place in Moscow of the conference of Allied foreign ministers, the first-ever Allied assembly of its kind, and curtain-raiser for the first encounter between the Big Three themselves five weeks later in Teheran. The British expressed a willingness to discuss 'any and every subject' and brought a detailed list to Moscow. The Americans wished above all to talk about the end of the war and their plans for collective world security. Stalin, recalled Churchill, 'made one suggestion and one suggestion only' – the consideration of measures to shorten the war.[61]

Italian questions were mentioned specifically on the British list. Besides the question of Russia's precise relation to the armistice, and to the administration of the country, there still lay open the question of the Political-Military Commission as first demanded by Stalin in August and requested again at the end of September. In the meantime another Soviet demand had appeared: for a share in the Italian fleet. All in all accounts had now to be settled up on the Anglo-American handling of the Italian collapse in the name of the 'United Nations'.

The key intervention was probably that of Eisenhower on 20 October. In their last note on the subject, the Soviets had insisted that the executive Armistice Control Commission set up under the 'Long Terms' (with the military commander as its president) would be unnecessary: the new tripartite Political-Military Commission would take care of everything. At AFHQ the situation appeared exactly the opposite: the military-run commission would have all the necessary power: the tripartite committee would simply be a hindrance. In spite of an earlier warning by Chief of Staff Marshall against any sharp rebuff to the Russians at that stage, Eisenhower's language was blunt:

> Allied C-in-C must continue to receive instructions, whether political or military, from the Combined Chiefs of Staff and from them alone.
> As regards the Allied Control Commission, experience in North Africa goes to show that so long as active military operations are being carried on, final authority regarding the political relations between the occupying armies and the local Administration should remain with the Allied Commander-in-Chief.
> When operations have ceased, the Commander-in-Chief's interest is reduced to the safety of any bases and the security of any lines of communication on which he may be relying, and normal diplomatic machinery can safely be allowed to function.[62]

There followed a stage-by-stage plan for the restoration of international civil control in Italy taken from a paper by Harold Macmillan, now British 'Resident Minister'. This centred on a new diplomatic *advisory council*, made up of representatives of the principal interested powers (except Italy). During the campaign, this council would watch over the activities of the Control Commission and advise the commander-in-chief in his capacity as its president on the internal and international situation of the country. Once the campaign was over and the commander-in-chief was satisfied that military control could safely be dispensed with, then this advisory council could supervise the transition to normal diplomacy.[63]

Eden took up this approach immediately and in the discussion of his own paper on the subject – which largely over-rode a confusing 'Four Nation Declaration' which Hull had brought to deal with armistice problems –

introduced a fundamental distinction between the general question of 'liberated territories' and the enforcement of the Italian armistice. Although Eden laid claim to a 'completely open mind' and a willingness to discuss 'any form of machinery for ensuring the close collaboration of the three powers', his proposals were clearly prejudiced in certain directions, as Molotov soon discovered on enquiring as to the fate of the British plans of early July. Conditions had changed since then, said the foreign secretary; 'some form of a clearing-house' was now the over-riding need; with the new advisory council on Italy to be set up only when the commander-in-chief felt free to relinquish his overall control.[64]

Molotov for his part outlined the Russian basic premises with force, concentrating on the new problems which derived from this first surrender, as they 'affected very directly the cooperation between our three countries'. Reaffirming that the Soviets lacked accurate information, or even a representative on the spot, Molotov declared that the Soviet Union 'attached the greatest importance' to what happened in Italy and wished in the first instance 'adequate guarantees' on the enforcement of the surrender and the eradication of Fascism. With these aims in mind he then read out a series of seven 'urgent political measures' which the Soviets wished to see applied to the internal situation, providing for the democratization and reform of national and local government by way of the elimination of Fascist institutions and the introduction of recognized anti-Fascist elements into the political life of the country.[65] Hull said that the points were at one with the political philosophy of America; Eden, in a telegram to the Foreign Office, predicted that it would have an 'excellent effect on the Soviet Government and finally bring them into line on our policy and actions in Italy, if we could agree to make the declaration proposed by Molotov.' The principles, Eden added, were unexceptionable and could be put into effect when the military situation allowed.[66]

In the immediately following session of the conference, on 23 October, the Soviets announced that they had come round to Eden's concepts, accepting a dividing line between the work of the Political-Military Commission – now to be set up in London – and the problem of the Italian armistice. It was a major victory for Eden and the Eisenhower–Macmillan approach, especially since it also implied full acceptance of the armistice terms and co-belligerency. And its price was low: Molotov simply demanded that the advisory council – henceforth to be known as the Advisory Council for Italy (ACI) – should be installed immediately rather than waiting until Rome was taken as AFHQ preferred; as for the seven points, the Soviets demanded little beyond the reluctant political efforts the Anglo-Americans were already making in Italy. The supreme commander in any event retained his jealous sovereignty on the timing of implementation, a right which the British were to insist on until the end of the war.[67]

Among the great tripartite gatherings of the war [writes Vojtech Mastny], the Moscow meeting stands out as the only one where issues were clearly defined, systematically discussed, and disposed of through genuine bargaining. No foreign conquests by the Red Army had as yet cast a shadow over the deliberations. Instead, the Western powers were the ones who had achieved such conquests in Italy – and these, significantly, enabled them to elicit the only important Soviet concessions.[68]

The extent of their loss became finally clear to the Soviets at the end of November, the occasion being the formal creation of the Advisory Council for Italy in Algiers. To emphasize the importance he attached to the original proposal for a Political–Military Commission, Stalin had nominated no less a person than Andrei Vyshinsky, deputy foreign minister, as Russian representative and this appointment was transferred to the new council. 'The Russian members, on reaching Algiers had the impression', Murphy reported to Washington, 'that Article 37 of the long-term Armistice Agreement with the Italian Government [on the establishment of the control commission] meant that the Soviet members were appointed automatically to the Control Commission . . . From our early talks with Vychinsky [sic] it became clear also that he thought the functions of the Allied Control Commission were to be decided by the Advisory Council.'[69]

The U.S.A. and the U.K. had little difficulty with the second point since the Council's terms of reference approved at Moscow envisaged that it would do no more than 'advise' the Allied commander-in-chief on the work of control as a result of 'watching' the machinery in action.[70] This was clearly part of the Eisenhower–Churchill strategy to guard the sovereignty of the military and in effect it forced the Council one step further away from the Control Commission on to a remote, non-executive plane. As for the problem of Russian representation on the Control Commission, the delegates in Algiers were told that only the CCS could approve appointments, while Article 37 merely provided 'in general' that the Commission would contain United Nations representation.[71] Eventually, in February 1944, Vyshinsky agreed to accept a consultative position – together with a representative of the Free French – on the understanding that no further members would be accepted.[72] This position Vyshinsky then handed down to a subordinate, A. Bogomolov, whose subsequent career in Italy was (with one exception) predictably inconspicuous.

The Russians had agreed to the terms of the armistice and despite Foreign Office fears had made no difficulties over co-belligerency. In Moscow they had also repeated their interest in a share of the Italian royal and merchant navies, and had been fended off.[73] What sort of suspicions must have been provoked then by the conduct of American policy in Italy with its series of resounding defeats for the Soviets, leading to their effective exclusion from any practical power-sharing in the theatre? Was it, as Mastny writes, 'the price Stalin seemed willing to pay for ending the war quickly'? John Gaddis reports that: 'American officials realized that the decision to minimize

Moscow's role in the occupation of Italy might give the Russians a convenient excuse later on to restrict Anglo-American activities in Rumania, Bulgaria and Hungary . . . but Roosevelt did not expect the Russians to allow their allies much influence in this area whatever happened in Italy.'[74] Thus when Romania was occupied by the Russians in 1944, the JCS noted with good grace that it was 'only natural and to be expected' that Moscow would conduct the surrender, precisely because of the Italian analogy and precedent.[75] But the Russians were to be the first into the field in the following year with an attempt to restore the balance in one place – Italy.

This was the environment from which the plans for liberated Italy emerged. The Moscow conference has been seen as a high point in Allied collaboration, not least because it produced a common declaration on policy in Italy. But the reality was suspicion and confusion: 'Churchill loathes the Russians', said a Foreign Office delegate to the Moscow conference, Oliver Harvey, who even alleged that the prime minister had tried to wreck the conference by presenting the military picture in Italy as even worse than it was.[76]

The greatest confusion lay in the American camp, whose representatives, unwilling or unable to make precise political choices in specific situations such as the Italian one, found themselves outdistanced and outmanoeuvred by the British, knowing where their interest lay and prepared to act on it. The Americans hoped to 'wait and see', undervaluing the significance and weight of the Italian problem, even as they were pouring large armies into the country.[77]

As 1943 closed Italy's status in international relations was defined in a way which was to change little in the subsequent three years. 'Co-belligerency' signified little beyond compromise and postponement: compromise between statesmen and military men, between British and Americans, between the recent past and the battleground of the present; postponement in the name of practical flexibility and unprejudiced freedom of action. Between the Italians and their newly-legitimized government, and between that government and the outside world, stood a special body, the Allied Control Commission – born with great labour on 10 November – which also existed, among other reasons, to free the Allies from burdens and commitments. There was no further talk of a dozen Italian divisions in the front line.

But certain choices had already been made. First there was one of method: the Allies had chosen to regulate Italy's external and internal arrangements according to military priorities and by military means. So whatever demands might come from Italian or domestic political forces beyond the pale of military awareness came far behind the fact that Italy was indeed a battlefield. Secondly, Italy was to be governed not by the United Nations, nor even by the tripartite Alliance, but under an uneasy condominium set up by the British and the Americans and dominated by the British. As we have seen, the evolution of this option was intimately, probably deliberately, connected with the preceding one, though what its implications were for the world interests and relationships of the powers concerned was not at all clear. Thirdly, an undefined responsibility had been assumed with respect to the King of Italy and Badoglio. Should they fail to hold in check their patch of territory, the British and the Americans would find themselves constrained to carry out what Churchill had said they must at all costs avoid, what the armistice defined as the ultimate sanction against the defeated enemy: the physical occupation of every square mile of Italy freed from German hands.

3 Liberators or occupiers? The Allies in southern Italy, autumn–winter 1943

THE NEW INVADERS soon discovered that between the abstract, high-altitude struggles over such problems as the enforcement of the armistice, and the physical realities of southern Italy in late 1943, there lay a world and more of difference. Naples had been entered on 1 October, where the Allies were greeted by 'screaming, hysterical people'. 'There was no question of war or enmity here,' the journalist Alan Moorehead wrote afterwards, ignoring the after-effects of Nazi terror;

> hunger governed all . . . What we are witnessing in fact was the moral collapse of a people. They had no pride any more, or dignity. The animal struggle for existence governed everything. Food. That was the only thing that mattered. Food for the children. Food for yourself. Food at the cost of any debasement and depravity. And after food a little warmth and shelter.[1]

As the military advance bogged down between Naples and Rome, so the Allied machinery for controlling and feeding the people behind the lines began to crumble. Naples during the winter of 1943–4, 'represents military government, let it be hoped, at its worst,' a veteran of the experience wrote later. 'During that period of time Naples was probably the worst-governed city in the Western world, and it was not much better a year later.'[2] At the time the worry and dismay of the authorities reached a high-point in the middle of December, when AFHQ telegraphed to the CCS to inform them that:

> Conditions in Southern Italy and Sicily are such that unless reasonable quantities of food are supplied very promptly we will experience sabotage, unrest and a complete cessation of those activities necessary to our advance.[3]

From the moment when the Allied armies first set foot in North Africa they had found themselves confronted with social and political problems which far outweighed in scope and significance any foreseen in the dense months of military planning preceding the invasion. 'The adjustments of modern society were so delicate and the impact of modern war so compre-hensive that an elaborate web of non-military activities had to be organized merely to protect the military advantages gained,' wrote the political scientist William Reitzel in 1948:

> coincidentally with military operations, the inescapable need for civil government presented itself. Nothing delayed for long the interest of the indigenous population in

food, clothing, work and some sort of social organization. This meant in effect that
the Allied Military Command was the final authority to whom these claims were
presented.[4]

They were not welcome. The Armies adopted the attitude of 'Maximum
returns with minimum responsibilities'[5] and inevitably subordinated as far
as possible all such considerations to the prosecution of the military effort.
Although it was foreseen by planners as a vital problem even before the
arrival in Sicily, the social environment in which the campaign took place
was something the soldiers preferred to ignore if they could, and while the
population was supplied with the minimum amount of attention thought to
be needed to prevent 'disease and unrest', and the country adapted as
dictated by the needs of the campaign, 'civil affairs' in general were
relegated to the status of a 'Cinderella' service suitable for Ancient Military
Gentlemen on Tour (the Allied Military Government of Occupied Territories, AMGOT, was thought to be their province), and a variety of other
elements from the middle levels of army life.[6]

In contrast the high-level organs of Allied control in Italy were invested by
the 'Long Terms' with heavy formal responsibilities. On their shoulders fell
the burden of imposing and enforcing the armistice, and of abolishing
Fascism. In addition they constituted the channels by which the Allied
governments made their wishes known to the Italian government. The
unwritten objectives were even more demanding: according to journalists,
the Allied managers were expected to reflect the intentions of the Allies
towards the liberated continent, and to demonstrate the capacity of the
democracies to reorganize war-torn Europe. The evolution of these commitments and their overall significance did not become fully clear until the end
of the war, when serious questions first began to be asked about the
character of this intervention, and its implications for the political development of Italy and other countries similarly treated.

Commenting on the Nazi use of terror to keep peoples in occupied
countries in order, Harold Macmillan said: 'civilised armies, defending high
principles, cannot find this easy way out. They start as conquerors but soon
find themselves trustees.'[7] Many of the essential dilemmas were seen by the
British and the Americans right at the beginning, even as Italy was being
invaded, and they exercised minds at the highest level.

To begin with there was the question of whether Allied control should be
prevalently civilian or military in character. A Department of the Interior
expert in Washington warned:

The civilians are in danger of losing the post-war world by default. They are in danger
of losing out because they seem to lack a comprehensive plan and a unified purpose.
The Army, on the other hand, has a plan and a purpose. The Army's plan is to train
administrators for the post-war world and thereby to control it. Furthermore, this
plan will monopolize all of the training and research facilities of the country by a
process of total absorption. . . . From a democratic point of view – from the point of
view of what the United Nations are fighting for – this situation is disturbing.[8]

Then a principle had to be established which would indicate whether the occupiers would assume full political and administrative control or delegate responsibility to cooperative local elements, bearing in mind the problem of purging Fascism's influence from the state. Churchill advised Roosevelt in June 1943:

> It seems wise to make [newly conquered regions] run themselves as much as possible. Malignant or prominent Fascists must be removed and we should be prepared to replace them with trustworthy administrators to the extent that these cannot be found for our purposes from the local population. I am sure that it would be a mistake to flood all these places with hundreds of British and American gauleiters, however well meaning and well trained they may be.[9]

Were the Italians to be treated as potential friends or permanent enemies?

> The advantage of an occupation of comparatively brief duration [wrote a State Department planner in July] is that it would suffice to carry out the disarmament of Italy yet would not arouse the deep-seated and lasting antagonism of the Italian people. With this end in view, the occupation might be terminated as soon as a government satisfactory to the United Nations assumed control. . . . The more drastic policy of continuing the occupation for a considerable period after the conclusion of peace would have as an object to fully impress on the Italian people the consequences of Fascist imperialism.[10]

How would political reconstruction take place if the military stayed in charge? A commentator in the *New York Herald Tribune* foresaw the difficulties with considerable accuracy:

> It would be painfully easy for an occupying force, in the interest of 'order', to freeze Italy's Fascist organization in authority. It is less likely that the Allied authorities would permit the opposite to occur – namely the riotous competition of anti-fascist groups for power – during the critical period of occupation . . . [to find a middle road] will require the most earnest efforts of men of vision, sympathy with legitimate Italian aspirations and, above all, knowledge of Italian conditions.[11]

But the problem of defining and deciding these issues immediately brought out the underlying difficulty, which concerned not so much *what* would be decided, or even *how* the decisions would be made, so much as *who* would settle them. The Russians were excluded by common Anglo-American consent, but between the British and the Americans power had somehow to be shared, and whether this was to be done on a basis of equality or inequality was still not fully clear. In Whitehall, however, there was no doubt: if the control machinery could be so constructed as to leave military affairs in American hands, this would 'make it easier to retain the direction of political and economic questions in British hands.'[12]

The Sicilians probably bore the brunt of the ambiguity of the British and Americans towards their new subjects more directly than any other section of the population, since the island was occupied before the armistice, and hence under AMGOT, the particularly chaotic military government of the first instance. The CCS directive for the occupation of Sicily stated:

The administration shall be benevolent with respect to the civilian population so far as consistent with strict military requirements. The civilian population is tired of war, resentful of German overlordship, and demoralised by the Fascist regime, and will therefore be responsive to a just and efficient administration. It should be made clear to the local population that military occupation is intended: (1) to deliver the people from the Fascist regime which led them into the war; and (2) to restore Italy as a free nation.[13]

On the other hand, General Administrative Instruction No. 1 told AMGOT officers:

You will be guided in your attitude towards the local population by the memory of years of war in which the Italians fought against your people and your Allies.[14]

Even when this difficulty had been resolved in favour of the CCS approach, the problem remained of reconciling the liberated, welcoming Italian people with the overwhelming presence of Allied control. The head of AMGOT, Lord Rennell, delivered a stern warning at the beginning of October:

The enthusiasm with which Allied troops have been received . . . must not be construed as indicating a desire to be governed by an Allied Military Government which, as I have before stated and desire here to restate, cannot in my view conduct a direct administration in Italy or do more than direct an incompetent Italian bureaucracy to govern a dispirited and apathetic people.[15]

The head of the military mission to the king, Mason-MacFarlane, complained in the same period that Victor Emmanuel was scarcely interested in administering the portion of territory allotted to him (known as 'King's Italy') until Rome was captured and, worse, His Majesty continued to assume that this would be imminent.[16] To other Allied administrators on the spot it soon became clear that without the support of the central machinery of the State, the king's government was inoperative, and radical revisions of the plans for speedy hand-over of responsibility had to be made from the middle of October onwards. First it was decided to continue military government under the Allied Armies throughout the liberated territories until Rome was taken. Then came the emergence of Mussolini's 'Republic of Salo' as a thoroughgoing puppet administration in the hands of an invader; at the same time the military advance in the South ground to a halt. '[In] consequence [said the head of the Military Government section of AFHQ, the American General Holmes], steps must be taken at once to develop the Italian Government.' All concerned agreed with Macmillan when he said that the best way to do this was to establish the Control Commission as soon as possible as a substantial umbrella organization under which the government could begin to take control of more territory, beginning with Sicily.[17]

The result was the birth, with great fatigue, on 10 November 1943, of the Allied Control Commission (ACC). Its first head was a Corps Commander from Eisenhower's early career, Major General Kenyon A. Joyce, who soon built it up to a staff of almost 1500 officers.

As initially brought into action [writes the British official historian], the Allied Control Commission was an integrated Anglo-American unit divided into four sections – Military, Political, Economic and Administrative, and Communications, each divided into a number of subcommissions. The Military Section was to contain six. . . . The Political Section was to have three. . . . The staff of the Political Section was to be largely civilian – mostly Foreign Office officials – in contrast to that of the other three, which was to be formed of officers of military rank. The Economic and Administrative Section was to be sub-divided into two directorates, each embracing a varying number of subcommissions. . . . The Communications Section was divided into three subcommissions.[18]

There was an immense hierarchy of specialized officers. Each of the 26 subcommissions had a head and a deputy, as did the four main divisions. Above or alongside them all were chiefs of staff, executive officers, intelligence people, security people and a large secretariat. However, the greatest complication of all was that high policy had decided that a 'scrupulous equilibrium' must be maintained between the two main nationalities involved. This meant that heads and deputies were often of different nationality, or that different subcommissions would be run on quite different lines according to whether they were in British or American hands. To house this super-bureaucracy along with its parent, AFHQ, took one of the largest Bourbon palaces in Europe, at Caserta near Naples, where military administrators began to be gathered from late summer onwards from wherever they could be found.

But this was not all:

Beneath the central hierarchy were large regional teams of civil affairs officers and specialist officers organised on AMGOT lines. These were intended to provide 'a thinly spread control over the local administrations in the field'.[19]

Meanwhile in the forward areas the armies maintained their own military government whose reign ceased only when the supreme commander judged conditions stable enough for the revived Italian government to take over – under a system of 'advisory control' maintained by the ACC.

'When the plan was first drawn up', said a Foreign Office functionary late in October 1943, referring to the scheme for a Control Commission included in the 'Long Terms', 'the conception was that [its] administrative and economic section[s] would exercise a *repressive* supervision over the Italian people and industry. Now that the policy is to make the Italians fight the Germans, to re-equip them and to make their war factories productive, a different emphasis is needed.'[20] In view of the sceptical attitude of the Foreign Office towards Italy's new status, it was no surprise that this change in emphasis was not forthcoming from London. But – beyond the establishment of 'King's Italy' around Brindisi – the military men and their advisers in southern Italy proved no more successful than Whitehall in adapting the plans for occupation at short notice to accommodate the uncertain rights of a quasi-Ally. 'The implications of co-belligerency appear to have been most

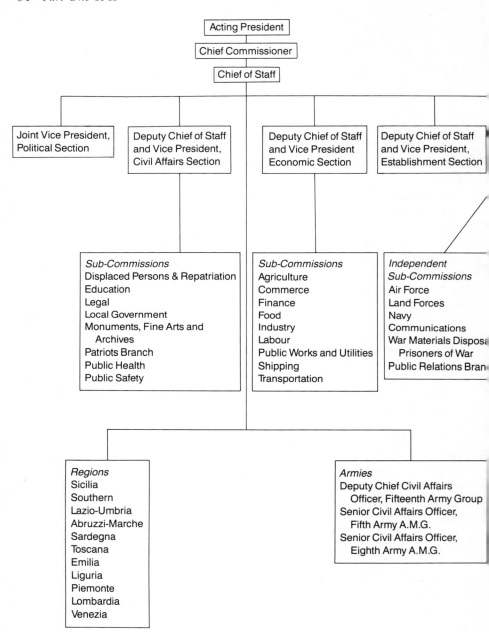

Fig. 1   A.C. organization chart, after the Allied Commission Desk Diary of January 1945.

imperfectly realised, and detailed control of every branch of Italian administration was insisted on,' writes the British official historian; '. . . it is difficult
to avoid the conclusion that, instead of thinking things out afresh, AFHQ
merely trimmed the organisation which they had designed for the military
government of the peninsula in the event of no acceptable Italian Government being available.'[21] In other words the structures of control set up in
Italy were those designed for total occupation in enemy territory. Whatever
mitigation of a harsh armistice was to be offered by such structures would be
arbitrarily defined by the victors: 'the Control Commission will in fact carry
out such provisions of the Armistice as we may care to insist on,' said the
Foreign Office.[22]

The complex processes which resulted in Italy's liberation being run by a
large military bureaucracy can best be appreciated if, in addition to the
attitude of the British and the inadequacies of the AFHQ planners, in
addition to the basic dilemmas listed above, we remember the one essential
factor of circumstance – time – which conditioned events. Other circumstances, particularly the lack of coordination between London, Washington,
Caserta and Algiers, also weighed heavily on the evolution of the structures
of control, which in the first instance were composed of a body made up of
two obsolete war-machines intermingled (as Harold Macmillan said, referring to the U.S. War Department and the British War Office[23]) under a head
formed out of the original military mission to the king in Brindisi. But more
than any other factor it was the delay in the advance through the winter of
1943–4 – cruelly repeated in the following year – which highlighted the
contradictions, the improvised nature of the solutions to the basic problems.
The risks were accurately predicted by Macmillan, who had told the Foreign
Office in September: 'I can foresee a great period of confusion during the
battles in Italy and the necessity for a considerable degree of Amgot in any
area which may be under our control.'[24]

THE FOREIGN OFFICE had also predicted that the administrative ability of
the government would be 'practically nil' when co-belligerency came into
effect. They were right:

> When we arrived at Brindisi [Captain Stone the later head of ACC, recalled], there
> was virtually no Italian Government and no administrative machine. There was the
> Italian Prime Minister, Marshal Badoglio, with two service ministers but without any
> other colleagues or any of the officials, archives, or even typewriters that are the
> apparatus by which administrations can be carried on. It is no secret that all our
> original communications from the Italian Government of Brindisi came in the form of
> letters written by the hand of the Prime Minister himself.[25]

There were, as Stone said, but two ministers in Brindisi in the first weeks –
military heads of the air force and navy – and a third in Naples, the former
'Minister of Corporations' of the pre-armistice weeks.[26] With political life
paralysed, Badoglio was unable to recruit anti-Fascist politicians when he

formed a new government early in November. Consequently it was composed of the two service ministers together with a number of under-
secretaries, who then became ministers as part of the government reinforce-
ment campaign when Sicily was returned to its jurisdiction in February
1944.[27] The help these 'transient and embarrassed phantoms' could give to
the Allies was of course minimal, lacking as they did the most elementary
tools of government. This situation was doubly unfortunate since the Allies
had placed supreme emphasis on the administrative benefits they expected
to get from collaboration with the indigenous State machinery in public
explanations of the type of control installed, and in their declarations in
favour of co-belligerency with the remnants of Fascism.[28] In the early
governments, individuals could be found who would accept responsibility
and somehow make the machinery work, and the early directors of communications and railways were retained at Allied request throughout the
occupation. But the majority resembled the education minister who, asked
by Allied officials in November 1943 what plans were formulated for his
ministry, replied at first, 'None'. He subsequently explained that 'his
purpose would be to re-establish the honest character of education, to get
rid of Fascist influence, and to return to where education would have been
had Fascism not intervened.' There could be no ministry, said the minister,
until Rome was reached, though 'an assembly who would begin to plan
with him' might be contemplated for the beginning of the New Year.' He
then asked that we continue to run education until Rome was taken . . . in
order to give him the opportunity of making a working administration. He
was told that he must not assume that his request would be agreed by us.'[29]

In deference to traditional British practice, the province was selected as
the lowest manageable level of Allied control. Here, says an American
official historian, 'the military government would operate by indirect control; it would utilize the existing Italian law – and also retain as far as possible
the existing local administration.' How were these procedures – fundamental to traditional conceptions of military occupation – to be reconciled
with the commitment to uproot Fascism? 'The Combined Chiefs of Staff,
asked to clarify the point, stated that the first objective of military government must be to maintain efficient local government,' explains the same
War Department historian.[30]

The element in local government most determining its efficiency had
already been identified by Allied planners before the invasion: it was to be
found in the person and institution of the provincial prefect. The essential,
indispensable relationship between the local Allied administrator and this
key figure of the Italian state was explained as follows by the head of
AMGOT in a pre-invasion argument with American planners demanding
his substitution:

> In this system, the Senior Allied Provincial Administrator . . . sits, not in the chair of
> the Prefect, but in a chair at his side and tells him what the Military Government

wants done. The Prefect then issues his own orders, to his own subordinates, in his own name, at the direction of the Provincial Administrators. Allied personnel lower down the scale sit in with and supervise the functioning of branches and divisions to ensure that orders given by the Prefect are, in fact, properly carried out.

Under this arrangement, continued Lord Rennell, local civil servants would be less disturbed, more obedient to their superiors, more easily reformed, and it would be possible to avoid the appearance of 'instituting a government which either looks like a colonial government, or gives the impression of being a prelude to annexation.'[31]

As the basis of Allied control on the ground, this scheme was first experimented with in Sicily and subsequently installed throughout liberated Italy. It was the visible symbol and the practical, operative expression of the interdependent relationship between the Allies as liberators and occupiers, and the permanent Italian State. Its immediate justification remained practical, but once co-belligerency came into force, juridical and political arguments added to its favour:

> If the governments of the United States and Great Britain chose to deal with Marshal Badoglio and the King of Italy, military government officers were, of course, prevented from ousting local officials whom they knew beyond all reasonable doubt to be Fascists, as long as such officials had the blessing of the Italian authorities accepted by American policy makers.[32]

It was this situation which tended to give the lie to Allied propaganda claims that by handing over the the Italian machinery they were encouraging self-determination and democracy:

> Every effort was made to impress upon the people the fact that it was their responsibility to govern themselves. Italians who came into the national and provincial headquarters seeking assistance were routed by experienced enlisted men to the appropriate Italian agency, and few if any complaints were received by Allied officials except through Italian channels. Provincial orders were frequently issued over the name of the Italian prefect, the order also indicating that it had been approved by A.M.G. In these and other ways efforts were made to push forward the Italian officials so that the people would look up to them and not the A.M.G. as the proper organs to which to turn in matters of Government.[33]

But the main difficulty did not come from the local population, whose initial friendliness more than any other factor carried the military government through its tumultuous early phases. The most serious obstacles were to be found in the State apparatus itself, as the scattered remnants of a decapitated machine sought in all directions for protection, legitimacy, and some form of direction. Since all appointments were vetoed by the Allies, and all communications between the local authorities and the centre, when functioning, were also controlled by them, the surviving elements looked naturally towards AMG. This was not, of course, what the Allied controllers had in mind when they urged delegation at all costs on their local representatives. In the resulting confusion Italian public officials refused to take on any kind of responsibility, while Allied military governors of limited experience found themselves caught between the chaos of the municipal authorities on the one hand and the detailed instructions coming from the armies or Caserta on the other.[34]

In this climate a *de facto* alliance very quickly sprang up between the Allied authorities in the provinces and what Lord Rennell called 'the most prominent "local" citizens'. It was they who provided new mayors and town hall officials and it was to them the AMG men looked as a way of communicating with local society at large.

The way forward was indicated by Lord Rennell after his experience of the first few weeks:

> I think it is desirable that, with the fatherly blessing if not the official approval of AMGOT which cannot make constitutional changes yet, a small council be set up in each commune to assist the mayor, take some of the responsibility off his shoulders and explain the necessity of unpopular measures to their constituents . . . Civil Affairs Officers . . . should be guided by the following suggestions:
> (a)   Representatives from a number of different classes and interests should be included.
> (b)   Consult the priests and the doctor, though you need not necessarily follow their recommendations.
> (c)   Try and get one of the more intelligent small farmers on the council.
> (d)   The schoolmaster often makes a useful member and acts as liaison officer with mothers of large families.[35]

The Church had a crucial role to play in such a strategy, as it immediately understood. 'The Roman Catholic Church authorities have been cooperative and easy to deal with,' Rennell wrote in an early report; 'I have heard two sermons to large congregations exhorting the people to obey and accept the Allied Military Government coupled with invective against the Fascist regime.'[36] The bishop in one Sicilian province succeeded in attaching a priest to the local Civil Affairs Officer (CAO) as his liaison officer, and offered the Church's organization throughout the province to assist the CAO's work.

These methods were not without their problems for AMGOT, by far the most conspicuous being that of deciding how the most prominent, honest, non-Fascist local citizens might be identified. Among the more remarkable documents of the entire occupation is one testifying to this difficulty. It originated in the American Embassy in Berne, and was designed to reply to State Department enquiries regarding 'parties, personalities and organisations . . .' which might be useful to the Allies in case of invasion:

> The following influential Italians are said to be pro-Ally and willing to work for the United Nations:
> Comm. Agnelli . . . Torino.
> Giovanni Rodrigueze, Porto Lonjone, Isola Elba – Mayor.
> Comm. Berlingieri, Rossano Calabro, large property owner and very influential.
> Conte di Lusio, Messina, large property owner and very influential.

Elso Battistini, Anversa, head of the Cammora.
Carmelo Albo, at present in jail, head of the Mafia.[37]

As Lord Rennell explained, the situation did not improve after the invasion:

> More than half the adult population of Sicily is illiterate and the choice of candidates for an unpaid office was small in many of the remoter communes. Moreover the Sicilians of any standing, whatever their political views, who were ready to cooperate by work and responsibility, as opposed to advice and criticism, were singularly few. . . . With the people clamouring to be rid of a Fascist Podesta, many of my officers fell into the trap of selecting the most forthcoming self-advertiser. . . . The choices in more than one instance fell on the local 'Mafia' boss or his shadow, who in one or two cases had graduated in an American gangster environment.[38]

There seems little doubt that the part played by the Mafia in filling the vacuum of indigenous authority in Sicily was greater than the head of AMGOT admits. 'American intelligence had seen to it that the Sicilian component of the invading force was as high as 15%', a British intelligence officer has since written in a book on the Mafia, and such noteworthy figures as Lucky Luciano, Don Calo and Vito Genovese appear to have used AMGOT as a bridgehead to return to Sicily, or to return to active life from exile or prison, after being unofficially enlisted in some cases by U.S. Navy Intelligence.[39] It was probably in this limbo world of semi-official advisers that the Allies' long-rumoured contacts with Sicilian separatism took place: there is no evidence up to now that interest in separatism enjoyed official support at any higher level (distinct, that is, from the sympathy of individual officers).[40]

But there were reactions against many of these developments. To begin with the local populations had overwhelmed the Allies with gestures of friendship, but already by the middle of August 1943, Allied officials had noted a change of mood. In large part this was attributed to 'the failure of the Allies to secure a reign of plenty, the absence of coal and fertilizers, broken communications' and the distance between continuous propaganda promises and the chaotic reality.[41] There were political factors too. At the end of November, the head of 8th Army AMG told his superiors that there was:

> undoubtedly a feeling of dissatisfaction amongst the people particularly in the back areas that the 'political choice' which they have been promised is not eventuating as quickly as they hoped. This feeling is accentuated probably by the fact that the form of government we are using is still totalitarian in fact, though we profess that it is not in theory.[42]

In King's Italy the government had not passed the first decree on de-Fascistization until the very end of 1943, and even this remained 'largely a dead letter', reports C.R.S. Harris. The results were illustrated by the Allied naval officer in charge in Brindisi:

> One thing is obvious to the most unbiassed observer and that is that all is not well in Brindisi. There is a feeling of unrest, of uncertainty, of surprise that the local Fascisti

are still allowed to hold the most powerful positions in the area, especially in local government, and moreover that they are using their powers to their own advantages and that of their friends, and to the detriment of the Allied interests.[43]

Commentators in the Allied press were sharply critical. 'Allied Regime in Italy Fails at Many Points', proclaimed the *Chicago Daily News*, suggesting that 'the whims of military authorities' were at the root of the trouble. Although such papers as the *News Chronicle* in Britain had insisted at the beginning that a clear distinction was to be drawn between 'our attitude to the Italian masses and our treatment of the ruling caste which has been running the war against us since 1940', American reporters found that by the autumn of 1944 a most comfortable *entente* had been struck up between this ruling caste and the new occupiers:

> conservatives are wining and dining American and British officials, exactly as they formerly wined and dined the Germans, absolutely convinced in their little minds that Britain and America will really rule Italy, and that the way they can save themselves is to curry favor with Englishmen and Americans. They love us. They do indeed. They love us exactly the way nightclub proprietors love millionaire playboys.[44]

LOOKING BACK on the Italian experience towards the end of the war, Harold Macmillan felt that the essential problem for the Allies had always been the same: that 'self-government for Italy requires that we should go away and leave Italy to her own disorder; good government for Italy requires that we should remain a bit longer and help her get organised.' But the resident minister was not at all certain as to how this dilemma could be resolved; 'Perhaps a compromise might be worked out . . .', he suggested lamely.[45] The area where the contradictions and disorder of the early stages of the occupation showed up at their worst was in the field of economics, where the Allies found the obvious tasks of feeding the living, putting people to work and making use of local resources for the campaign far harder than they had imagined. And then there were the bigger, longer term questions of rebuilding and 'rehabilitation'. As Macmillan forecast, it was 'one vast headache, with all give and no take'.

Two crucial developments conditioned the history of the Allied approach to Italy's economic position: firstly, the material situation in the liberated areas was much worse than the Allies had ever been led to expect by their scanty intelligence estimates; secondly, the military campaign lasted far longer than anticipated in any of the early forecasts. It was these circumstances which threw into stark relief the other failures: the irrationality of much of the early planning, the incapacity of most of the Allied control organizations, the lack of coordination – where not open conflict – between the military and the civilians, between planners and executors, between propagandists and allocators of shipping space, between British and Americans.

The soldiers arrived in Italy with a blanket formula designed to cover all their civilian responsibilities. The 'prevention of disease and unrest' was the first normative standard supplied by the planners, and its purpose was above all to minimize: to minimize expenditure of time and money, to minimize disturbances behind the forward lines, to minimize the tasks of feeding, controlling and recuperating all those unlucky enough to find themselves in the path of that 'hot rake of war' Churchill had promised for the entire peninsula. In addition the military government and armistice directives imposed on the armies the responsibility of developing and exploiting local resources for the use of a campaign, a seemingly logical task which implied a moderate resumption of economic activity according to criteria laid down by army technicians. Coles and Weinberg describe the turn of events succinctly:

> The question was not whether Italy could aid the Allies in the future but whether, within the limits of the supply program, the Allies could aid Italy sufficiently to make it usable for present military operations. . . . The basic economic problem was control of inflation. The roots of the evil went back to the Fascist regime, which had spent lavishly to finance Mussolini's military exploits. The already weakened system of price and rationing controls collapsed with the invasion and, though the Allies continued all of them, the system could never be rebuilt. Nor did the reduction of controls to a few basic foods work much better. The inflationary spiral continued, wage increases were allowed and then disallowed, and farmers preferred to hoard wheat rather than sell at official prices.[46]

Roosevelt's initial impulse had been to regard the feeding of the population as a charitable act which would soon be appreciated by the world at large, but it was soon swept away in the disruption of Sicily. On 19 October 1943 a protest demonstration against wage and price levels in Palermo – where black market prices were 1000 per cent of Italian official prices – was fired on by Italian police, leaving 14 dead. Lesser incidents continued thoughout the South and Sicily during succeeding months.[47] The American press reacted by pointing out that supply was not simply a military or even a moral affair, but a basic element of the Anglo-American political 'package', with important immediate and long-term repercussions elsewhere. At the beginning of September the *New York Herald Tribune* reported that Italy was likely to require a vast supply of oil, coal, chemicals, metals, tools and food if any form of rehabilitation was to begin, and the attitude of the Allies towards these needs might be taken by countries still in the Nazi orbit as 'a yardstick to measure their own chances of economic survival should they break away from German control. If Italian needs are met such countries as Hungary, Rumania and Bulgaria will probably be less hesitant to throw off the economic bonds binding them to the Nazis.'[48]

But in the second half of 1943 there were few signs of any long-term approach to the economic devastation of Italy. The British War Office had already made clear that it was not interested in the business of reconstruc-

tion, and the American War Department likewise shrugged off all respon-
siblities not related to the immediate needs of the moment, on the assumption that civilian agencies would take them over when the battle had passed
on.[49]

The crucial declarations made to the Italians after the fall of Mussolini, at
the time of surrender, and at the Moscow conference said nothing about
their economic future, neither did the Combined Chiefs of Staff Directive for
Sicily, the 'Long-Term' surrender document or the master-plan laying down
the functions of ACC,[50] and only on the level of propaganda were promises
lavish. That there was another level of economic thinking at work is made
clear by a note in the secret high-level Whaley–Eaton Newsletter:

> Churchill has made it abundantly clear that Britain is not fighting this war in order to
> engage freely hereafter in a vast humanitarian campaign to transfer into the farth-
> ermost places an Anglo-American standard of living. Neither is the United States,
> despite the slogans of wartime. It was the Hitler thesis that the time had come for the
> 'have-not' nations to take away from the 'have' nations a part, if not all, of their
> possessions. It may be assumed that the 'have' nations will not voluntarily give away
> that which they are spending unlimited blood and treasure to prevent being taken
> from them by force.[51]

The same report revealed however that the Italian financial system had
been found to be on the point of collapse, implying that 'the credit of Italy
will probably have to be restored (old currency virtually wiped out) and the
price structure will have to be remade', and from the battle zone itself
pressure was already coming for a reappraisal of economic objectives by the
middle of October. The basic 'disease and unrest' formula was not brought
under discussion; instead the attention of the planners in London and
Washington was directed to the need for a set of long-term economic aims
on which sights could be fixed as soon as possible. 'To take an extreme case,'
said a War Office man in North Africa, 'we might play merry hell with Italian
finances now in order to win the war against Germany and flood the country
with worthless money just as the Germans did in the Balkans. Clearly this
would be unacceptable in any constructive long-term plan. But it might be
quite in accordance with a short-term plan.' The suggestion in this case was
for a statement along lines which might 'encourage Italy to rehabilitate
herself as a nation in such a way as to become a useful entity in whatever
political or economic form may be required by future world conditions, and
to assist her in preparing for this process,' and it was implied that this meant
reconstruction of utilities, of industries and agriculture.[52]

The first agency to take a serious estimate of the overall economic
situation was not an Allied one at all, but an American team under Adlai E.
Stevenson sent out at the very end of 1943 by the Foreign Economic
Administration (FEA), the executive organ controlling wartime economic
operations overseas. The declared purpose of the four-man mission was
strictly technical: 'to investigate the nature and extent of the civilian econo-

mic needs of Italy with special reference to rehabilitation and reconstruction,' and to assess the possible contribution of the FEA. Most of the mission's conclusions were also technical, concerned, for example, with the immediate problems of prices, inflation, production and distribution in industry and agriculture. Its recommendations dwelt heavily on the confusion and inefficiency of the Allied organs of control, particularly the Allied Control Commission and Allied Military Government, whose circumscribed resources meant that they were totally lacking in the means to make the Italian economy self-sufficient, a necessity which the mission considered the prime objective of economic policy. But Stevenson also asked a number of key political questions, all the more pertinent since few in Washington were able to give a convincing answer to them: 'Is this primarily a British sphere of interest and responsibility? If it is are we going to participate actively and energetically in the direction and operations of ACC. . . . What funds are to be used?' The report was highly critical of the widespread compromises made with Fascist local government in the name of effective administration and denounced the gulf separating the Italian people from the government of Victor Emmanuel and Badoglio:

> [The mission] cannot fail to point out that, in its opinion, the present unhappy political situation will constitute a formidable obstacle to orderly and effective realization of our economic aims and operations.

On the strictly economic level the mission declared that it was impossible to formulate any precise long-range economic policies for Italy, at least as far as America was concerned, and they settled for urging a short-term emergency plan. This centred on a supply programme to prime the pump of local production, to be managed by capable civilians. A more responsible awareness of the long-term difficulties in military quarters was demanded by the FEA team, and greater coordination in the civilian ones. But there were still too many unanswered questions:

> how far are we going to go in rehabilitation? Are we going to supply just seeds, tools and services to rehabilitate agriculture? Are we going further and help with the restoration of the fertilizer, power and transportation industries, bearing in mind that they have a value to the Italian economy beyond food production and distribution? What about the food processing and clothing industries. What funds are to be used?[53]

With a lengthy exposition on the causes of inflation, which was largely attributed by Stevenson's team to uncontrolled troop spending at inflated exchange rates, an interminable debate was set in motion, lasting, without any noticeable effect whatsoever on the price spiral, until the very end of the occupation. Each ACC department contributed to a report refuting the FEA analysis, and laying the blame squarely on the Italian government deficit, said to be increasing at a rate of $2\frac{1}{2}$ billion lire a month. The FEA replied in kind, defending its original position while acknowledging that efforts were being made by the managers of the Control Commission.[54]

On the other hand such were the difficulties surrounding the supply of goods – the other essential ingredient in any inflationary situation – that they could hardly be contemplated. Those who pressed for as broad a definition as possible of the 'disease and unrest' formula found themselves writing memoranda to prove that candles were indeed a military necessity, and even when a product had received this label it was impossible to alter in any way its allocation in the shipping patterns. 'Thus, illogical as it may seem,' say Coles and Weinberg, 'it was easier for AFHQ to get thousands of tons of wheat than for it to obtain agricultural or industrial machinery occupying less cargo space and designed to reduce the need for imports by increasing local production.'[55]

The army, on the other hand, received more than it could consume. Before long, writes the economist Vladimir Petrov, the markets in liberated Italy were 'filled with American merchandise; canned food, wheat, sugar, cigarettes, uniforms and underwear, razor blades and army blankets were seen everywhere.' With the connivance of almost every level of the army command, much of this material found its way to the black market; an estimated 60 per cent of the total tonnage unloaded in Naples disappeared in this way, bringing handsome profits for certain Allied soldiery and local operators, and further disruption to the local economy. Southern Italy between 1943 and 1945 became 'a world of monopolies', in the words of Bruno Foa, a Federal Reserve expert at the time. The position of farmers was strengthened against that of town-dwellers and that of commodity manipulators against all:

A class of *nouveaux riches* emerged almost overnight from the city slums . . . and spectacular profits were made by shrewd or reckless operators at all levels of the social structure. Those were days when a truckload of goods smuggled across the Military Police roadblocks would make a man rich overnight, while the bulk of the city population subsisted on a little black bread and dried pea soup.[56]

In Washington bureaucratic battles broke out for supervision of economic policy in liberated Europe and cut off any real hope of a unified, coherent operation on the spot. They continued in spite of the promptings of Stevenson and others who felt that discord only served, among other things, to leave the field to the British. The details of these conflicts were rarely trivial, since they involved the basic principles of America's foreign economic policy for the war and its aftermath, as the various protagonists liked to point out. A State Department economic adviser wrote in October 1943:

whether non-military economic operations in liberated areas are to be conducted by the military or by the civilians is certainly a question of foreign policy having the most far-reaching implications. Our relations with the governments of liberated countries, the attitude of Russia toward military government, the future role of UNRRA and the effective prosecution of our long-term economic objectives are only a few of the policy matters intimately related to this question.[57]

Partly as a result of political and jurisdictional rows between the War Department and the FEA, it was impossible to settle on a nominee for the head of ACC's Economic Section (a post awarded to the Americans in the division of labour inside the Control Commission at this time). None of the nominees ever stayed in Italy more than 90 days, and there were to be long gaps between the departure of one candidate and the arrival of the next. On the other hand the British – once they had decided that the consequences of economic chaos in Italy were too serious to ignore – did no better. They considered inserting their own man in the vacant slot, but the problem was the same: no suitably qualified candidate could be found anywhere in the imperial machine.[58]

But the lack of qualified men and the bureaucratic infighting were only part of the reason why the Allies' economic operations were in chaos by the end of 1943. From the beginning there was an absurdly large gap between the number and complexity of the plans and the reality of southern Italy. A typical example was the area of labour relations, where the Allies were expected by the logic of their military needs and their declarations to (a) use workers in whatever way needed to promote the military effort, and (b) rebuild and reform labour relations in accordance with democratic ideals and the de-Fascistization priority.

As supreme commander, Eisenhower had been provided with a detailed technical guide drawn up in Washington covering every aspect of the civilian and military labour problems likely to be encountered in Sicily. In forwarding it to the War Department's Civil Affairs Division, its formulators indicated that it was a combined effort of the Civil Affairs Division itself, the Office of Economic Warfare, the Department of Commerce, the Law Committee of the Office of Foreign Economic Coordination (predecessor of the FEA); in addition the 'Treasury, State and Justice Departments and the Lend-Lease Administration participated and their suggestions were incorporated in the guide'.[59]

An AMG labour officer described the situation in which the guide and the post-Fascist labour vision were applied:

> The entire labor staff in the early days of Sicily consisted of one officer. . . . The head of the subcommission on labor was for a long period an officer who in civilian life had administered unemployment relief. . . . He was naturally helpless in strike negotiations because he had never participated in them before. His successor was an American with an anti-labor bias and no knowledge of the fundamentals of the trade. He had to be eased out of responsibility.[60]

Yet at home the message of liberation was being proclaimed: 'Allies Free Sicilian Workers to Bargain as They do Here', declared the *New York Times* on 6 September 1943. 'The Allied Military Government abolished today all fascist labor and corporative organizations . . . and is substituting a free labor movement', explained Herbert Matthews. Lt Colonel Charles Poletti, a prominent New York Italo-American, was reported to be setting up new provincial labour offices whose tasks would range from employment provision to vocational training, from cost-of-living studies to mediation and arbitration. However, Matthews admitted in the same article that existing collective contracts between workers and employers would be continued 'in the interest of stability', and that in social assistance, 'where the Fascists were ahead of Britain and America', the same institutions would carry on with a change of name and head.[61]

But the factors which weighed most heavily on the relationship between the Allies and the workers and peasants of southern Italy were not the fault of abstract planning or overblown propaganda. The extended presence of military restrictions and the scarcity of food and effective ration controls must have weighed much more heavily, problems which immediately involved wage rates and hence inflation. AMGOT's report for November 1943 described the prevailing tendencies succinctly:

> During the month considerable labor unrest was evident, traceable to two causes: (a) Lack of adequate supply of food at reasonable prices; (b) Wages insufficient to maintain a minimum standard of living. . . .
> An example of the kind of situation that arose is that of the Società Generale Elettrica della Sicilia. On 8 November, 650 employees of the Società Generale Elettrica della Sicilia in Palermo left work to search for flour substitutes leaving 50 essential workers at the plant. At the conference that day, the workers insisted that their action was not a 'strike' but a human and necessary attempt to obtain food for their families. At the same time increased wages were demanded. The workers returned to work when it was explained that efforts were being made to make food available and that a wage increase was under immediate consideration.[62]

THE MOST COMPREHENSIVE survey of the situation at the end of 1943 was provided by Harold Caccia, previously one of Harold Macmillan's assistants, now a vice-president in the Control Commission. This list of disasters covered almost every aspect of the scene and emphasized the alienating effect on the Americans, who were saying quite openly that 'the British had better be left to sort out the Italian mess because they will have to live with the aftermath.' More immediately, said Caccia, there was starvation and crime in the country, the impotence of a people and a government. The people were embittered by the realization that the Allies did not believe Mussolini alone had started the war, and that they were held responsible, while the government was given no practical opportunity or resources to alleviate the armistice.[63]

Caccia's worries were widely shared. In a letter already mentioned, the naval officer in charge in Brindisi concluded: 'The Badoglio government is mistrusted and considered incapable of putting things right even if it wanted to do so. . . . The danger lies in one of the rabble parties attempting to take control . . . the time is ripe for us to declare our hand and take a decided course of action.'[64]

In London the secretary of war, P. J. Grigg, told the Ministerial Committee on Armistice Terms and Civil Affairs (under Clement Attlee) in December that 'the present state of civil affairs in Italy was chaotic'.[65] Some worried over the sheer dimensions of the machinery, others over the political consequences. Macmillan was as harsh as any on the first point:

> Planning of ACC by academic methods thousands of miles from the scene of operation, without comprehension of the situation regarding transportation, accommodation, light, communications likely to exist in conquered and largely devastated territory, has produced an organisation . . . ill-conceived, ill-staffed and ill-equipped for its purpose. The exaggerated insistence of exact Anglo-American parallelism has led to too much weight at the top. It is also over-staffed throughout.[66]

As for the effects on the Italian government, Lord Rennell was left in doubt 'whether any Italian Government would ever survive being overlaid by such a nursery governess,' while Harold Caccia thought that the chances of reconstructing the government on broader lines after Rome was taken would be seriously prejudiced by such an apparatus: 'Certainly it is more than doubtful whether prominent Anti-Fascists will agree to service for any length of time in a government which will in effect be a Colonial administration.'[67]

As for the local population, a prominent American expert on Italy, H. Stuart Hughes, looked back afterwards and remembered how the people of the South had been the 'wards of the Allies – scorned, misunderstood, suffering from every kind of shortage and privation.' Yet they were out of danger and free to recuperate as best they could. 'For them the war had really ended with the arrival of the Allies; what followed was a painful and mostly incomprehensible epilogue in which they felt they had no part.'[68] It was perhaps a fitting comment on the first phase of the liberation of Italy.

PART TWO 1944

4   The politics of the Italian problem from Monte Cassino to the liberation of Rome, January–June 1944

MARSHAL PIETRO BADOGLIO was a figure whom many would consider fate had not, in the end, treated too badly. He had survived the collapse of Fascism, Italy's change of sides as a power in the middle of a world war, the breakdown of the State and the unique humiliation of running a government from a hotel room in a seaside resort. Now he was considered indispensable by the prime minister of England and the president of the United States, and by their generals too. Yet he was not satisfied. At the end of January 1944 he told Reuters' man Cecil Sprigge: 'If you ask me what advantages Italy has gained from "co-belligerency" . . . the answer would be "absolutely none", but this cannot be said.'[1]

The Foreign Office too was unhappy about 'co-belligerency' which, they said, 'means trying to treat the Italians as friends and foes at the same time' Specifically,

[it] has put us in a series of positions where we have had the choice of virtually going back on our own word to the Italian Government or sacrificing some essential interest of our own with adverse results on the war or on our relations with our allies.[2]

In the American camp distraction and equivocation seemed to be prevailing at the beginning of 1944. Roosevelt had told the JCS in November that the Army divisions in North Africa, Sicily and Italy should be the first to be sent back to the U.S. He felt 'that we should get out of France and Italy as soon as possible, letting the French and the British handle their own problem [sic] together.'[3] Yet little over a month later Roosevelt was expressing to Churchill his firm wish for joint control of the situation (to the exclusion particularly of professional diplomats): 'I wish you and I could run this Italian business. We would not need any help or advice.'[4]

After the lost opportunities of the post-Salerno period (specifically the lack of collapse of the German south-eastern front) and Stalin's decisive approval of American strategic plans at the Teheran conference in November, the American military could feel confident that the balance of judgments and events was swinging in favour of their plans for the cross-Channel invasion and for its support by a landing in the South of France. Although Churchill and the British staff used every opening to insist to the Americans and to Stalin that their objectives in Italy were limited to the seizure of Rome and its surrounding airfields, and that these could be obtained quickly, there could by now be no illusions: fighting in the

Mediterranean and in Italy in particular had sunk well down on the list of priorities.[5] One of the consequences was that from that moment on American preoccupations in Italy, as far as they could be defined or were defined, began to change character. Although still maintaining their emphasis on the short-term and pragmatic problems, although still characterized by reluctance and contradiction, the considerations which slowly emerged as most important related to defining a specifically American approach to the political and economic questions found inside the country.

The first signs of this tendency appeared in the fact-finding mission sent over to Italy by the Foreign Economic Administration. What influence the Stevenson report had on the halting course of subsequent American economic policy towards Italy or on the reorganization of the ACC, already under way, is hard to say. But its political message can only have added weight to the growing conviction of Washington that in continuing to underwrite the government of the king and the marshal they were not only being tarred with the brush of illiberalism, but were also dealing with a political agent liable to default from one moment to the next. Hull demanded drastic pre-emptive action, telling the American representative in Algiers at the end of January that 'the reorganisation of the Government of Italy should no longer be delayed,' and he urged not only that liberal forces should set up a government immediately, but that Victor Emmanuel should be forced out at that very moment.[6]

Among men on the spot eager to point to the realistic, democratic alternative, none was more prominent and energetic than Herbert Matthews, the correspondent of the *New York Times*. In a long discourse in the State Department towards the end of January, Matthews came out strongly in favour of a group of liberal politicians in Naples calling themselves the Committee of National Liberation. 'They are the kind of Italian statesmen that we as Americans should and would want in authority in a new Italy', Matthews declared. But he felt that a first step in the right direction would be a clear American statement emphasizing the right of the Italian people to choose their own government, and that the U.S. was supporting no particular political regime.[7]

However, American diplomats closer to the scene knew that the Allies could not have it both ways – public detachment while privately hoping that one group would prevail – since the liberal forces of Naples were so split on the basic problems of the moment as to threaten total deadlock. This implied that the Allies would have to choose one of the formulae suggested by these forces and 'use their influence to secure its general acceptance', a State Department official surmised; '[T]wenty years of Fascism have so destroyed the fabric of the Italian State that its rapid recreation along democratic lines without outside help is difficult to envisage.'[8] Italian politics, in other words, was now becoming a serious problem in the conduct of America's war in Italy.

While Americans struggled to define their approach to the prevailing political uncertainty, Churchill was insisting on the one he already had defined after co-belligerency: full support for the king and Badoglio, with space for some liberal elements to reinforce their legitimacy, but with all major changes postponed until the liberation of Rome:

> In Rome lie the title-deeds of Italy and of the Roman Catholic Church [he had explained to Macmillan in October]. Badoglio and the King reinstated there will have a far better chance of rallying such elements of Italian strength as exist. There is the place for us to make our deal and for them to issue their prospectus.[9]

Churchill maintained this view right through the winter, notwithstanding the difficulties and disappointments which postponed the arrival in Rome. He also maintained it in spite of the doubts of the Americans and of his own subordinates. Macmillan knew that Badoglio was unable to broaden the political basis of his rule as the liberals refused to recognize the authority of the king: it was one of the few things they were agreed on most of the time. The Foreign Office felt that the temporary nature of British support for the two veterans had to be emphasized, while the Psychological Warfare Executive in London, looking for principles on which to base propaganda, proposed that absolute political impartiality should be maintained, with full assurance given on the free political choice which awaited the Italians at the end of the war. On the ground, however, the propaganda agencies gathered round the Psychological Warfare Board (PWB), and many Allied officers and journalists sympathized openly with the liberal and Left forces. Churchill was not impressed, insisting that the king and Badoglio had delivered their fleet into Allied hands and were still the determining factors in the loyalty of the Italian army and people. As for the newly reappeared politicians, about whom Macmillan and Murphy too had considerable doubts, what little was known of them provoked only scorn and distrust.[10] Among all the Allied observers one unspoken premise reigned supreme: that political reconstruction would have to begin from scratch, with the Allies themselves keeping a close watch on developments and having the last word, as least as long as the war went on.

From the moment when Allied armies had first set foot on Italian soil signs of political life had begun to appear. But the identification of the true and honourable opponents of Fascism for the purposes of a democratic restart proved to be far from an easy task. '"Anti-Fascists" Crawl Out in Naples; Most Liars, Bums', the *Chicago Daily News* cruelly reported in October 1943. The Allied armies, however, would not be taken in, said the Chicago paper, having sure criteria for recognizing the genuine material from the fraudulent mob.[11] Once the resumption of political activity had been sanctioned by the Moscow conference, various forms of awakening in this field were distinguished by Allied observers. There was the Naples Committee gathered round the internationally famous figure of the philosopher Benedetto Croce; here the nuclei of six parties could be identified: Communists, Socialists, Christian Democrats, Labour Democrats, Liberals and Actionists. There was the return of Count Sforza at the end of September, a figure well known as the leader of the exile groups in America and thought to enjoy the favour of the State Department. This veteran nobleman had journeyed to Italy via London, where he had been entertained by Churchill and in return had apparently promised to support the Brindisi government (but unfortunately had provoked in the prime minister a violent personal antipathy). There was more generally a certain stirring among the intellectual and politically aware classes of the towns in the liberated areas. Commenting on this an AFHQ observer of November 1943 added

> a sprinkling of what may be termed 'natural' or spontaneous political activity, usually of the Leftist variety, among certain elements of the working classes, forming around individuals of the constitutionalist idealist or agitator stamp who continued to work underground during the late regime and in many cases underwent great suffering for their opinions.[12]

As for the parties, the Socialists and Communists were thought by this commentator to be 'definitely Leftist . . . but far from extremist', while the Action Party appeared as 'a party of personalities rather than ideologies.' As for the rural masses, they were said to be 'without political consciousness except opposition to the regime itself,' but should a Catholic movement develop in the country it seemed clear that it would be formed around the Christian Democrat party.

In Naples Croce and Sforza were discovered to be 'really conservatives' by Murphy, but this did not prevent the American political adviser from taking seriously their warning that the small Communist Party could expand rapidly if economic misery persisted and the government remained weak. Change, if delayed, could provoke a 'great disillusionment' among the people, they said, while Murphy himself worried that anti-Fascists in the North might be tempted to set up a separate government if liberation were long delayed.[13]

Anti-Fascist forces in Rome were deeply shocked by the flight of constituted authority and the collapse of the Italian army, and they saw in both events crucial implications for their own future. The United Freedom Front met on 9 September and changed its title to the Committee of National Liberation (CLN) on the French model. Ivanoe Bonomi was confirmed as its president and a call was issued for all Italians to rally 'to the struggle and to the Resistance, and to reconquer for Italy the place it deserves in the community of free nations.'[14] Soon afterwards the Rome CLN decided that by their flight the king and Badoglio had forfeited all legitimate authority, and that henceforth the CLN itself should be considered the authoritative future government of Italy.[15]

For two weeks after the surrender Rome was an 'open city', in chaos and confusion, without authorities or order. As the Germans surrounded the city most of the Italian generals who had not fled with the king simply left for home, as did the mass of the soldiery. Only at the southernmost gate of the city was token resistance put up, by an armoured division together with some 2000 hastily armed civilian volunteers. But the Germans quickly put an end to this situation, fastening complete martial law on the capital after 23 September; even the *Carabinieri* detachments in the area were arrested and deported to Germany.[16]

The lack of substantial opposition to the German takeover profoundly dismayed the anti-Fascist leadership, especially the Left. Pietro Nenni, the Socialist leader (and Spanish Civil War veteran) liberated from island exile at the beginning of August, had felt that if some part of the army could hold out for eight or nine days with the support of an armed population, Rome might become 'a second Madrid'. With the immediate collapse of this illusion, Nenni was left lamenting anti-Fascism's 'lack of political efficiency' and 'the lack of political education of the masses'.[17] As the German armies took hold, Nenni and his CLN colleagues regrouped clandestinely and with difficulty. Almost isolated from daily life, this tiny group of personalities nevertheless felt confident enough by the middle of October to issue a call for an anti-Fascist cabinet to be formed (in the South), for the abdication of the king and for a popular consultation on the fundamental institutions of the State – monarchy or republic? – at the war's end. Reaching AFHQ by newly created Resistance channels in northern Italy and Switzerland, the call was immediately transmitted by the supreme commander to the CCS. Eisenhower commented:

> Committee's program sound and liberal. Committee much more representative than Naples group. Sforza has little following among three largest parties: Socialists, Communists, Christian Democrats . . . Allies not interfering in political situation, but Bonomi solution the best to date for all concerned.[18]

NENNI HAD CONCLUDED his brief lament on the missed opportunities of the summer, saying that 'the only hope now' (13 September) lay with 'partisan guerrilla warfare'. In the same days action in this very direction was being taken in towns and villages throughout northern and central Italy. To the mountains of Tuscany, Emilia Romagna, Liguria, the northern Veneto and above all Piedmont drifted small groups of men forming themselves into poorly armed bands ready to learn the hazards of guerrilla life: hit-and-run attacks from alpine hideouts; forced marches and retreats to avoid capture; sabotage and ambush; constant fear, hunger and cold in the bad winters of 1943–4 and 1944–5.[19] This was the story of Resistance everywhere but the Italian Resistance – still the least known outside the country itself of any in Europe – possessed from its beginnings in September 1943 a number of features which distinguished it from other experiences.

Firstly, it began not from a popular revolt against Fascism or the tradition-al State – which collapsed under the weight of their own errors – but as a rebellion against a foreign invader and his local puppets. This had the effect of limiting the potential political impact of the movement: would it then be simply a minority force for national freedom or a mass movement for national renovation? Adding to the weight of this difficulty was the fact that Resistance was largely a northern phenomenon – and involved only a minority in the North at that – cut off totally from the South, where the war had ended and where the traditional State was picking itself up from the dust with the aid of the real liberators of the country, the Anglo-American armies. Yet another complication was the Resistance's relatively late start, with the Allies already in the country and by autumn 1943 beginning to think of the claims they would stake in the political battles likely to break out as the war ended: of this international dimension of the liberation the Resistance and its leadership knew almost nothing.[20]

On the other hand the Resistance could count on a number of assets which quickly gave it political and organizational effectiveness. Right from the start the armed bands were supported in the cities by all-party Committees of National Liberation (CLNs) similar to those in Rome and Naples. Gradually these bodies achieved regional status and even came to recognize the coordinating role of the Milan-based CLN of Upper Italy (CLNAI). With some notable exceptions (the so-called 'Autonomi' or Autonomous groups), the bands themselves took on party-political colouring – particularly the Communist ('Garibaldini') and Actionist ('Giustizia e Libertà'), formations – as they evolved militarily into fully-fledged 'divisions' and 'brigades'. Overall unity continued to be maintained, if at times with great difficulty, via the CLN's, which would eventually multiply and propose themselves as alternative local and even national governments (in the case of the Rome and Milan Committees).[21]

Secondly, the Resistance could count on support from parts of all sections of the population. To the first bands went ex-officers and soldiers of the disbanded Italian army, draft dodgers from Mussolini's puppet 'Republican' army, long-time anti-Fascists, veterans from the Spanish Civil War and on occasion Allied soldiers released from Italian prisoner-of-war camps.[22] But the appeal to voluntarism echoed a long-established Italian minority tradition, so that in the larger organizations could eventually be found not just manual workers and peasants but also students, professional men, white-collar workers and so on. Together with the mountain bands, urban guerrilla units (GAPs) were founded on the initiative of the Communist Party from November 1943 onwards and in 1944 took an important role in organizing strikes and sabotage in the larger industrial centres.[23]

What unified these various elements was the moral force and by now established tradition of *anti-Fascism*, understood not simply as rejection of a particular regime in a particular historical phase, but as a prospect for rebuilding social life and political institutions along modern, progressive lines recognizable in other advanced industrial societies. The official Left called this process 'completing the bourgeois revolution'; others saw it as a relatively restrained form of political rededication which would cancel out the excrescences of Fascism and renew the pre-Fascist parliamentary tradition. Inevitably the future of the country's constitution became a central issue and there was agreement that a choice would somehow have to be made soon after the war: a crucial 'appointment with democracy'.[24] But beyond this point Resistance anti-Fascism dissolved in individual minds into as wide a variety of currents as is politically possible, from libertarian anarchism to Catholic populism, from unrestrained Stalinism to Manchester-school liberalism. Consolidated and enriched by 20 years of exclusion and exile, anti-Fascism nevertheless proved to be a strong enough home-grown plant to withstand the violent storms of the 18-month struggle in the North, expressing its underlying unity through the six parties and their CLNs. Although much of the moral force and renovating energy of the Resistance was subsequently wasted or at least neutralized, as we shall see, in the first national elections of 1946 these parties together gathered over 80 per cent of the vote.[25]

A fourth asset on which the Resistance could count was of course the Allies themselves, but their help turned out to be ambivalent. The British and Americans each possessed organizations specifically designed to support Resistance movements with men, matériel and information, and to coordinate their activities with the main armies; in the British case the London- and Cairo-based Special Operations Executive (SOE) quickly got to work and under an arm called Special Force (SF) would send in more than 500 agents up to May 1945. The American role in this field was in the hands of the far less experienced or developed Office of Strategic Services (OSS), the extent of whose activities is still by no means clear. Relations between the two services have likewise proved a difficult area to penetrate and in general the overall contribution of these organizations to the measure of success achieved by the Resistance has remained a controversial point between survivors and between historians (often the same people). It appears certain that the British Special Force largely dominated the Allied presence in the North, with the Americans occasionally to be found in Piedmont, Emilia Romagna, Tuscany and elsewhere.[26] It also seems clear that Special Force had its own view of how the Resistance should make its contribution to the war, based partly on experience in the Balkans and France but also on the natural outlook of the officers involved.[27] Even before Special Force discovered that militarily the Resistance would be heavily indebted to Communist Party organization and energies, the Milan CLN leaders Parri and Valiani were being told in Switzerland in November 1943 that their ideas of a politicized mass-movement supporting partisan 'armies' were not welcome: plenty of small-scale sabotage, information gathering and preparation for the final offensive of the main armies was what was demanded.[28] Politics, it was felt in Special Force and AFHQ; should be avoided or at least postponed until the war's end, thus ignoring the fact that without its political push the Resistance could not exist or develop. As in the Balkans and France, the Allied Commands (though the Americans to a much lesser extent than the British) were making the mistake later admitted by one of their commanding officers, Bickham Sweet-Escott:

> it was the people inside the occupied countries, not only in Yugoslavia and Greece, but also in France, Italy, Burma and elsewhere on whom we had to rely for the action which the Services asked of us. These people were not necessarily or even mainly, the people who hoped that when the war was won things would go back to being just what they were when it began. . . . They were risking their lives for war aims of their own which differed in many important respects from ours. Rarely was this elementary truth grasped by the Foreign Office and more rarely still by the Services.[29]

The result was that in the North direct help in the first winter was 'meagre and slow', and contacts developed only where pro-Badoglio elements could be found, in the slowly-emerging, non-party 'Autonomi' bands.[30] In the South small but sincere efforts to assemble volunteer forces from ex-army personnel and other anti-Fascists found very little encouragement from AFHQ, with the most serious attempt, a 'national' (non-monarchic) brigade under a retired general, being officially dissolved out of respect for royal sensibilities.[31] In the event the Allies' experience with the various partisan formations differed very greatly from place to place, according to a range of contingent factors of which political colouring was only one. But as long as the CLNs in the centre and North of the country continued to coordinate the struggle and represent its most profound aspirations, Allied liaison officers had somehow to come to terms with them: politics could not be delayed or avoided.[32]

IN THE MIDDLE of January 1944 the main force of the Allied armies arrived at the foot of Monte Cassino and were to remain there, some two hours drive north of Naples, for over four months. A few days later came the Anzio landings, 'a story of high opportunity and shattered hopes', as Churchill said in his memoirs, in which 'a lightning thrust by two or three divisions' was turned into a desperate effort to defend 70,000 men and 18,000 vehicles from being thrown back into the sea through lack of Allied boldness, and the speed with which the Germans reacted and regrouped.[33] The blow to Allied prestige, to British prestige in particular, was hard, since the prime minister had been the main promoter of the enterprise and had even spent Christmas in Carthage planning it with the generals, and since both the supreme commander, Harold Maitland Wilson, and the commander of the Allied Armies in Italy (AAI), Harold Alexander, were British, Eisenhower having left at the turn of the year. It was against this background that the political forces anxious to proclaim an alternative to the immobility of Victor Emmanuel and Badoglio and even to the monarchy as an institution decided to meet at Bari.

The Bari congress (28–29 January 1944) was the first such meeting for over 20 years, and from it came a resounding call for the abdication of the monarch as a preliminary to the eventual installation of a democratically elected republic. In reality Left and Right in the congress were divided on the precise solution they wished to see to the institutional hiatus, the Left – including representatives who had crossed the lines from the North – having initially demanded that the assembly proclaim itself an 'extraordinary government' with all powers, pending a post-war national referendum. The problem was passed to a new 'Executive Junta' created by the conference and based on the political groupings of the Naples CLN, hence containing Communists, Socialists, Actionists, Christian Democrats, Labour Democrats and Liberals.[34]

The meeting of the Bari congress created a considerable stir in southern Italy, and in the Anglo-American press, and there was much anxiety in Allied military government circles over its possible outcome. Here too the British were now firmly in charge, with the direction of the Allied Control Commission in the hands of the head of the first Allied mission to Brindisi, Lt Gen. Sir Noel Mason-MacFarlane. It was from these levels that instructions came which, writes Charles Delzell, 'circumscribed the congress with many restrictions, limiting the number who might attend, forbidding any broadcasts, and not allowing spectators or Allied military personnel to attend. Military police cordoned off the Piccinni Theatre where the congress met. Some people wondered if the Allies feared a revolution.'[35]

The principal British fear, at least at first, was a naval mutiny. Admiral McGrigor, senior British naval officer in nearby Taranto, thought the Italian fleet might mutiny in response to the congress:

> It was not quite clear [wrote Harold Macmillan in characteristic fashion] whether they would adopt this course because:
> (a) they were monarchists and wished to protest against the views [likely to be expressed] at the Congress;
> (b) they were republicans and wished to show their sympathy for the said views.[36]

The reassurances of Macmillan were delivered to Admiral Cunningham, the (British) naval commander-in-chief in the Mediterranean, who was told:

> that although I [Macmillan] was quite prepared to accept the view that the Italian fleet would mutiny, I did not believe that this would be as a result of the congress at Bari, but rather due to the natural propensity of all fleets to mutiny. This seemed to satisfy him.[37]

Macmillan's own description of developments on the abdication issue, made without reference to the incidental threat of mutiny, produced a one-line riposte from Churchill: 'The Navy is what really matters.'[38]

The king and Badoglio were not pleased by the reappearance of political energies beyond their control. In the middle of February 1944 His Majesty told MacFarlane that 'he had heard stories that the Allies wished him to abdicate in favour of the Crown Prince, and to install a government representing the Bari Congress parties. He hoped there was no truth in these rumours . . . .'.[39] Meanwhile the king's supporters and the government had made 'every effort to sabotage the [Bari] Congress,' PWB reported, and there were constant protests by Badoglio that he could not carry on 'if we [the Allies] permit and broadcast expressions of opinion which are definitely illegal under the laws of the country which he is governing.'[40] MacFarlane for his part took these protests seriously, even recommending censorship of 'criticism likely to bring the Government into disrepute or statements likely to provoke disorder and dislocate administration. . . . The opposition have been told quite clearly that they will get their chance when we reach Rome.' General Wilson on the other hand was not so dogmatic, fearing that if the Allied answers to the opposition junta's demands (a programme 'as moderate as anything with which we are likely to be faced') were long delayed, and if the Allies insisted on maintaining the status quo until Rome was reached, the 'parties will no doubt turn towards more positive action to gain their ends. Some of them might even welcome arrest and subsequent martyrdom.' As it was, said Wilson, the opposition could not make any changes without Allied assistance, hence 'we are at the moment in a particularly advantageous position to obtain anything deemed in our interest, including, naturally, the reaffirmation of all Badoglio's commitments. This would not necessarily be the case to the same degree in other circumstances or in Rome.'[41]

This partial change of heart was a direct outcome of the publicity success of the Bari congress and, inevitably, of the new delays on the road to Rome. The ACC thought it appropriate at this point to make a direct approach to the new 'Junta', asking for a concrete proposal. They were told, says the British official historian, that:

> The King should abdicate immediately and be succeeded by the Crown Prince [Umberto of Savoy], who must, however, agree to delegate the exercise of his constitutional powers to a Lieutenancy of the Realm [which would] . . . proceed immediately to the constitution of a representative government of anti-Fascist parties. The delegation of powers would remain in effect until conditions permitted the calling of a constituent assembly, regularly elected by the whole Italian people, which would thereupon decide the form of the constitution.[42]

The parties, who had just been prevented by ACC from inviting the employees of the State to repudiate the authority of the king and his government, hinted that impatience was spreading in the North with the southern stalemate, and that more radical solutions might be contemplated there.[43]

In his message to the CCS Wilson therefore endorsed the Junta's programme, knowing that it would be sympathetically received in American circles. But in the same days Churchill was bombarding Roosevelt with messages to the effect that no change whatsoever was needed or desirable:

The present regime is the lawful Government of Italy [and] . . . will obey our directions far more than any other that we may laboriously constitute. On the other hand it has more power over the Fleet, Army officials etc. than anything else which can be set up out of the worn-out debris of political parties, none of whom have the slightest title by election or prescription. A new Italian government will have to make its reputation with the Italian people by standing up to us. They will very likely try to wriggle out of the armistice terms.[44]

Convinced that Roosevelt shared this point of view, Churchill repeated it, in somewhat less brutal terms, to the House of Commons on 22 February, insisting that 'when you have to hold a hot coffee-pot, it is better not to break the handle off until you are sure that you will get another equally convenient and serviceable, or, at any rate, until there is a dishcloth handy.' The ten-minute strike organized in Naples by the junta to protest against this speech was immediately banned by ACC, which instead allowed a public meeting – and even for this earned a rebuke from the prime minister.[45] In the North one of the future 'fathers' of the Italian Republic, Ugo La Malfa, told his fellow Action Party members that 'the inaccuracy of [Churchill's] appreciation of the situation was so enormous that some kind of adjustment of the Anglo-Saxon outlook to our point of view must be possible.'[46]

The Allies were thus split among themselves, with their more imaginative representatives on the spot together with the Americans, favouring liberalization, while the British in London insisted on maintaining the status quo. Churchill seemed to be thinking in essentially tactical terms, but inside the Foreign Office resistance to concessions was strategically oriented. No one doubted the need to reinforce the political authority of the Badoglio government – at least inside Italy. But whether the proposals regarded Italian participation in the war against Japan, an Italian volunteer force, the restoration of territory from ACC to Italian jurisdiction or Italy's signing the Atlantic Charter – all measures suggested by Italians or Americans in the spring of 1944 – the typical British response was always the same: the Italians were 'trying to wriggle out of their position as a defeated enemy.' They would have to be 'brought up with a severe jerk otherwise when the time comes we shall never be able to enforce the territorial provisions of the peace treaty which we ultimately conclude with Italy.'

In the case of Italian participation in the Japanese war, an idea which may have originated with Badoglio, the same hard reasoning prevailed: rejection, since it would 'increase our sense of obligation to Italy and put them in a better bargaining position at the peace table.'[47] As for Italian adherence to the Atlantic Charter, suggested by Washington, there was, according to the Foreign Office, the problem of Allied public opinion, 'whose feelings towards Italy will inevitably continue to be determined for some time to come by their recollection of Italy's record in recent years,' so that the only effect of an Italian signature 'would be to bring the Charter into disrepute.'[48] The Badoglio cabinet had itself made a declaration in favour of the Atlantic

Charter with special emphasis placed on reconstructing links with the victims of Fascist aggression. Eden was furious:

> This is all lies. Italians greatly enjoyed attack on Abyssinia, Good Friday assault on Albania and, above all, stab in the back delivered to the French. It was only when war went badly for them they began to have moral scruples . . . I am all for a rough and tough reception to such stuff.[49]

The one person in the British hierarchy qualified by position and familiarity with the Italian situation to protest against such outbursts was Macmillan. In reply to the judgement on the Atlantic Charter, Macmillan pointed to the manifest contradiction between getting the Italian government to 'make themselves generally more respectable' and the discouraging treatment handed out over such problems as the restoration of territory to Italian jurisdiction and the Atlantic Charter. The resident minister's well-known wit rose even above the occasion: 'If St. Paul had adopted this attitude to the Gentiles, Christianity would have remained a small Jewish sect.'

Macmillan saw a fatal dualism in the British line: 'Confession and penance are no doubt appropriate commandments to [the] shriving of a sinner. This I can certainly explain. But I feel it awkward to refuse absolution altogether, however tactfully.' As for the memories of English public opinion, was it not better that attention be directed towards the present? The public outlook 'will be determined, I hope, by observation of Italy's present performances as much by recollection of her past record . . . That is how I understand the Prime Minister's phrase "working her passage".'[50]

Meanwhile between Badoglio and the six parties of the Junta a state of deadlock had developed, revolving round the question of the entry of the parties into the government, which was made conditional upon the king's abdication and the selection of a new prime minister. Up to that point the king had agreed only to 'retire', and only when Rome was reached; with Churchill's endorsement, even this commitment began to evaporate and the southern anti-Fascists 'found themselves tied up in a semantic argument with the King and Badoglio, as enervating as it was inconclusive';[51] and as far removed from the daily problems of the war-torn southern towns and villages as any political question might be.

In the North in contrast there were dramatic developments directly involving large masses of people. The armed Resistance had grown from an estimated 9,000 to 20–30,000 by this time and working links had been established between the CLNs, the party underground organizations and the bands in the hills. In conditions of growing hardship which included economic shortages, Allied bombings and the large-scale threat of deportation to Germany, the CLNs were able to organize – using Communist Party cells and experience – widespread, coordinated strikes which paralysed Turin, Milan, Genoa, Florence, Bologna and elsewhere at 10 a.m. on 1 March. The cities of Milan and Turin with their large industrial populations were quickly reduced to a state of siege, and the immense Fiat-Mirafiori plant was totally halted. The lessons of these events were eloquently drawn by the *New York Times*:

As a mass demonstration nothing has occurred in occupied Europe to compare in scale with the revolt of the workers in Italy. It is the climax of a campaign of sabotage, local strikes and guerrilla warfare that has received less publicity than resistance movements elsewhere because northern Italy has been more cut off from the outside world. But it is an impressive proof that the Italians, unarmed as they are and under a double bondage, will fight with reckless courage when they have a cause to fight for. They might have acted with more spirit in the South, also, if they had not been called upon both to surrender unconditionally and to fight at the same time. The political situation in Italy has been bungled from the beginning, and the atmosphere has not been lightened by the offhand way in which the President announced the disposal of the Italian fleet, or by Mr. Churchill's statement that he supported the Badoglio regime because a more representative government might not be so ready to carry out the terms of the armistice, terms which have not yet been revealed by either the Allied governments or Marshal Badoglio.

The rising of the northern workers suggests that the Italians, like the French, may have something to say about their own government and even about their own fate in the final reckoning. It is another sign that the Europe that will arise when Germany is defeated may have ideas for the future that will not always fit into the plans of the Great Powers.[52]

The Communist underground leader Pietro Secchia wrote a stirring 'Reply to Churchill' in the party's clandestine newspaper in the North, affirming that 'with the great battle of the first of March, 1944, Italian popular forces, led by the working class, have hit Nazifascism hard, have said no to Badoglio, have given an eloquent riposte to Churchill.'[53] The March strikes were one of the high points of the Resistance in the North and seemed to justify the methods of the Communist Party and its factory cells; but on one point there was soon to be embarrassment, for within a matter of weeks Secchia and his comrades found themselves saying 'yes' to Badoglio.

THE SUDDEN announcement of an exchange of diplomatic representatives between the Soviet Union and the Badoglio government on 8 March struck like lightning in the fog of intrigue, dissension and apathy spreading in the South. The move had probably been initiated by Vishinsky before his departure in January (though the Russians had expressly told the ACC of their desire for closer links in December) but was now presented as the result of Italian initiatives.[54] In any event its immediate import seemed clear to all concerned on the Anglo-Saxon side: an attempt to by-pass and sabotage the Allied organs of consultation and control, the ACC and ACI. Eden told the British ambassador in Moscow of the suspicions inevitably aroused, of mutual obligations of collaboration ignored and of the 'deplorable effect here'. Macmillan termed it a diplomatic success 'old-style' and pointed to the Soviet intention of using Italy as a base for operations in the Balkans, while other members of his staff emphasized the probable desire of the Soviets to increase their influence in the North, where the trends in the anti-Fascist forces seemed overwhelmingly leftwards and republican.[55] Amid the general clamour Churchill's reaction was quite different:

> I am glad Vishinsky's realistic views have prevailed in Moscow [he wrote to the British Ambassador Clark Kerr]. The Russians are wise to have a full-scale Ambassador to Italy and I see no reason why we should rebuke them for it. . . . The best medicine for this tangled situation is a decided victory on the Italian front and I am quite content to wait till one is gained.

For Churchill in fact it was more important that the Russians had come out in favour of Badoglio and against the junta than that their procedure had been rude.[56]

Molotov intervened within a few days in any case to explain the motives of the Soviets. The foreign minister began by denying that on the international level the ACI and the ACC represented the exclusive channels of communication between individual allies and the Italian government, though Molotov insisted that what was intended was a *de facto* relationship rather than the creation of formal diplomatic links. More important overall was the Russian desire to balance out the inequality in effective representation in Italy due to the massive Anglo-American presence on the ground and in the ACC.

But the most significant part of Molotov's memorandum dealt with the Soviet view of internal political relationships in Italy. In a situation of imminent crisis and collapse, he claimed, dissension split the Allies in Italy and the forces supposedly interested in aiding the Allied campaign. Instead of uniting for the struggle Badoglio's group and that of the Junta wasted their energies fighting each other: '. . . it is impossible not to realize that on the side of the permanent executive Junta is a tolerably broad union of democratic elements expressing a tendency to direct activities side by side with the Allied democratic countries against Hitlerite Germany and the Fascist gang of Mussolini'. For Molotov the task of creating unity could not be deferred, certainly not until the liberation of Rome, while the institutional question by comparison could indeed await the declared will of the Italian people. To the insistence of Churchill in favour of Victor Emmanuel and Badoglio, Molotov replied that 'the Badoglio government still has not demonstrated as much as could be desired its capacity for carrying on the struggle against Fascist and pro-Fascist elements,' and added that the survival of this government should be linked to its ability to unite with the junta and listen to some of its desires.[57]

Leaving aside considerations of diplomatic nicety, the Soviet move can be understood without great difficulty. If the history of the Military-Political Commission of 1943 did not in itself offer a legitimate pretext for an attempt to challenge the inequality of representation (and power) in Italy, the continued exclusiveness of the Anglo-Americans and the dwindling relevance of the Advisory Council for Italy – which had taken on a purely formal existence since its establishment in November – must have done so. Although outraged, the Foreign Office had in fact discounted the possibility of direct Russian representation before the Moscow conference, and from February onwards had installed its own full-time 'High Commissioner' alongside Macmillan, in the shape of Sir Noel Charles, a career diplomat previously H. M. Ambassador in Brazil (though this was a unilateral not a bilateral arrangement).[58]

But it was reported almost immediately that the Russians were talking of further concessions. The source of this news was Prunas, Badoglio's foreign secretary, who did not hesitate for a moment to use the weapon of blackmail now placed in his hands against the stubbornness of the British and the Americans. Hardly a single area of Anglo-American sensitivity was left untouched by the proposals Prunas attributed to Bogomolov. The Soviets, it appeared, wished to exploit the fact that they had not arrived in the country with a suffocating military government. They might even wish to go beyond co-belligerency altogether, exchanging diplomatic representatives after an armistice which would guarantee Italy's eastern frontier, among other things. Could the British and the Americans do anything to match such favourable treatment? Prunas asked MacFarlane. Would they be willing to give some positive meaning to co-belligerency?[59]

Until this moment the Foreign Office had presumed to deal with the crisis by ignoring the new Soviet representative in Italy, whenever he arrived, in the belief that this would make him look ridiculous. Now the British were obliged to fall back on the fervent hope that the Soviets would not in fact come to the point of supporting an Italian request for Allied status.[60] In the event nothing was produced by the Russians; a full ambassador was not appointed to Rome until the end of October, after the other major Allies had exchanged diplomatic representatives. Nor did Moscow attempt to counter the Anglo-American rebuff to their attempts to set up a small operations base in Italy for liaison with Tito. The half-dozen aircraft and few score personnel proposed were regarded in the West as the thin end of a wedge which could easily come to threaten empire sea and air communications: 'It may prove difficult to dislodge the Russians from this area after the war,' the British chiefs of staff noted.[61] Soviet influence in any case had other much more potent means of penetration: it was precisely at this point that there returned to Italy from Moscow one of the most prestigious figures of the Third International, the leader of the Italian Communist Party, Palmiro Togliatti.

What the recognition episode demonstrated was that each of the major powers had by this time begun with varying degrees of enthusiasm to seek space for long-term unilateral policies in Italy, preferably to the exclusion of the others. Between the British and the Americans there was a total conviction that Italy's future hopes lay in the West, but beyond this basic point of agreement there was, by the spring of 1944, little more in common.

'The Americans are already very sensitive to their position in the Mediterranean since the departure of General Eisenhower,' wrote Macmillan at the end of March. 'The Russian game is, I am convinced, to try to drive a wedge between us and the Americans.' For this reason Macmillan thought the Soviet recognition of Badoglio would have the useful side-effect of consolidating Anglo-American unity, which he saw as threatened by collapse.[62] The Americans had not, however, been conspicuous in the events surrounding the recognition. Hull refused to discuss the move in public and Roosevelt even denied that it had any international implications.[63] But interventionist domestic critics were now saying openly that the Russian initiative had been facilitated by American passiveness in European affairs. What should be done, declared the *New York Times*, 'is to sharpen and strengthen our own official American convictions about what we wish to see happen in the immediate future in those European areas where the troublesome political problems now arise. . . .'[64] Hull's overall response came in a major foreign policy speech on 9 April, which spelled out the liberal principles America was fighting for but also placed heavy emphasis on tripartite collaboration. In the case of Italy, said Hull, principles were to come first and a political broadening of the Badoglio government was promised, but without any specific indications as to timing or method.[65]

Even before the crisis the Americans had made it clear to London that they did not regard Churchill's 'coffee-pot' speech as an adequate reply – or a reply they could identify with – to the proposals of the Junta. The American director of the Combined Civil Affairs Committee based in Washington had stated his preference for the Junta's proposals at the end of February on the basis of the warnings from Wilson that chaos would develop if the life of the Badoglio government was prolonged much further.[66] After the Soviets had made their move Roosevelt telegraphed to Churchill saying that the time was ripe for a declaration of support to the Junta, though whether this initiative was directly related to the processes started by the Russians is still not completely clear, in spite of Hull's speech. According to Murphy it was the faith of Hull and Roosevelt that Italy 'provided the first real testing ground of Big Three cooperation' that lay behind American approval of the return of Togliatti.[67] But whatever the sentiments at the top, the prevailing reality on the ground was tension and suspicion, increasing not only between the British and the Russians, but also between British and Americans. The U.S. representative in Algiers went so far as to wonder aloud (and with some justice) whether Wilson's management of the ACC in the recognition crisis had been based on instructions from the Combined Chiefs of Staff or orders from the prime minister.[68]

ON ONE POINT the British did clearly give way to American pressure. At Murphy's instigation and in line with American views which had crystallized at the beginning of the year, a joint delegation visited the ancient Savoyard on 10 April to inform him 'personally and unequivocally that the time had come for him to retire,' and in front of pressure of this kind Victor Emmanuel had little choice.[69] Two days later he announced his intention to retire to private life upon the liberation of Rome when all powers would be handed over to his son Umberto, designated Lieutenant of the Realm. As the Americans pointed out

> the mere policy of preserving the status quo until after the liberation of Rome is in fact favouring the position of one group of Italians, and . . . the weight of Allied authority in Italy is such that we cannot avoid the responsibility of supporting one of the various solutions. Furthermore we are opposed to a policy, in those areas of Italy restored to Italian administration, calculated to suppress normal political activity.[70]

The most immediate impact of the Soviet recognition, with its criticism of political arrangements inside the country and its hint that Badoglio and the Junta should be uniting instead of manoeuvring against each other in a vacuum, was this: that it forced the British and Americans to decide conclusively what their attitude should be to the so-called 'institutional question'. Although the two sides had hoped to put this choice off for as long as possible – for quite different reasons – events had caught up with them. But they were not entirely unprepared.

Well before the armistice, the Anglo-American Allies had with varying degrees of enthusiasm decided that '[T]he House of Savoy, despite its compromised position with Fascism, remains in theory the legitimate source of authority in the Italian State,' as the State Department said, and hence would constitute the 'least objectionable' choice of official interlocutor for the United Nations when the collapse came.[71] But the difficulties were not hard to foresee. State Department planners wrote in August 1943:

> The problem is to determine what form of permanent national government in Italy will be acceptable to the United Nations as a basis for recognition . . . [owing to the commitment in favour of free Italian choice of a non-Fascist government] what definition of 'non-Fascist' the United States may wish to apply [must be decided] and . . . whether the United Nations may wish to assure before recognition that the new government holds promise of stability, conforms to the requirements of international security, and gives expression to the liberal principles of the Atlantic Charter and the Four Freedoms.[72]

If judged by these criteria, a constitutional monarchy did not look at all like a sure bet. The doubts were multiplied by the character of Victor Emmanuel himself, who was thought to have 'never enjoyed the popularity of his predecessors' and to be 'tainted in the minds of many Italian anti-Fascists with the stigma of his essentially unconstitutional act in elevating Mussolini to power.'[73]

Once in the country, and with the armistice and co-belligerency crises behind them, the Americans found their scepticism confirmed at every level. The legitimacy of the monarchy and the king appeared to make them indispensable, especially since alternative political forces were few in number and 'a Republic could scarcely be established without disorder on our lines of communication', as Eisenhower's chief of staff told Murphy and Macmillan in October.[74] But Murphy waxed eloquent on the disadvantages:

> In Brindisi remains a discredited King clinging to the vestiges of his diminished authority and desperately, tenaciously saving his dynasty from total eclipse. . . . The King repeated over and over that he was an old man living in the past but he did not even hint that Italy in her tragic situation needed more vigorous leadership . . . politically I find that he stands for a governmental structure having a democratic and liberal facade concealing a highly centralized authority built around the person of the King.[75]

But there was vigorous braking action from the British. Churchill's attachment to the 'handle' of the 'coffee-pot' of Italian politics has already been demonstrated; it was ostensibly based on the question of the loyalty of the armed services and the doubtful loyalty of the liberal groups in Naples. On the institutional question Macmillan had this to say:

> In the interests of Italian unity and the preservation of a stable economic and political system, the Monarchy seems to the majority of informed opinion to play an essential role. It is therefore wise to seek the most hopeful course for the ultimate as well as temporary preservation of the monarchical principle.

According to Macmillan, the king favoured a regency and a constituent assembly to decide the fate of the monarchy after the war, a proposal which threatened to split the parties, leaving the Left in opposition.[76]

Matters moved quickly only after the Soviet intervention in the first week of March and Togliatti's arrival at the end of the month (the two events were not of course formally connected). The Communist leader astonished all by immediately declaring his willingness to serve under Badoglio and the king; on 10 April Victor Emmanuel was persuaded by Mason-MacFarlane, Macmillan, Charles and Murphy to withdraw into private life upon Rome's liberation and announced this intention on the 12th; a new six-party government containing among others Croce, Sforza and Togliatti was formed less than a week later. This government immediately accepted the armistice clauses (without being allowed to see them), pledged not to reopen the 'institutional question' until the end of the war, and set in motion the project for a constituent assembly consisting of elected party delegates first noted at the Bari congress.[77]

Not the least delighted at this turn of events was Badoglio, who found himself courted on all sides and in possession of a measure of authority he could hardly have dreamed of six or seven months previously. He had 'behaved splendidly' said Sir Noel Charles, who looked forward to an enduring Badoglio–Togliatti partnership.[78] The CLNs in Rome, Florence and elsewhere, particularly their republican Action Party members, swallowed the new arrangements specifically in the hope that this combination would not endure, and doubts were expressed in particular over the fitness of Crown Prince Umberto to be the first representative of liberated Italy as Lieutenant General of the Realm according to the plan. To satisfy the demands of the anti-Fascist forces Badoglio made grandiose commitments: to de-Fascistization, to aiding the Resistance, to begin economic reconstruction. But the government was confined to the small town of Salerno, and lacked the physical, administrative and juridical resources to make the slightest impact in these areas. In the event it was destined to last only six weeks, but its real significance was historical and political: anti-Fascism had compromised with the traditional State and the defenders of Fascism, and this compromise had been engineered above all by the Communist Party. A quite new phase in Italy's liberation was opening.[79]

THE IMPACT of the Soviets on the institutional question, directly transmitted by the newly arrived Togliatti, immediately changed the complexion of Italian politics as far as the British and Americans were concerned. Eden told the War Cabinet of his worries over the rise of Communist influence, and in private foresaw large-scale Soviet designs on Eastern Europe and the Mediterranean. Churchill insisted at first that Italy was exclusively an Anglo-American theatre so that there was nothing to worry about, but the prime minister soon began to change his mind, at least as far as internal arrangements in Italy were concerned.[80] In the middle of May Charles reported a conversation with the leader of the PCI in which Togliatti had pointed to the difficult problems of the monarchy and of Badoglio's position as the key questions to be resolved upon arrival in Rome. Togliatti was said to favour the continuance of the government until the North was liberated, though the king's retirement was an absolute necessity and the auspices for his son none too good. Churchill was furious:

> I do not like Togliatti's attitude. Having boosted the King and Badoglio into a certain position, he now wants to ruin them and no doubt the Communist gang will sing their part. Thus they will pulverize every form of government that can be set up. It would be well to give them some very sharp pricks when they show these tendencies and let them know the limits within which their advice is needed. If the whole manoeuvre of the Communists has been to try to get Italy into their hands by breaking down every alternative structure, you [Charles] should not hesitate to use language suitable to the rights and dignity of Britain which has done four-fifths of the fighting against Italy from the day she entered the war. Do not take it all lying down. A good row with the Russians is sometimes a very healthy episode. A Communist Italy under totalitarian rule is fundamentally opposed to the policy of Great Britain and I think also of the United States.[81]

The Foreign Office commented timidly: 'Togliatti is an Italian though Russian trained. . . . The Prime Minister has always been rather wedded to the idea of keeping on Badoglio but we should perhaps not regard him as absolutely indispensable if a suitable substitute can be found.'[82]

Togliatti saw his first task on arrival as to 'break the isolation and impotence of the anti-fascist forces'.[83] By imposing on his party a reversal of its attitude to Badoglio and agreeing to postpone the discussion of the institutional question along the lines suggested in Molotov's memorandum, Togliatti opened quite new perspectives and opportunities for the PCI and for those other parties in the Junta willing – with good or bad grace – to follow this lead. Within a month of his return from Moscow, he had been made minister without portfolio.

Among the Allied authorities no one doubted the weight of Togliatti's contribution in resolving the political impasse,[84] but what implications did this bring for the future role of Communism and/or Russian intervention in Italy? What would be the likely weight, or the degree of autonomy of the moderate forces if the PCI could assume the lead so easily? What might be the long-term intentions of the party, and how might its growing prestige in the eyes of the masses – and in the Resistance in the North – influence the political expression of a people liberated from more than 20 years of totalitarian repression?

Suddenly these questions dominated every perspective on the Italian problem, every aspect of Italy's external and internal situation. A good deal of time was to pass before Allied analysts were able to offer particularly precise or convincing answers to them, even to their own satisfaction. What mattered was that henceforth no consideration or revision of the treatment of Italy could afford to ignore them. In the equation of Italian politics they had become the xs and ys which would not disappear no matter how many times the equation was added to or multiplied on this side of infinity.

During the spring of 1944 indeed evidence began to flood in of the growing power and presence of the PCI. Sir Noel Charles concentrated on this phenomenon and the inevitable suspicions of Russian intentions in the long term to the exclusion of almost all others in his first report to the Foreign Office as British 'High Commissioner', while his newly arrived American counterpart, Alexander Kirk, estimated that the PCI had 20,000 members in Naples in mid-May and 100,000 in liberated Italy as a whole. In a single day the party was known to have received more than 100,000 lire in legitimate subscriptions, to which were 'almost certainly' added subsidies from the Soviets, the ACC reported. Even professional men, officials and officers were swelling the party's ranks, the ACC believed, and even if most were doing this for 'insurance' purposes, the result was a new 'double prestige' for the party. Yet another factor to be considered was the westward advance of the Red Army which captured headlines throughout the spring, and meant that through influence on Yugoslavia, Italy might soon have Russia on her eastern border. Although the Party itself was preaching a line of cautious firmness, the thought of the broadest implications produced apocalpytic tones in the judgment of the ACC:

> These cumulatively powerful influences are superimposed on a country already ripe for that swing toward extremes which is the inevitable corollary of a shattered economy and the threat of inflation.

More than twenty years ago a similar situation provoked the March on Rome and gave birth to Fascism. We are now about to stage another March on Rome. We must make up our minds and that quickly whether or not we wish to see this second March developing into another 'ism'.[85]

The Foreign Office on the other hand brought a more subtle mixture of intuition, past memories and shrewd calculation to the business of prediction:

It is questionable whether Italy will turn Communist after the war. Extreme Left Wing opinion in Italy in the past has tended more in the direction of anarchism and unorthodox Communism than to a Communism subservient to direction from Moscow. The larger Russia looms the greater will be the attraction of Moscow. On the other hand from the point of view of her economy Italy cannot depend on Russia but must turn to the Allies. I think that our policy towards Italy can only be guided at the present time by the paramount importance of ensuring the success of the military operations and by the hope that in the post-war period our influence will gradually extend at the expense of any temporary swing towards Moscow.

Eden sympathized with this analysis but felt that policy based on 'a pious hope' was 'not substantial enough'. The Department, he ordered, 'must apply its mind to develop something more constructive, hard as the task is.'[86]

When the Department applied its mind during May 1944 a more activist approach did appear, with a significant new emphasis placed on the presumed link between the material condition of the Italian people and their swing Left-wards. The deputy under-secretary, Sir Orme Sargent, in explaining why halting the slide to Communism was the number one priority in Italy 'momentarily', emphasized that:

Communism is beyond the control of Badoglio and his Government, however much we may strengthen it. The causes of Communism lie elsewhere, e.g. deterioration of economic conditions; the effect of Russian victories; and local propaganda, which, inter alia, exploits the fact that unlike the British and Americans, the Russians are not killing Italian civilians and bombing Italian towns.

Sargent then outlined a list of possible concessions, beginning with adjustments in Italy's international position. These ranged from the granting of Allied status, the offer of a preliminary peace treaty or Lend-Lease aid, to participation in the United Nations Relief and Rehabilitation Administration (UNRRA) and adherence to the Atlantic Charter ('Please, not this one,' begged Eden). Sargent urged that particular attention be given to economic questions: altering an unfavourable exchange rate, controlling troop expenditure, stepping up supplies: measures like these, Sargent thought, would 'enhance the popularity of the British people and army, and . . . would be a first step towards building up a useful member of the European family under British direction.' The only alternative was to continue on a negative line, with the likely result of 'the spread of Communism in one form or another, coupled with the danger – a real one – that the Soviet Government will exploit the situation to the detriment of British influence and authority in Italy.' For Sargent the only real possibilities lay in the direction of economic concessions and, on the diplomatic level, a preliminary peace treaty. On this latter project, first mooted before the end of 1943, the Foreign Office now set to work.[87]

The rise of the Communist question, challenging Italy's position in Europe and the Mediterranean, and dominating the path to the political future, thus brought about a qualitative change in British and American approaches to the country's problems. Sargent's analysis of the situation foreshadowed much of Allied, and especially American policy towards Italy in subsequent years, with its premise that Communism would gain influence rather than direct power, that the Italian State was not equipped to deal with the question at the roots, and above all that *economic* causes, and hence economic remedies, were the key to the Communist Party's mass influence: a 'communism of the belly' as Don Sturzo, the founder of the Catholic Partito popolare (forerunner of the Christian Democrats) had once said.

Since that time a vast amount of effort has gone into fathoming the PCI's real intentions, objectives, tactics and strategy at this point in 1944, but it is the variety of conclusions which strike the observer rather than their power of explanation. Clearly there was some form of direct link with Soviet aspirations, which have been characterized authoritatively as an attempt to reproduce the 'Czech model' in Italy, a reference to the December 1943 pact between Stalin and Benes (Head of the exile government in London) which would give the Soviets extensive powers to bring about internal political changes in the country in exchange for military, political and economic support. This precedent was apparently referred to by Soviet negotiators with the Badoglio government, and has led the émigré historian Vojtech Mastny to see in Togliatti's return a bid for a special kind of influence: '[R]ather than holding the power in [his] country, [he would] hold the key to its balance, which would then be manipulated conveniently from Moscow.'[88]

But of course the British and Americans were already in the country, determining the conditions under which political life would restart and extremely watchful of Communist moves in all their forms. A number of observers have seen in Togliatti's flexibility a decisive reconciliation to this reality, a recognition even of the incipient division of Europe into spheres of influence with Italy formally in the western camp. In the context of Italian history since 1944, in which the PCI has played so large a role, the 'turning point' (known as 'la svolta di Salerno' after Togliatti's first speech on his arrival) has come to assume great significance, the moment when a far-reaching compromise was made with the traditional State and when Togliatti decided that the PCI should be a mass party, aiming at power through the traditional mechanisms of parliamentary politics and supremely concerned with anti-Fascist and national unity.[89] This approach has the advantage of looking at PCI choices in their own language and terms, as a product of Italian Left-wing history – a viewpoint which Allied observers at the time found almost impossible to adopt – but it undervalues the dynamic of interdependence between Italian internal politics and Anglo-American interests, which although already started was vastly expanded by the recognition crisis and its aftermath.[90]

For it was at this point that a real sense of urgency began to appear in parts of the American camp for the first time over the situation which had emerged from the process of Italy's liberation,[91] and it was at this moment too that the conviction began to spread openly in the southern Italian ruling class that their salvation lay not with the heavy-handed and vindictive British, nor with the dangerous Soviets, but with the benevolent, remote United States of America.

'BADOGLIO said that he wanted to talk frankly and confidentially to me,' Murphy reported to Washington in April. The marshal spoke again of the recent Russian recognition of his government. 'You Americans must not leave me in a position where without warning I might be subject to a further proposal from the same source looking to an alliance with the Soviet Union. . . . If you permit me I think that for the longer term the U.S. is making an error in surrendering (or so it seems to me) its influence in this region.' For Badoglio the objective circumstances in which Italy found herself pointed to one solution only, but first there had to be some induce-ment for the proposed new patrons:

> The Mediterranean will become the pivot in the future of a huge new European-African politico-economic set-up in which Italy will play a certain role. Your Soviet ally and Great Britain seem to see and appreciate this. Why do you withdraw? We Italians like to deal with Americans and we think we know that our economic future is bound with the west. We can hope for little or no material support from the Soviet Union for many years to come and also but little from Great Britain. But what happens? You withdraw your good Eisenhower and the sympathetic General Smith, and General Wilson whom I esteem takes over. It leaves my people with the impression that the U.S. is abandoning Italy to Great Britain and the Soviet Union.[92]

Other American representatives in Italy, such as Harold Tittman, chargé d'affaires in the Vatican, conveyed the views of their Italian friends, who unanimously felt 'like the great majority of Italians, . . . that Italy will be obliged for the most part to count on the U.S. for help in restoring her internal situation after the war.' In a typical report by one of Tittman's acquaintances ('a moderate and a fervent Catholic') dated March 1944, the U.S. was invited to accept 'a magnificent base in the heart of Europe and the Mediterranean for the extension of a civilizing influence and for profitable economic penetration', based on American capital investment as soon as possible 'to take advantage of propitious monetary and psychological conditions' (i.e. the very low exchange value of the Italian lire). The report included a complete plan for political reconstruction too, based on monarchy and 'democracy' but rejecting universal suffrage and government by 'anti-fascists'. Alcide De Gasperi was named as a potential political leader and the writer did not fail to mention the 'communist abyss' which awaited the country should America fail to come to the rescue.[93] From the provinces the widely ranging agents of the Offices of Strategic Services reported similar sentiments:

> many reasonable and intelligent Italians of the upper and middle classes stated their belief that the only salvation for Italy in the post-war period is that the country come under American influence for an indefinite period.[94]

The various components of the American executive at first reacted disjointedly to these pressures, which soon seemed to assume the dimensions of an organized class campaign. The military, engaged in planning the capture of Rome, thought of sending an advanced detachment for feeding and controlling the city in the hope of gaining useful political and propaganda side-benefits. General McNarney suggested in a JCS meeting that the Vatican should be approached since, 'The Vatican would exert control over more people in Italy than the government itself and therefore it would be an advantage to establish proper relations,' a thought seconded by the Chairman, Leahy. The impression that the Vatican was the determinant factor in Italian politics was, of course, as much Roosevelt's as that of the military.[95]

The leading American civilians in the field, Murphy and Kirk, exposed as they were daily to political and personal pressure, soon produced a definite plan in favour of the new Badoglio government. The U.S., they declared at the beginning of May, should take the initiative in discussing the possibility of Allied status for Italy. But the reply of the State Department to this suggestion might have been written by the British, so close was it to Foreign Office arguments on the subject up to that time. In its message of rejection the Department mentioned first the impact on such allies as the French, the Greeks, the Yugoslavs, and then went on to warn of the 'far-reaching consequences in tending toward the disintegration of the whole machinery of the Allied Control Commission and the terms of the armistice, far in advance of that date when Italy, as a defeated power, shall inevitably become signatory to a peace treaty with the Allied nations.'[96] In spite of the promptings from the field and the alarms of the Soviet recognition episode, policy in Washington was still remote and passive, as Robert Murphy recalled in his memoirs, content to 'trail along' in the wake of the British, who by this time, he said, had 'practically [taken] over the administration of the country, challenged only by the Communists.'[97] But after the liberation of Rome on 4 June, only a few days after Kirk and Murphy received their disappointing reply, the State Department too began to think more critically about the nature of American interests in Italy.

THE ALLIED break-out from Cassino and Anzio finally began on the night of 11 May, but nearly three weeks hard fighting ensued before the enemy was cracked south of Rome (itself only 30 miles from Anzio), and began retreating north of the capital. Although military logic suggested that the bulk of the Allied armies should go round the city, its allure drew in General Mark Clark and a good many of his soldiery. It was, as Churchill told Alexander, 'a vast, world-wide event' not to be minimized, and the festive crowds which welcomed the liberators confirmed that a historic event in Italian history had also taken place.[98] Roosevelt issued a striking call for the Italians to take their future into their own hands and reunite their country with the world community:

> Just as the entire civilized world regards Rome and the other historic cities of Italy as their inheritance, so, I am certain, the people of Italy have never been more deeply aware than now that the cause of the civilized world is their cause too and calls for the dedication of all their powers of heart and mind.[99]

More concretely the armies at the front were told by AFHQ that the importance of the liberation of Rome was above all political, rather than military, and preparations were set in motion from the last week of May to bring about the long-awaited contact and hopefully fusion between the government of Badoglio and the anti-Fascist leaders gathered in the Rome CLN. Sir Noel Charles recommended that food be rushed into the capital to guarantee a good reception for the aged marshal and the new lieutenant general of the realm, and somehow avoid a political crisis. As for the situation of the parties at that moment, it was summed up as follows by the British High Commissioner:

> It would seem that the Left parties are continuing the steady task of preparation to meet future events in attending to the day-to-day practical needs of the country and in decrying their 'Fascist' enemies. The Monarchists are being apathetic and apart from Marshal Badoglio have no leader. The intellectual liberals and Action Party who should be leading the moderates are busy exchanging words and the Catholics who should form a leaven are more ineffectual than they should be; they will, however, naturally become more powerful as soon as Rome has been liberated.[100]

But the political processes set off by the liberation of Rome did not meet up with Sir Noel Charles's hopes or expectations, since within days Badoglio had flown to Rome, met a front of total hostility from the Rome CLN and had forthwith tendered his resignation – to the lieutenant general, Prince Umberto. The following day – 9 June – Bonomi had formed a new six-party government, including Togliatti, De Gasperi, Sforza and Guiseppe Saragat, the future president of the Republic, for the Socialist Party. The only Allied representative present at the crucial meeting in the Grand Hotel was General Mason-MacFarlane, whose efforts seem to have been limited to excluding Count Sforza from the position of foreign minister. Mason-MacFarlane explained to Caserta:

1. During the first conversations in Rome it became clear that Badoglio would have met with a strong and very active and vocal opposition and could not form an all-party government. These conditions would have seriously handicapped the tranquillity and administration of the country.

2. All parties, on the other hand, had a common readiness to serve under Bonomi on the conditions required by me as regards the obligations taken by the previous governments towards the Allies and also in respect to the institutional question . . .

4. Both Bonomi and I did our best to persuade Badoglio to accept a post in the Cabinet. However, the Marshal was altogether unyielding in his determination to retire from the scene.[101]

'Both Allied Governments were thus presented with a *fait accompli*', says the official British historian discreetly, 'which aroused considerable indignation in London. . .'.[102] Churchill was in fact furious, loudly denouncing 'this extremely untrustworthy band of non-elected political comebacks' and the hapless British representatives Charles and MacFarlane who had permitted 'this disaster' to go ahead unchecked. Churchill ordered the change of power to be suspended and the return of Badoglio to office while the ACC and the various governments in the Advisory Council to Italy were consulted. Towards MacFarlane the prime minister turned executioner: 'he will never have any post of the slightest military or political responsibility again', and soon afterwards Mason-MacFarlane was replaced at the head of ACC by the American Captain Ellery Stone.[103]

But in Washington the State Department had immediately taken pains to dissociate itself from the British line and had insisted that from the negotiations with the Rome CLN onwards MacFarlane had been acting solely under instructions from London. The suspension of the new government and particularly the effective veto on the name of Count Sforza as foreign minister – apparently a personal initiative on MacFarlane's part – did not represent the position of the U.S. government, the State Department declared, though in public Hull denied that Whitehall was backing Badoglio.[104] After a direct appeal by Churchill, Stalin gave his sanction for the removal of the new cabinet, but from Roosevelt came a detailed argument in favour of it. For the Americans the immediate priority was to allay criticism at home and abroad directed against the compromise supported since the days of the armistice with the most prominent remnants of Fascism. As Roosevelt pointed out, the need to broaden the government politically had long been recognized while any attempt to impose vetoes would only look like interference. The State Department was apparently willing to accept the new government without conditions, but in the end Churchill succeeded in imposing – via the ACI – two reservations: firstly, formal recognition was demanded of all the armistice terms and other commitments accepted by the Badoglio cabinets; secondly, there was to be a ban on reopening the institutional question. Ivanoe Bonomi and his colleagues complied without question.[105]

The American press saw a clear break with the past in the formation and composition of the new administration. 'Old Men in Italy Inspire New Hope for Democracy', announced the *Chicago Daily News*, alluding in somewhat equivocal manner to the veteran, pre-Fascist air surrounding Bonomi himself and certain of his colleagues. A leader writer in the same paper expressed the sense of the new satisfaction:

> In our former policy there was too much expediency and not enough principle. For how could we claim to be fighting Fascism while ourselves compacting with Fascists and near Fascists? The CLN has done us a service.

From now on, wrote the *Christian Science Monitor*, the armistice, which was a political and military mistake, was a bar to popular rule in Italy.[106]

In reality the liberation of Rome meant much more for Italy's relations with the rest of the world than the military and political events suggest, crucial as they were. Rome was the centre of the State, of finance and of communications. Those who wished to make or remake links with Italian commerce and industry, with the press or with the power centres of the bureaucracy and the Vatican were no longer required to make hazardous contacts across the lines or to overcome the obstacles of an embattled and disordered army administration; with the right contacts and a little dealing in the appropriate circles they could begin to move in to the capital freely (while the government itself, in a bizarre reflection of Allied restrictiveness, was to be confined to the province of Salerno until mid-July). In the short term the most visible result of this process was a notable expansion in the news and comment on Italy appearing in American newspapers and magazines.

Whatever the expectations or illusions may have been, when seasoned American reporters such as Allen Raymond of the *Saturday Evening Post* took stock of the situation in the middle of 1944, the results were not encouraging to the American establishment, either in Italy or at home. 'We run third in Italy', proclaimed Raymond in a long despatch published in the middle of June. The PCI was the group whose prestige had risen most in recent times, thanks to the victories of the Red Army and the persistence of the party itself. But the most powerful influence was that of the British. Not only did they predominate in ACC but they were using it to guide the rebirth of the trade unions, to supervise the armed forces and distribute Allied food. Yet most of this food was American in origin, Raymond reflected, so why was America as a power and an influence running third?[107]

Comments of this kind produced a particularly strong effect in the confines of the U.S. Treasury Department, where Henry Morgenthau Jr. described the situation as he saw it with an eloquence all his own:

> I am very much disturbed the way things are going in Italy. It looks to me as though they are headed straight for Bolshevism, and we go through all this process and liberate the country, lose an enormous number of American soldiers, and when we are through we may have a much more chaotic condition than when we went in there. . . . At present we have spent ninety per cent, roughly, of the money. But

every time we have got to move, we have to consult these English people with the result that it takes months. . . . By the time you get through you have people dying on the streets. I would much rather stand up publicly and say, 'In order to keep Bolshevism from spreading through Europe, I, the Secretary of the Treasury, am willing to recommend that we take the whole job, that we will bill each country what we think their share is, and have a final settlement round the peace table. . . .' I want action. I want to give these people the chance to be decent people. That is what we went in there for.[108]

But these feelings were still not strong enough to produce a definite American plan for the country, still less a strategy for putting a plan into action; even after Rome's liberation the British were still in charge.

5   Staking claims and making plans: British and American approaches to the Italian question, June–December 1944

WHILE Morgenthau fulminated impotently in Washington and anxiety mounted among the Americans on the spot, the British were showing a much more obvious level of interest in the country. In line with Sir Orme Sargent's desire to rehabilitate Italy as 'a member of the European family under British direction', at least to the extent of blocking off the new Communist danger, work went on on the idea of a preliminary peace treaty, and the first designs were sent to AFHQ at the end of May. The scheme which circulated in the British camp in Italy and elsewhere in the empire indicated that as soon as the military position permitted and the Allies were convinced that 'the Italian government had sufficient authority to speak on behalf of the whole Italian people', negotiations would be set in motion. In reality, as the evidence makes clear, the intention at first was never to *conclude* such a treaty but simply to float an idea whose buoyancy might help sustain the authority of the Badoglio government for a time. Since the military position in May was that the Allies were still south of Rome, while the representativity of the government obviously could not be tested until full-scale national elections were held, the offer with its conditions should immediately have appeared as false.[1]

The contents of the document were nevertheless fully detailed and almost as harsh as the armistice itself. While reserving all rights under the surrender and on issues to be decided at the final peace conference, the British were already demanding the renunciation of all colonies, of Italian islands in the Mediterranean and territory on the frontier with Yugoslavia.

In return the Italians were offered (though not in the treaty document itself) the status of an 'associated power'. The ACC was to be limited to administrative tasks and more territory was to be restored to the government. There was a suggestion that some of the many thousands of prisoners-of-war still scattered in various parts of the empire might be returned. Economic concessions were particularly prominent: the restoration of trade and a significant increase in general supplies and consumer goods were promised. Macmillan pointed out that these measures were still bargaining points, while any delay might mean having to give them away.

And it was this latter conception which dominated the thoughts of those who seriously believed the treaty applicable in the summer of 1944. The main object of the exercise for them was to 'consolidate the penal clauses of the ultimate settlement while it was in our power to confer benefits which would offset their severity,' and strong words were used to ensure that the Americans in their generosity did not hand over *gratis* benefits which the British were willing to give only to gain acceptance 'of the many unpalatable conditions.'[2]

The strategic situation after the fall of Rome in June reinforced to some extent the arguments of those who wished to see a treaty applied right away. When the departure of a substantial portion of the American forces in Italy for the South of France took place at the end of June, the British were left with the prospect of relying to a much greater degree on Italian help in the front line than they had ever thought of doing before. Precisely for this reason authoritative elements in the Foreign Office insisted anew that 'we must impose our conditions while we are in a position to make them relatively palatable.'[3]

But as long as the pace of the Allied advance continued at the heady rhythm of summer 1944 an even more appalling prospect presented itself, namely the liberation of all Italy with its attendant consequences of dislocation, chaos and political restlessness on a vast scale:

> there would be the most terrific problems to face, [a member of the Foreign Office Southern Department wrote]. It would be advisable to throw as much as possible of the responsibility for coping with these problems on the Italian Government, in order that, if things went wrong, it would not be the Allies but the Italian Government who would take the blame. This was an argument in favour of concluding a preliminary peace treaty.[4]

The cool cynicism of such an approach appeared to offer other advantages. Without the Allied organs of control, the ACC and the ACI, and British responsibilities towards the United Nations under the armistice, there would be the opportunity to hew to a purely British line in Italy, which would 'enable us to secure certain concessions from the Italians in return for concessions made by us.' There was no risk that Italy in her condition of that moment could offer anything like the presence necessary to make such a deal a balanced one, as the Foreign Office well knew, but the problem still persisted of having an ex-enemy as a co-belligerent. Everyone had a cause to be lenient except the British, reflected a Whitehall analyst, but in the end one was bound to ask: to what extent should the past and the future be considered in proportion to one another?[5]

Here indeed was the heart of the matter. As should be clear by now, the entire British approach to the political problem of Italy had up to that time been defined in terms of the past, in terms of the damage and affront caused to the empire and its prestige by the 'Italian' – not Fascist – adventures of 1935–40. In this sense the single-minded formulators of British policy maintained a dour coherency which no challenge or criticism could crack. But by the middle of 1944 the principal English participants in the drama had lost sight of the quantitative or qualitative 'threat' which Italy as a power could now possibly represent to their interests (presumably understood in terms of the status quo pre-1935, or at the latest pre-1939)[6] and hence were unable to define in any precise, non-arbitrary way a positive role for Italy in a post-war international system. Nevertheless the shape of the future was clearly discernible, and it was a future of competition, preferably friendly but perhaps not, between Britain and the other two great powers of the anti-Hitler alliance. Smuts had already told Churchill at the end of 1943 that Britain would have to fight to stay in this race, and in the light of the Red Army's successful advance into central and eastern Europe in the spring of 1944, coupled with what the prime minister called the 'difficulties in Italy . . . owing to Russian intrigues' (i.e. the recognition of Badoglio and the return of Togliatti), he wrote to his foreign secretary suggesting that 'broadly speaking the issue is: are we going to acquiesce in the Communisation of the Balkans and perhaps of Italy?' With the United States involved in some way, there would have to be either a showdown or a deal with the Russians, Churchill and Eden decided, and they immediately set in motion a project to secure recognition of respective 'leads' in the various countries involved (particularly Romania and Greece), Roosevelt grumbling all the while that they were opening the way to a share-out of sphere of influence which would prejudice things for long after the war. The basic criterion for 'taking the lead' in this plan appeared to be: who was doing most of the fighting?, a question not difficult to answer in Romania or Greece, but not nearly so clear in Italy. There the British and Americans shared responsibility equally at all levels, and even if the British empire was 'doing four-fifths of the fighting' as Churchill had said, it was the United States which did most of the paying and supplying, as Morgenthau had said. Besides, these abstract agreements were of little use in running the day-to-day situation, fraught with the destruction and misery of war, the intractability of the military campaign and the waywardness of the local population and its would-be political representatives.[7]

For Anthony Eden the Italian problem was, at this point in the war, one of the most intractable with which he had to deal. 'An unhappy fate seems to hang over Italian affairs', he complained at one point, and at another, 'Nobody helps much; indeed there will be satisfaction in many quarters if muddles grow worse and they will be laid by all, P.M., Macmillan and soldiers at door of Foreign Office.'[8]

King George VI himself visited the front in July, but by far the most significant event in the whole history of British intervention in Italy in these years was the long sojourn by Churchill in the month of August. The prime minister's immediate reasons for going to Italy were military. Firstly there was the need to offer some psychological compensation to AFHQ for the loss of 7 divisions to the 'Anvil/Dragoon' landings on the French Riviera demanded by the Americans. From then on the Allied Armies in Italy were to be almost wholly from the British empire (and almost equal in number to

Field Marshal Kesselring's 14 divisions), and so there was to be a boost for British generalship as such. As Michael Howard has put it, Churchill 'longed to see what he described as "the most representative Army of the British Empire now in the field" end up in a blaze of glory.'[9] Shortly after the liberation of Rome the optimism of the commanding general, Wilson, had indeed reached the point of promising the liberation of Florence by the end of June, a bridgehead across the Po by early August and arrival in southern Hungary by the end of September.[10] But in the trail of such feats would come the wreckage of Italian politics and towards this aspect of things Churchill showed himself 'very tough', the accompanying Foreign Office official P.J. Dixon recalled. 'Italy had done us great damage [Churchill told Dixon] and must be punished and ground down. I asked him what "working [her] passage" meant. Answer, 3 or 4 years. I tried to counter these extreme views but without much success.'[11]

But on his arrival in Italy Churchill found 'a great deal here which is not satisfactory. They talk of a great scarcity in the poor quarters of Rome.' The ACC was without an authoritative head since MacFarlane had left, under a very heavy cloud, soon after the capture of Rome, and for Churchill the fact that the Committee of National Liberation had formed a new government in liberated Rome without seeking the approval of any of the Allies demonstrated that there was no effective British control; the positions of Macmillan and Charles were too anomalous.[12]

After the initial shock of Badoglio's removal had worn off, the British had soon realized nevertheless that the new government possessed distinct merits. Firstly it offered a link with pre-Fascist traditions through its members who had been active during and after the First World War (notably the prime minister himself, Bonomi), and in addition it promised to defend the existing institutional bargains. So the job of reinforcing the authority of the Rome cabinet presented itself in much the same terms as in the era of Badoglio. The first plans to emerge from Churchill's entourage clearly emphasized this need to support Bonomi, 'in order to arrest [the] disintegration of [the] Government and drift to the left.' The means were to be the same as before: reorganization of the system of control ('This should have the effect of giving Charles [the] effective hand in Italian affairs which he now lacks'), and a preliminary peace treaty.[13] But Churchill, who had other problems and other men on his mind, did not agree.

In the preliminary discussions Churchill had already made quite clear that he was against the preliminary peace proposal. For him its savage territorial demands would serve to weaken rather than strengthen the government and since this government had no mandate from the forces of the North, the temptation would exist – when the North re-entered the political arena – for these forces to repudiate the territorial provisions as an electoral manoeuvre. As for the threat from the Left, Dixon reported that the prime minister's 'present inclination seems to be not to rate the danger from

Communism too highly, since it is doubtful whether the Soviet Government's present policy would favour the Communisation of Italy.'[14]

However, during Churchill's sojourn in Italy, the Warsaw rising took place, producing a new wave of suspicion and alienation against Stalin in the Anglo-American camp. 'And if the Russians were not quite so good as had been thought,' wrote Dixon, 'then perhaps the Italians were not quite so bad.' Churchill's attitude was seen to soften every day, especially after contact with huge and cheering crowds, and in his parting message he went so far as to claim that for this people, 'I have always had, except when we were actually fighting, a great regard.'[15]

There was to be no preliminary peace treaty. Instead there was a public lecture on the nature and practice of liberal democracy and a stern reminder that:

> When a nation has allowed itself to fall into a tyrannical regime it cannot be absolved from the faults due to the guilt of that regime, and naturally we cannot forget the circumstances of Mussolini's attack on France and Great Britain when we were at our weakest, and people thought that Great Britain would sink forever – which, in fact, she has not done.[16]

There was a proposal that Italy 'should be regarded as a friendly co-belligerent and no longer as an enemy state' (without infringing on the powers of the supreme Allied commander), and there was to be a relaxation of economic controls in the belief that, with the aid of relief organizations like UNRRA, disturbances 'such as food riots' could in this way be prevented. There was a firm intention to shift power from the ACC to the Italian government, while the ACC might become simply the Allied Commission (not the 'Commission of Aid and Guidance' as Churchill first suggested). As much as anything else, all this was done, said Churchill, because 'I think the Americans would like to have a more conciliatory gesture made to Italy.'[17]

The British maintained their intense interest in the Italian situation throughout the late summer and autumn of 1944. Churchill was followed by Attlee at the end of August and other visitors included George Hall, parliamentary under-secretary for foreign affairs, L.S. Amery, secretary of state for India and a trade union delegation led by Will Lawther of the National Union of Mineworkers. The attention of these gentlemen – at least as indicated by available documentation – seems to have been directed almost exclusively towards the forces of the Left, the Communist Party, the Socialist Party and the trade unions, a policy which most probably owed its inspiration to a Foreign Office finding in July that what the 'Democratic' (sic) parties needed was 'the direct inspiration of British politicians'. A plan was accordingly devised to encourage Labour Party visitors to Italy, avoid the danger of a similar initiative by the American Congress and separate out purely British propaganda from the joint control of the Psychological Warfare Board at AFHQ.[18] Among the more striking visions of British strategy produced in this period – but not dissimilar in its basic premises to these propaganda tactics – was the paper entitled 'The Future of Italy' produced by the Foreign Office Research Department (FORD) in the middle of August. Since this document is not the sort we are used to reading in British histories of the Second World War, the FORD analysis is worth quoting at some length.

The opening judgments were nothing if not approximative:

> If the Allied Governments are going to wash their hands of Italy as soon as the country has been freed of Germans, it looks as if chaos will reign for an indefinite time. Italy will, apparently, be free to choose any form of democratic Government but will not be allowed to return to a Fascist Government. It is presumed that by 'Fascist Government' any form of dictatorship is meant.

The social and historial impressions on which this verdict was based followed next:

> The Italians have always been very cynical in their attitude towards their Government, not always without reason, and after 20 years of Fascism will, in all probability, be more so. The average Italian does not follow, with any real interest, what the Government are doing in relation to their advertised policy. He does not, in any way, feel part of the Government as Englishmen do . . . Italians of most classes are much more apt to seize on some political figure who touches their imagination, regardless of what party he belongs to and even what his ideas on policy are, and follow him blindly. Thereafter everything he says is acclaimed regardless of what he does. Unless, therefore, Great Britain remains in control (i.e. a virtual dictator) and large-mindedly and firmly guides Italy along democratic lines, Democracy looks like having a very poor chance.

The lack of any outstanding leader combined with institutionalized corruption and unstable government had shaken the confidence of 'educated and responsible' Italians, who were 'beginning to doubt Italy's capability of governing herself . . . and are themselves suggesting that Great Britain should retain control for some time to come.' The document foresaw a return to a form of Fascism should the people refuse Communism and lose all faith in any other form of government. If, however, the British way of doing things could be made plain to the Italians, an alternative to extremism might yet find favour:

> On the other hand Italy will need a loan if she is to recover, and if it came from Great Britain and was administered by H.M.G.'s 'advisers' [sic] to the Italian Government it might help to make the advantages of British control more obvious to the man in the street . . .
>
> Once the Italian people had realized the advantages of a democratic Government under British control, they might take greater and more realistic interest in politics and Democracy have a chance to take permanent root in the country in the future.[19]

But the War Cabinet had decided in August that 'in no circumstances can we agree at the present to any programme of rehabilitation for Italy', while Eden had also ruled out UNRRA aid as a possible concession.[20] How then could this opposition be reconciled with the desire to maintain the lead, even a form of complete control of the country? On what basis of authority was this leadership to rest, and what currency of power could the British use? 'We live here in the dark shadows of mystery', Macmillan wrote to Eden in September.

> We cannot reconcile the contradictions in our Italian policy. Sometimes they are enemies: sometimes they are cobelligerents. Sometimes we wish to punish them for their sins: sometimes to appear as rescuers and guardian angels. It beats me.[21]

NEVERTHELESS, concrete choices had to be made, and with economic means of influence ruled out, the British concentrated on constructing political bridgeheads. Eden thought these should pass through the Allied Control Commission and exercise a restrictive function, but the Foreign Office staff concentrated on more positive forms of action. Their attention centred on the activities of what they called 'the liberal centre bloc', which included elements of the monarchist groups, the Liberal Party, the Labour Democrats (Bonomi's own shadowy party), the Christian Democrats and, possibly, sections of the Partito d'Azione, in a word 'the moderates'. 'It is unfortunate the [non-Communist] parties cannot agree on a united democratic line,' Charles told London after the Rome crisis had subsided; 'their leaders, I think, would welcome visitors from the U.K. whom they could consult on questions about moderate political thought and the democratic evolution of our Country. This seems to me an opportune moment for such visits.'[22] Fortified by a determination to get the 'non-communist progressives' to strike out and show initiative, the Foreign Office and Charles decided that the 'direct inspiration of British politicians' was needed, and began to think of a programme of visits and other measures which might allow a revised British policy to make its weight felt in Italian political life. But in the middle of July such notions were brutally crushed by Eden, with an outburst to the effect that Charles had forgotten 'which country was our Ally and which our enemy in the war that is not yet won. But the British people haven't forgotten nor have I.'[23]

From that moment on British representatives in Italy and the Foreign Office confined their moves in favour of 'the moderates' to discreet conversations and informal gentlemens' understandings. Former prime minister Orlando was a privileged beneficiary of such attentions from the moment when Charles found him 'very impressive and livelier than Bonomi', and with a 'better understanding of the Allied point of view than any other leading Italian.'[24] While a manoeuvre started by the lieutenant general, Prince Umberto, in favour of an alliance between Badoglio and Orlando to challenge the Bonomi government was blocked by Stone of ACC (who reportedly wanted no more sudden changes),[25] the Foreign Office welcomed conservative combinations at lower levels. Informed of the incorporation of a small conservative group from Naples (De Nicola's Partito della Democrazia Liberale) into the Liberal Party, a Whitehall commentator said: 'This is good news since thè Right will certainly not rule if it is divided and subdivided.'[26] Churchill's discussions in Rome produced the sensation that 'it would be in our interests to bolster up the position of Bonomi and his Right-Centre followers,' but the Foreign Office thought that vague gestures from outside in this direction were not enough; what such groups should do was 'to produce some sensible programmes of their own which has a popular appeal.'[27]

This succinct recommendation demonstrates the continuous preference of Allied managers for conservation by autonomous action weighted towards *reform*, though it ignored the effective dependence of the moderate parties on the Allies for that guidance and support which might enable them to develop the capacity for promoting autonomous reform. On a different level the instruction also illustrates a fundamental difference in mentality and outlook between the various sides: put very simply, one might say that while the parties were struggling to define what they might be, the British and Americans worried above all (and not surprisingly) about what they might do.

In general the six main parties which participated in the government after April 1944 and struggled among themselves to determine the new direction of Italian political life, appear to have ignored the presence of the Allies as far as possible, an impulse which was turned into a quite futile strategy of action when the North was liberated and the parties were acting (temporarily) via the CLN structures.[28] In Italian historiography the first substantial attempt at a survey of the period which gave due weight to the real hegemony of the Allies with respect to political life was that of E. Aga-Rossi Sitzia, *La Situazione Politica ed Economica dell Italia nel Periodo 1944–45: I Governi Bonomi*, published in 1971. Here we read that only with the liberation of Rome did an effective reorganization of the parties take place, capable of recreating the substance of political life after years of clandestine and fragile contacts. But in all the parties present at the time there was

uncertainty and confusion, not only in their analyses of the current situation but also in their short-term objectives. The generic nature of their theory and the poverty of their ideological weapons, true also of the Left, helps to explain the substantial weakness of the parties at the level of government and the absence of a common understanding on the programme of reconstruction. In addition inside each party there were misunderstandings and differences due to the gap between old and new generations, between the experiences of the exiles and of those who had stayed behind, between the traditionalists and the advocates of experiment. The problems of government policy were relegated to a secondary level in this phase of clarification and definition of ideological positions.[29]

This was particularly true in the case of the Socialist Party, an element whose composite make-up and unpredictable loyalties gave rise to some hopes that it might be recruited if not to the moderate camp at least to that of the 'non-communist progressives'. Nenni's anxiety to maintain contacts with the British Labour Party was earnestly encouraged by Charles, who thought that 'some counter-poise to Soviet propaganda' might thereby emerge, but the unity of action pact signed by the Communists and Socialists in August 1944 was severely disillusioning:

> Thus we see an extreme left bloc being formed and the Communists continuing their plan to swallow up their 'next-of-kin' and preparing themselves for real battle against their political enemies.[30]

Nenni's exhortations at the Italian Socialist Party (PSI) congress in September in favour of a 'socialist republic' (in maximum contrast to Togliatti's demands for a 'progressive, democratic republic') were given short shrift in London: 'This is all very silly', sniffed a Foreign Office observer, to which a colleague rejoined: 'But then the Italian Socialist Party is a remarkably silly party. It is living in a world of its own making, using language coined in the '20's and doomed to be eaten up by the much more astute . . . Communist Party.'[31] However, the Socialists could not be written off quite so easily. Shortly after the party congress, Nenni joined a group of high Allied officers at dinner and made a strong impression:

> The conclusion which represented itself to those who listened to the discussion [said a report which found its way to the State Department] was that Nenni made the follow-ing plea: 'If you are afraid of Communism and would like Socialism to act as a counter-poise you should see to it that the Socialists get some material help. At present they are left standing by the Communists who have the whole support both moral and material of Russia behind them.'[32]

In public of course Nenni was never more diligent than in these weeks in asserting the importance of unity with the PCI, in denouncing the rigours of Allied control, and in demanding 'All Powers to the CLN', a claim inevitably seen in Allied circles as revolutionary in intent. Nenni was nevertheless allowed to come to the Labour Party congress in London in December, 1944 ('We should like Italian political life to evolve on British lines . . .', explained the Foreign Office), and declared himself tremendously impressed by the Labour Party's unity and dedication to the war effort. But Macmillan wrote the Socialist leader off as an animal 'like the chameleon [who] takes his colour from his immediate surroundings,' and the Socialist Party as a whole could never be regarded by the Anglo-Americans as a reliable pillar of the moderate forces.[33]

IN REALITY two contingent factors were uppermost in the minds of the Rome politicians which cut across British efforts for influence: firstly, it was self-evident that the war would come to an end within a few months, and the Allies and all their paraphernalia including the embarrassing Control Commission would then go away; secondly, that the liberation of the North, and the role of the CLNs in it, would be the decisive event for Italy's political evolution and the place of each of the parties in it. To the extent that the

Rome leaders thought seriously about Italy's international relationships, it was to the United States that they looked for succour and support, not to the British. This was demonstrated at the end of July by the long personal communication which Bonomi delivered to Secretary Hull through the Americans in the Political Section of ACC. It contained a comprehensive list of complaints on Italy's treatment by the Allies. From the anachronistic nature of the armistice regime to the denial of a substantial Italian contribution to the fighting, from the recently announced refusal of Italian participation in international organizations such as the International Labour Party Organization (ILO) and the Bretton Woods Monetary Conference, to the economic impositions of a low exchange rate and uncontrolled troop-spending, the account was complete, and resoundingly denounced the 'indefinite subjection of a civilised people like the Italians to a state of tutelage.' Particularly vibrant was the protest against the position of the Italian colonies and the prisoners-of-war still in Allied hands.[34]

Hull's reply, the British official historian informs us, was 'a model of diplomatic repartee.' In other words Hull defended the existing arrangements in a way exactly consonant with British preferences. The armistice terms, said Hull, 'were being applied solely for the purpose of furthering the prosecution of the war against Germany', and he suggested that if the Italian government had ideas for alternative arrangements they would be received with interest in Washington. For Hull the *de jure* status of Italy was secondary to the *de facto* relationship with the U.S. created by the country's contribution to the war effort. Italian participation in the war was still conditioned by memories of Fascist aggression, said Hull, but a technical mission to discuss the many economic problems could certainly be contemplated, as long as it was understood that the formal definition of Lend-Lease operations excluded any hopes of Italian participation. As for the ACC, the freedom and sovereignty of the Allied commander had to remain the prime consideration.[35]

In reality in the subcutaneous layers of the Washington administration a ponderous development of awareness, of orientation towards problems such as those found in Italy, was taking place. Certainly there was no unilateral intervention by the Americans to match the visit of Churchill in August, and on the level of diplomatic representation no continuous effort was made parallel to that of the British; on the contrary Kirk went out of his way to maintain as low a profile as possible in Rome. But as James C. Dunn, the director of the State Department's Office of European Affairs put it in July: 'in general, it may be said that we are entering the post-war period in our political relations with Italy.' For Dunn a broad series of factors pointed in one direction: namely the end of the armistice regime and the return to 'a basis of peace with Italy.'[36]

'What is our policy towards Italy?' asked the State Department in the form of its Policy Committee in the middle of July. Since the answer provided reveals many of the assumptions underlying the American vision of Europe in mid-1944, assumptions based on political premises which were to change little in succeeding years, and is directly comparable with the FORD paper already mentioned, it too, is worth quoting in some detail:

> It is American policy to desire and to promote the political independence of other nations. We do not believe that an ordered and peaceful world can be created upon the foundations of an international society in which certain states are subject to their more powerful neighbors. This policy applies to Italy. We do not want to see that country fall under the domination of any third power. During a time when we occupy a particular position of authority in Italy, as a result of military operations, we should support and encourage elements and aspirations which will develop the Italian nation into a democratic and constructive force in the future Europe.

Then came the economic theory which would underpin this political model:

> American policy is based on the premise that the economic well-being of a country is a prime factor in its internal stability and in its peaceful relations with other states. We believe that the economic dependence of one state upon another is not conducive to such well-being and may ultimately have disturbing political implications. Therefore it is sound American policy to help Italy again become self-supporting and economically independent as quickly as possible.

The primitive ways of traditional European imperialism were roundly denounced:

> The United States does not accept the theory of economic and political 'spheres of influence.' While, for geographic reasons, this country's interest in Italy may not be as great as that of certain other powers, it has, nevertheless, a very real interest in the development of normal and mutually profitable trade relations, in the protection of American property and investments in Italy, and in insuring that Italy becomes a positive force for peace and cooperation in the post-war world. The blood sacrifices made by American men from Sicily to the Alps cannot be ignored in the determination of our interest in, and our policy toward, Italy.[37]

In the name of constructing a peaceful, independent nation in Italy other elements in the State Department were planning, as we shall see, a drastic overhaul of the machinery of state. The Foreign Economic Administration was building up an economic planning and intelligence staff to manage a revival of the national economy which would have 'lasting effects in that country,' and 'be watched with close attention not only in this country and in Italy, but [in] all the world,' while American trade-union groups were mobilizing money and high-powered delegations to guide the Italians in their struggle to build new anti-Fascist trade union structures. These developments will be considered in detail in appropriate chapters, but they should be related in the first instance to what was happening in Rome at this time.[38]

From the eminence of his pontifical chair, Pope Pius XII directed the attention of Roosevelt's personal emissary to the Vatican, former U.S. Steel president Myron Taylor, to the 'possibility of the spread of Communism in

Europe and a very real danger of its development in a strong way in Italy, especially in the period of political and social reconstruction.' On several occasions, said Taylor, the pope had expressed a desire that the Allied armies 'would not leave Italy for a long time to come. That their presence would have a stabilising influence upon the people and the politicians.' According to the *New York Herald Tribune*, Rome business men were pessimistic about the future, foreseeing a strong trend to 'the Reds'. The Allies, they declared, ought to stay for five years or more since the Italians themselves were incapable of self-government. 'But the U.S. will go isolationist, the U.K. will leave, then we'll have civil war and communism,' they predicted gloomily. It was not difficult to find members of the new anti-Fascist government who shared the same sentiments and had no hesitation in expressing them, even in apocalyptic tones. Cerabona, the Social-Democrat minister of communications, told the Office of Strategic Services (OSS) that he thought the Allied occcupation should last 'for centuries' though he then added that he was thinking in economic rather than military terms. Italy ate Allied food and wore Allied shoes, Italy was being rid of German oppression by Allied arms, Cerabona reflected. Reconstruction would be impossible without Allied, and especially American, assistance. 'American capital was essential,' said the minister. He was then asked by his interviewers why he assigned the leading role to America rather than Britain:

> the Minister gave two explanations. First of all, he said, there was the fact that the Italians were utterly pro-American, a sentiment based largely on their belief in the indescribable wealth and consequent generosity of America. And secondly because it was in America's interest to have a practical means of access to Europe's markets and a base for political influence. Isolationism was no longer possible.[39]

It was Kirk's responsibility to act as the transmission belt conveying these solicitations to the Washington hierarchy. Although the British felt that Alexander Kirk was an element likely to weaken rather than strengthen Allied control ('a solvent', he was termed on one occasion), the American political adviser was quite capable of reading the signs of the times. In forwarding the Cerabona interview to the State Department, Kirk added that 'many Italians harbour misgivings over the withdrawal of Allied officials as territory is transferred to the Italian administration,' and as time went on Kirk grew more and more resentful both of British predominance in Italy and the lack of positive measures in Italy's favour coming out of Washington.[40]

Kirk's own recommendations about this time would have meant a quantitative leap in American intervention in Italy. In a despatch in early September he demanded a supply of highly qualified American advisers to transform ACC and the Italian ministries plus American business, agricultural and industrial experts 'when and where required throughout the country.' Even the military presence should stay, 'at least as long as any other [army] remains on this soil.'[41]

In spite of everything said until then about the virtues of indirect rule this was a recipe for neo-colonialism, but it was nothing more or less than what was being urged daily upon Kirk and his colleagues by their contacts in the bourgeoisie of Rome and the South. Although signs of a more activist approach were appearing in Washington by the end of August, the immediate objective of the State Department planners remained the construction of 'essential safeguards against the possibility of renewed Italian aggression', as an important new policy document explained at this time.

In this analysis the geographic position of the country alone put her in a position to 'wage wars against African peoples and minor European states,' and the only real deterrent to such a geopolitical menace could be material and juridical restrictions on the one hand and large-scale internal adjustments on the other, aimed at the roots of minority megalomania. Ideally such adjustments would be composed of:

(a)   Such a political reconstruction of Italy as would prevent the possibility of domination by any one class or group, and through the establishment of democratic institutions would permit the pacific and constructive sentiments of the mass of the Italian people to find political expression.

(b)   An economic reconstruction designed to create an expanding economy which will offer the Italian people genuine opportunities for their economic betterment.

(c)   Establishment of such political and economic relationships between Italy and the rest of the world as would undermine any widespread popular support in Italy for imperialism by offering the Italian people a genuine opportunity for an honourable part in pacific international activities.

There then followed a detailed and comprehensive plan for the realization of these guidelines which, if enacted, would have left hardly any aspect of Italian life untouched. From the Church–State relationship to educational development, from the composition of the armed services to the powers of local government, from the reorganization of financial and fiscal controls to the regulation of labour and industry, everything was covered. Italy's colonies and frontiers were also dealt with one by one. All that was missing was any consideration of the idea that Italians might have views of their own on these problems.

It was a plan to warm the heart of any American internationalist, be he Republican or New Dealer. Leaving aside the theoretical premises of political strategy embodied in the July and August statements, two kinds of historical conception prevalent in the minds of the State Department planners are worth pointing out. Firstly there was the attention paid to the *structural* condition of Italy, and it was from this direction that the impulse came to deal with 'the pressure of [Italy's] population on its limited resources and the need for providing outlets for the creative energies of the Italian people.' The search for foreign raw materials and markets, and for outlets for surplus population, had been among 'the strongest of the forces which [have] been used to impel that country along the path of imperialism,' the analysts felt (although they were also aware that the overseas possessions had in fact proved an economic liability).

The second 'historical' consideration was one consciously and permanently sensed throughout the Roosevelt administration with regard to the European situation. This was the need to avoid at all costs the supposed errors which had provoked the forces of revisionism and revanchism in Germany after the First World War, and those of isolationism in the U.S.:

> [The] recognition and establishment of a positive role for the Italian people in peaceful world reconstruction should be advertised to them. If the peace appeared to them to be purely negative, it would tend to make Italian national feeling focus in opposition to the treaties, and in opposition to the powers making the peace.[42]

Meanwhile against the elaborate abstractions of Washington the pressure of the present was mounting. The British mine-workers' delegation reported in September that conditions were 'quite impossible to describe.' Money had lost all meaning and the people were left without food or organization: 'There is no real basis for the social life of the population,' the delegation declared.[43] As the Allies advanced across the Arno valley to the foothills of the Appenines, towns were liberated faster than their populations could be fed. In June Cardinal Spellman had promised that U.S. troops were the 'advance guard of America's charity.' By September American military government officers were facing up to the tremendous and appalling threat – to use the words of one of them – that combat troops would have to be used to control starving crowds.[44] However, it was up to the soldiers to face this contingency; for the others – journalists, diplomats, staff of the Allied control bureaucracy – politics came first. 'They argue that, if large-scale rioting and social disintegration occur in the first country placed under Anglo-American control, the blow to the democracies' prestige would have repercussions throughout Europe,' Anne McCormick reported in the *New York Times*.[45] Not only was Italy a test of the Allies' 'capacity to reorganise the Continent', but the political position of the U.S. in the post-war period was seen to be at stake.

Throughout August and September a barrage of criticism aimed at the practical inactivity of the Roosevelt administration mounted. La Guardia, the Italo-American mayor of New York, threatened to stop his weekly propaganda broadcasts to Italy 'unless I have something to say;' while George Baldanzi, a CIO leader newly returned from Italy, told the *New York Times* that his two principal impressions had been the desperate economic situation of the country and the need for an American policy: 'Thousands of our boys have been killed or wounded here in Italy and yet the only policy seems to be to bomb, fight, and win the war and then go home. As everybody knows, the British are playing a predominant role in the present set-up while the U.S. shows no interest.' Confusion and resentment were spreading, Anne McCormick warned again at the end of the month, and everywhere people were asking 'what will America's policy be?'[46]

THE DEVELOPMENT of an Anglo-American position 'adequate to the total situation and yet free from those precise commitments that spelt political controversy at home or malicious misinterpretation abroad' – the words are William Reitzel's – came with the Hyde Park Declaration, pronounced at the president's home in up-state New York on 26 September 1944, with the British prime minister present. This large-scale programme of aid and relief was divided effectively into two parts, one political and one economic. Under the first heading came measures intended to shift responsibility from the Allies to the Italian government and to give the government some visible recognition of its new authority. Thus the ACC would become the Allied Commission (AC) and the exchange of diplomatic representatives with the Allies was to be allowed. The means to establish a degree of autonomous responsibility were provided under the economic clauses and appeared much more imposing than the political concessions:

> First and foremost, to relieve hunger, sickness and fear UNRRA would send medical aid and other essential supplies [writes the British official historian]. At the same time, first steps would be taken towards the reconstruction of the Italian economy – primarily with a military aim, in order to employ Italian resources to the fullest extent in the struggle against Germany and Japan.[47]

A milestone had undoubtedly been erected along the way to the full reinstatement of Italy in world affairs and Macmillan baptized it the 'New Deal' for Italy. But this milestone bore no indication at all of the distance still to be travelled or even of the units of measurement: 'We all wish to speed the day when the last vestiges of Fascism in Italy will have been wiped out,' the Declaration vaguely concluded, 'when the last German will have left Italian soil, and when there will be no need of any Allied troops to remain – the day when free elections can be held throughout Italy, and when Italy can earn her proper place in the great family of free nations.'[48]

For the Americans, two quite different levels of interest were reflected in the decision in favour of Italian rehabilitation. Beyond the considerations of propaganda and the betrayal of public ideals, the collapse of Italian society threatened to open the way to some form of Communist advance, as almost every observer had agreed. What was still unclear was the content of this threat. Ideologically and politically it meant presumably the growth of the PCI; but on the strategic level it was the Soviet advance westwards and southwards which spelt instability and danger in Washington. The State Department's explanations of the new declaration concentrated on its internal implications:

> if, by our providing help at this critical period, Italy can achieve economic and political conditions favourable to the development of democratic institutions and policies . . . our investment in effort and money may be well worthwhile.[49]

Other Washington observers saw the Declaration's international function; for *Newsweek*, for example, it reflected 'a growing concern with the mounting prestige of the USSR,' (as well as 'an effort to halt the drift towards communism').[50]

Beyond all this, the Allied campaigns of the spring and summer of 1944 were by September approaching their long-awaited climax: both British and American intelligence estimates put the latest probable date for a German collapse as December and no one doubted (in private, at least) that the Red Army's contribution to this situation had been overwhelming. Thus the Hyde Park Declaration was – for the Americans – part of a recognition process which saw the planning of the post-war system and its alternatives as an immediate priority.[51]

For certain groups in America, immigrants from the fringes of Europe, the question of Soviet influence was of immediate political interest, and as the presidential elections of November 1944 approached they mobilized to remind the Roosevelt administration and the opposition of their own commitment in America's response to the Russian advance. Although no ethnic community matched the massive campaign of the Polish-Americans, the movement of the Italian groups in New York and elsewhere in favour of expanded aid and political support to Italy soon assumed dimensions which the candidates could not ignore.[52] As Don Sturzo had reminded Assistant Secretary of State Berle in September many Italians too had an interest in restricting the Soviet's freedom of manoeuvre in southern and central Europe, and in any case were utterly dismayed at the lack of Allied action on the basic problems of relief, transport, prisoners-of-war and co-belligerency.' [The] wreckage of war lay exactly where it had fallen,' declared Don Sturzo, to which the unfortunate Berle could only reply recognizing that 'the underlying situation is unhappily there.'[53]

The electoral motivation behind the Hyde Park statement has seemed so clear to observers past and present as practically to exclude all others. As 6 November approached a Gallup poll showed New York state to be 51 per cent Republican and 49 per cent Democratic and certainly no occasion was missed to remind Italo-Americans of Roosevelt's concern for their native land. A troop pay credit – first announced at the beginning of October as part of the Hyde Park plan – was brought out, dusted down and republicized, especially on Columbus Day, the community festival of the Italo-Americans. On that day, reported the *New York Times*, 50,000 of them bore the emblem of the House of Savoy down 5th Avenue for the first time since the war began, watched by 1 million others. At a Columbus Day dinner Roosevelt's rival Dewey claimed that while Italo-Americans represented only 4 per cent of the population, they made up no less than 10 per cent of the armed forces, and he ended with a defiant assertion: 'Liberated Italy is today a friend and an ally, not just a cobelligerent.'[54]

The Foreign Office found the whole pre-electoral exercise 'nauseating' and 'repulsive'. 'Only wish the Greek vote was heavier,' wrote one observer in Whitehall and others worried that for the Americans at that time 'anything is justifiable that brings grist to the Presidential mill.'[55] In this frame of mind Whitehall was not likely to regard the Hyde Park concessions with indulgence. Over-riding strenuous Foreign Office objections, Churchill had pushed forward his own line in policy discussions with Roosevelt, telling the president that he was 'distressed and disquieted by the tales I heard of serious food shortages in some parts of Rome and other great towns.' There were other menaces too: 'Unemployment looms big in Italy. We may also soon have the populous North flowing on to our hands.'[56] Churchill's own proposals revolved round the need for an effective relief scheme and for a change at the top of the ACC in favour of a politician rather than a general. When the list of concessions emerged its continuity with these proposals (and others gone over by Churchill and Macmillan in Rome) was clear; as the prime minister told Sir Noel Charles, the premise for the discussions with Roosevelt had been that 'Italy is henceforth regarded as a friendly cobelligerent and no longer as an enemy state.[57]

Under these arrangements Macmillan emerged as the new head, or 'Acting President', of ACC, with an important mandate to work out a plan for applying the reforms. The Foreign Office was pleased: 'We should thus acquire a dominant position in the ACC and so be able to protect our special interests in Italy'; as long as Macmillan was president, 'British influence in Italian affairs will obviously be predominant.'

On one other most important point the Foreign Office also obtained satisfaction: there was to be no revision or even any mention of the armistice terms. To the suggestion from Hyde Park that such a revision be promised in the Declaration, the Foreign Office replied that this would call everything into consideration, and in addition involve consultation with the Russians. Then again there was the problem of the secrecy still surrounding the armistice documents; 'Parliament would certainly press to see the terms if their revision is announced,' the Foreign Office warned with effect.[58]

In Rome, where various gradations of opinion on Allied operations in Italy had been crystallizing since the liberation, the Hyde Park Declaration was received with approval but not with enthusiasm. 'The [Italian] people have noted with satisfaction this commitment,' wrote Pietro Nenni in *Avanti!*, the Socialist Party paper, 'and hope that it will rapidly be translated into concrete facts.' Within a matter of days the government had sent to Admiral Stone as executive head of ACC a long list of demands aiming at a decisive reorientation of the relationship between ACC and the Italian authorities. As the British official historian reports, 'the upshot of the reforms suggested was that the Commission should . . . be transformed into a joint Italian-Allied body largely civilianised, and that the Allied officers attached to various Italian Ministries should be withdrawn. The service sub-commissions should be separated from it and organised as a military mission.'[59]

At the beginning of October Roosevelt, over-riding more British protests, promised a significant increase in the basic bread ration in Italy and 1700 new trucks for its distribution. The troop pay credit deal was announced a few days later. Yet 'in words of greater bitterness than any yet uttered by an Italian public figure,' said the *New York Times*, the veteran philosopher Benedetto Croce spoke out in the middle of that month demanding nothing less than Allied status for Italy. Italy's moral condition was so low, declared Croce, that the Russian treatment of Romania, where national forces were immediately conceded participation in the war and the country was not saddled with collaborationist politicians, was regarded with envy. Herbert Matthews, the *New York Times* correspondent, commented that Croce's statement drew its force from the fact that 'it truly expresses the feelings of every thinking Italian . . . Italian morale has never been so low, nor her leaders so discouraged as today.'[60]

Croce was simply one of the first to understand that of all the measures and 'concessions' announced in the previous weeks none represented more than a palliative with respect to the immediate material situation of liberated Italy. To appease inflamed opinion at home and abroad certain gestures had been made by the Anglo-Americans, but of the essential nature of the relationship between Italy and the Allies, the dependence, the subjection, the ambiguity, nothing had changed. Discussions of the details of the new arrangements 'flashed to and fro between London and Washington for month after month,' C. R. S. Harris reports, while the Germans stopped the Allied advance in the mud of the Gothic Line and winter began to descend. The public pronouncements had been made, but in the headquarters of the military, executors of whatever action might be intended, there arrived no instructions. And in spite of further promises by Roosevelt, the amount of wheat shipped, already known to be inadequate, was actually cut by 20 per cent at the end of the year.[61]

THE MIDDLE of October found Churchill in Moscow with Stalin, and there, on the fringes of the meeting which produced the famous percentages deal and in which Churchill declared that Britain 'must be the leading Mediterranean Power', the prime minister attempted another bargain, a bargain which revealed just how far certain American fears matched reality. Churchill said at one point that he wanted to talk kings and assured Stalin that in no case would Britain try to force kings on Italy, Greece or Yugoslavia. 'Britain did not care for the Italian King,' Stalin was told,

> but above all they did not want civil war after the troops had been withdrawn or before their arrival. Britain would like the Soviet Union to soft-pedal the Communists

in Italy and not to stir them up. Pure democracy would settle what the people wanted, but he did not want to have disturbances in Turin or Milan and clashes between the troops and the people. The Italians were in a miserable condition. He did not think much of them as a people, but they had a good many votes in New York State. This was off the record. [sic]

The P.M. went on to say that he did not want to have trouble in Italy before the United States left it [the minutes record]. The President was their best friend. They would never have such a good one. That was why he petted the Italians, though he did not like them much. He had not meant that the Soviet Union should influence the Communist vote in New York. He was referring to the Communists in Italy.

Naturally Stalin was not prepared to concede so lightly that Togliatti was at his direct disposal, for purposes of agitation or any other:

Marshal Stalin remarked that it was difficult to influence Italian Communists. The position of Communists differed in different countries. It depends upon their national situation. If Ercoli were in Moscow Marshal Stalin might influence him. But he was in Italy, where the circumstances were different. He could send Marshal Stalin to the devil.

Stalin cited what had happened in Bulgaria:

When the Red Army entered Bulgaria, Bulgarian Communists proceeded to form Soviets. The Red Army stopped it. The Communists arrested the Bulgarian police and the Red Army freed the police. However, Ercoli was a wise man, not an extremist, and would not start an adventure in Italy.[62]

The sober Churchill did not, he said, think much of the Italians, but in the warm afterglow of a Moscow dinner they did not look so bad:

The P.M. considered that the Italian people, who had been misled by their rulers, were harmless and friendly. He had been impressed by the warm reception which he had received from the Italian populace during his recent visit.

Eden was sour, warning Churchill that appearances could be deceptive and claiming that the traditional Italian foreign policy was 'blackmail', but Stalin was even sourer:

they had behaved badly and deserved no consideration. . . . Bad as the Italian leaders were the Italian people could not be absolved from guilt. It was the Italian people who had thrown up Mussolini.

In comparison with Stalin, Churchill began to appear as a benefactor, even if a reluctant one; unless the Allies extended some help to them, he said, they would simply starve. To this Stalin replied doubting whether the economic situation was really so serious.[63]

IF THE ITALIAN problem had simply consisted of a contest for influence between the British and the Russians, as some sectors of American opinion imagined, the Churchill–Stalin conversations of October would have resolved any lingering doubts. Gone were the recriminations over lack of consultation and information, unequal representation and other similar grievances, and no claims or mutual accusations were exchanged. Instead there appeared to be implicit acknowledgment of the newly established ascendancies and a free hand for Britain in Italy. There was little sign even of concern for American interests, which caused predictable irritation in Washington. By the end of the year opinion polls were showing that Americans distrusted Britain even more than they distrusted the Soviet Union and a diffuse sense of uneasiness was spreading through the press and Congress at the apparent return to spheres of influence, alliances and balances of power – the very arrangements Hull had declared dead and buried before Congress on his return from Moscow at the end of 1943.[64]

The British, and Sir Noel Charles in particular, found these tendencies wholly incomprehensible:

> It is difficult to fathom the reasons why the Americans are apt to feel that British control of Italy has as its purpose to reduce Italy to the status of a British economic dependency. I can only explain it by the fact that most Americans are, as Don Sturzo says, hopelessly ignorant about Italy. Americans too, do not seem to be happy unless they have a grievance against us. That England should be accused of trying to make Italy into a dependency, economic or political, is incredible, since with due respect, we appear in our policy to show a certain indifference to Italy's fate.[65]

But after the Moscow meeting the British began to think more openly and concisely about the disposition of their long-term interests in the European area and the Mediterranean. As Harold Macmillan worked to produce a plan which would turn the Hyde Park design into concrete directives, his assistant (and head of ACC's Political Section) Harold Caccia drew up a comprehensive map of British long-term interests in Italy. As the Foreign Office noted at the time these efforts were not unrelated.

'Italy is a country which we can get at and in which we rather than Russia should naturally expect to exert predominant influence.' This was the central theme of Caccia's opus, repeated with variations in a long accompanying letter by Sir Noel Charles, who said: 'We have the opportunity of attaching her to us without the expenditure of great effort or wealth'.

For Caccia the British currency of influence consisted of 'the loan of brains and organising ability as much as in the provision of finance and material'; or as Charles put it: 'by showing willingness to help and sending a fair amount of material and technical help, we can maintain the position which our strategic and permanent interests require.' Resentment among the British people should not be allowed to go unchecked for the sake of these interests, Charles asserted, especially since 'Italy's traitorous proclivities may have assisted us more recently.' For Caccia the past meant an Italy 'too strong'; now she should be strong enough to stand up to her eastern neighbours but no stronger. 'For much the same reasons of our own self-interest,' Caccia went on, 'it would be to our advantage that the internal regime in Italy should be of a moderate and democratic kind. Fascism did not suit British interests. No more would Communism.'

Given the historical weakness of the Italian State and Italian political immaturity, it might even be necessary to adjust British claims to consolidate the new balance:

> For instance, we accept that a monarchical regime is capable of being an element of stability inside Italy. As the monarchy derives much support from the armed Services and in particular from the Navy, its chances of survival would be sensibly reduced if, for instance, we decided practically to disband the Navy.

The pillars of economic support for such a strategy would of course have to be provided by the United States; 'if they do this, they will indirectly be serving our interests and we should welcome and encourage rather than contest any such development.'[66]

As William Reitzel wrote not long afterwards:

> The British, in fact, had fallen into a policy of 'as if,' taking positions *as if* there had been no change in the distribution of power resources and *as if* American power in the Mediterranean was a demonstrably permanent factor.[67]

At the time Myron Taylor wrote from the Vatican that an axiom of the wartime emergency had been the need for Britain and the U.S. to cooperate 'to the limit': 'If there is any break in such relations, both countries must suffer,' Taylor believed, 'but Britain would suffer more greatly than the U.S.' Taylor's note was a long a bitter complaint denouncing the arrogance and selfishness of the British not only in their attitude towards the Italians – which he described as 'cold, unforgiving and at times actually cruel' – but also in their conduct *vis à vis* the Americans.[68]

Such damning comments added authoritative weight to the momentum of complaint being generated in the same period by the American press, intent on reminding the executive of the gulf which had opened up 'between visible American power and the purposes for which it was being used.' Typical was Herbert Matthews' late November protest that Allied rule was still that of the iron hand, while the British – assumed to be backing the monarchy – and the Americans were so afraid of revolution or civil strife that they would support the forces of conservatism against any supposed threat. Whatever Anglo-American wishes might be, Italy was inescapably a test case on the future Europe, said Matthews.[69] 'The country is half-slave and half – well, we cannot call it free, but the trend is in that direction,' declared the *Christian Science Monitor*, pointing out at the same time that the promises of Hyde Park remained unfulfilled.[70] The comments of Dorothy Thomson in the *Chicago Daily News* were more concisely political, and intended for British consumption in particular:

> The legitimate attempt of Britain to extend her influence in Europe is to be welcomed, provided that that attempt does not uphold a neo-Fascism on the backs of reactionary opponents. Whoever wants continual influence in Europe must back the trends rising out of the masses of the European peoples, and not try to set the clock back.[71]

THIS AND SIMILAR statements from many prominent commentators at the beginning of December formed part of the massive barrage of American criticism which fell on the British intervention in the cabinet crisis now developing in Rome. The rumblings of crisis had been heard ever since the beginning of autumn when attempts by the Left – Communists, Socialists and Actionists – to stimulate the government into a more energetic line of action, particularly in the field of epuration and in its relations with ACC, had been met with prompt threats of resignation by the prime minister. On these occasions Bonomi never failed to tell the Allied authorities that he feared an extremist take-over, thus lending substance to the claim of the Left that Bonomi and the conservatives had been intriguing to gain the support of Churchill while he was in Italy.[72]

Harold Macmillan was convinced that behind the immediate events of the crisis (revolving round a proposal to somehow submit the problems dividing the parties to the northern CLNs for solution) lay the intrigues of Count Sforza and the cynicism of the Left, which wished 'to get out of the government in order to leave the disagreeable job of a hard winter on short rations to the Moderates'. Bonomi himself told Admiral Stone that his decision to resign resulted from left-wing demands for control of the Epuration Commission (which Bonomi wished to dissolve), of the Ministries of the Interior and of War, and for the Foreign Ministry to be placed in the hands – it was thought – of Count Sforza. When undenied rumours began to arrive in London of Communist pressure for the resignations of the Minister of War Casati, of the Liberal Under Secretary of Foreign Affairs Visconti Venosta, and for a renewed epuration, there was no hesitation. Charles was instructed to tell Bonomi that 'on no account' should Sforza be admitted to a ministerial position, while the resignation of Visconti Venosta would be considered 'regrettable'. The inclusion of the Versailles veteran Orlando in the new government was urged. The Americans, it was decided in Whitehall, might be kept informed in general of British moves, except for those against Count Sforza.[73]

The storm which immediately broke around the heads of the British government when this intervention leaked out represented more than a decisive turning-point in Anglo-American relations in Italy. The newly appointed Secretary of State Stettinius was forced to improvise a riposte appropriate to the clamour and in this first major policy statement of Roosevelt's new administration, there was both a reply to the particular questions of the Italian case and a restatement of general principle. As far as the U.S. government was concerned, said Stettinius, the formation of the new cabinet was a purely Italian affair, requiring no interference from outside and no opposition to particular individuals such as Count Sforza. For the secretary of state this was the meaning of the self-determination theme in the Atlantic Charter, and as such constituted a principled approach to the political problems now emerging in liberated Europe. This statement received an authoritative endorsement from Congress when Senator Tom Connally, an influential isolationist, announced his approval.[74]

In the heated discussion which followed in the international press, the almost unanimous condemnation of the Eden–Churchill line (defended by Churchill in the Commons on 2 December) represented little more than a starting point. Few doubted that the incident had dimensions embracing problems far beyond the immediate case of Italy, and it was clear too that fundamental choices in foreign policy were at stake. But beyond these obvious points of reference nothing was certain. What did the State Department mean? asked the *Christian Science Monitor* after the Stettinius initiative. Was this a warning to Britain and to Russia? If so, why was the dispute between the Allies so open? Could such a drastic reconversion to Atlantic Charter principles really be so all-inclusive? How, in fact, could non-interference – 'hands off' – be enforced on others?[75]

Herbert Matthews insisted in the *New York Times* that America's policy of non-intervention was a positive one, but then went on to ask whether it could really mean that Italy was going to be left to the British. When the same question was applied to Greece, the situation looked somewhat different: 'It is fantastic for the British to veto Count Sforza as Italian Foreign Minister without consulting the Americans and the Russians,' noted the *New York Herald Tribune*, 'it is equally fantastic that the British should now be left to struggle single-handed with Communist revolution in Greece without the active support of American and Russian policy.' The ACI and the European Advisory Commission were both 'fading into cyphers,' the New York paper believed, and new alliance machinery was needed, although it also felt that Stettinius's statement had 'almost for the first time [declared] an active American policy in the reorganisation of Europe: something which has been consistently missing through all the vagaries, clouds, confusion and expedients that have previously characterised our foreign policy.'[76]

British commentators did not for the most part share these preoccupations. The *Daily Telegraph* saw the Stettinius move as 'hint' to Russia against interference in liberated countries, while only the *Manchester Guardian* attacked British unilateralism openly and directly: 'It would be better to have pure and unadulterated AMGOT than a representative government which represents nothing except the wishes of the AC (British Section).' The most violent attack of this sort came from Michael Foot, who proclaimed from the pages of the *Daily Herald* that 'Sir Noel Does Not Speak For Britain,' and went on:

> Our victorious armies carry the banner of liberation. They are greeted with flowers and song and rejoicing. And in their wake comes some caricature from the Foreign Office with a brief-case full of vetoes, a kind message for the nearest monarch and the smell of Chamberlainism lingering about his person.[77]

In the Foreign Office there prevailed an atmosphere of astonishment and outrage. The secretary of state's pronouncement was felt to be an act of 'calculated unfriendliness towards us . . . all the more wounding in that the Soviet Government have so far scrupulously abstained from any similar conduct or comment.' The prime minister was 'deeply hurt' and said so in no uncertain terms to Roosevelt. The general impression created now was 'deplorable' and an offensive was immediately set in motion to extract from Stettinius an apology and an admission of the harm done. This satisfaction was almost immediately conceded by the hapless secretary of state who did not find an opportunity to vent his feelings for some time, and then in a quite different context.[78]

Reactions to the British veto in Rome were predictably disparaging. The Socialist leader Nenni, playing to the full his role of most vocal critic of Allied operations in Italy, called the move 'intolerable', and insisted that the Allies should not and could not limit the initiative of the country in the name of a misplaced faith in the capacity of the right to restore order.[79]

In Florence the regional CLN newspaper *La Nazione del Popolo* protested that the new democratic revolution promised by the Allies and the parties had not been born, and there was indecision and lack of faith in the battle against internal reaction.[80]

The PCI on the other hand kept its eyes firmly fixed on the immediate realities of the internal situation. If we are to believe in the 'most secret sources' of Sir Noel Charles, one possible reason for this was to be found in a conversation held between Togliatti and a member of the Soviet embassy in Rome at the end of November. Togliatti was warned on this occasion that he should not expect assistance from outside. Ministerial crises were also expected by the Soviets in Belgium, Poland and France, but until the imminent meeting of the Big Three had produced a new directive, the PCI should lie low. The Foreign Office was taken aback once again, finding the attitude expressed by the Soviet diplomat 'quite staggeringly "correct"'.[81]

In any event the reasons and circumstances which had driven Togliatti into his earlier alliance with the established conservative forces had not changed, and it was these which the party underlined in its private and public pronouncements in favour of participation in a new cabinet under Bonomi. The immediate result of this approach was the resolution of the government crisis, with the Socialists and the Actionists now choosing to remain outside the government in the hope of maintaining thereby their own liberty of action. In Harry Hopkins' words, the remaining elements which constituted the new cabinet represented 'a union of the conservative right and the extreme left.'[82]

The crisis was over, but its dilemmas were to linger on longer than any of its principal actors or commentators imagined. Its peculiar tension and depth were due largely to its timing. As the Yalta conference approached, together with the final collapse of the Third Reich, political choices for the reorganization of post-war Europe took on a new urgency. For Americans this was a moment of particular emotion. Since the alternatives in foreign policy had been effectively reduced in the public mind to two: intervention or isolation, 'hands on' or 'hands off',[83] it was now up to the proponents of these lines to give them some content, based either on a reinterpretation of traditional American principles or on precise indications of policy and method.

The British drew their own conclusions from the crisis and had no doubt which priorities were imposed by the exigencies of power. At Allied Force Headquarters in Caserta a level of communication and common operation existed between British and Americans which now served as a vital channel of reflection on the new situation. Through it the British attempted to expose official Washington to what they believed to be two unrefutable facts of international life at that time: firstly that 'isolationism is dead, whether the American people like it or not', and secondly that a realistic view of British interests and commitments in the world demanded that Americans 'resist a temptation to lecture the British from a pulpit of moral superiority.'[84]

'It has been most interesting to observe the reaction of various British military officials in the Anglo-American milieu of AFHQ to public statements of the Secretary of State regarding the Sforza case and the Greek situation,' noted Carmel Offie, assistant to the American political adviser at AFHQ in a noteworthy memo to the State Department at the end of December. Besides emphasizing the two lessons mentioned above, the British, Offie reported, demanded from Washington a 'sympathetic and realistic view of British traditional policy and commitments in Europe and the Far East.' As far as Greece was concerned, there was a longstanding political and strategic interest which meant that 'as a Mediterranean power (we, the British) have got to live with the Greeks'. In a situation like that prevailing in those days in Athens there was no room for moral quibbles:

> They state they may have been unwise in doing what they did in Greece, both from a local and wider Balkan point of view, but they insist they did it after consultation with the American Government and all they ask is that American authorities should not take this opportunity of abusing them as anti-democratic reactionaries up to old imperialistic games, brutally suppressing the spontaneous and popular will of the Greek people as expressed in terms of bombs and guns. That, they say, is nonsense.

As far as Italy was concerned, nothing had changed: that country was still 'in the position of a defeated enemy working its way home by a degree of co-belligerency.' The future autonomous development of ex-Axis powers could not come 'until the end of an occupational period,' consequently the Allies 'must retain the right to reject any man as a member of the Government of Italy, Germany or Japan who they think would be prejudicial to the aims for which the war is being fought,' although it was admitted that such decisions could only be inter-Allied (and it was forgotten that there was almost nothing concrete against Sforza other than Churchill's personal prejudice).[85]

The immediate reaction to these views showed little awareness of the fundamental questions raised. Commenting on the Offie memorandum, James Clement Dunn limited his observations to the immediate necessity in the Italian case to appease public opinion, and emphasized that 'co-belligerency', as understood by the Americans, signified a constructive approach to the elaboration of a future role for Italy in Europe. Missing was any reference to the short-term nature of the original arrangements, or to the political pressures inside Italy (or, for that matter, inside Greece) which required new methods of management distinct from the direct repression of the early days. The fact that talk of the 'defeated enemy' contradicted flatly the spirit and declared intentions of the Hyde Park Declaration was likewise ignored.[86]

But it was at this time that the search began in earnest for an active and autonomous American policy in Italy, one which could express a visible difference between the naked and regressive application of power as practised since the beginning by the British and now by the French (who were reported from the north to be massing on the Franco-Italian frontier with large-scale designs for occupation by force after the German withdrawal), and the positive aims and principles for which Americans had been persuaded to join in the war. Early in the new year Harry Hopkins visited Naples and Rome on his way to Yalta, making a rapid but thorough survey of the situation in liberated Italy without even informing the British of his presence. His verdict left no room for misunderstanding: it was 'essential for the U.S. Government to stop being merely a silent partner of the British in Italy.' Instead of automatically acquiescing in British decisions, the U.S. should insist that the Allies give the Italians greater political responsibility. Because of her military presence in the country, it was impossible for America to escape the responsibility for military decisions concerning political matters, 'even though it was the British who were really making these decisions.' In a Rome press conference, Hopkins declared openly that on the basis of previous impressions he had not liked the general situation between the Allies and the Italian people and government, and that nothing he had heard since his arrival had changed his view. In private Hopkins pointed to the key problem of food, whose remedy he thought was easily within the reach of available resources.[87]

For its part the Foreign Economic Administration had revised its entire programme for Italy within a matter of days of the Stettinius statement, declaring openly that 'recent disturbing events in Italy' meant that 'American influence [would] have to be strengthened and American responsibility somewhat enlarged.' The FEA demanded a new and more liberal directive for supplies, an aid programme similar to if not actually part of the Lend-Lease programme, and the immediate setting-up of an FEA mission which could be sent to Italy within a few months.[88]

The Combined Civil Affairs Committee sitting in Washington was the scene of the first direct American attempts to assert an alternative approach to the Italian problem. When the committee met in the middle of December to discuss Macmillan's plan for implementing the Hyde Park 'New Deal' for Italy, it split. Formally the plan was endorsed. But the American members insisted in a minority report that 'the directive as now written falls so far short of what we believe could be reasonably done at this time that we feel it amounts only to a relatively feeble gesture of no permanent or significant value.' Particular objection was made to the condition that every new government submit formally to the terms of surrender, a penalty whose continuation the British insisted on absolutely. The group believed that the conclusion of a tripartite preliminary peace treaty was an urgent political and psychological priority, especially since the will of the Italians to fight alongside the Allies – after a year of resistance in the North – could no longer be doubted. This was going to be the last occasion of self-abnegation for the sake of the alliance which, the Americans declared, had characterized their behaviour on Italy up to that moment. The meeting in fact marked the start of an American campaign in favour of a preliminary peace treaty which was not abandoned until the entire picture had changed many months later.[89]

Whatever the quality of American ideas in British eyes (which regarded with scorn the new treaty proposal[90]), certain directions had by now been chosen in Washington, which could rely in the last analysis on the *force majeure* of supplies and money to impose them. Inside Italy the restoration of democratic institutions was beginning to be seen as dependent on positive political intervention and an aid policy designed to cut the ground of oppressive material conditions from under the feet of the Left. In addition the open approval given by the State Department to the representativity of the second Bonomi government meant acquiescing in the suppression of the move to consult the CLNs and signified an explicit choice in favour of one group of Italians rather than another. As Herbert Matthews pointed out, the favoured group was the Right, led by a prime minister who was also identified with the monarchy.[91]

The dominant reality of international life in 1944 was of course the massive increase in the power and influence, the new presence of the Soviet Union. Whatever pangs of conscience the Western Allies may have felt at their late support of the Russians in the struggle against Nazi Germany, the question of where the balance of power would eventually come to rest was now an active one, especially if the decline of British capabilities in the Mediterranean – as demonstrated by the Greek fiasco – was to be taken seriously.[92] The new activism in the American approach to the Italian question could not be detached from this context of deepening instability in the Mediterranean area. At the same time the tasks to be faced in Italy began to be easier to define: they involved the development of an explicit, independent line of action, capable of applying a new system of stabilization effective at once inside the country and with reference to Italy's position in the Mediterranean and Europe. To cite William Reitzel once again:

> An implicit objective of Allied policy was accordingly shaped. The 'development of democratic institutions' became less of a verbal formula and more of a positive intention to construct a system securely tied by interest to the West. It is not necessary to prove that such an aim was officially envisaged by the American government. It is only necessary to note that the rehabilitation of Italy was begun under conditions which inevitably pushed policy decisions in this direction.[93]

6 Material conditions and the rise of the Left: the economics of the war in Italy in 1944

THE ITALIAN FRONT was by the end of 1944 totally stagnant, with the entire country except for certain portions of the South under military occupation of one sort or another and a great swathe across the centre a war zone. In vast areas survival was not a moral or political question but a physical one with semi-starvation and the rubble of war an experience shared by entire populations for months on end.[1] Bureaucrats and planners in Caserta, Rome, London and Washington knew very well what the situation was and worried about it: they feared a total social collapse, with incalculable impact on their own authority and prestige inside Italy and the world at large, with the risk that the Italian State would be submerged, and with the danger that the Communist Party would profit directly or otherwise: many in AFHQ argued that this was one of the most striking lessons of the Greek crisis. But neither the British nor the Americans were organized in such a way at this time to have much impact on social or economic reality; neither the plans nor the structures were capable of tackling the conditions caused by a liberation process such as this.

One source of intelligence on the everyday living standards of the liberated Italians was intercepted mail. In May 1944 the Italian Division of the Foreign Economic Administration in Washington learned in this way that in Sardinia:

> Food riots are reported from the provinces of Cagliari and Sassari. At the end of January a food riot took place in Sassari and lasted three days. From the same town a writer mentions 'a prelude to revolution' and 'today it continues more furiously . . . all the roads are blocked . . . the Red Flag is waving at the head of the people, violences [sic] took place against the police.'

Another typical excerpt said:

> According to a letter from Carbonia . . . in all the houses people are dying of 'starvation' . . . 'The other day along the roads of Iglesias forty dead were found, and the next day twenty.'[2]

The Foreign Office was also well informed on this subject, to the extent of knowing that *if* the promised March deliveries of sugar and cheese had ever arrived in Naples, the total daily calories available to each individual would have been 615, compared with 1378 on German rations (Allied food planners in London aimed at a basic average level of 2000 per day in their calculations for post-war Europe).[3] Sir Orme Sargent saw a fundamental reorientation of policy implicit in this sort of news and demanded 'analysis of the whole question of economic and financial conditions in Italy in connexion with the recent growth of Communist influence, [and] in view of the impetus to Communism which inflation and a shattered economy may give.' Sir Noel Charles was inclined to blame troop spending and the exchange rate for the state of things, but Sargent was severe with such a view, which he thought might let the Italian government 'get away with the idea that inflation is solely due to the Allied occupation, nor should the Italian communists be allowed to foster this impression among the Italian people.' For the short term Sargent recommended enforced taxation and a redistribution of the load of Allied military expenditure;

> From the long-term point of view [continued Sargent], the objective must be to restore Italian industry to comparative prosperity within as short a period of time as possible, and in the interval to provide consumers' goods . . . the ultimate problem of getting occupation costs in Italy paid and such reparations as are considered possible will be a formidable one, in view of Italy's present economic and financial situation.[4]

In Washington the planners had begun with a set of simple minimum objectives dictated by the obvious exigencies of the wartime situation:

> To prevent Italy from becoming an economic drag on the United Nations, primarily by enabling that country to meet its basic needs through domestic production and the exchange of goods with foreign countries.[5]

But by the end of 1944 FEA, State Department and Treasury experts were reaching conclusions similar to those of the Foreign Office, and they were profoundly upsetting ones to that body of opinion which had assumed that the interim period between the end of hostilities and the take-off of world prosperity due to American free-trade policies would be relatively brief. When Hull had formulated America's post-war economic policy in May 1944, the focus had been, as Gabriel Kolko emphasizes,

> on its trade goals rather than emergency aid to a starving Europe that was fighting the war with far greater sacrifices than those of American businessmen, farmers, and exporters anxious over their future profit margins . . . Widespread starvation was a much more remote consideration than ripping down the accumulated pre-war trade barriers and the special war-time licensing and government bulk-buying practices that the British, French and Russians threatened to continue in the postwar period.[6]

The man who brought the prevalent American mentality of expansion to Italy was Henry F. Grady, an eminent businessman and politician who had already accomplished a number of important missions for the U.S. government during the war, and whose presence in Italy at the head of ACC's Economic Section was regarded at first by the British as a signal that the United States meant serious business in its share of occupation policy. Grady's obscure departure after a matter of weeks ensured that the policies he advocated, as exclusively unilateral as any the British proposed, would not be carried out in the foreseeable future:

> our national contribution [in Italy] . . . [must] be made, so far as possible, the means of furthering our national policies in the international field, designed for the reconstruction of a world of expanding economic activity and peaceful development, unhampered by excessive trade restriction, special spheres of influence, and the other concomitants of the economic imperialism which must ultimately lead again to war.[7]

Just how these policies – which Grady termed the 'development of Italian initiative and responsibility' – could be applied in Italy no one knew. As Robert Murphy told James Clement Dunn in June 1944: 'I have never seen a concrete analysis or statement of our economic objectives.' Murphy was convinced that the British in contrast did have economic aims in Italy, but he refrained from stating them even indirectly, and Eden, upon reading this letter, asked his civil servants outright what British economic policy was.[8]

The Americans had great difficulty in finding candidates for the invidious post of head of ACC's Economic Section, and for most of 1944 it was left vacant. Protests from every level, AFHQ, ACC, the Political Adviser's Office, the Foreign Office, were to no avail. By June the hapless Mason-MacFarlane was speaking out 'with considerable feeling and bitterness' over the absenteeism of the nominal incumbent, the Hon. Henry F. Grady, who had arrived in January 1944, had departed in March and according to MacFarlane had not been heard of since then, except when he had published an independent personal assessment of the Economic Section's work.[9] The American political adviser, Alexander Kirk, pressed hard for a replacement, stating that the job was 'the most important civilian task in Italy and one that can be best performed by a civilian.' Technical knowledge, experience and ability were the requirements, said Kirk, and he considered Grady's successor O'Dwyer (who stayed six weeks) to be under-qualified, though by this time Kirk had decided that ACC itself should be taken over by an American civilian economics expert.[10] From then on no new head of the Economic Section was officially appointed until March 1945, when a former chief Italian buyer for Macy's department store who was on the spot for some months was given the job, to be succeeded within weeks by a 27-year-old graduate, Harlan Cleveland, who proved to be one of the few 'young, enthusiastic Rooseveltians, creatures of the New Deal . . . passionately concerned with Italy's problems', and much praised by the later UNRRA staff, ever to arrive in the country.[11]

With AFHQ and ACC lacking an economic overlord to match Macmillan's weight in political matters, it was up to the bureaucracies in London and Washington to read the danger signals coming in thick and fast from Italy by late 1944. 'Industrial wage rates increased between September 1943, and September 1944, by from 55% to 100% in different categories,' said a memorandum drawn up for the War Cabinet's Ministerial Committee on

Armistice Terms and Civil Administration in October. In the same period the cost of living in Naples had risen 321 per cent, said the report, which also included graphic figures on the situation in Rome:

Percentage of food available in	Sept. '43	Jul. '44
Rationed market	10.9	3.4
Free market	23.5	22.6
Black market	65.6	74.0
	100.0%	100.0%

Price Index in	Sept. '43	Jul. '44
Rationed market	100	127.6
Free market	100	397.8
Black market	100	465.0[12]

By this time the Foreign Office had decided that 'concessions' to halt the Communist advance were not enough; instead much more drastic intervention was required, namely 'the most rigid control of production, prices and distribution, coupled with strictly enforced taxation at high levels and energetically conducted savings campaigns . . .', and a set of measures was accordingly recommended to the Rome cabinet.[13] But the Foreign Office had few illusions; only a strong government could enforce such measures and there was little chance as the Foreign Office saw things of the Rome authorities of that time summoning up the organizational capacity or willpower demanded. The inevitable consequence was clear: the Allies themselves would have to be prepared 'to put into practice and administer a widespread and rigidly enforced system of control over the entire economy.'[14]

In Washington the State Department planners elaborating a global design for the treatment of Italy in the summer of 1944 found themselves obliged to make a space for 'certain measures to meet emergency conditions which are not in harmony with [our] long-term objectives.'[15]

In the long-range view, the key aim was to be 'the development of an expanding Italian economy designed to improve and render secure the Italian standard of living,' the State Department explained. This meant the dismantling of autarky and its production system, and a return to 'multilateral, non-discriminatory foreign trade,' with industry and agriculture reconstructed by Italians 'along the lines of production best suited to the resources and aptitudes of the Italian people.' The use of American financial assistance to obtain 'political concessions' during reconstruction was firmly ruled out.[16]

The short-term plan on the other hand envisaged not only an expanded programme of economic first-aid, but also the rehabilitation of those industries 'which in the past have formed an important part of the Italian economy,' together with 'reorganization of the taxation and fiscal systems . . . improved fiscal, monetary and financial controls, and reconsideration of the exchange rate.' In addition there was a demand for 'continued regulation of imports and exports'.[17] The essential difference between the two views was that the emergency plan inevitably involved direct American intervention in the near and not so near future at every level of the Italian economy. The U.S. (or for the emergency period the Allies together) would supply the plans – not forgetting America's own national economic aims, the State Department urged – while the authorities in Rome would carry them out and rally public enthusiasm for them.

But when Allied visitors repeatedly described the incapacity, inefficiency and ignorance of Italian economic administrators,[18] it was clear that there would have to be drastic and direct intervention – in spite of the urge to transfer the load. Certain steps were taken by the control machinery, but the obstacles to the kind of emergency plans envisaged in London and Washington were not to be surmounted during the occupation, and they were obstacles produced in part by the Allies' own methods of operation on the spot.

THE KEY AREAS of economics which lay entirely in Allied hands, not requiring efforts of management or reform by Italians, concerned supplies, troop spending and credit. Not until very late in the occupation, when a new historical phase had opened, were there signs of efforts in these fields equal to the emergency and equal to the exhortations being made to the Italian government to overhaul itself and look after its own responsibilities. Although apparently technical, each of these problems involved fundamental political considerations, and they illustrate the political priorities of the occupying powers not only with respect to Italy, but also in reference to much broader areas of interest: first the British, then reluctantly and haltingly the Americans, began to see a revolutionary threat in the economic chaos of post-Fascist Italy, and began to reorder their own operations there in this light. But because of the arrangements desperately improvised to cope with the wartime emergency, this reordering proved to be no easy task.

As we have seen, the supply question arose from three main problems: real technical difficulties, military exclusiveness and the peculiar British attitude to the treatment of Italy characterized in no small part by vindictiveness. Yet even when the American administration was free to put forward its own policy to correct these distortions, there was hesitation and postponement. The FEA proponents of Lend-Lease aid for Italy, for instance, were unable to persuade either the State Department or the president that Italy was a vital defence interest of the U.S., in spite of the fact that American armies were fighting there, and in spite of the Lend-Lease Supplemental

Appropriations Act, which furnished the legal basis for the Army's large-scale relief operations in Italy. Hull told Bonomi that the definitions of Lend-Lease aid excluded operations in ex-enemy territories, while the U.S. Treasury was included to favour this concession, but uncertain. Since the high-level U.S. Treasury meetings are the only discussions concerning wartime Italy which have left a verbatim record, the reader may appreciate the atmosphere conveyed by the following debate on the Lend-Lease topic:

> HENRY MORGENTHAU JR.: Why should we go along?
>
> MR GLASSER (*an assistant secretary*): It will, I think, further the U.S. policy in Italy. If there is anything that will bring us back some of the prestige we lost in Italy, this will do it. It is the best way of doing it to regain the prestige. We will have to do it anyway.
>
> MR CURRIE (*State Dept, after reporting that Dean Acheson, chairman of the Department's Liberated Areas Committee, wished UNRRA rather than Lend-Lease aid, proposes a loan*): We keep that pretty clean, treat it as a commercial loan, extend no more than we think Italy will be able to pay in the future for the heavy type of reconstruction goods – utilities, factories, raw materials, possibly; and then for the intermediate class of essential civilian supplies – not straight relief, and yet not strictly speaking in the reconstruction category – we put that on a cash reimbursable Lend-Lease basis. The only catch is that the cash would be lire, and what we would eventually get out of it would depend on the final settlement.
>
> MR BELL (*a Treasury assistant*): . . . why should we go in for reconstruction when the war is on in all its fury and we need our supplies here for munitions?
>
> MR CURRIE: I think it is to our interest to get that economy self-sufficing and operating again as soon as possible, otherwise we will have to carry those people indefinitely.
>
> MR BELL: Granted, it is to our interest; but it is also to our interest to build tanks and guns.
>
> MR MORGENTHAU: I want to know more. How am I going to vote? Is it that important?[19]

Although the Lend-Lease administrators were convinced that their operations contributed to the industrialization of devastated or 'backward' countries, thereby making them better long-term customers for U.S. exports, commercial circles objected that Lend-Lease was a barrier to private trade. In Italy's case they hoped that as in South America, a distinction could be drawn between military supplies and non-military goods, with the latter left to private industry.[20] In fact such a distinction was eventually made, when the Hyde Park plans were formally implemented in January 1945 in a scheme which sought to boost the supply of consumer goods, and looked forward 'in somewhat distant fashion owing to the shippping shortage' to the resumption of private trade. The British official historian presents this choice as an improvised, strictly technical affair, although the two designs – that of the traders and that of ACC (whose economic section was headed by a fervent freetrader, Antolini) – coincide exactly. However, there is as yet no direct evidence of a connection between Italy's exclusion from Lend-Lease and the manner in which private commerce was resumed.[21]

The obscurity surrounding the American decision against Lend-Lease pales in significance, however, when compared to the dense fog of ambiguity which enclosed the ill-famed exchange rate of L.400 = £1, L.100 = $1, fixed before the occupation started and unchanged when it ended. The first rate established was that applied by the British in their occupation of Italian territory in East Africa in 1941 (at L.450 = £1), and in spite of insistence by FEA and by the U.S. War Department that it be drastically lowered for the occupation of the Italian mainland, to prevent inflation, it entered at almost the same level with the invasion, and the issuance of printed 'Allied Military Lire' (AM Lire)[22]

Even in British circles there were protests. Questions were asked, and rebuffed, in the House of Commons, and in the British financial press. Eisenhower too objected, suggesting a rate of L.80 = $1. But in the United States opinion was divided, Assistant Secretary of the Treasury White suggesting that a lower rate 'would be favourable to "Italian fascists" and . . . Allied soldiers deserved a better break.'[23] U.S. Treasury experts pointed out that the lira was in steep decline due to speculation and the collapse of price controls before the invasion, and worried about the prices the Allies would have to pay for Italian exports if revaluation were carried out. Argument on the subject went on unceasingly in AFHQ and ACC (where it was known of course that any Italian exports in the foreseeable future were likely to be miniscule). Harold Macmillan and Henry Grady pressed separately for the rate to be reduced to 200 lire to the pound, and Macmillan went so far as to include this proposal together with tougher regulations on troop spending in a list of economic reform measures of May 1944.[24] But when Badoglio pressed for revaluation, he was told that government deficits ruled out any such concession, or any other which might give the lira 'a value which is obviously too high to be maintained over a long-run period.' In September 1943 the British Treasury had predicted that inflation was such that the rate would be too low within a short time, and this line of argument was maintained by Whitehall until the end of the occupation, in spite of the echo which Macmillan's suggestion found in the plans of certain sections of the Foreign Office aimed at eliminating the conditions Communism was supposed to feed on.[25] By August 1944 revaluation had disappeared from the list of concessions discussed with Churchill in Rome, and by the spring of 1945 – according to a British Treasury visitor – the complaint was no longer heard. In his opinion a realistic rate at that time would have probably been L.800 to the pound.[26]

By that time uncontrolled troop spending (which gave the ordinary G.I. a real disposable income not far from that of a top Italian functionary) had already contributed its own weighty share to the inflationary damage. In this sphere the Americans, who put far fewer brakes on their troops than either the British or the Dominion commands, had to bear to brunt of the blame, since no serious plan seems even to have been considered by the War Department. When the American troop pay credit deal was announced in

October 1944, a debt was paid in the propaganda count as well as in the financial one, but the inflationary spiral had taken grip and was not to relent for many months. Probably none of the many arbitrary elements in Allied policy in Italy caused more hardship than British punitive action against the lira and American casualness over troop spending.[27]

But with the troop pay credit, the admission of Italy to the UNRRA fold and the Hyde Park declaration, followed by Roosevelt's unilateral promises on food and transport,[28] a new phase opened in the politics of economic action as in other spheres of Allied operations in Italy. It was in this time that the new priorities of stability and prosperity suggested by the State Department in August received official definition and endorsement in Washington, and henceforth economic policy tended to become a long-term affair with an ever more sharply defined political profile. At almost all levels there was consensus on the role of economic aid in halting the advance of 'extremism', and extensive commitments made in official declarations began to pass to the planning stages in Washington. But the application of these designs on the spot proved to be subject to the tortuous processes set off by the new power struggle of late 1944 between the British and the American sides in Italy (as well as to the confusion on the ground). In spite of the underlying agreement on the methods required to oppose the Left, in spite of the sentiments of those who wished to see the United States pick up its inevitable burden as soon as possible, the assertion of American priorities did not pass easily or quickly within the Anglo-American camp.

On supply questions the British were as tough as ever. The minister for war reassured the minister for foreign affairs that in reality the Hyde Park Declaration had changed very little: 'All that is intended,' noted Sir P.J. Grigg, 'is that the existing "prevention of disease and unrest" standard which has hitherto been applied shall be interpreted less rigorously,' adding that the new levels of supplies coming in were 'unlikely to be very considerable'.[29] Given the direct responsibility of the secretary of war for civil affairs and hence for supplies sent through military channels to the liberated areas, this was a prophecy which could be made with confidence.

But the Americans were by no means always consistent on questions such as these, in spite of their verbal promises. Churchill's growing anxieties as to the degree of American commitment to European welfare were justified, as a private British official visitor to Assistant Secretary of War McCloy discovered in December 1944. From this conversation it emerged that the U.S. War Department had lately decided to disregard the claims of Europe for civilian supplies until the war in the West was won, when shipping could be released to make up for the sacrifices endured in the meantime. The Washington embassy official who talked to McCloy described his personal reaction as follows:

I said that whilst I understood the reasons for which such a decision had been taken it seemed to me that a very grave risk was being run. To put it bluntly, in order to win the war were we not imperilling the political and social fabric of European civilization on which the future peace of the world depended? This drew from Mr. McCloy the immediate rejoinder that it was a British interest to remember that, as a result of the complete change in the economic and financial position of the British Commonwealth which the war had brought about, we, in the U.K., depended at least as much upon the U.S. as we did upon Europe. Was it wise to risk losing the support of the U.S. in seeking the support of Western Europe? This was what was involved.

The shocked embassy representative tried to press McCloy into discriminating between 'the case for Europe' and 'the manner in which the problem of getting civilian tonnages should be tackled,' and was reminded in reply of the great difficulties of the war in the Pacific, where there was a risk of 'complete collapse' in China:

> Against this background [continued McCloy] and against the strongly held views of the U.S. Navy it would be fatal for us to argue that the war in the Pacific should be retarded in order that the civilian populations of Europe should be fed. If we were to do so there would be a leakage both from the War and Navy Departments and we should be accused in all the isolationist press and elsewhere, as we have already been accused in the case of Italy and Greece, of endeavoring to use American resources to promote British imperial interests in Europe.

The basic question of course still remained: how could shipping be obtained to supply liberated Europe? The prospects could not be more stark, said the British representative:

> Unless raw materials were provided for Belgium and France and more food for Italy, the political and social position in those countries seemed to me likely to deteriorate to a point from which it could not be rescued by the hasty provision of additional supplies at the end of the European war, since by that time a new political situation must have been created.

McCloy's reply can hardly have been reassuring. What was needed, he said, was a renewed effort by the existing machinery: 'Resources would . . . have to be strained as they would to meet an unexpected counter-attack by the enemy.'[30]

As the Foreign Office pointed out, this was an 'extremely revealing' discussion. McCloy's further admission that the Japanese navy and air force had been largely destroyed seemed to demonstrate to the British that certain sectors of American official opinion, if not all, were prepared to risk the engulfment of Europe by revolution and Soviet Communism but not an improbable Japanese victory in China.

In Italy, of course, the food shortages grew worse, as did the price spiral. The labour subcommission of ACC had discovered as early as May (1944) that 'the answer on the labour front is food, not wages', and later its director declared that the continual wage demands 'when examined, were invariably demands for more food.'[31] Inflation in the liberated areas was approximately 3,500–4,000 per cent by the end of 1944. In Greece in the same period it passed from over 1500 times the 1941 level to over 2000 million times.[32] The December insurrection of 1944 had come shortly after the first substitution of the currency, and in the aftermath of its repression several more attempts were made under British direction. If, as Wray Candilis claims, Greece offered an important experience in teaching American planners of the gravity of European conditions (and their possible consequences), the effect of this situation on the British was much more immediate. While in London Keynes and his colleagues were looking to inflation and food shortages as the crucial economic problems to be faced before there could be talk of free trade and prosperity, Macmillan – political overlord of both Greece and Italy – did not hesitate to warn in Caserta that identical trends left uncontrolled in Italy would produce consequences identical with those of Greece.[33]

'It is my opinion that the Allied Control Commission is not capable of operating the Italian economy in a manner which can successfully avoid inflation', said a U.S. Treasury expert after a visit to Italy, in the knowledge that the ACC had set up its own Anti-Inflation Committee. He went on:

> Perhaps the Italians can't either, but an Italian Government which has the confidence and support of the bulk of the people is the only type of government which can be capable of managing internal economic affairs as to attain and maintain financial and economic stability. Therefore, it is necessary that the Allied Control Commission transfer to the Italian Government greater responsibility and authority for the management of Italian economic and financial processes.[34]

If a social and political breakdown was to be avoided, it was up to the unloved Control Commission to do whatever was necessary until a thoroughgoing plan of rehabilitation could be organized.

7 Military necessities and political purposes: the evolution of Allied control

> We were very keen, we had lots of experts, we made a great quantity of plans, we imported a lot of food and materials; we set up all sorts of commissions and boards and committees. We started to govern (or try to govern) and regulate (or try to regulate) every aspect of Italian life.

THE ITALIANS, continued Macmillan in a newspaper article in 1948, had listened and appeared grateful, 'but [they] were waiting for us to leave.'[1]

From the spring of 1944 onwards, Macmillan began to urge the dismantling of ACC and Churchill too urged that wider responsibilities be shifted to the Italian government in the judgments he pronounced during his visit to Rome in August 1944.[2] Yet it was not until Macmillan wrote his post-Hyde Park report that the highly ambiguous compromise which had emerged between liberation and occupation was faced critically. The OSS stated at the end of December (1944):

> Allied leaders have now frankly admitted that they intend to maintain strict control in Italy. It is clear that any Italian government must face Allied review of its policy and administration. Three probable results may be expected from this policy: a) governmental action will be slow; b) the government will appear to be weak and uncertain; c) popular pressure for legislation will often be counteracted by foreign controls. Under these circumstances, it is somewhat doubtful if any government can be expected to meet with popular approval.[3]

The Control Commission had been reorganized at the beginning of 1944, but neither its size nor its powers of intervention were reduced. Essentially the changes eliminated the distance between Allied Military Government in the field, which continued to be handled by the armies themselves, and the supervising Control Commission, which organized overall 'civil affairs' policy on behalf of the supreme commander, and above all kept a watchful eye on the activities of the Italian government at all levels, deciding, among other things, when areas were considered sufficiently stable to be 'handed over' to the direct jurisdiction of the government itself. The three key sections of the Commission, administrative, economic and political, were all directed primarily towards this guardianship role, the latter, headed by the Englishman Harold Caccia and the American Samuel Reber, being charged with the control of the government's foreign relations. The fourth section, 'Regional Control and Military Government' dealt directly with the army AMGs and Italian local administration, and was headed by the British

Brigadier Maurice Lush (formerly of the Sudan colonial administration) with the title of 'Executive Commissioner', supervising a team of 'Regional Commissioners'. Below the main sections continued the many subcommissions, from communictions to finance, from education to displaced persons, a total of twenty-four. Above them there ruled the chief commissioner and his deputy, acting together for the 'President' of the Control Commission in the person of the supreme commander. As we have seen, Lt Gen. Noel Mason-MacFarlane was the figure occupying the chief commissioner's post in the period up to the downfall of Badoglio, for which he was obliged to carry a perhaps disproportionate share of responsibility. He was succeeded by his deputy, an executive from ITT at that time in the U.S. Navy Reserve, Captain (later Rear-Admiral) Ellery Stone, who was destined to soldier on until the very end of the Allied presence in 1947.[4]

The February reorganization of the Commission, 'though it eliminated some of its more patent organizational inefficiencies, did not really go to the heart of the matter', says the official historian of Allied rule in Italy: '[The] Commission never wholly escaped the deformities arising from the confused conditions which attended its birth.'[5] Italy was under 'bondage', Badoglio complained to Kirk in May, insisting that he headed a government responsible before the country but without power, while ACC had all the power but no responsibility to the country. ACC officers nonetheless often took their labours extremely seriously, so much so that a visiting *New York Times* reporter felt that although the organization was only six months old in April 1944 'the problems of its work-a-day world have tended to age it prematurely.' He went on:

> There is no doubt that the slow Allied advance is complicating civil affairs. They were complex enough to begin with, but failure to occupy Rome has made everything much more difficult . . . the ACC, charged primarily with seeing that the terms of the armistice are carried out, is going about the vast secondary program of civil affairs in an atmosphere strongly characterized by a feeling of tentativeness, of impermanence.[6]

Allied Commission executives insisted that 'the presence of one Allied officer in an advisory capacity may make all the difference between order and disorder and is probably worth many hundreds of Carabinieri or troops in the enforcement of law and the maintenance of stability.'[7] But it was precisely this situation which the resident minister and acting president of AC attacked most vigorously in his post-Hyde Park report. Although Macmillan did not allude to the fact that almost one-third of AC's staff remained at their posts in areas nominally restored to government control, he did state that 'in many cases, they are the same officers who were functioning during the period of military government,' and as a result, 'the change from "direct" to "indirect" rule is . . . obscured.' In Macmillan's view the regional officers were 'insufficient to govern but sufficient to interfere. And their presence tends to weaken the sense of responsibility of the Italians themselves.' These arguments were well supported:

> For instance, during the recent riots at Palermo, it was the Italian Prefect who was responsible for calling out the troops, which he did somewhat precipitately. We had a Regional Commissioner who was powerless either to act or to restrain action. And the very presence of a Regional Commissioner in Italian administered territory allowed the Italians to pursue the congenial plan of throwing upon us – in the public opinion of the world – a responsibility which belongs to themselves.[8]

THE ALLIED OFFICERS responsible for 'civil affairs' thus had many heavy obligations, whether they were acting under AMG with full powers close behind the battle line, or in the second stage of 'advisory control' when the armies had moved on. Who were these men and what did they make of their unusual duties?

In the spring of 1944 the newspapers and periodicals of New York 'dogmatically recommended' to their readers a 'rarely moving and beautiful . . . little masterpiece,' by a rising *Time-Life* star named John Hersey. In *A Bell for Adano* Hersey described how a young American major 'tried to rebuild the life and spirit of a war-torn Italian village.' A *New York Times* critic called it 'without question the finest [novel] about American participation [in the Second World War] that I have seen'; several editions were printed and there were stage and film versions.[9] In the novel we find many familiar ingredients of the occupation story of 1943–4. Military arrogance is represented by a bullying general who torments peasants and shoots their mules (thought by some to be modelled on Patton)[10] and by navy men who would let the population starve rather than alter the regulations to allow the fishing fleet out. There is inflation, the black market, venal Fascists, rowdy troops and a quartermaster who says: 'we're just winning this damn war for the British Empire.' Above all there is the solitary figure of Major Joppolo, 'town major' of Adano, a former clerk in the New York city administration:

> There were probably not any really bad men in AMGOT [Hersey's foreword explains] but there were some stupid ones. You see the theories about administering occupied territories all turned out to be just theories, and in fact the thing which determined whether we Americans could be successful in that toughest of all jobs was nothing more or less than the quality of the men who did the administering.
>
> That is why I think it is important for you to know about Major Joppolo. He was a good man, though weak in certain attractive, human ways and what he did and what he was not able to do in Adano represented in miniature what America can and cannot do for Europe . . . America is on its way into Europe. You can be as isolationist as you want, but there is a fact. Our armies are on their way in.
>
> Therefore I beg you to get to know this man Joppolo well. We have need of him. He is our future in the world.

As a man with a mission, Joppolo himself lacked nothing in zeal and national pride (his United Nations status passing quite without mention). As he told the remaining town officials soon after entering Adano: 'now that the Americans have come, we are going to run the town as a democracy.' Presuming that the assembled company might feel threatened by this unwritten proclamation, coming on top of numerous written ones, Joppolo offers to explain:

> Democracy is this: democracy is that the men of the government are no longer the masters of the people. They are the servants of the people. What makes a man master of another man? It is that he pays him for his work. Who pays the men in the Government? The people do for they pay the taxes out of which you are paid.
>   Therefore you are now the servants of the people of Adano. I too am their servant. When I go to buy bread, I shall take my place at the end of the line, and I will wait my turn. . . . If I find that any of you are not giving the type of service that I desire, I shall have to remove you from office.[11]

To prepare the Joppolos of the future, a School of Military Government had been set up in 1942 by the U.S. Army in the University of Virginia, its development being watched over by the president himself. In answer to a specific question, Roosevelt was told that of the 49 pupils in the school's first class, 53 per cent could claim no government experience whatsoever, only 8 per cent had foreign experience of any sort and the average age was 48.1 years. A great many of them had been 'reserve officers of long standing', the president was told, and had reached the status of the '"professional veteran" type, organized patriots, political and social conservatives', dumped in the school by commanders anxious to be rid of their least useful subordinates.[12] An American recruit told of his enrolment in military government as follows:

> Geez, Maj, it was like this. I was a quartermaster. Well, Maj, you know how it is. The boys just got around and found a ready market, and we went shares. But then they caught up with me and put the squeeze on. They said: 'We're going to give you a break. Court-martial or Civil Affairs.' . . . A guy has no choice – and so that's why I'm here![13]

The British on the other hand relied on word-of-mouth contacts, personal patronage, men who had done business or owned property in Italy, on a civil affairs school in Wimbledon described as 'rather a farce' by Eden, and above all on former colonial administrators.[14] At the top this produced a robust collection of men with banking and business connections with Italy, Foreign Office officials and 'misfits of the Lieutenant Colonel type' as Murphy and Macmillan said on one occasion. At the bottom were to be found the least influential products of the Officer Training Corps, men who 'would be contented with a job as a town major or with AMGOT, where they could look forward to comfortable billets, an obliging girl-friend and reasonable profits on the Black Market,' as a rugged fighting-man contemptuously recalled.[15]

Few of the civil affairs officers either of the upper or lower levels have left records of their experience. Perhaps this was because, with General Joyce the first head of the Allied Control Commission, they did not 'care a whoop', but as the official historians Coles and Weinberg, Lord Rennell and above all John Hersey seek to demonstrate, there were at least as many who took the job seriously, whatever their qualifications, and understood why they should do so.[16] The question of the civil affairs officers' attitudes, generally and individually, is one the mass of documentation produced by the occupation leaves unanswered on the whole, though it seems reasonable to suggest that outside headquarters the single officer, left very much on his own, ruled according to his own personality, his own prejudices, and his own civil and military background. This autonomy of the local officials explains much of the variety of experience recounted by indigenous observers from province to province, in the North as well as in the South, and before writing off the hapless corps of military government men altogether we should not ignore the subjective situation of an individual called upon to assume full *de jure* and *de facto* responsibility in cases like that of Naples, where at a certain point one officer only was available for assignment to an area covering 27 communes with a combined population of 500,000.[17]

However, beneath the surface of the particular situations, certain common processes were at work, and it was these which left whatever general imprint remained, not just the personality of the transient Allied representative.[18] An Allied official familiar with many aspects of the war in Italy, Max Salvadori, has summed up precisely the problems facing the military governors, and the tendencies set in motion on their arrival:

> The immediate problem which confronted the Town Major on his arrival was to establish some sort of contact with the population. . . . [of the British and American officials], the majority were not so much Italo-Americans as Sicilian and Neapolitan Americans; they half-knew a bit of Italian and acted as if they knew everything (they usually hated the British); the British had either lived in Italy or had learned Italian in school or in special courses. British and Americans alike knew they must not make use of people who had held positions of responsibility as Fascists, but frequently yesterday's Fascist . . . was today's anti-Fascist, and without a certain capacity for discrimination which was not simply rare but altogether lacking, it was impossible to discover the Fascist behind the ex-Fascist.

Salvadori explains what happened upon the civil affairs officer's arrival at his destination:

> The usual thing was for the Town Major and other AMG officials to contact immediately the most senior member of the clergy . . . and the local commander of Carabinieri. . . . The result was that quite often and quite willingly power was monopolised by the official coalition of Allied authorities– ecclesiastical authorities – commander of the Carabinieri, a coalition which I would call 'Badoglian'.

Up until the liberation of Rome, says Salvadori, very few AMG officers had the slightest idea 'of what Fascists, proto-Fascists, frondistes or anti-Fascists were or had been, nor of what the CLN was or the parties which composed it.' The British were scarcely more successful than the Americans at identifying ex-Fascists, and both British and Americans tended to equate anti-Fascists with Communists, and being clearly prejudiced, for various reasons, against Communism, they were anti-anti-Fascist. The local notables played on this sentiment with success, from the Roman princes who took over completely poor Admiral Stone . . . to the petty landowners of the villages who took over the ignorant minor official sent by AMG. There were exceptions![19]

There were constant recruitment difficulties at all levels of the machine, and those who appeared often left much to be desired. Robert Murphy told the State Department so in as many words, adding:

From what I have seen of a number of . . . officers, decent and conscientious Americans as they may be, they are obviously not all stars, and some of them I think are fairly well down the ladder in point of efficiency, language qualifications, and knowledge of European conditions.

This problem, said Murphy, was not confined to the Americans:

As Mr. Macmillan points out, many of the British officers . . . are frustrated colonials of Lt. Colonel type who are in this assignment because it was not known where else they could be put, and some of them are a bit sour on life.[20]

Differences in promotion systems exacerbated these problems, and there appears to have been so much underlying sensitivity on this issue that an order emerged forbidding any officer to talk to any man more than two ranks lower than himself. Here again there were striking contrasts between the British and the American sides: Myron Taylor in the Vatican complained to Roosevelt of the 'astonishing fact that the British side included a Lieutenant General, three Major Generals, and eleven Brigadiers . . . [while] the American side had but one Brigadier and even he was not at headquarters.'[21] But as Murphy emphasized in the letter cited above, much of the dissatisfaction among officers, at least on the American side, sprang from 'lack of a well-defined notion regarding our objectives in Italy.'

In the absence of such a notion, 'military necessity' was the concept prevailing inside ACC, which meant – complained Anne McCormick in the *New York Times* – 'not the most but the least' which could be done to maintain law and order.[22]

Myron Taylor was among the bitterest critics of the Commission as constituted:

The Allied Control Commission has, seemingly, failed in three respects. It has not made a success of its political affairs, its attempt to 'rule' Italy (though it was hardly created for any such purpose). It has not been able to provide a sufficient amount of food for the hungry millions of Italians and, lastly, it has not brought in enough transportation to carry even what food there is to the places where it is to be distributed. A recent issue of *Time* called the ACC 'a mumbling Anglo-U.S. bureaucracy superimposed on the Italians; composed of four-fifths British brains and four-fifths American supplies – and neither is adequate.' To this one of the American officers at ACC headquarters was heard to remark that while it would be hard to show that the Americans had furnished even one-fifth of the brains, he knew damned well that the British could not show that they had furnished one-fifth of the supplies.[23]

Taylor talked of 'hard feeling and inefficiency' in the control structures, and attributed the troubles overwhelmingly to the British attitudes.

MEANWHILE the government devoted a not inconsiderable portion of its scarce energies to complaining of the changes the Allies had brought about. Badoglio and his colleagues were disturbed above all by the Allied impulse to brush aside prefects, questori and other local functionaries, and promote inferiors for purely practical reasons. The minister of the interior, Reale, confessed to Badoglio in March 1944 that 'it was possible that they [the new incumbents] could give some satisfaction in the tasks assigned to them,' but that 'at a time when every effort must be made to normalize the life of the various provinces . . . it is necessary that their administrative direction be in the hands of persons of proven capacity and attitudes, who by means of their competence and experience, can apply a new rhythm of vitality to public life.' Consequently the Allies received an official protest, in which they were accused not only of having disturbed the pension and promotion scales, but above all of having acted 'without any consideration for the structure of Italian administration.'[24]

Thus the 'hand-over' of responsibility, when it occurred in liberated areas, was an extremely ambiguous affair from the administrative as well as from the formal political/juridical point of view. As the executive commissioner of ACC told the April 1944 monthly conference of his organization:

> Direct government is easier than advisory control. There is an inevitable slowing down when the Italian Government takes over. AMG with Allied officers in charge and with their resources can do much more than Italian officials who are acting under orders of a Government which itself is in no easy position.[25]

At the top 'desperate efforts had to be made to build up a technically efficient administrative machine', reports an official historian, efforts which were not helped by splitting up the ministries and ACC itself between various towns in the South as a result of accommodation difficulties in the early phases. Nevertheless, the Control Commission exercised 'minute supervision' of the government's activities, says C.R.S.Harris.[26] A representative instruction of an ACC subcommission to its corresponding Italian ministry defining their relationship is provided by a letter of the labour subcommission to the Ministry of Labour of March 1944:

> As a matter of policy, it is understood that the Ministry will not make any changes in laws, decrees, ordinances or policies affecting labour or labour organizations, and will not make any major personnel changes or any change in personnel appointed by Allied Military authorities without prior approval of the Labour Subcommission. In addition, the Ministry will keep the Subcommission advised of any labour shortages, disputes or programmes which may affect work being performed for the Allied

Military Forces, or which may affect labour policy in areas now under direct control of the Allied Military Forces.

To facilitate the clearance of these matters, a Liaison Officer for the Labour Subcommission is stationed at ACC Rear Headquarters and will visit the Ministry regularly every day . . .[27]

But the government behaviour which provoked the most profound dismay in ACC headquarters involved de-Fascistization, or more precisely the lack of it. The veto over official appointments – a right not included in the armistice – was established by MacFarlane after repeated proof of government hesitation in the field of the purge. But this was only the beginning of the problem, which Allied officials encountered on a daily basis at every level.

An education officer thought that the tendency of his minister to reappoint banned Fascists was not due to ideological disposition, but because of ties of kin: the victims were relations or relations of relations. However, others noted the general hesitation of ministers to dismantle the structures of the Corporate State (if only for fear of the consequent mass unemployemt of functionaries), and that a promised Ministerial Commission on the project had, by July 1944, never even been appointed. At first Allied controllers were uncertain over the extent to which pressure was desirable. One leading AMG officer felt it necessary 'to go slowly in the removal of Fascist officials', but his assistant was quoted as saying that the Allies were 'laggard' in the field and that British and American news correspondents were becoming 'increasingly critical'.[28] The War Department's Civil Affairs Division was told at the end of December 1943 that 'generally speaking' the only realistic policy had been to abolish the outstanding Fascist measures and institutions, 'and to wait the formation of an Italian Government capable of tackling the problem.'[29]

Thus the Allies were brought face to face with one of the fundamental objectives of their presence in the country, and the question of how it was to be realized. As in most other fields of activity calculated to reinforce and reform the government, initial zeal had died away after several months of confrontation with the reality of southern Italy and its ruling class. But in the spring of 1944, there came a spur to renewed efforts in de-Fascistization as in so many other areas of activity:

One of the ways in which we can both work to eradicate Fascism in Italy and, to some extent, take the wind out of the Communists' sails [wrote the Foreign Office], is by keeping the Italian Government up to the mark on defascistization . . . one might ask Sir Noel Charles to keep an eye on the situation and encourage the Italian Government to take effective measures.[30]

But not even the anti-Communist motive was sufficient to resolve the underlying ambiguities and contradictions of the Allied attitude towards de-Fascistization; there was much suspicion in the British camp for instance when particular Left-wing bogeys such as Sforza, the Communist Scoccimarro and Nenni the Socialist became successively heads or assistant heads of the Government's 'epuration' commissions, although there was little action.[31] The underlying attitude of the British was defined by Sir Orme Sargent as follows:

> If Count Sforza starts trials and executions à la Pucheu we shall not like it. If, on the other hand, there are no executions, there will be a great number of people who will say that nothing effective has been done to destroy Fascism, and indeed they may prove right. It looks as though it is going to be a choice between a bloodbath, which will really destroy Fascism entirely as we know it, or a temporary exclusion from public life of a few minor Fascist officials, which will leave Italian belief in Fascism untouched and ready to come to life again in more favourable circumstances. Meanwhile its latent force will be strengthened by giving it a few living martyrs.[32]

Here again Eden's attitude complicated the British line since he was apt to write off Italian declarations of anti-Fascism saying: 'One can't object to the Italians saying that they disown Fascism but one need not and should not believe them.'[33]

The raillery of American observers at Italian upper class posturing in front of the Allies was apparently not translated into any form of vigorous action by official Washington, so that the task of keeping up the façade of Allied de-Fascistization was left to ACC/AMG. But at this level the contradictions multiplied. The energetic regional commissioner of Palermo, then Naples, then Rome, Poletti, made the epuration field a personal speciality, and also made sure – said Sir Noel Charles – that his activities were reported in the American Press.[34] This zeal was far from popular on the ground, and when Poletti extended his attentions to private industry there was an immediate outcry from Badoglio, who accused him of 'Sovietizing' Italian factories. At the bidding of the Interior subcommission of ACC, Poletti's actions in this field were summarily annulled.[35] The upper echelons of the Control Commission were exposed to pressure on this subject not only from authoritative official sources. The elder statesman Orlando, a favoured Allied interlocutor, was also critical: 'the old Fascist Prefects of towns [have] been turned out of office: why? they were civilian bureaucrats and were loyal to Fascism because it was the legal government; they [have] been replaced by politicians of varying shades of opinion.'[36] And this view found a direct echo in ACC; one of its 'top three' officers vetoed a long-sought anti-Fascist nominee for the position of prefect of Naples saying, 'it would be a curious thing to appoint a man to a governmental post who has spent his life in fighting his government.'[37]

AMG was then said to be 'immeasurably relieved' when the Italian government completed preparations for its own 'epuration' programme and was thus in a position to assume the burden itself, but the decree setting these preparations in motion was not published until the end of October 1944, and its various ramifications – especially with respect to epuration in the provinces, where committees of 'local personages' were called for – still under consideration on the eve of liberation. Nevertheless ACC claimed to be satisfied with its efforts:

> If the accepted policy is to remove only the ardent fascists in a position of authority and to regard the average civil servant as of necessity a fascist . . . then the proportion of persons dismissed, 4%, is consistent with a reasonable purge . . . Epuration may have been slow but that is partially because it has been careful; the spirit in which it has been carried out has been excellent; on the whole it has been effective and it has not left a feeling of resentment.[38]

DE-FASCISTIZATION of course was not simply an end in itself, an abstract propaganda priority dispensable as more concrete demands were made of the Italian State by the Allied controllers. Sweeping under the carpet, or allowing the sweeping under the carpet of the problem of Fascism among the personnel of the State did not contribute to resolving the difficulties of re-establishing working institutions in Italy. For reasons which should by now be clear, the Allies had neither the intention, nor the desire, nor the capacity to carry on running the country themselves for a day longer than necessary, and they looked to the indigenous machinery to resume its traditional duties as soon as possible. But as a first step towards encouraging autonomous political reconstruction, there had to be intervention of a reforming and modernizing kind: only in this way could the conditions be created which might eventually bring 'stability' and a consensus which would reject extremism. At AFHQ and ACC, and in London and Washington all saw the need for reforms of some sort, but there was considerable divergence on the scope and content of the changes needed. The most far-reaching proposals came from within the State Department, and contemplated nothing less than a complete reconstruction of the State apparatus on the principles of regionalism and enhanced popular participation.[39] The scheme, fully detailed, seems to have been quietly suffocated in London and ACC in 1945, but there was no shortage of reform energies on the spot.

The most activist agents of reform were, inevitably, the officers of ACC, who were obliged to live day by day with the Italian State administration as it emerged from Fascism. If we take the non-military subcommissions listed in the structures of ACC as of February 1944, we find that at least nine of these – the bulk of the administrative and economic sections – were involved in more or less substantial reform plans, either initiated by themselves or under discussion with the government, at various periods of their existence.

A typical small-scale example was the experience of the education subcommission, one of whose officers, G.R. Gayre, left an unusually complete account in later years. The powers of this officer had been by no means negligible; they had included 'the appointment of all professors, rectors, presidii or deans of faculties, the publication and revision of textbooks and the [determination of the] form the schools are to take.' In their enjoyment Gayre wished only to 'be left in peace [by Poletti and ACC] to carry out this great task of rebuilding and reform.' Nonetheless it was Gayre's hope that the institutions would reform themselves: 'That is the real basis of a democracy. We are not imposing our ideas upon them.'[40] This theme was interpreted by Gayre's successors in ACC as 'assisting . . . the Italian Government in its attempt to organize its schools in a way which will foster healthy living, good citizenship, decent world attitude, and economic efficiency, while preserving the best cultural traditions.'[41] They were perplexed by the seeming negativism of the task of destroying Fascism, in contrast with the much more desirable aim of 'teaching democracy'. The difficulty lay in the fact that:

> Schools require teachers, and teachers cannot teach democracy until they are taught democracy. It requires a generation to make teachers who can, *if* they can, remake society.[42]

The most serious reforms promoted by ACC itself concerned the forces of law and order. Although the judiciary was seen to have lost much credibility and to have suffered from various forms of Fascist influence, there appears to have been no serious plan of overhaul beyond epuration and 'setting an example'.[43] The prefects, the polizia and the Carabinieri on the other hand received a good deal of attention. The significance of these local institutions in the early plan of occupation has already been seen, and from that time on a long-term strategy began to be defined intended to restore morale, efficiency, reliability and authority. This plan moved constantly upwards in the list of Allied priorities in Italy, as the 'internal threats' to security appeared to loom ever larger, and the result was that by 1946 the internal security forces were more numerous than those for external defence.[44]

All the Sicilian prefects were removed sooner or later (i.e. those who had not fled before the invasion), and the process was repeated in the South on a reduced scale, where the Allies put more faith in a purge supposedly started by Badoglio.[45] In Catanzaro the Allies arrested the prefect, the podesta (mayor, politically appointed), the vice podesta and the director of prisons. While podestas – as party officials – were removed on a very wide scale, the Carabinieri – as a traditional corps of the State – enjoyed Allied favour, since it was thought that they were a continuing institution, originating well before Fascism, and hence constitutionally respectable. Considerable efforts were made to restore the self-respect and credibility of this corps, beginning with combined town patrols, in which British or American military police were seen working together with the Carabinieri.[46] On the other hand the ordinary police (polizia) were felt to have been 'much more corrupted by Fascism . . . and therefore took longer to bring to a state of even moderate efficiency,' says the British official historian; 'A number of their chief officers, Questori, had to be interned.'[47] However, when Naples was reached, this distinction was apparently not applied. The Allies were confident enough to call together in the first stages the chiefs of the several police services, to accept their assurances of cooperation, and to give each policeman accepted for service an armband 'identifying him as a representative of the AMG civilian police service.'[48]

In this way immediate practical needs were met, the policy of indirect control vindicated and the authority of the traditional forces of law and order recognized. But the agents concerned were far from reassured on their long-term place in society; their own self-respect, operating autonomy and legitimacy remained suspect as long as the Allied civil affairs officers remained on the spot – whether as military governor or advisory controller'.[49]

The dilemma which Macmillan first spotted of 'self-government versus good government' was thus felt very keenly in the Allied command; what was lacking was the political will to resolve it, or even to promote some of the lofty plans such bodies as the State Department were so adept at producing. Later, when these problems reappeared in much more dramatic form in the case of Germany, American political scientists reflected on some of these earlier experiences, admitting the 'poor results' obtained in Italy and recognizing the paradox of 'democratization by force'. Military government, said Merle Fainsod, was 'a regime of force. If it is tempered at all, it is by virtue of a self-denying ordinance which the victorious power imposes on itself.' The comments by the economist E. F. Penrose on the German situation were also intended for general application:

> if it is desired to lead and confirm a people in the path of democracy, the aim will not be achieved by displaying the apparatus of military government before their eyes. If it is desired to demonstrate a better way of life and conduct to a people, the aim will not be achieved by planting in their midst an army made up largely of raw youths, separated by thousands of miles from the restraint of family and neighbourhood, subject to new temptations against which nothing in the experience of the majority of them is proof, and consuming liberal rations while the indigenous peoples are desperately short of the basic necessities. In such conditions . . . little ground is left for hoping that the prestige of the occupying powers will be as great at the end as it was at the beginning of the occupation.[50]

The remarks seemed tailor-made to describe the situation of Allied military government in all its forms in the southern and central Italy of 1944.

8 The road to the North: Italian politics and the Resistance Question after summer 1944

FROM THE LIBERATION of Rome onwards, new sections of opinion began to make their weight felt against the awkward presence of the control apparatus, namely the Italian government, parties and press. On the whole politicians and political commentators preferred to ignore the effective suspension of their authority in these months; indeed the credibility of the parties was unlikely to be enhanced if they too considered their government 'a synod of politicians formed under Allied auspices', as a British Treasury observer wrote, or 'not governments at all, but local administrative instruments of Allied control', as the *New York Times* held.[1]

Although it has not been possible to make an exhaustive survey of the Italian press of those years – some newspapers are extinct, many have left few traces – it seems clear that only one major newspaper referred repeatedly and critically to the effects of Allied control, and that was the Socialist organ *Avanti!*, whose Rome edition began publication within a matter of days of the liberation of the city. Whatever Pietro Nenni's motives,[2] it was his newspaper, and often his column, which drew attention to the lack of an Allied plan for the country which might substantially involve the Italians, to the obstructionism of the Allies on the ground, and to their permeation of all civil and political life.[3] *Avanti!* also warned against appearing as beggars in Allied eyes, exhorting its readers not to flood Allied officers with requests, demands or offers of special favours. At the Socialist Party's congress in Naples in September 1944, Nenni demanded that 'the gigantic machinery of ACC be reduced to a control function where reasons of military necessity really exist,' and in the conference's final communiqué there was a request for

> the progressive demobilisation of the financial, economic and administrative organs
> of ACC, in order to restore to the country its autonomy in decision-making.[4]

Nenni followed up with a vibrant appeal from the columns of *Avanti!* entitled 'Let Us Get On With It!'.

Individual political personalities interviewed by Allied representatives did not hesitate to convey a similar message. The rector of the University of Naples, Omodeo, a prominent Action Party member, said:

> it is all very well to control all political and economic activities, but the Allies should
> tell the Italians exactly what they want and what can be expected from them. The

> Italians always have the impression that they are drifting along, without any stability or direction, whether it is in politics, economics or finance.[5]

A leading Christian Democrat, Guido Gonella, added that

> he did not believe that members of the government or newspapermen or the people thought that the Allies were *wilfully* creating difficulties for the Italians . . . he did think that many held the view that these difficulties resulted from a certain degree of *neglect* on the part of the Allies. There were many things which were difficult to explain and which remained unexplained – no petrol to transport food to Rome but plenty of jeeps flying around with parties of soldiers and girls in them; sailing boats that did not use coal or oil not permitted to be used for the transport of food and so on – and it was really a necessity of the first order to make clear to the people to what extent their discomforts were connected with the requirements of war.[6]

A high Allied official had told Count Carandini, 'what we want of you Italians is that you work'. 'But work with what?' asked Carandini, 'Cement industries . . . were all requisitioned. There was no petrol allowance to enable the earth to be ploughed, food to be transported, materials moved . . . There were no facilities whatever to enable the government to carry out its tasks.'[7]

Protests at the official level were not lacking. The most substantial was that included in Bonomi's long message to Hull of August 1944, already mentioned, which recommended:

> The ACC should be relieved progressively of at least three-quarters of its duties and directed towards a system at once less oppressive and less patently indicative of interference and intervention in all sectors of Italian life.[8]

Concrete proposals were submitted by the Rome government in October and November 1944 after the Hyde Park Declaration and the renaming of ACC as the 'Allied Commission'. They envisaged the transformation of the Commission into a single civilian body based on joint Italian-Allied cooperation, the elimination of the subcommissions and sections not directly related to the war effort, and the removal of Allied officers from government territory. But AC was sceptical; Admiral Stone recalled that the prime minister had recently asked him personally not to remove Commission officers from government areas until conditions there were more settled, while the directors of certain subcommissions insisted that 'no functions of AC should be discontinued in Italian Government territory.'[9]

What irritated Allied controllers most in responding to these pressures was the gap between the attitudes and posturings of all the parties and their action in the government. Ignoring the effects of their own presence, Commission chiefs had often denounced the attempt to run the government by all-party committees, saying that 'practically nothing is done unless someone from outside gives orders, which he is presumably not entitled to do.' When Bonomi's first government fell in November 1944 a comprehensive AC attack was mounted, denouncing the effect on the war effort of the refusal of the ministries to make any policy decisions:

In the middle of a war with the pressing problems that have to be solved in this country, the cynical disregard of apparently all parties for the necessity of making their political aspirations subservient to the war effort which has led to the failure to form a government, can only increase the difficulties of the Italians themselves, decrease their dignity and prestige among the Allied Nations and do irreparable damage.[10]

This state of affairs was aggravated by the repeated complaints of AC's regional commissioners that the government was not always 'able to provide for the civil administration when territory is transferred to its jurisdiction', so that in the very days in September when the 'New Deal' directive was being read to the country, AC sections were calculating how best to develop in the government the elementary capacities needed to carry on the running of its domain.[11]

'What we clearly need is that Italian politics should not intrude into English or American politics, nor adversely affect the war effort,' Harold Caccia declared. The progress of events in 1944 demonstrated that by non-obtrusion into English or American politics, the Allied managers meant not only domestic politics or foreign policy in general, but also their separate national policies towards Italy. The reluctance with which the Bari anti-Fascist junta was accepted, the extreme suspicion provoked by the rise of Communist power, the conviction that the fall of Badoglio reflected the weakness of Allied control, the impulse to shift blame for chaos in the liberated areas on to the indigenous government, all these facts testify to the unilateral and exclusive conception of Allied authority which dominated the policy of occupation. From the first moment to the last, Italian governments sought participation or representation in the control organs, and from the first moment to the last they were rebuffed.[12] The essence of the situation was later described with great precision by William Reitzel, who explained that the basic responsibility of the Control Commission

> was to cushion the future against the unrestrained play of party feeling; and its ultimate right of veto, even when unexercised, was a powerful factor in giving direction to political activities.

The means by which the play of party feeling was to be neutralized were perfectly understood by Bonomi, who

> in July [1944], was able to secure agreement among competitors for power by pointing out that no-one of them would be acceptable to the Control Commission if he appeared as the sole claimant to political authority.

The Italian political field '*had to be left clear for complete control by ACC*', says Reitzel. Thus

> when the State Department described the new Bonomi Government of December 1944, as '. . .supported by a majority of the political parties, comprising the CLN, and thus maintains a representative character,' the phrase must be understood to mean that a coalition had been arrived at in which competing political doctrines were so

carefully balanced that none could give effective direction to more than the routine work of Italian government.

This arrangement had particularly important implications for the position of the Left:

> The final result was to draw a line between the Control Commission and the parties of the Left, especially the Communist Party. An appreciation of the ease with which Togliatti . . . could upset the fiction of a freely operating Italian government inevitably led the Control Commission to look on the Communist Party as a dangerous and unpredictable element and to support the Christian Democrats by every means at its disposal.[13]

But with their entry into Tuscany the Allies met their first serious challenge to these arrangements.

THE LIBERATION of Florence in August (1944) presented the Allies with an entirely new and unprecedented situation. In the words of the OSS Research and Analysis Branch:

> When the Allied armies arrived in Florence they encountered, for the first time in a major Italian city, a nearly complete administrative organization established by determined and purposeful anti-Fascist forces. A provisional system, worked out to the last detail, already was functioning as an unchallenged *de facto* authority under the auspices of the Tuscan Committee of National Liberation, which regards itself as the legitimate representative of the Italian Government and aspires to Allied recognition as such.
>
> The duration and intensity of the underground struggle in northern Italy have produced highly developed resistance organizations with a considerably more independent outlook than in the South. For eleven months prior to the liberation of Florence, the Tuscan Committee of Liberation, which includes all five of the Tuscan anti-Fascist parties, directed the clandestine press, organized strikes, and sabotage, and functioned as the high command of partisan military activity in that region. . . . While the Germans were still in Florence the mayor and city council took possession of the municipal offices, and they were dealing with the public when AMG officials arrived.[14]

The committee now looked south for recognition of its achievements and found that Allied journalists at least were inclined to grant it. A correspondent of *The Times* praised the realistic spirit of self-help evident in Florence, adding: 'the impression is ever more common in Italy that the Government can only be reconstructed on a local basis. . . . A new beginning can only be made by the formation of regional administrations in which lack of experience is compensated by local knowledge and enthusiasm.'[15] On a strictly practical level the Allies were at first disposed to appreciate the concrete facts which the Florentine committee could point to: the appointment of provincial and city councils, the committees for various aspects of administration including transport and food, the mobilization of the population. But there were inevitably worries over the spirit underlying these actions and the eventual objectives, especially since no Florentine would accept appointment to office by the Allies without the approval of the committee. Since the relationships and the equilibria established between the parties were also involved, the question of jurisdiction was particularly delicate. At first AMG tended to ratify the committee's actions and appointments without asking too many questions, producing a most co-operative attitude on the part of the committee, as the British official historian writes; 'but when AMG appointed a Prefect from outside – a career official who had only just been made Prefect of Ancona – the trouble began.'[16]

The committee took objection to the prefect firstly on the grounds of his dubious past, secondly on the challenge to their appointments and sovereignty. Underlying this stance were fundamental political and historical considerations which made the episode a test-case of crucial importance (as all concerned realized). An eminent Florentine historian of law, F. Calasso, wrote that the intentions of the Committee were

> to transmit [to the Allies] the new and extraordinary powers created spontaneously from the break with a world in its death throes, on the assumption that these powers would be restored as soon as circumstances allowed.[17]

But the Allies and Bonomi made common cause in defending the prefect. The committee was told by AMG that

> at present the Prefect should not be considered as an effective representative of the Italian Government, but as executor of the orders of the Allied command, since Florence is still in the battle zone. . . . The CTLN should continue as in the past to collaborate closely with the Allies, carrying out its consultative functions fully recognized by the Allies, without worrying over the opinion of the Prefect. . . . When the Italian Government arrives in Florence, the CTLN should then deal directly with the Italian authorities.[18]

The selection of the prefect for Florence, considered 'the most important administrative appointment the ACC has had to handle since the fall of Rome' by the ACC Local Government subcommission, was argued on the basis of principle, namely 'that of encouraging Italian initiative and retaining the goodwill of vigorous democratic forces in the north without sacrificing necessary over-all Allied supervision' (or the authority of the Rome government), as the OSS explained. ACC's Regional Commissioner in Florence described the CLN as 'a sensible body representative of public opinion' and declared that 'he would only consider a man acceptable to the Committee.'[19] However, the head of the local government subcommission in Rome reminded his colleagues that 'the C-in-C at the Regional Commissioners' conference said "Administration must be carried on to the exclusion of politics",' and later insisted that the prefect's nomination 'must go out as an order from the Regional Commissioner and AMG'. When the prefect offered to resign, Bonomi and ACC refused the resignation, asserting that he must be kept in office, 'at any rate until such time as the CLN was brought to heel.'[20]

By the end of January 1945 the Regional Commissioner was satisfied that the CLN was much less influential, though still inclined to presume powers it did not possess and to ignore the official local government machinery. At the same time he felt that the Allies could do no more, and that indigenous authorities must take over. As F. Calasso concluded shortly afterwards:

> the Allied authorities [in contrast with the CLN] assumed they were taking over the traditional ordinary powers of administration, as regulated by the laws of the land, laws which the Allies saw simply as the Italian statutes, which they found in effect and intended to respect, and which for us on the other hand constituted the instruments of a twenty-year-old oppression we thought we had destroyed.[21]

The explanation for this state of affairs, and for the entire attitude of the Allies towards the political forces they found on entering Tuscany, is to be discovered in the detailed comments of the participants at the chief commissioner's conference which took place in Rome on 22 August 1944. The gathering included the regional heads of all the areas under ACC control, AMG representatives, directors of the ACC subcommissions and its vice-presidents, together with the top-level controllers of the Commission. Among those absent was any Italian representative. Among those present was the supreme Allied commander, General Wilson, whose remarks indicated first of all that in his view the 're-establishment' of the country depended on food and employment. The SAC then went on:

> The administration of the country must be regarded in all respects, and I would ask you to keep your eye tallied on the administration book and not led off behind the play of politics. The prestige of the two great English-speaking nations is bound up in your work.[22]

Admiral Stone on the other hand emphasized the ideological outlook to be aimed for, suggesting that the Four Freedoms 'are not mere idealism. They are practical essentials to the conduct of the war in Italy.' Specifically they buttressed 'the policy of support and assistance' which the Allies and the Control Commission were carrying out for the benefit of the Italian government:

> I need not remind you that this Italian Government was approved by the Allied Governments and we in Allied Control Commission are committed to do all that we can to support it in carrying out the hard tasks that lie before it. This, to my mind is the dominant aspect of this second phase into which we have now entered.

Various interventions at the conference indicated that when this principle was applied as directed to local government problems, the results left something to be desired. The regional commissioner for Calabria reported that the formation of town councils was hindered by the tendency of prefects to appoint them in collaboration with the Carabinieri; 'and this virtually makes the CC.RR [Carabinieri] the political boss for the area concerned.' In Sicily there was reported to be a serious problem arising from corruption and 'a mental sit-down strike' in government offices, 'on the

basis that the island was little concerned with the war.' The executive
commissioner concluded that it was 'easier to govern than it is to advise
other people to govern'. The CLNs as such were not mentioned at any point,
not even by AMG and ACC officers of Tuscany, who said simply: 'The
people of Tuscany do a great deal to help themselves. They are realistic,
generally honest, and industrious', or praised the 'useful work of the
Patriots' in 'the prevention of wrecking, general intelligence and reorganisation of local administration.' The 'new problem' created by the Patriots
(so-called not by chance)[23] contained implications which could not, however, be so lightly dismissed. A representative of the newly established
Patriots Branch said:

> Many questions have been asked of the political tendencies of patriot bands. After
> speaking to a large number of patriots in various corners of the country I personally
> feel that in the great majority of the cases these men have been fighting first to defeat
> the Germans, second to destroy Fascism and third, in the case of some of them, to
> build up a new Italy. Most of them have at this stage of the war very little idea of the
> aims and ambitions of the six political parties in Italy but they are keenly alive to the
> fact that something drastic must be done about politics in the very near future and,
> being mostly young and active men, they are keenly susceptible to influence and
> require a lead from the Italian Government. Some of them will undoubtedly be of
> importance in the new Italy and they are a great responsibility for us all.

But in Tuscany the Allies were confronted with a resistance movement
which presented itself as a military and political *organization*, not simply as
the summation of a number of scattered bands or groups, and in an initial
spirit of pragmatism and of 'retaining the good will of vigorous democratic
forces in the North' in the words of the OSS, they made concessions. AMG
arrived in Florence with nominees for all the principal civil positions: most
were members of the aristocracy recommended by the Rome government.[24]
After a period of confrontation, however, CTLN (CLN of Tuscany)
nominees were accepted for a number of key posts in the local administration, including that of mayor. While the government gave no encouragement to these initiatives and took its stance *vis à vis* the CTLN on the position
of the prefect, the Allies (in the form of AMG) extended the practice to a
number of towns in Tuscany, even arriving at the recognition of locally
appointed 'political' prefects in such cases as Grosseto, Lucca and Massa
Carrara.[25]

For those on the ground indeed the experience of liberation and Allied
control in Tuscany was distinguished by its extreme variety from place to
place. In Grosseto the provincial governor gave full practical recognition to
the CLN and installed a relationship of exemplary collaboration; in Livorno
AMG–CLN relations were cordial, all CLN nominations were accepted and
among other distinguished visitors, Cardinal Spellman of New York personally congratulated the committee on its work. The prefect on the other
hand was heavily inclined against the committee.[26] In Arezzo, Siena and

Viareggio, however, there were serious difficulties with the CLN, which ended with the committees' forcible dissolution by AMG. 'Several measures taken by Allied authorities have been interpreted by the population as efforts to drive the local committee out of existence,' the OSS reported on the Siena case; '[at] one point the offices of the committee were closed by Allied officials and its sign taken down.' However, the AMG-appointed prefect built up a city council in consultation with the CLN, while in Pisa the administration was quickly restored by a career officer despatched from Rome.[27]

As E. Rotelli, a constitutional expert, has emphasized, the treatment of Tuscany and its CLNs was a paradigm of the subsequent handling of the North and its political forces.[28] That is why we have given particular attention to the outlook of the committees there and the reactions of the Allies at the time. In the first instance practical considerations and the none-too-subtle tactics of Army AMGs, using the freedom of manoeuvre conferred by military necessity and military convenience, allowed the CLNs to remain in function in many cases and to see their nominees and activities recognized, at least temporarily. The subsequent installation of government officials was not primarily an anti-CLN manoeuvre, but a direct continuation of the long-standing Allied Commission priority of shifting responsibility and reinforcing the central government's authority. Such an approach, by its very logic, demanded that the 'vigorous democratic forces' of the North be brought round sooner or later to take the initiative themselves and to support the constituted authorities. As the British official historian notes, the autonomy of the local CLNs and their tendency to look to the northern supreme committee in Milan, the CLNAI, 'made it all the more urgent to reconstruct the representative organs of local government . . . so as to direct their energies into channels which would give them some foretaste of the re-establishment of democratic institutions.[29] The neutralization of the CLNs' political force was then attempted by considering it as a single interest group, on a par with others, to be inserted into the traditional provincial and communal councils as reconstructed by the local AMG officer and his prefect: 'care was taken in selecting the membership [of the councils] to give representation to local interests other than the purely political, so as to include elements to represent labour and agriculture as well as industry and commerce,' says C.R.S. Harris.[30] The balancing of local interest groups in the renewed structures of local government, along the lines first experimented with in Sicily and the South with the committees of prominent local citizens, was a common response in Tuscany to the presence of the CLNs (where they were not abolished), and one destined to show the way forward for the problems of the North. One of the results was that by the end of 1944 significant hesitations were beginning to appear in the outlook and action of the CTLN with respect to the Allied controllers in their region. The committee – after considerable discussion – called off a project to hold a regional CLN assembly. After its own experience and with the disturbing examples of Allied (specifically British) ruthlessness in Greece and Belgium in front of them, the CTLN members thought that any attempt publicly to promote the representative character of their institution would be interpreted as insubordination by the Allies. The regional committee settled for a conference to publicize and revitalize the work of the CLNs throughout the area.[31]

WHILE ALL THIS was going on the Allied command was gradually coming to appreciate the scale and significance of the Resistance movement spreading behind the so-called Gothic Line along the Appenines.[32] Ever since the March strikes large-scale Resistance activity had been on the upswing, swelled by hopes of an imminent end to the war in Europe, by hatred of Mussolini's futile but dangerous regime at Salo and its German protectors, and by increasingly effective organization: from June the CLNAI possessed its own military coordination capacity in the form of the 'General Command of the Corps of Volunteers of Freedom' (CG/CVL) under the future prime minister Ferruccio Parri and the future president of the Communist Party Luigi Longo. At the end of May Alexander told *The Times* that the movement was holding down up to 6 of the 25 German divisions in the country, and on 6 June he issued a famous proclamation inviting the partisans to be ready for insurrection during the summer.[33] Mussolini's spies estimated that 25,000 'rebels' were fighting in Piedmont, 17,000 in Emilia and northern Tuscany, over 14,000 in Liguria, 16,000 in Venezia Giulia and 5,000 in Lombardy, with the overall total including other zones reaching perhaps 82,000.[34] It was 'the great partisan summer', when the country regions of the Po Valley began to participate alongside the towns and cities, and when the youngest generation of 20-year-olds joined ranks with the veteran anti-Fascists. Among its greatest achievements was the liberation of most of the Alpine passes along the French frontier and the winning of at least 15 'partisan republics', isolated areas cleared of Germans and Fascists in which the first experiments in local self-government were begun.[35]

Macmillan told the Foreign Office in August that the 'Italian resistance has paid and is paying first class dividends', while Charles put the number of partisans at anywhere between 100 and 200,000. SOE in London pressed energetically for increased supplies to be dropped to the brigades, telling the diffident Foreign Office too that the movement was 'fighting extremely hard', and in October the minister of economic warfare, responsible for all pro-Resistance activities in Europe, took up this thorny question with Churchill himself, saying that the 'Italian Maquis' had 'done a magnificent job, far better than I ever expected; in fact just as good as the French did.'[36] The number of partisans estimated by the minister (Lord Selborne) was 150,000, a figure which he claimed could be doubled if the supply of arms in air – bedevilled by rivalry with the Americans and the claims of Yugoslavia –

could have been improved. Churchill was sympathetic, saying it was 'of the utmost importance to keep the Italian Maquis in the field' but by this time the military situation had turned very sour and other considerations began to appear more important than the Resistance's undoubted military capacity.[37]

Soon after the CLNAI had acquired a military command in the CG/CVL it applied to Rome for a professional military adviser, mentioning the name of General Raffaele Cadorna, the only staff officer to attempt a defence of Rome in September 1943. As AFHQ had suggested just such a move on several occasions, Cadorna was parachuted into northern Lombardy in mid-August. His reflections after some weeks in the North have come to be taken as a milestone on the road to Allied awareness of the political nature of the Resistance movement:

> It appears that the Allies continue to consider the partisan war as a normal military campaign, refusing to recognize its predominant political character. It must be stated very clearly that the resistance movement could not have existed without the political organization and that in this partisan warfare the Communist Party is predominant. The encroachment of political factors do not disappear by ignoring them. It is better to give them due consideration.
>
> The Communist Party, which gives the lead, does not try in the least to hide its intention of seizing the reins and setting up a regime similar to the Russian . . . They declare openly that they wish to lean upon Russia and Tito and will rebel rather than submit to the orders of the Western Allies.[38]

Special Force commanders in Italy continued to think that politics could be separated from the 'manoeuvres' of the parties connected with the Resistance but their message was equally alarming:

> The activities of Communists in the occupied zone are unfavourable to the operations of the Allied Commander.
>
> The growth of armed Communist bands and the retention of their arms and their formations will constitute a menace to internal conditions and to such Allied control as it may be desirable to impose.

The Communists had numerous advantages, the report went on: a leader with Russian cash, intelligence and diplomatic support behind him, the success of Tito's forces, an experienced organization with a clear programme, even the sympathy and interest of the OSS; there could be little doubt too that the Communists were saving their arms and ammunition for 'later purposes'.[39]

British observers at all levels took these warnings increasingly seriously as time went on, especially in September when the great autumn assault on the Gothic Line began and there were high hopes of the final breakthrough. But SOE/SF were not thanked for their watchfulness by the Foreign Office, which felt that in continuing to supply the Resistance they were recreating in northern Italy the 'conditions which they created so enthusiastically in Greece',[40] a message repeated with increasing shrillness from London as links between AFHQ/SF and the Resistance structures became more and more formal during the winter.

In reality the Communist Party's line to its members had already been defined in July 1944, and sounded as follows:

> Only the participation of all the people in the insurrection will guarantee victory and it is this participation which is the essential prerequisite for the democratic renewal of the country. The re-education of the Italian people, the radical elimination of Fascism and its economic roots, these will only be possible if all kinds of employees, not only workers, actively intervene in political life, in first person, as conscious creators of the new democracy. The first act of intervention of the Italian people in the forging of its destiny is the war of liberation. . . . The assumption of power before the arrival of the Allied forces is essential for the political direction and future development of the Italian people.[41]

For the PCI, events in Greece confirmed how dangerous any interpretation of this approach would be in terms of armed *revolution*. A letter from Bologna diffused throughout the party's clandestine network at the end of 1944 said:

> Greece shows that the PCI and the advanced democratic forces must not allow themselves to be isolated by reactionary acts of provocation intended to weaken and defeat them; they must not allow themselves to be isolated by the Allies, especially as long as the enemy still treads Italian soil. Only the Fascist remnants, only the most reactionary and regressive elements of the possessing classes, those responsible for Fascism, have any interest in a rift inside the CLN or between the Allies and the national anti-fascist forces.
>
> The PCI will do all it can to avoid civil war, because it is in the interest of a people and country ruined by Nazi-Fascist destruction and threatened in its national unity so to do. Anyone who declares that on the moment of liberation there ought to be a civil war, even harder and more difficult than the one just finished, is a glib extremist, a dangerous element incapable of fending off Fascist provocations which appear in every sort of disguise.[42]

In other words 'the Greek approach' was to be banished by unity of action, and the anti-Fascist revolution was to be transformed not into an armed insurrection for socialism, but into 'a struggle for a parliamentary democratic republic', using the mobilized force of consensus built up during the Resistance months.[43] But the Allies, concerned above all to neutralize any threat to their permanent design in favour of the pre-constituted authorities in Rome, were not convinced.[44]

For its part Special Force concentrated on stepping up the number of its missions to the various brigades and had 33 on the spot by the end of October (18 British, 15 SOE-trained Italians), with no less than 50 waiting to go in, according to Lord Selborne.[45] There can be little doubt that these missions preferred to work with the Autonomi non-party bands or at least those dominated by the Right-wing parties, which deliberately set out to attract SF favour. It was a Liberal leader, Edgardo Sogno, who was SF's 'chief organiser' in north-west Italy, and there were (and still are[46]) constant allegations that formations such as his received preferential treatment in the matter of supplies.[47]

Formally, however, all concerned were agreed that this tactic was too provocative, and instead efforts were to be made to build up the coordinating and balancing capacity of the CLNAI. A Berne-based representative of SOE said '[A] synthetic political committee such as the CLNAI comprising members of all the leading parties, makes for unity of command and serves as a brake on single party ambitions', and the SF liaison officer Max Salvadori advised similarly: in relation to the 'Patriot' movement he wrote, 'it would be advisable to create such a balance of forces . . . that no particular force hostile to Great Britain or unsympathetic to it can obtain the upper hand.' In AFHQ eyes this balancing role was General Cadorna's primary function – freely acknowledged by the general himself – and from the autumn onwards every effort was made to reinforce the CLNAI's authority and legitimacy in this direction, while taking care to leave it under no illusion about its future as a possible alternative government at the moment of liberation.[48]

ALL THESE CONSIDERATIONS went into the preparation of the Allies for the North, an effort considerably accelerated in the autumn of 1944 in parallel with the military campaign, which was expected to be the last one in Italy. Admiral Stone was instructed by Macmillan that while Special Force and OSS officers behind the lines might try to persuade local committees and resistance bands to preserve order in their bailiwicks in the period before the Allied arrival, there were to be no commitments made to such forces, not even to the CLNAI 'whose representative character is purely conjectural even though it has to some extent been encouraged by the Italian Government to regard itself as their agent.'[49] As a result Stone told the soldiers that while the advice of local CLNs should be taken and temporary appointments recognized:

> Care will be taken, as is now done, to prevent these committees setting themselves up as alternative government, and every effort will be made to preserve the structure and machinery of Italian local government.

This was the kernel of the Allied political strategy for the North. Filtered down to SF missions in the field, it was translated into the following instruction:

> You will have no political authority whatsoever and you will not give official recognition to the assumption or execution of power by any party or group of parties.
>   You will inform the Committee of Liberation that the Rome government has the full support of the Allies and that the Regional and Local Committees should not question its authority.

To which was added a rider whose significance should by now be clear:

> You should give your moral support to all groups and parties which constitute a

potential source of law and order, and you should withhold it from all extremist movements, whether political or military.[50]

In this way SF missions became, as their leader in Piedmont has stated, 'advanced patrols of AMG to be sent to every regional capital,'[51] knowing however that the CLNs offered a potential bridgehead for control from above and were in any case too strong to be ignored or summarily liquidated.[52]

Plans for the occupation of the north-west of Italy were, however, drawn up on a very special scale, commensurate with the risks Alexander saw there: 'Conflict between Partisans and Fascists, internal political factors and economic dislocation,' not to mention the serious risk of French incursions. A large-scale parachute landing was planned for Turin in the case of sudden German withdrawal – using 240 aircraft and the same British brigades employed at Athens.[53] In the event the military and political problems alike were postponed by the successful German defence of their territory in the North, and the Resistance forces, swollen beyond Allied desires and convenience by the autumn offensive, had somehow to be bottled up. While PWB received instructions to 'play down very gradually' the efforts of the Resistance, Macmillan and his colleagues turned to the political problem of the CLNAI, particularly its ominous degree of autonomy with respect to themselves and to their cherished if evasive government in Rome.[54]

The subsequent struggle to impose Allied and Italian government control on the Resistance structures was conducted on two levels: firstly (and this was the most important and effective method) by the strict separation of military from political considerations; secondly by reinforcing as far as possible the authority of the CLNAI as a *unitary*, supervisory body guaranteeing the loyalty of all its dependent organs to the Allies and the government, and by taking all precautions against the failure of this authority. As General Cadorna reported in October:

> The present position is considered to be satisfactory from the point of view of the Allied armies, in that while the CLN achieves a large measure of political unity and common policy, the control of operations remains with HQ AAI, acting through its British and American operating agencies.[55]

As the body supervising and guaranteeing the Italian government, ACC wished to assume no responsibility whatsoever for such arrangements, whose unpredictable political consequences Macmillan often underlined, and plans to 'infiltrate' its officers with Special Force missions were dropped:

> The reason for this change of policy [the executive commissioner explained to regional commissioners planning for the North] is that it was considered most important that AC should not be in any way concerned with whatever local government might be set up during the period before the arrival of Allied troops and the establishment of Allied Military Government.[56]

As the Turin historian G. Perona emphasizes, the overall strategy aiming, as Macmillan said, to 'get control over these movements right from the start', could only be consummated by a global accord, one which assured the military cooperation of the Resistance while avoiding 'playing the partisans up into a separate government.'[57] This was the meaning of the negotiations which began in Caserta on 14 November between a team of CLNAI leaders (including Pajetta of the Communist Party, Parri, Pizzoni, the non-party president of the CLNAI, and Sogno, though he was not a member of the committee) and the Allied command. It was soon clear that the credibility of the operation depended on two factors: the real loyalty of the CLNAI to the Rome government, and the effectiveness of the committee's authority over its own constituent parties and local structures. As long as there were doubts on these scores there could be no thought of political concessions.[58] Special Force was convinced of the usefulness of an organ where 'the aims of each party can be balanced, and if possible coordinated,' but the Foreign Office, overwhelmingly preoccupied with the Greek situation, saw great danger:

> Has the [CLNAI] sufficient authority? If it has and if we employ it as paymaster it is essential that we should not once again create a Frankenstein monster as in the case of EAM in Greece, and that therefore we must establish a firm control over the CLNAI so as to prevent its being captured by the Communists. This probably means General Alexander appointing a chairman with dictatorial powers and perhaps also a Commander in the field, who would have authority over all the partisan bands.[59]

The Foreign Office demanded (as did the Political section of AC) a political head for the committee to be responsible to Bonomi, and a military head answerable to Alexander, with full Italian government participation in the accord:

> we hoped at any rate to bring them as far as possible under the direct control of the Italian Government for political purposes, instead of allowing them to evolve as an independent political authority. Hence our desire to see a tripartite agreement.[60]

With Kirk's support, Macmillan wrote off such preoccupations as 'legal pedantry', and pushed through a firm, comprehensive agreement which guaranteed military and financial assistance to the CLNAI until the moment of liberation, when the committee would 'exercise its best endeavours to maintain law and order and to continue the safeguarding of the economic resources of the country until such time as Allied Military Government is established.' At that point 'CLNAI will recognize [AMG] and will hand over to that Government all authority and powers of local government and administration previously assumed.'[61]

Macmillan and Alexander were satisfied: the military agreement was the one that counted, since it fixed the exchange rate of power in terms overwhelmingly favourable to the Allies: money against military coopera-

An Allied military tribunal at work, applying the law of the land. (Original photograph from the Office of War Information collection, National Archives, Washington D.C.)

*Signing the 'Armistice of Cassabile', 2 September 1943. Seated: Lt. General Walter Bedell Smith;
left to right: Commander M. Dick R.N., General Lowell Rooks U.S.A., Captain D. Haan, British
Army, G. Castellano and F. Montanari of the Italian Foreign Office, Brigadier K. Strong,
A.F.H.Q., at rear. (Original photograph from the Office of War Information collection, National
Archives, Washington D.C.)*

*Italian Carabinieri on traffic duty at Allied Road Control Point, November 1943. The original
caption notes: 'Italian policemen wear British uniforms but retained their own caps'. (Original
photograph from the Office of War Information collection, National Archives, Washington D.C.)*

Reading Allied Proclamation no.1 in a south Italian village, October 1943. The posting of this proclamation was the first duty of the Allied Civil Affairs Officer on taking over a new area. (Original photograph from the Office of War Information collection, National Archives, Washington D.C.)

(overleaf) After the battle for the Gothic Line: destruction south of Pesaro, September 1944. (Original photograph from the Office of War Information collection, National Archives, Washington D.C.)

Meeting of the Advisory-Council for Italy (ACI), April 1945. Left to right: Chief Commissioner Ellery W. Stone, French Ambassador M. Couve de Murville, U.S. Ambassador Alexander Kirk, Representative for Greece Georges Exintaris, Genl. A. Kislenko of the Soviet Union, British Ambassador Sir N. Charles, Sloven Smodlaka of Yugoslavia. (Original photograph from the Office of War Information collection, National Archives, Washington D.C.)

Bonomi's first government meets in Rome, June 1944. Bonomi is fourth from right, Togliatti at bottom right, De Gasperi at head of table. (Original photograph from the Office of War Information collection, National Archives, Washington D.C.)

High hopes for the soundness of the monarchy in an Office of War Information picture and caption of March 1944: 'Prince Steno Borghese watches as refugees leave farm house to be evacuated from area. The Prince has been appointed Mayor of Anzio-Nettuno area by Army officials to help AMG in their dealings with civilians.' (Original photograph from the Office of War Information collection, National Archives, Washington D.C.)

Original OWI caption reads: 'With 5th Army, San Andrea area, Italy. Italian civilians who have fled the battle zones seek haven. They wait here for the arrival of the AMG authorities who will shelter and feed them during the chaotic days the war passes over their homes. 19/5/44'. (Original photograph from the Office of War Information collection, National Archives, Washington D.C.)

Lt. Genl. Sir R.L. McCreery, 8th Army Commanding Officer, reviews partisans at a demobilization ceremony in the Udine area, June 1945. 'General McCreery told the 6,000 Partisans that they had done a good job in helping liberate their country', says the original OWI caption. (Original photograph from the Office of War Information collection, National Archives, Washington D.C.)

tion and the full takeover of AMG on liberation. The formal political considerations they considered entirely separate and secondary, to be left to the government and the CLNAI to settle between themselves. A subsequent agreement between these two parties satisfied the extreme diffidence of both Rome and the Foreign Office by ensuring (at least on paper) that, as Bonomi said, the committee 'remains in a subordinate position and does not have the least character of a *de facto* government.[62]

A military, political and juridical stranglehold had from this moment been clamped on the development of the Resistance movement, an act of submission by the North quite disproportionate to the effective relationship of strategic power at that time between the contracting parties.[63] But there was still no certainty that all would go according to this plan, and that temptations would not emerge, as in Greece, to essay a breakaway on the definitive liberation of the North. 'Speed in getting ourselves established is the essential factor; without this there is a real danger of extreme Communist elements taking control regardless of AMG or the Italian Government', said a joint note from the British and American political advisers at the end of January 1945.[64]

The longed-for final advance had been stopped in the mud, rain and gales of the battle for the Gothic Line, and the military campaign practically shut down for the winter at some points only fifteen miles from Bologna and the Po Valley plains. The Resistance movement had been keyed up to its highest pitch during September waiting for the final signal to release the great insurrection. When the signal never came, bitter disillusionment set in, adding to the physical and psychological difficulties of clandestine survival in alpine winter conditions. It was in this context that the final episode of the drama between the Allies and the Resistance was played out for that year, an episode which carries to this day a stigma of suspicion and rancour. This was the announcement by radio on 13 November, in General Alexander's name, of the end of the serious hostilities for the time being, with an invitation to the partisans to 'save their munitions and matériel until further orders', and 'prepare for a new phase of the struggle against a new enemy, winter'.[65] A former SF liasion officer in Liguria, Basil Davidson, in an extremely critical account of Allied attitudes, has written that the broadcast 'as well as told the partisans to disband, and to the enemy to come up and finish them off while they were doing it', and in the days afterwards this was the effect in the North. Other commentators have blamed not the message, but its diffusion by radio, or have suggested that the Allied commander ingenuously did not foresee all the consequences.[66]

Whatever the truth of the matter – which Alexander tried to amend with increased supplies and a counter-message – nothing could have further alienated Allies and Resistance, especially when the results of the CLNAI team's trip to the South began to spread through the northern leadership. There were serious defections to the South, across the lines, and to the life of passive waiting. In this moment of deep crisis it was the Communist Party which again proved most effective in changing tactics and finding new ways of carrying on the struggle; at every key moment and in every crucial situation this problem of the PCI and its strategy reappeared, the decisive one from the Allies' point of view in all their many problems in Italy.

PART THREE 1945

9   The end of the wartime Alliance and the approach of liberation

1945 WAS THE YEAR when Italy staked her claim as a major battleground in the Cold War. William Reitzel wrote afterwards:

> The correct estimate that the Left-wing parties did not constitute a majority, and so did not have to be accepted as representing the will of the Italian people, did not alter the fact that they were in a strong position to force a crisis whose repercussions would run far beyond the borders of Italy. After 1944, the situation from week to week based as it was on a complex interaction between Italian instability, the conduct of the war and relations with Soviet Russia in neighbouring areas, remained consistently delicate.[1]

The country seemed to be moving towards the centre of a circle of deepening instability in the Mediterranean area, with events in Greece and Yugoslavia in particular prompting the most disturbing questions about Soviet and British objectives in southern Europe. The Soviet deputy foreign minister Litvinov had told the American journalist Edgar Snow in October of his anxiety over the state of the wartime Alliance, especially his fears of British plans for a division of Europe into blocs, in other words 'a revival of British traditional diplomacy in Europe. . . . Britain has never been willing to see a strong power on the continent . . . without organizing a counter-force against it.'[2] A few weeks later, at the height of the Greek crisis, Churchill wrote to his confidant Smuts that 'if the powers of evil prevail in Greece, as is quite likely, we must be prepared for a quasi-Bolshevised Russian-led Balkans peninsula, and this may spread to Italy and Hungary.'[3] Inside Italy there was the ever more pressing enigma of the PCI's attitude, so warlike and unyielding in the North, so efficient, reassuring and diplomatic in Togliatti's behaviour in Roman political circles. Sir Noel Charles for one was baffled: 'I do not pretend to know what the final aims of the Communists are. I wonder if anyone knows!'[4]

But if this was the problem at the forefront of attention as the liberation finally approached, it must not be thought that other problems were less urgent or substantial. Besides the conduct of the war itself, compromising Allied (especially British) prestige and increasing reliance on the Resistance, there was the tense struggle to define national aims in the country, as the prospect of rehabilitation and reconstruction began to open. The Four Freedoms, the Atlantic Charter, the United Nations plans were little use in guiding action on the ground, any more than the elementary certainty that Italy's future would be inextricably bound up somehow with 'the West'.

For the United States the end of the war was expected to give the green light to long-nurtured plans aimed at constructing a new, integrated world order functional to the dramatically rescaled needs of American capitalism, but also believed to be of general benefit to mankind. Revolving round the themes of collective security, free trade and the raising of living standards 'everywhere', these visions were much more clear and concrete in their economic part than in their politics, except to the extent that Americans considered all social unrest and extremism to be economically rooted.[5] But in 1945 it was not evident how these aims and beliefs could be applied to the chaos of war-torn Italy, though the urge to clear decks and start afresh by means of a preliminary peace treaty was already making itself felt.

The tired and irritable managers of British imperial interests, on the other hand, had to reckon what a treaty might cost them materially. Some perceived that British survival itself would be tied to American aid in peacetime as well as in war; others aimed to salvage something of an independent British sphere in Europe if not further afield; many thought of using the realism of the first view to get the Americans 'embedded' in the new conflicts of power in Europe and the Mediterranean. Italy paid the cost of these contradictions in continuing British hostility, and in the refusal of the British governments of 1945 to use even a minimum of their infinite power over public opinion to rehabilitate the image of the ex-enemy and open the way to a definite revision of the rights of the Italian people in their national and international affairs.

But essentially Italy's status as a sovereign nation depended on the state of play between all three victors, and as soon as the wartime alliance lost its first and only raison d'être, all sympathy and shelving of differences disappeared. The Russians increasingly compensated for their effective exclusion from Italy by claiming that their relationship with the conquered territories of eastern Europe was directly analogous to that of the Western Allies with Italy. If then the Americans and the British seriously intended to demand that the Russians loosen their hold on those eastern territories, they were bound to minimize the real situation of dependency in which Italy languished. Since the potential substance of this Soviet claim had been recognized in the West ever since the days of the armistice, it was up to Britain and the U.S. to establish their side of the argument by offering a different model of control in Italy, of which the first requirement was that it should be indirect and delegated.

Here was yet another reason for dismantling the Allied Commission and the other machinery of Allied control; it fed the long-standing urge to shift responsibilities and burdens on to the locals' own shoulders and hence the desire for a preliminary peace. One of the main reasons for promoting a treaty therefore was to strengthen the Rome government. But the British and Americans could only justify the conclusion of an early treaty to themselves if the Rome government looked solid.

This was just one of the dilemmas inherent in the political situation in Italy, which at its worst seemed to threaten a total rupture between the North and Rome, and the installation of a separate northern government supported by a Communist insurrection and hence bringing Tito's and Stalin's power directly into the country. Even if this apocalyptic scenario could be avoided, there was still the fundamental quandary of the so-called 'institutional question' over which the CLNAI parties, in the midst of the German occupation, wrangled bitterly during the winter. To Allied minds this question was abstract, and a good deal less significant than encouraging the opponents of Communism, rebuilding the State and managing the return to free elections. It was not enough to declare repeatedly that the Allies stood behind Bonomi: without damaging the prospects for self-determination, the conditions had to be created from which *stability* would emerge, meaning in the first instance, it was now clear, law, order and freedom from want. First, however, the Allies had to get into the North and finally defeat the Nazi-Fascist armies.

IN AMERICA meanwhile fears were mounting that the situation in Italy could get out of hand before the North was reached. 'Italian people are literally dying of cold and starvation before your eyes by the thousand,' the controversial representative from Connecticut, Mrs Clare Booth Luce, told a press conference early in the new year, to which the administration replied by stating that an expanded Allied supply programme to aid restoration of the Italian economy was now seen by all concerned to be 'advisable'.[6]

One group far from indifferent to this situation – and its political implications – was the Italo-American community of New York. The Italo-American Labour Party Council (which claimed 300,000 members) passed a resolution at a large-scale meeting at the end of January urging more aid and immediate application of the Atlantic Charter to Italy. The resolution stated that Italy's internal conditions and rehabilitation transcended her immediate boundaries and similar international interests. The council's desires, it was claimed, sprang not only from hope for Italy, 'but, above all, from our devotion to America as the hope of the world in its aspirations and strivings for the triumph of democracy in war and peace.' The council claimed to have raised $167,000 to support 'free' trade unions, $1½ million in clothes and $7000 for food, medicine and clothing.[7] But in presenting the resolution to James Clement Dunn, Luigi Antonini, president of the council, dwelt exclusively on the geopolitical significance of the demands. 'What is needed,' Antonini explained, 'is more American "moral" – that is "political" – intervention to "balance" British and Russian "intervention".' The British, said Antonini, were 'running Italy', but they were 'short-sighted', interested only in maintaining the monarchy, so that they took in known Fascists for administrative posts on the basis of their administrative experience. The entire policy was simply 'giving Italy into the hands of the Communists.' The time had come to 'put teeth in the Atlantic Charter.'[8]

Few were as frank about their overall intentions as Antonini. From the columns of the *New York Herald Tribune* the former assistant secretary of state, Sumner Welles, denounced in more disinterested but no less damning terms the lack of any semblance of a coherent or constructive policy in the fact of the appalling conditions known to exist:

> If the recent policy of studied insult, and of flagrant administrative inefficiency and neglect, pursued in varying degrees by the major powers, is persisted in, Italy will be plunged into a long-protracted period of hopeless anarchy.

For the Big Three there was no more serious problem in Europe than that of Italy, Welles concluded.[9]

Further bitterness was injected into the situation by Churchill. Here was the prime minister in the House of Commons in mid-January insisting, 'once and for all that we have no political combinations in Europe or elsewhere, in respect of which we need Italy as a party. We need Italy no more than we need Spain, because we have no designs which require the support of such powers. We must take care that all the blame of things going wrong is not thrown on us.'[10]

A muffled cry of renewed martyrdom arose from Rome. Churchill's words 'seem deliberately contrived to discourage and to depress,' wrote *Italia Libera*, organ of the Action Party, and Herbert Matthews reported that Churchill's 'slap' was 'considered here as the hardest and most discouraging blow that has yet been struck against a people who are almost used to being kicked around verbally in London'.[11]

In spite of mollifying afterthoughts by Churchill, the Italians had never 'felt so aggrieved with us since Allied troops arrived in this country,' said Sir Noel Charles, warning of the dangers of a rebirth of the anti-English sentiments of Mussolini's time.[12]

Had the Italian public known of Whitehall's reply to the American suggestion of December in favour of a preliminary peace agreement, their sense of grievance might have deepened even further. The firm refusal of Eden was formally motivated by doubt that neither the non-elected Italian or the Allied governments could gain any benefit from such a concession. The furthest the British were prepared to go would be outlined in the imminent Macmillan proposals for implementing the Hyde Park Declaration; 'We think that the fact that the Commonwealth has borne by far the greater share of the Italian war entitles us to ask that our views be respected,' the State Department was told.[13] But a more realistic view of sentiment in London is given by comment on a statement made in Rome by Harry Hopkins to the effect that American public opinion could not tolerate the thought of people in liberated countries starving to death. Couldn't Hopkins understand the difference between an ex-enemy and an ally? asked a Foreign Office mandarin.[14]

The Americans realized that behind the unbending insistence on the exclusive right of the British Empire to determine the future of Italy lay a challenge to their own right to demand a different policy. Argument inside the State Department as the new year opened had swung between those who were 'not only critical but despairing of "Allied policy" [sic] in Italy', and who insisted that Americans were effectively excluded from policy-making, and those on the other hand who sought to defend the American contribution up to that moment without suggesting any alternative.[15]

For Henry Morgenthau, the strong-willed U.S. Treasury Secretary, this difference did not even exist. In an emotional meeting which saw Morgenthau and aides and American representatives of the Finance subcommission of AC on one side, and delegates from the British Treasury and the Washington Embassy on the other, the secretary made two blunt charges: firstly that in implementing Allied policy, AC followed an exclusively British line; secondly that the British 'were interested in maintaining Fascists in power,' a feeling, said Morgenthau, widely shared in Washington. Not surprisingly, the British representatives 'displayed some degree of perturbation'.[16]

Unfortunately no one on the American side could document these charges, in spite of the repeated mention of them by U.S. officers returning from Italy. An approach was nevertheless made to Macmillan, who provided the predictable 'most emphatic and unequivocal denial' of Morgenthau's allegations, and the Foreign Office wrote them off as characteristic outbursts from a man reluctant to attend to the business of his own 'rather insignificant' department.[17]

Resentment in the British executive departments against attacks on their own attitudes, and against American generosity to Italy, reached an all-time high in the first weeks of 1945. 'Where they differ from us is their love for courting the public and making extravagant promises,' said a Treasury official.[18] But the Foreign Office warned that American aid might be needed now more than ever; 'the more we can encourage them to have a feeling of continuing responsibility for the maintenance of stability in Europe the better.'[19]

Some heat was taken from the argument by the arrival in Italy at the end of January of the long-awaited directive implementing the Hyde Park Declaration, and bringing certain structural changes in the Allied organs of control to increase the area of autonomy of the Rome government. Stettinius had opposed publication of the directive on account of its weakness, and senior officials in Washington told the British openly that they took it for granted that the U.K. wanted to 'keep Italy down.'[20] As a result the Foreign Office felt obliged to provide Eden with a tranquillizing statement for use if necessary at the Yalta conference. This claimed that the differences between the principal occupiers could in reality be reduced to a question of timing; whereas the Americans had 'never really felt themselves at war with Italy, [and] wish to go full-steam ahead,' the British were bound by the feelings of public opinion and doubts as to the survival capacity of the Italian government to go more slowly. The Americans were once again firmly reminded of their inability to provide their share of high-level staff for the control machinery.[21]

Not until Roosevelt had intervened formally with a letter to Churchill was a measure of calm restored. Here it was agreed that there were no basic differences on Italian policy since both wished to

> foster her gradual recuperation by developing a return to normal democratic proces-
> ses, the development of a sense of her own responsibility and the other steps so
> necessary in preparing the long hard road of Italy's return to the community of
> peace-loving democratic states.

Only trouble-makers could profit if despair set in, the president believed, hence a determination to pull together was absolutely necessary. But Roosevelt was not to be deflected from implying that certain essential differences did persist, and that weighty concessions had been made by the American side. The new directive, he said, 'was greatly watered down and much of its substance lost,' and only in the hope that 'some agreement on further steps' could soon be reached had the U.S. gone along.[22]

Yalta

IN THE CLASH of imperial interests which took place at Yalta, the British emerged as the victors, at least so far as Italy was concerned. Each Ally arrived at the conference with a more or less articulated approach to the Italian question in mind. In the event, Italy was hardly even mentioned between the walls of the Livadia Palace, and the ways and means of British hegemony suffered no challenge beyond that of Roosevelt's letter, written as the conference closed and without reference to it.

Yet the terms of much of the discussion at Yalta had a good deal to do with Italy's objective status at that moment. Hopkins in Rome had stated that the old Rooseveltian notion that politics could in some way be 'postponed' until the end of hostilities had been abandoned: the condition of liberated countries, he believed, was from that time on an integral part of military plans.[23] Yalta witnessed the transformation of this old State Department appreciation into a concrete design, intended – as in the arguments in favour of the Political-Military Commission of late 1943 – to enlist both Soviet and domestic political support at a time when both were needed as never before.

The outcome of this feeling was the Department's proposal for a 'Provisional Security Council for Europe,' whose purpose would be 'to supervise the re-establishment of popular government and the maintenance of order in the liberated states in Europe and in the German satellite states, pending the establishment of the proposed general international organization of the United Nations.'[24] There was 'growing evidence of Anglo-Soviet rivalry on the continent of Europe,' the president was told in his briefing paper for Yalta on liberated countries. And this rivalry was due less to territorial problems than to competition for influence over provisional governments.[25]

In Washington Roosevelt had been told by his staff that the general mood of European peoples was to the Left, 'and strongly in favour of far-reaching economic and social reforms, but not, however, in favour of a left-wing totalitarian regime to achieve these reforms.' Consequently provisional governments had to be sufficiently progressive to satisfy these moods, and to meet Soviet suspicions, Right-wing enough to exclude the risk of Communist dictatorship. America therefore should actively participate in machinery designed to guarantee support to those governments who would, firstly, preserve civil liberties, secondly 'favour economic and social reforms.'[26]

In Italy the State Department looked to the CLN – as already constituted at the national and local levels – to provide the required model of stabilization:

> As long as Italian governments, regardless of changing personnel, continue to be based upon the foundation of the Committee and to reflect in a generally equal manner the political parties represented therein, Allied basis for recognition will continue to be sound.[27]

When the conference got under way, it appeared at first as though the political confrontations of the summer of 1943 were to be re-enacted. The Western side once again produced a plan for tripartite control in Europe (opposed in practice, as before, by the president). The Soviets repeated their worries over the 'unconditional' nature of the surrender: would Allied support of pro-Fascist factions in Italy after the invasion mean the eventual preservation of the Hitler government in Germany? asked Stalin. The strongest echo of the past came in the discussion of the American declaration on liberated Europe. Molotov greeted the proposed scheme benevolently, but demanded explicit support 'to men in those countries who took an active part in the struggle against German occupation' (Stalin provocatively offered to exclude Greece from this provision). Eden and Stettinius were taken aback, and when the measure was hammered out between the foreign ministers, they made common cause in rejecting it. The principle of non-intervention was evoked in justification, and the difficulties of sorting out resisters from collaborators. Above all, claimed Stettinius, there was the problem of American domestic politics, where such a suggestion would not be understood.[28]

Two quite opposing views of social reconstruction in post-war Europe confronted each other at this point, one based on renewed forms of liberal democracy and inter-class collaboration, the other on anti-Fascist merit.

Two different currencies of power were involved: in the Western case tradition, moral prestige (the British) and new plans for prosperity and security (the Americans); in the Soviet case, strategic effort and sacrifices in the war. Stalin told Tito at this time: 'This war is not as in the past; whoever occupies a territory imposes on it his own social system. Everyone imposes his own system as far as his army has power to do so. It cannot be otherwise.' But after many years of reflection, Milovan Djilas, present on that occasion, decided that this was precisely where Stalin had gone wrong in 1945: 'it is the fatal, unforgiveable error of conquerors to ordain the destinies of men and nations according to wartime views and circumstances.'[29] The two visions of West and East were clearly incompatible without the common anti-Hitler bond: the Soviets were convinced that Britain and the U.S. sought to rob them and their Communist Party allies in the various countries of the fruits of their victories; the Western powers saw an attempt to impose the Soviet system by force on the wrecked traditional societies of central and southern Europe. At Yalta then, instead of establishing machinery to police Europe according to Anglo-American sensibilities, the Soviets withdrew their collaboration. An empty agreement on consultation was the result and this was incorporated in the final version of the Declaration on Liberated Europe. Within a matter of weeks it was a dead letter. What remained were the American concerns from which the plan had sprung, and these were to find other outlets, in Italy as in the rest of Europe.[30]

'NOT ONE single word of relief,' groaned the anti-Fascist press in Rome after the Yalta conference had ended. The only hope for Italy was for peace and serenity after her sufferings, said the Action Party's *Italia Libera*. The Communists said little on Italy's disappointments but instead looked to the new weight of the Soviets in international affairs, and saw a demonstration that 'there are no such things as indissoluble contrasts between the United Nations.' The Action Party paper also believed that common action was now the rule, and that the Americans had prevented an Anglo-Soviet division of Europe, thereby refuting Guiseppe Saragat's assertions in the pages of *Avanti!* that the world was henceforth split into three irreconcilable blocs.[31] The conviction was beginning to spread that even after 16 months of relentless hardship and sacrifice, nothing had changed in the Allied relationship with Italy. The effect on Italian morale was well described by Anne McCormick in the *New York Times*:

> We are still outside Bologna, and the fact that the Italian front has been almost static for 5 months while the decisive battles are waged elsewhere has had effects that should not be minimized on the material and moral state of Italy as well as on the Allied attitude to that unhappy land.
> During these long months all other decisions seemed to be held in suspense, too. One had the impression that the Allied Commission was cumbrously marking time,

waiting for directives, waiting for events, running round in aimless circles while the economic and social situation went from bad to worse. It is difficult to avoid a suspicion that the civil administration is being turned over to the Italians because the Allies want to be relieved of problems they cannot solve.[32]

The 'New Deal' directive on Allied control (supposedly implementing the Hyde Park decisions of September) was finally announced by Macmillan in February. The State Department had already decided that the statement was so unsubstantial that it was not worth public endorsement, and now began to press for more tangible signs of positive thinking on Italy's future. Whitehall reacted to these urges by turning its back on everything which had passed between the British and the Americans in the previous three months, and began to overhaul the list of impositions to be included in a possible British peace treaty, starting out from the position that all Italian rights as regards frontiers, colonies, fleet, and so on were to be renounced.[33]

In the following weeks each of the various elements of the British official machine supplied its own view of a possible settlement, views which differed little from each other in their underlying vindictiveness and in their overall aim of pressing Italy back into place in the imperial scheme of things current in the 1920s or early 1930s. The Post-Hostilities Planning Staff, for example, felt assured that without raw materials or wealth of her own Italy would not be in a position to threaten world peace for some considerable time; 'nevertheless, Italy, owing to her geographic position, constitutes a factor which influences our strategy in the Eastern as well as the Western Mediterranean. It is therefore important that Italy should not again come under the control of a hostile or potentially hostile power.' On the other hand, 'she should not be so militarily weak that she would fall an easy prey to the influence of a hostile power.' Above all, 'Italy must not be in a position to threaten our Mediterranean communications.' To this the Foreign Office added its own belief that:

> The Italian Empire was the product of strategic calculation and Italy's pretensions to be a Great Power. We have a strategic interest in preventing Italy's return to the Red Sea area and the future security of the Mediterranean will probably require the establishment of United Nations bases and facilities in the former Italian territories in North Africa.

The Colonial Office too worried about Africa since, 'in the eyes of the Colonial Empire, and particularly in East and West Africa, the Italians, ever since the attack on Ethiopia, have been regarded as aggressors no less than the Germans. Moreover Colonial troops have taken an active part in the military defeat of Italy.' The Dominions Office pressed for India's interest to be taken into consideration, particularly in view of her contribution in men and supplies, while the Board of Trade moved to ensure total Allied control of any future trade negotiations.[34]

Only from those on the spot did a more differentiated and positive approach appear. What was needed was a programme to 'safeguard our future material interests and avoid sowing seeds of irredentist dangers,' said Sir Noel Charles, a programme preferably based on a number of key points:

(1)   Reference should be made and attention paid to the difference between 'demo-cratic' and 'fascist' Italy.
(2)   The extent of democratic Italy's future cooperation with us in the Mediterranean depends on our treatment of her now.
(3)   Italy is willing to make amends for fascist depredations and hand over all land seized subsequent to the last war.[35]

Charles insisted that the Italians were convinced that they had worked their passage – 'the patriots are playing a very big role in the actual conquest of Northern Italy' – and needed to be shown that Britain was not the least friendly of the Allies, a point repeated by Italy's new representative in London, Count Carandini, who told the Foreign Office in one of his earliest conversations that since America would go away after the war, 'he was convinced that in the long run England would be the best friend to whom Italy might turn'.[36] Endorsing Charles's points, Macmillan suddenly pronounced a damning overall verdict:

We are playing our hand very foolishly with regard to Italy. There seems to be a kind of childish animosity towards the Italians which does not do us or them any good. Can you not exorcise this spirit from Whitehall?[37]

But it was Macmillan who revealed to Kirk – in strictest secrecy – the real limits in which the British were bound to operate on the treaty issue, as well as on all those other questions which brought Italian autonomy into general discussion. The problem was – Kirk told Washington – that, 'from the financial standpoint, Great Britain is not (repeat not) in a position to assume the burden of the expenses of the British armed forces in Italy, which are now charged to occupation costs under the armistice'. Kirk made the obvious point that such a line meant British opposition to *any* fundamental change in the armistice regime in the foreseeable future. More broadly, claimed Kirk, 'acceptance of the [principle] that the immediate financial interests of one government alone can dictate basic policy towards another country is bound to retard the orderly process of national and international recuperation'.[38]

BEFORE these arguments could be drawn out any further, Alexander's spring offensive had finally got under way, promising the long-awaited liberation of the North. But reports from behind the lines on what the Allies could expect to find when they arrived were far from reassuring. Special Force No. 1, the British liaison organization with the Resistance movement, told AFHQ in January that:

Many reports have reached this HQ from British missions in Northern Italy during the last few months which leave no doubt that those who control Communist bands are preparing to seize power by force when the Germans are expelled by the Allies.

Recalling the situation in Greece, this review claimed that the Communists were fighting, 'not for patriotic motives, but for the eradication of all traces of Fascism,' implying also,

> the elimination of all elements who actively oppose their intentions towards a finally liberated Italy. Those who are not Communists are inspired by patriotic motives, which include the destruction of Fascism; but, latterly, we have evidence that they regard their formations as potential adversaries to the growing Communist power.

If Special Force was correct, Togliatti's efforts in discouraging criticism of the Western powers in the name of unity of action were not meeting with success:

> Certain of their less discreet leaders have made damaging references to the Allies, whom they branded as enemies of a new socially reconstructed Italy. Against this, they pour praises on the Russians whom they recognize as the true friends of the future Italy.[39]

Harold Macmillan did not neglect the connection between the immediate moment of demobilization and the overall political strategy:

> Although [the North] would be under AMG in the initial stages, I was anxious to strengthen the hand of the Italian Government and to increase their prestige in every possible way. It was vital to neglect no method which could prevent violent action by the Communists.[40]

While the movement was fighting the aim should be 'to confine supplies to food and clothing, to regulate the quantities'; the instant it was over, 'to see that British and American task forces moved as quickly as possible to the important centres.' In the final analysis, however, as recent Greek events demonstrated, 'nothing matters except disarmament. The political questions are [an] excuse for retaining armed power', Macmillan told his diary. Among the tactics used in Italy to keep the military potential of the brigades under control and facilitate disarmament was the incorporation of some of the largest into the Italian army combat groups, now fighting south-east of Bologna. More important in the north-west was the direction by Allied missions of their energies into 'anti-scorch' efforts; the defence of the factories, power stations, transport facilities, etc. against last-ditch German sabotage.[41]

Nevertheless, at the beginning of February, SF and AC threatened to stop further supplies of arms and money to the CLNAI and its brigades until they were sure that a special fund was not being built up for 'post-liberation revolutionary purposes', and the alarm spread to the CCS, who issued a warning against 'any attempt [by the CLNAI] to set itself up in opposition to the Italian Government in Rome' on the strength of the December accords.[42]

The most diffident agency of all was the Rome government itself, which in the middle of March 1945 sent (with the approval of the Allies) the under-secretary of the Ministry of Occupied Territory, the Liberal A. Medici-Tornaquinci, to the key CLNs in Milan and Turin to extract new promises of obeisance and repeat the warnings over Allied attitudes. The under-secretary found identical, hardened opinions in both regions: 'acceptance, even with reservations and through gritted teeth, of AMG; preconceived and manifest hostility to the national Government.'[43] With considerable energy Medici-Tornaquinci described the difficulties under which the government laboured ('the lack of facilities, of communications, of cash'), and was not surprised to find its activities 'almost unknown'. By dint of relentless negotiation, the under-secretary succeeded in bringing back from the North two theoretically important agreements. The first concerned the insertion of the CLNs in 'expanded consultative organs' which were in fact to be the new town councils and would include representatives and 'technicians' from agriculture, industry, the Church, education, etc. on the Tuscan model. The second agreement sounded no less important: the CLNAI promised to apply, during the insurrectional period when it exercised *de facto* power, the laws of the State. In this way, said Medici-Tornaquinci, there would be 'formal assurance, even in the insurrection, of the principle of the continuity of the State.'[44] But there remained the burning issue of local government nominees: to what extent would local figures, particularly CLN members, be permitted to enter the official administration? A heated confrontation on this subject took place in the spring of 1945 between Bonomi and the AC, the prime minister insisting on the sanctity of the traditional structures and the career functionaries, Admiral Stone telling the government that 'it would be quite useless to appoint any nominee who is not acceptable in the locality',[45] and since AMG would be first on the spot flexibility would be the rule in the first instance, as Macmillan's colleague Hopkinson made clear to the acting president's conference at the beginning of March:

> In many districts 'shadow' Governments had been set up and the various portfolios had been distributed among the leaders of the different parties [Hopkinson reported]. In most cases the Committees represent the six parties which, up till last December, were represented in the Government in Rome. . . . On the whole it seemed that for the time being there was a remarkable degree of unity of purpose in the Committees and party differences had been sunk in the common desire to chase the Germans from Italy and punish their Fascist collaborators. These Committees were assisted in their operations by the Allied authorities and the giving of such assistance had necessarily implied recognition of the value of those operations.

According to the SAC–CLNAI agreement the committees would hand over all powers to AMG as soon as its men set up office, but the problem was that the legitimate government of Rome supported by the Allies 'might not have the entire confidence of the Committees of Liberation in the North, or at any rate their influence there was subject to fluctuation.' The reasons were clear: there was the North's conviction that its contribution to victory had far exceeded that of the South, and that it had paid far more dearly for it. The Rome authorities furthermore had shown scant capacity to set reconstruction in motion, to deal with the basic economic problems of the moment or to press on with the purge of Fascists. Consequently – and this was the ultimate fear of all – the temptation might well arise to promote a breakaway movement, based on the CLNs and dominated to a greater or lesser degree by the Left. For the Allied planners the only realistic solution to this danger lay in the application of the SAC–CLNAI accord, accompanied by 'the absorption at a very early date of members of the local Committees of National Liberation into the civil administration operating under Allied Military Government', as in Tuscany.[46]

Macmillan was optimistic: 'it was fashionable to believe that there was going to be a great deal of political trouble and even revolution in the North,' he told the March conference. 'However he [Macmillan] was of the opinion that we should find a great deal of invigorating and beneficial aspects of Italian life in that territory and that the people would be more active and powerful than any we had yet come across in Italy.'[47]

'In my opinion,' said Alexander Kirk on the eve of liberation, 'security in the initial stages, at least, will depend upon an effective display of military authority.' Like Macmillan, Kirk was not intimidated by any immediate danger from the power of the PCI:

> There is some discussion of a possible attempt by the Communists to seize power by one means or another at the time of the liberation of the North, but this possibility would appear to be ruled out by Togliatti's success to date in extending the strength and influence of the party by 'democratic' processes.

But in the longer term there could be far less confidence. If, as seemed quite probable to Kirk, the unified CLNAI structure broke up, or if the CLNAI became a Leftist front organ, then 'the struggle for power between the "state" as supported by the Christian Democrats and the Liberals, and the "people" as upheld by the Socialists and Communists . . . can be expected to be intensified, and the possibility cannot be overlooked that this divergence may lead to local disturbances and perhaps even to civil war.' Such a scenario could only be avoided, Kirk thought, by ensuring the *effective* authority of the Bonomi government, and since the situation was likely to be aggravated very seriously by rising hunger and unemployment, this meant continued Allied support to the Rome authorities in some form or other, and adequate rehabilitation and assistance, 'especially from the United States.'[48]

BUT TWO more international crises erupted on to the scene before any of these forecasts could be tested. Just as the Trieste question came to a climax in the north-east – with Tito's forces apparently poised to seize the city and hold it by force as a prelude to annexation – so the forces of de Gaulle attempted their own large-scale manoeuvre in the north-west.

The Trieste/Venezia Giulia question had been high up on the list of Allied priorities ever since Churchill had come to Italy in August 1944 to establish direct contact with Tito and sound out his intentions on the subject in the light of the fact that his forces were already operating in the area, and were cooperating with Italian 'Garibaldini' (Communist) partisans. On that occasion Churchill had laid down the lines of policy for the eventual occupation of north-east Italy as he saw them, an integral part of British policy to Yugoslavia as a whole. These were: (a) imposition, after the German collapse, of AMG with the surrender of Italian sovereignty until the Peace Conference; (b) maintenance of military lines of communication from the port of Trieste up through to the Austrian border; (c) cooperation of Yugoslav forces with these plans; (d) the creation of a united Yugoslav government to organize this cooperation and open the way to the establishment of democracy in the country; (e) non-involvement of the Allies in internal Yugoslav political battles to the extent that they did not compromise the anti-Nazi struggle.[49]

But difficulties soon broke out in all directions: between the British and the Americans, between the military at AFHQ and the political overseers in London and Washington, between Tito and the British, and between Tito and the other major element in the united national government plan, the exile cabinet in London round King Peter and the prime minister Subasic. There was disagreement in the first place over the extent to which military arrangements would prejudge the political issues, particularly since the Italian government was to be deliberately excluded, with consequent offence to Italian public opinion. Then from the U.S. came strong objection to linking the military plan to overall political aims for Yugoslavia, especially since the British had clear and detailed hopes in the area while America did not. Then again objection was made to the nature and degree of cooperation expected from Tito, especially since the partisan leader soon declared that his forces would expect to participate in administering these frontier zones after the liberation. Of one reality the Allied command became more and more aware as Special Force missions reported back from the area in late 1944: that so severe were the risks of conflict between Italians and Slovenes (the local Slavic population around Trieste), and between Tito's forces with its PCI brigades and the non-Communist brigades (notably the substantial 'Osoppo' division, largely Catholic or non-aligned), that it would be extremely difficult for any Allied force, army or AMG to impose its will on the area without becoming caught in the middle. When events in Greece demonstrated just how serious this risk was, the impulse to come to an agreement with Tito increased.

It was in this context that the famous 'percentages' agreement was made at Moscow between Churchill and Stalin, which apparently shared their influence 50–50 in Yugoslavia, thus leaving space for British hopes of a multi-party system in the country. But when AFHQ finally produced a definite plan for military government in Venezia Giulia, at the end of November, it was found to weigh heavily in favour of the partisans, since it

aimed essentially to freeze the situation as of the moment of liberation –
therefore including Tito's forces present throughout the region – and
evidently hoped to win his support for this regime. A variety of concessions
were included which kept the Rome government well at bay and made
space for local representation (e.g. in police recruitment). But while this plan
was being floated came news from the British missions of formal links
between the Slovene forces and the Garibaldi brigade 'Natisone', which
would henceforth no longer recognize the authority of the CLNAI, but only
that of the Slovene IX Korpus. Even more alarming was the news that
Togliatti had pronounced himself strongly in favour of this form of collaboration, and in general of Tito's occupation of the eastern Giulian
regions, where, said the Communist leader, a 'profoundly democratic
situation' might well be created, 'different from that in the rest of liberated
Italy.' Togliatti also insisted, however, that there should be no talk of formal
annexation: the sovereign status of the region would be decided by local
self-determination after the war had finished.[50]

At this point the military confessed that they were unable to do any more,
passing the initiative directly to the political-diplomatic levels. Here the
powerful impulse to maintain British influence in Yugoslavia, and above all
keep Tito neutral or passive *vis à vis* Greece soon produced a new proposal:
that of a demarcation line to the west of which the Allies would hold sway,
while to its east Tito would freely instal his own administration. To have any
chance of getting the marshal's approval, said the Foreign Office, his
frontier claims should be recognized in deciding where the line should go,
even if this meant shifting the frontier to its 1914 position and thus placing
Trieste, Fiume and Pola in his hands. This project Eden took to Yalta where,
however, it was ignored by the other two powers. Eventually the State
Department pronounced itself opposed for reasons of principle, and so the
hapless British had no alternative but to pass the buck back to Alexander and
AFHQ, where hopes still lived on for the constitution of a unitary government which might solve the Allies' problem for them. But with time
pressing and the spring offensive about to open, the supreme Allied
commander could not afford to wait on this eventuality, and so he personally flew to Belgrade at the end of February to establish, if nothing else, a
working arrangement with the partisan leader. The result was ambiguous:
to Alexander's suggestion that he establish AMG throughout the region,
Tito replied that he was already in control of much of it and intended to
make formal claim for the region centred on Trieste; he was, however,
willing to respect the need for Allied lines of communication, even to the
extent of placing his troops and administration under Allied command in
those specific areas.

As the final push gathered speed, Alexander found himself caught
between two incompatible pressures. From the combined bodies in
Washington came strong but imprecise promptings to instal AMG wherever

possible, with or without local participation, and with or without Soviet support. On the ground the Slovene forces were pushing as far west and north as they could. Into this cauldron Alexander sent General Mark Clark's 15th Army Group, with instructions to reach Trieste as fast as possible, and if nothing else secure the port areas and the roads and railways leading north and north-west from the city. While the German resistance finally gave way (not without attempting a separate peace manoeuvre[51]), the 'race for Trieste' began.[52]

THE SIMMERING THREAT of trouble between French and Italians on the Piedmont frontier – reported to AFHQ by the northern Resistance with growing alarm from autumn 1944 onwards – suddenly burst forth in April 1945 when Free French forces occupied the Valle d'Aosta and surrounding regions with openly declared annexationist aims. Since September 1943 De Gaulle had concentrated his attention on the liquidation of the Italian communities in Tunisia and Corsica, expelling the leading members (lawyers, doctors, teachers, journalists), breaking up families and absorbing the remaining 'amorphous mass' into forced labour. Now the bill of 1940 was presented on Italian soil, with the warning that henceforth north-west Italy was under permanent strategic threat.[53]

The general strategy was in effect to set up – after German withdrawal – a vast French zone of occupation in Piedmont and Liguria, as Pierre Guillen reports. More important than the seizure of certain local zones were, however, the overall political objectives:

> to expunge the humiliation imposed by the Anglo-Americans who, in September 1943, had excluded France from the armistice negotiations and who, since that time, had practically left her out of the conduct of policy towards Italy; to forcibly reinstate a French presence in Italian affairs on an equal footing with the Anglo-Saxons; to obtain a lever with which to press French claims at the time of the peace settlement.[54]

A foothold had already been gained with the occupation by French authorities of the island of Elba, and the Free French navy had pressed to participate in operations in the Gulf of Genoa which included Italian naval disarmament. Now De Gaulle told his local commander Doyen to carry out 'a war of movement capable of rapid progress far from your present base', and by the beginning of May the objective had become Turin, liberated by the Resistance on 27 April.[55]

The extreme agitation of Rome and Caserta in reaction to this dangerous new threat was not simply a product of the frontier problem. The British of course had long justified their attitude to Italy with the notion that an ally should not be worse treated than an ex-enemy, while systematically excluding the French from real participation in the control of Italy and thereby exacerbating French revanchism. For the Americans there was the embarrassment of seeing a recently recognized ally in open violation of Article 1 of the Atlantic Charter, which rejected all territorial aggrandizement. For the

Allied commanders there was a new factor of tension and complication at the moment of liberation, which might serve to justify Resistance claims to retain armed power and at the same time legitimize moves by Tito on the eastern frontier. Alexander reacted by countering force with force, and in the middle of May there was real risk of armed confrontation between French and American troops in the frontier zones. But De Gaulle was in no position to risk his relationship with the Americans, especially at a time when another serious crisis had developed in his relationship with the British, and the arrival of an ultimatum from Truman at the beginning of June, threatening to cut off all supplies to the Free French forces, produced the required results. In less than a week an agreement had been signed at Caserta for the withdrawal of French troops from the contested areas, and De Gaulle was forced in subsequent months to reappraise his entire strategy for eliminating the Italian menace to French soil, and Italian influence in the Mediterranean.[56]

10 The Liberation and its aftermath

THROUGHOUT the Po valley, in the major cities of the North from Venice to Turin, in almost every town worthy of the name, the scene during the last two weeks of April 1945 was much the same: a partisan insurrection followed by the definitive withdrawal of the German armies, a bloody settling of accounts with neo-Fascist remnants, the installation of the CLN administration, then a few days later, the arrival of the Allied armies and Allied Military Government. The speed of events took armies, military governors and Resistance forces alike by surprise. In spite of the strenuous efforts made by the Allied command to avoid a 'revolutionary interval', a period between the disappearance of the enemy and the entry of AMG when the long-feared breakaway movement might establish itself, many zones and medium-sized towns and villages were left in the hands of the Resistance administration for periods up to two weeks, with results which profoundly surprised the political watchdogs of AFHQ and ACC.

Admiral Stone reacted swiftly, ordering on 1 May a review of policy in the light of 'the outstanding successes of the patriots in liberating their towns from Nazis and Fascists, the good administration, according to initial reports, set up by the CLNs, the execution of Mussolini and many of his accomplices, and the surrender, in some cases to the patriots, of a great bulk of the German forces.' With great relief Stone ordered 'the greatest delegation possible' to the CLN authorities, and reminded his officials in the field that 'above all . . . it is our duty to administer rather than to intervene in the political future of Italy.'[1]

Those who felt responsible for the political future of much more than Italy were not prepared to take such a detached view of things, and began to look again at their plans for the future stability of Europe. 'Department notes increasing number of northern Italian communities headed by mayors described as "militant Communists" or Socialists,' Kirk was told in the middle of May on one of the apparently few occasions when his advice was sought by his employers:

> Appears that these two groups are dominating northern Italy to the exclusion of right-wing Socialists. Appears also that these mayors may not enjoy spontaneous support of majority of people but perhaps seized positions by force and then confronted AMG officials with *fait accompli*. . . . Pattern developing in Europe of

attempt by Communists to wield an influence disproportionate to their real numbers and eliminate their opponents either by public stigmatism or epuration if possible.[2]

Kirk was instructed to find out the means by which the Left gained control and its proportional strength. His reply tried to be reassuring. The PCI and the PSI, he reported, were strong in the major industrial cities of the North – Milan, Turin and Genoa – and enjoyed 'a large popular following' in the surrounding regions of Piedmont and Lombardy, while the Christian Democrats were strong in the country. As for the tactics of the Left parties, there was 'as yet no evidence that they have succeeded in obtaining a share greatly in excess of their proportional strength.'[3]

Even while reports of the liberation of Genoa and Milan by Resistance forces had been coming in, it had been immediately clear to Kirk that a decisive shift had occurred in the centre of political gravity inside the country, even beyond that already discounted in Allied forecasts. The authorities, said Kirk, would undoubtedly have to 'give far more weight to public opinion than has been necessary in similar circumstances in southern Italy',[4] but the State Department's observations had already shown what sort of official conclusions would be drawn if this opinion turned out to be overwhelmingly republican and Leftist.

IMMEDIATELY AFTER the final insurrection – and before the Allied armies arrived – the CLNAI in Milan issued triumphant decrees on 26 April announcing its takeover on behalf of the national government, summoning the northern citizens to obey its authority, and demanding the formation of a new national executive corresponding to the changed situation. In Milan no mention was made of the transfer of powers to be carried out on the arrival of AMG, but in Rome Bonomi was careful to publish in these same days the agreement of December.[5] Meanwhile the CLN of Lombardy met to discuss, as its minutes record, the 'take-over of power'. The CLNAI took note that there was no surrender treaty for the Repubblica Sociale Italiana of Mussolini, and demanded that neo-Fascists surrender to the CLNs, to be tried under a judicial system created by them (and not by arbitrary action). As the CLNAI's decrees stated:

> At the moment of occupation the Allies must find themselves in the presence of a fully-functioning system of political justice, that they have no interest in interfering with.[6]

In Milan and Turin there was talk of dissolving the national army and replacing it with partisan formations. On the ground, the Resistance experiences of the partisan republics in certain country areas, of the Agitation Committees in the cities, of the regional, provincial and communal CLNs, and of the occasional popular junta, were consolidated, and there was a blossoming of local committees, of cooperatives, of factory CLNs, of district, neighbourhood and even street CLNs.[7] The pre-revolutionary atmosphere in many areas was accompanied by a violent settling of accounts with the Fascist remnants – CLNAI orders notwithstanding. Contemporary esti-mates speak of 20,000 killings in northern Italy in this period, most of which took place in the second half of May, and in such cities as Bologna and Genoa 20 to 30 bodies were often picked off the streets by early-morning police patrols.[8] The atmosphere in one city in Emilia-Romagna – Ravenna – was dramatically described by a Communist delegate to a regional CLN meeting at the end of May:

> The [Allied] Governor thinks an insurrection is going to happen. Not a single night passes without 3 or 4 or 5 deaths. The Governor has had to turn to the partisan commanders because only they can keep control, the population listens only to them. . . . It is almost impossible to maintain control over the population, which is frustrated over the incapacity of the local institutions to satisfy its needs.[9]

The dramatic days after the liberation were to be remembered by an entire generation, with exaltation or fear depending on which side of the class barrier individuals found themselves at that moment. 'A state of near anarchy exists at some points,' a State Department visitor to the North reported in May. 'Fiat, Turin, who normally employ 120,000 people is a typical example. Here workers have to all extents and purposes taken over the factory. About 4000 people are actually employed in the factory but during my visit practically no work was being done. Factory is patrolled by armed liberationists. Management is virtually ignored.'[10]

Italian sources, such as Valerio, head of the important Edison electrical company, usually self-appointed informers, were never more active than in describing the fearful revolution which would erupt on the day the Allied troops left, Valerio himself declaring that: 'Today the primary necessity is the immediate construction of a strong force for public order, composed of some 100,000 men, capable of overpowering an armed population.'[11]

Valletta, the Fiat managing director, narrowly escaped being shot out of hand on the factory floor. He was unanimously condemned as a collabor-ationist by the regional CLN, but when the time came for his arrest he was well prepared. The Communist leader Giorgio Amendola recalls:

> when our partisan formation went to arrest him, we found in the villa where he had taken refuge, an English liaison officer, who presented a safe-conduct pass for Valletta, since he had played a double game, naturally; he had not only collaborated with the Germans, but had maintained his contacts with the English, had rendered great service to the English.[12]

The director of a large Genoa factory (where the red flag flew from the chimney-stack), told two PWB officers in a clandestine meeting that the atmosphere in the factory was 'if anything slightly more strained than it was during the last days of Nazi-Fascism, alone the colour of the flag and the form of salute having changed. He [the director] is as shackled as he was under the former regime and has to watch his words and actions just as carefully.' As for the attitude of the workers towards the Allies, the director said:

> The Communist workmen consider the Anglo-Americans to be their ideological and capitalist enemies (the phrase 'National Enemies' was used) who are very much the same sort of labour slave-drivers as were the Fascists.[13]

Confirmation of all these views was provided by Rocco Piaggio, owner of shipyards, sugar refineries and soap factories, and a leading industrialist in Liguria. According to Piaggio, the country was heading 'straight for Communism', and the situation would precipitate the day the Allies departed. Fascism, a similar totalitarian dictatorship, had trained the Italian people to be 50 per cent slaves, whereas 'they will become 100% slaves under Communism.'

> In his despair at the future of Italian industry [the PWB interviewer reported], Piaggio said that he hoped the Anglo-Saxons, as part of the settlement of Italy's war indemnities and debts, would take over the ownership or control of the great industries of Italy (including his own).[14]

The Allied authorities had their own criteria for judging such alarms, which did not hesitate to raise the spectre of imminent insurrection in such centres as Milan and Turin. As AFHQ Operations Division reported to Washington in July, there was 'no adequate evidence to substantiate such rumours which largely emanate from industrial and right-wing elements anxious to stir up anti-communist feeling.'[15] Even known anti-Communists such as Camerana, vice-president of Fiat, confirmed that rumours were being deliberately spread, and from numerous other sources it was apparent by mid-June that 'a definite reaction against some of the excesses of the first few weeks' had set in among the workers, as an AFHQ visitor to the North reported. An important Piedmontese woollen manufacturer told the American consul general in Genoa in June that there had been 'a marked reduction in Communist fervour' in his area, and that he was confident that the danger of a Communist takeover was past.[16]

But the situation remained critical, with fears of financial collapse in industry, of mass unrest when temporary blocks on redundancies were removed, and of a breakdown in law and order if the government was unable to make its presence felt. Reports soon began to appear of a clandestine Right-wing industrialists association formed with the objective of fighting Communism, if need be by force. Its methods were to be:

> (a) by an intensive press and propaganda campaign, which includes the corruption of Communist leaders and writers;
> (b) by force of arms.

Expenditure of L.120 million per annum was foreseen for press activities, and the money was to be deposited in the Vatican City and invested as a hedge against inflation.[17]

Sir Noel Charles believed the reports of Right-wing conspiracies to be true, as did AFHQ, and the Foreign Office agreed that activity of this sort was extremely dangerous: 'This was exactly how Fascism had begun, and it would indeed be the end of Italy if we were again to see the forces of the Right and Left engaged in warfare against each other. It must be our task to prevent the crystallization of such a division.'[18]

ADMIRAL STONE had decreed on 1 May that 'a light rein with a firm hand should be the order of the day', and emphasized that 'CLNs must be treated with courtesy due to their political position and their past labours.' But there was a reminder too:

> every effort should be made to impress upon the people and the authorities that AMG is the temporary forerunner of the Italian Government, and that AMG is working in the closest cooperation with that Government at the Headquarters of this Commission.[19]

For those concerned in the cities and villages of northern Italy this was the most brutal shock of all. In general Resistance military and political forces had had very little information on what to expect on the arrival of the Allies, or on the contacts between the CLNAI and the Allies, and as to the activities of the Rome government there was almost total ignorance. The resulting confrontation destroyed many illusions and left enduring bitterness. A left-wing witness from Emilia recalls:

> Those weeks after the liberation were weeks of joy, but also of anxious and vain expectation that a substantial measure of social justice would be applied. The Allies blocked even the most modest initiative which seemed to prejudice the principle of private property. Their stay as occupiers was therefore more than welcome to the forces of conservatism. . . . They left Reggio and the other cities of the North certain that the CLN would never have effective power and that political life would be channelled according to their criteria.[20]

The power of the CLNAI in Milan lasted five days. On 2 May AMG was set up under the ubiquitous Poletti and the sovereignty of the CLNAI formally abrogated. By 12 May AMG had reorganized justice to ensure that all measures against Fascists were treated exclusively according to government law (AMG itself remaining as far as possible outside the process), and on 19 May the truck which deposited the copies of the *Gazzetta Ufficiale* in the storeroom of the Prefectura brought into force all the laws outstanding on the Italian statute-book, old and new. The Milan population, totally unaware of what these laws might now be, complained that in trusting in the authority and hence the decrees of the CLNAI it had been deceived.[21]

In the first instance the Allies had been impressed by the practical and organizational capacities of the local forces: 'Where necessary the people started repairing utilities on their own initiative, in remarkable contrast to the behaviour of the Southern Italians,' Vth Army AMG reported from Bologna.[22] 'In almost every instance the CLN has proved to be sensible and cooperative,' said a first-hand VIIIth Army observer, a judgment confirmed from the Veneto, where all ten prefects were local nominees, and 'it was obvious that any attempt to introduce career Prefects from the South would be resented. The men now holding office have given an impression of keenness and a desire to help in the reconstruction of their country.'[23] AC Headquarters experts were less enthusiastic, noting in the case of the questori (police chiefs) that 'most of them [have] little or no former police experience,' as the Public Safety commission remarked in July. The sub-commission's policy could be summed up in a few words: 'Career questori from the South are resented but appointments are being made as the situation tempers sufficiently.'[24]

In the case of prefects, this approach was not so easy to apply. In Central Italy, AC noted that from two to seven months had been required for the government to supply a career prefect, and suspected that the individuals' own fear of the conditions they were likely to find in the liberated areas explained much of the delay. AC's confidence in the government in this direction was not increased by a remarkable suggestion from Bonomi (who was also minister of the interior) in January 1945, that personnel dismissed by AMG as security risks might be reappointed by the government (pending epuration proceedings) in its own territory, in cases where the individual concerned was not 'gravely compromised', thus releasing officials for the North.[25] In June the civil affairs section of AC found itself constrained to tell its regional commissioners of the government's incompetence in this field, and urged them to appoint non-career men rather than block the local administration. As the Commission noted, 'for the purposes of AMG, the Prefectures get along just as well with local men of energy, decision and brains. Our only reason for sending career officials down is to set up the kind of administration the Italian Government wants and which will ease things for them when they take over.'[26]

Thus circumstances and instructions combined to give the local AC/AMG officers a great deal of autonomy, leading to a confusing variety of situations which the CLN structure was once again unable to challenge on any significant scale. As an AMG provincial governor in the Apennines between Parma and La Spezia complained, the CLN pyramid of command 'hardly exists, because the central CLN has no means of enforcing its orders upon its lesser brethren.'[27]

After the CLNs had attempted to by-pass the authority of AMG by such methods as calling conferences of political prefects, definitive decrees were issued by the Allied authorities annulling all CLN legislation and arrogating all executive, legislative and judicial power to the military government. This event coincided with a decisive meeting of party leaders in Rome (on 2 June), which sanctioned the end of CLN authority and practice – though there was no connection between the two events (the problem of the Allies does not appear to have exercised the participants to any noticeable degree).[28] From that time on the action of Allied governors was less and less diplomatic whenever the CLNs showed signs of taking any form of political or social action. But such instances were infrequent by the middle of June, as attention had shifted to the political struggles going on in traditional fashion in Rome. A bitter epitaph to the early phase was written by a Milanese observer in early June. His complaint concentrated above all

> on the psychological side of the question. The moral liquidation of everything that was best, historically new, in the Resistance and the insurrection, namely a clandestine government which made laws and created respect for them, fills one with anguish and sadness. Those who struggled against Fascism now find a new obstacle in front of them: centralisation. That is the enemy now.[29]

'WITH THE FORMATION of the Parri Government the political danger from the Resistance had ended,' says the British official historian; '[Parri's] appointment automatically disposed of the tension between Milan and Rome.'[30] Instead of a brief revolutionary interval between the departure of the Germans and the arrival of the Allies, there was a long counter-revolutionary interval between the liberation and the resignation of the Rome government in early May, and the formation at the end of June of an alternative cabinet corresponding somehow to the new conditions. During this time 'all the powers of an occupying force' were held with determining effectiveness by the Allied controllers, notwithstanding the oft-invoked 'spirit' and the letter of the 'New Deal' directives. As AMG beheld its efforts of these weeks shortly afterwards, its commanders permitted themselves a certain satisfaction:

> It is agreed by all but the Italian extremists that AMG did a necessary and effective job at the time of the occupation. The first few weeks were disorderly and the political tension was high. Nearly all factions accepted AMG as an impartial stake-holder until the internal political difficulties could be settled, at least to the extent of forming satisfactory governments at the provincial and communal level. This has been done in the great majority of the provinces. The administrative personnel is consistently of a higher order and more efficient than in the South. The only impediment has been the political one which has been pushed far enough into the background so as not to be a major factor in the local administration at the moment.[31]

In these few, laconic phrases is contained the essence of the liquidation process which the Resistance movement and its political organs underwent in the weeks after 25 April. Almost 30 years later, Pietro Secchia, a member of the PCI's northern directing committee, wrote:

> Young people today [1973] who read certain romanticized histories of our war of liberation have the impression that we held *power*, and that we were unable or worse, unwilling, to retain it (for some unknown reason), to bring about if not the proletarian revolution, which was quite out of the question, at least a regime of progressive democracy. The fact is that on account of the conditions in which the war of liberation developed in Italy and in Europe, *we* (when I say, 'we' I mean the anti-fascists, the CLNAI) never held *power*, nor were we capable of capturing it.[32]

At the time this was by no means apparent, or at least it was not admitted. And the frustrations and disappointments of this crucial period should not be attributed exclusively to the Allied presence, though measures such as insisting that northern CLN members could come to the South only on request of the government, while banning a visit to the North by the government itself (as the central CLN), can hardly be considered as positive contributions.[33] When the CLNAI did come south a tortuous and increasingly squalid process of cabinet selection began, which AC watched closely but on the whole kept out of. What followed was the work of the politicians themselves.

'Vile humours' of all sorts had in fact been building up in the bodies of the parties since the winter, and the difficult outcome of Bonomi's first crisis in November had given a foretaste of how hard the reconciliation of North and South, State and CLNs, Left and Right, would be when the moment came. In its style the post-liberation confrontation was in fact very similar to every other government crisis in the history of unified Italy to this day: a long-drawn out series of manoeuvres, conducted by diehard professional politicians far removed from the press of the country's most urgent daily problems, with as its outcome a delicate, temporary compromise loftily phrased to allow each participating group to take from it what it wished according to its own interests and intentions.

In its substance, however, the transition from Bonomi to Parri was a far more serious and significant moment in contemporary Italian history than the unedifying intrigues accompanying it seemed to imply. On the solution of the fundamental problems of reconciliation just mentioned each major party had a distinct series of views (though these revolved round methods, not specific proposals), first set out in the North in a series of letters exchanged between them from November 1944 onwards. Put very briefly – in the order the letters were issued – the Action Party stated that at the centre of all preoccupations should be the reconstruction of the State, creating new autonomous regional and communal bodies for the revitalization of grass-roots democracy; the Communist Party agreed, adding though that this new democracy ought to be based on the diffusion of the CLN principle and on the new 'mass organisations of a unitarian nature (trade union organisations, women's organisations, professional organisations, and so on)', which in fact the PCI was already constructing. When the Partito Socialista Italiano di unità proletaria (PSIUP) socialists gave their views, the first Bonomi government had fallen and been reconstructed – without the CLNs or the Socialists, and in spite of specific hopes that they would contribute. This meant that the Communist proposals were unrealistic, according to the Socialist analysis, and so the only hope lay in stimulating the Left forces themselves, in particular the working class. As usual in this period, the PSIUP thus placed itself to the Left of the PCI. The major conservative parties, the Christian Democrats and the Liberals, replied in February. Their comments, though separate, had much in common, and largely concen-trated on criticizing the positions and behaviour of the Left: they rejected the notion that the CLNs had an intrinsic merit which would justify continuing their lives beyond the insurrectionary period, and stated that political activity should be based on the interplay between a majority and an opposition. This would give rise to an 'evolutive order', and there were severe warnings against the risk of an unconstitutional coup d'état. The Liberals distinguished themselves as the most conservative element in the spectrum by praising the role of the crown in the current situation and embracing the dream of a return to the classic night-watchman State of the nineteenth century.[34]

However, a series of factors were missing in this range of analyses. The international situation and the role of the Allies were ignored, as was the need for an economic dimension to these visions; in particular, says the historian Franco Catalano, 'hardly anyone gave a thought to the peasants, who still formed the majority in what was essentially an economically underdeveloped country.' Even less attention was given in these debates to the real situation of the country at the end of the war, the 'devastated, hungry, frantic land' which one of Tito's lieutenants, Milovan Djilas, had seen on a visit there. In reality when the long-awaited contact finally came in Rome at the end of May, little serious attention was paid to the grand objectives stated in the 'five letters debate', so called: they were seen as fundamental to each party's identity, rather than as ends round which to organize political action. With the great fear of revolutionary chaos and upheaval abating, the party leaders concentrated instead on the cause dearest to their hearts, which was the consolidation of the position of the parties themselves, their machinery, propaganda, electoral prospects and alliances. Seen from this perspective the man most likely to succeed appeared to be Alcide De Gasperi, the Christian Democrat leader, with his links to the Vatican, his potential mass base of Catholic voters and his distinguishing 'sense of the State'. It was to this figure that Togliatti increasingly directed his attention after the liberation, insisting – in line with his very first statements on returning from Moscow – that anti-Fascist and popular unity was as necessary as ever, and meant seeking the basis for a long-term collaboration between the Communist and Christian Democrat parties. Nenni, not to be outdone, began rapidly moving his position to the Right during the crisis, hoping to emerge as a mediating prime minister. But he was disappointed.[35]

In Rome the CLNAI demanded action on the purge, on reconstruction, on agrarian reform, on a non-nationalistic foreign policy, as well as moves towards the recognition of the moral and political authority of the CLNs.[36] This was one set of one political demands. Another was that discussed at the party leaders' meeting of 1–2 June. This mentioned the return to legality, the commitment of the parties to the relaxation of political tension, the 'needs of production and social justice', anti-Fascist unity and the 'historical' role of the CLNs. But the underlying political issue was expressed quite differently by Allied observers and their interlocutors among the parties:

> Representatives of the Right and Centre parties state, privately if not in public, that the Socialist-Communist block aims at creating a one-party State, the hallmark of dictatorship [said a high-level PWB report of July]. To permit the Left to come to power would be equivalent to signing their own death warrants. Consequently the political activities of right and centre are directed primarily towards preventing the Left from extending its control.
>
> The Left parties consider they have majority backing, especially in the North. They are determined to obtain that position of power and responsibility which they believe is due to them. In the event of this being denied, certain elements are prepared to use non-constitutional and violent means. Any criticism made of their activities or curb placed upon them, is apt both in conversation and in their Press to be branded as a relic of Fascism to be done away with.[37]

Ambassador Kirk's worries over the dangers of a civil war between the forces of the 'State', represented by the Christian Democrats and Liberals, and the 'People', symbolized by the Socialists and Communists, should be considered in this context. They reflect the fact that the struggle was not 'simply' between freedom and totalitarianism, as Churchill would have it, but, in A. Giobbio's words, 'between those forces created and brought forward by the Resistance, and those belonging to the old political class, those whose very existence was defined by raisons d'Etat'. In this situation it was inevitable – given the constantly reiterated premises of Allied policy in favour of the constitutional State – that a party like the Liberal Party should be considered 'the key to the situation' by the Foreign Office on the now reopened institutional question, and thought to have 'views . . . very much in line with our own' when it put the choices in terms of totalitarianism versus liberty.[38] Yet in mid-1945 this was still not enough to guarantee a total convergence of thought and action between 'the moderates' and the British and Americans, as the evolution of the political situation would soon demonstrate. Neither did the lugubrious pre-civil war atmosphere of the months after the liberation suffice to prompt the Allies to undo some of the effects of the international stalemate, or to aid Parri on his impossible path between the hopes of the Left for a new democratic *method* (not programme), and the suspicion of the conservative parties and the Roman bureaucracy.[39] Togliatti chose to sacrifice all – including the new method and the reform of the State – to the preservation of unity at the summit between the main anti-Fascist currents. To what extent these sacrifices – reminiscent of the clandestine period – were conditioned by the *growing* hostility to the PCI, especially in an international climate of ideological polarization which the party had not foreseen, remains to be investigated.[40] While the Socialist Party was already being seen by some observers as the second largest after the Christian Democrats, the Action Party, which had made institutional reform a reason of life, now had its moment after leading the attack on Pietro Nenni's candidacy as prime minister.[41]

In June a new all-party government finally emerged after weeks of slow-motion political grappling, headed by the Resistance and Action Party leader Ferruccio Parri. This was the first post-Fascist government of the entire nation, and it contained the leaders of the three strongest parties, the Socialist Nenni, the Communist Togliatti and the Christian Democrat De Gasperi, under a man of the northern Resistance whose moral authority could not be contested.[42] While the monarchy and the Right wailed – 'this is not a change of government in Italy, it is a change of regime,' Orlando told Kirk – cautious satisfaction and considerable relief prevailed in AFHQ and the capitals. 'We have got what promises to be a good Italian government and we must try to help that government weather the storms ahead,' said a Foreign Office official commenting favourably on Parri's plans for the reform of local government and attempting to discourage the Americans from imposing their own.[43] Allen Dulles, head of the OSS in Switzerland, expressed the feelings of many when he said that Parri was 'a man of courage and principle, modest and unassuming to a degree that is almost a fault in a Prime Minister. . . . As a politician he is probably a novice, and I question whether he will prove to be ruthless enough to grapple with the difficult situation facing him. However, you can count on his honesty and fundamental friendship for us.[44]

But not even Parri's most enthusiastic Anglo-American supporters, the Left-liberal press, could disguise the overwhelming difficulties the new prime minister faced, and while such papers as the *Christian Science Monitor* concentrated on the need to rush aid and supplies to the new government, others stood back and surveyed the depressing picture which remained after 21 months of Allied liberation and occupation.

'Nobody wants a job that carries responsibility without power and depends on outside powers who don't know what they want,' Anne McCormick wrote in the *New York Times* in a long feature article on the appearance of 'Generale Maurizio' (Parri's nom de guerre) in Italian politics. 'The Cabinets that have been functioning since the armistice of September 1943 were not governments at all, but local administrative instruments of Allied control. Now the whole country is liberated, but nearly half the territory is still under military government, and the rest is only nominally under Italian rule.' The armistice remained unpublished, and the country was without economic power or resources: 'Italy has no ships, no material for reconstruction, no access to Lend-Lease, no assistance from UNRRA except to a limited number of children and displaced persons.'[45]

The long silence of the British press on Italy's problems, understandably complained of by Carandini, was broken by the *Manchester Guardian*, which in a substantial editorial explained why Italy's predicament carried implications hardly less far-reaching than the British general election itself:

In Greece we interfered to stop a revolution, with the result (which no doubt the government did not intend) that we have put back reaction in its place. In Italy, more complex and more important, the issue is still in doubt. But for many Europeans, and especially perhaps, for the Russians, this will be seen as a test-case. Shall we and the Americans (for they are also responsible) allow the new forces in Italy, Republican, progressive, even revolutionary, to go their own way or shall we again intervene (no doubt from the best of motives) on the side of reaction?[46]

Disappointment inside the CLN structures was bitter. The regional president of the Lombardy CLNs, the Communist Sereni, told a CLN assembly: 'We have no governing power; our authority is [moral], and it is on that authority that we must base our action.' In later years the spectre of a fundamental missed opportunity began to appear. In 1965 the Communist leader Giorgio Amendola wrote that, '[After] the liberation there developed throughout the working class movement, including undeniably in the Communist Party too, a tendency to see as inevitable the dissolution of the CLNs, and to bet everything on the electoral game. From that there could come nothing but bitter disappointments. And come they did.' The former Action Party activist Vittorio Foa stated in 1973:

The mechanism by which the democratic and revolutionary energies of the Resistance were absorbed consisted in coopting at the top levels of the traditional State the men and forces of renewal. Instead of the national assembly of CLNs, requested by the Action Party to focus opposition to the pressures of the Allies and the reactionaries, we had the Parri Government, which in its construction consisted of a kind of stabilising influence since it coopted the Resistance in the highest levels of the conventional State.

The same was true of the preliminary, non-executive assembly known as the Consulta, which came into being in Rome at the end of September to plan the constitutional choice. Of its 400 members, 110 were recognized men of the northern Resistance; most of the rest were 'old anti-fascist ex-parliamentarians, of conservative and out-dated mentality', as the historian E. Piscitelli writes.[47]

Whatever the hopes of Allied reformers may have been, there was, in other words, still no sign of government by consensus, of government led by 'the moderates' based on 'a sensible programme of their own with popular appeal' even with a Resistance leader in power. 'We have granted freedom of speech and writing; we have ensured freedom from hunger; we have not ensured freedom from fear,' said the executive commissioner of AC in May:

Among the majority of the people the fear of Communism remains. Complete eradication of that fear may not be possible in the present political turmoil in men's minds. But it must be admitted that the two democratic Allies have stood by in this country and watched the spread of Communism and still more the spread of fear of Communism. We have failed adequately to present to the Italians the other alternative – a democratic way of life.[48]

Alexander was more specific; he warned of the mass of uncollected arms and mentioned areas, even in the South, where the local head of Carabinieri said that he could not guarantee security. Government measures to quell disturbances were inadequate, said Alexander; incidents kept recurring and the Allied command was seriously preoccupied:

> any further deterioration . . . is likely to have the most serious consequences. In this connection it should also be stated to the Italian Government that their ability to maintain law and order must inevitably be an important factor affecting any decision of the Allied Governments in regard to the return of further territory to Italian control.[49]

ONE AREA where territory would not soon be handed back to the Italian government was Venezia Giulia, where on 1 May Tito won by less than 24 hours the race to enter Trieste. It was, however, to the New Zealanders of the 15th Army Group that the Germans surrendered and the Allied troops immediately set out to occupy the militarily significant sections of the city – ports, roads, railways – while the Yugoslav army set up its own administration in the rest. This ambiguous overlap then spread to the rest of the region as other Allied forces marched north and east to the Austrian border, where Tito's men were also waiting for them. The tension was extreme: neither the Allies nor the Yugoslavs were willing to recognize the other's authority in the region, and there were heated exchanges at the highest levels on undertakings not honoured and promises not maintained. Alexander Kirk went so far as to compare Tito's posture to that of the Japanese prior to the Manchurian invasion, and Mussolini's pre-Abyssinia: the 'first act of postwar aggression' would be that of Yugoslavia, said Kirk. Macmillan in contrast thought of Greek precedents, implying that the problem was not 'no annexations', but 'no communist take-overs'.

As Alexander and his generals squared up to the possibility of a full-scale military confrontation on the issue, Tito insisted that the problem was exclusively political, and in fact it was hard to deny by the middle of May that Alexander had no longer any need of communication lines to Austria, since the Allied installation there was proceeding satisfactorily and had access to other supply routes. The question thus was reduced directly and unequivocally to the single point: whose authority would rule in Venezia Giulia?

There could be no question of installing AMG. Tito was setting up his own police force, popular tribunals and administrative organs, and to force AMG on to these would require the use of arms. The British ambassador in Belgrade, Stevenson, thought that the Yugoslavs would not go to extremes if they could avoid them, and a compromise on the arrangements along the Austrian border, where Allied forces were distinctly superior, seemed to bear him out. The most important element of doubt in Belgrade, according to the British ambassador, was the amount of Soviet support the Yugoslavs thought they could count on. In AFHQ it seemed that the only solution was to seek a purely tactical *modus vivendi*, but when this approach also failed – in spite of direct contacts with Tito suggesting a clear line of demarcation just east of Trieste – there could be no avoiding a full-scale international dispute. And that meant involving the two powers the British had hitherto wished to keep away from the problem, the United States and the U.S.S.R.

During the month of May therefore, while Allied troops mixed incongruously with the formidable elements of Tito's army and alarming reports began to accumulate of the methods used to establish full Yugoslav control over local society, a large-scale diplomatic and military front was established by the British and AFHQ, involving shifting troops to the area, arranging battle plans and support from Eisenhower, and enrolling the active support of Truman for an unequivocal stand. To what extent the Soviets were brought into the picture at this point has never been clear, but their silence on the issue was notable, and according to some historians was probably the decisive factor in the Yugoslav acceptance at the end of May of the demarcation line proposed by AFHQ, on condition that the forms of Yugoslav presence were maintained, especially on the level of civil administration. Only after this climb-down by Tito did Stalin make public his support of Yugoslav claims.

In June therefore two agreements were reached between AFHQ and the authorities of Belgrade defining the broad areas of responsibility and the operational details of the AMG which would be set up in Trieste and its environs west of the demarcation line. Essentially the intention was to instal an Allied system as already applied thoughout Italy, treating the Yugoslav presence in the same consultative and pragmatic way that the CLNs had been treated elsewhere, while undoing as far as possible their administrative effects. On 24 June AMG officers began to move in to start this process, and it appeared that the worst risks of a military clash had for the moment passed.

But the way forward was far from clear. From the local populations came news of serious dissatisfaction with this solution imposed from above, dissatisfaction which according to some military observers the Yugoslavs were sure to exploit with propaganda and underground activity. In Belgrade in fact there was no sign of any intention to relinquish the original objectives and there was outright resistance to Allied plans for the liquidation of the Yugoslav political and administrative innovations in Trieste. The June accords were not particularly clear in this area and there was plenty of room for tension and misunderstanding. Finally it was evident that these solutions could represent only a temporary blocking operation, and when, in a new message at the end of June, Stalin criticized Anglo-American actions and defended Tito's aims on the familiar ground of anti-Fascist merit, the British and Americans knew that there would have to be a settling of accounts at the highest level. In this way the Venezia Giulia issue was put on the agenda for the forthcoming Allied summit in Berlin itself, at the palace of Potsdam.

Two Italian representative bodies with a direct interest in the situation were particularly discomfited by all this. One was the Italian Communist Party which, while maintaining as far as possible its support for the 'advanced model of democracy' based on Italian-Slovene unity prevailing in Trieste, was finally forced to choose sides. The result was the creation of a Communist Party of the Giulian Region, with Italian and Slovene members, but whose purpose was the defence of popular democracy (not its diffusion), with reference to the situation in Italy. The territorial claims, said the local Communists, were entirely secondary to this priority, and in fact the party generally preferred not to take up a position on the prongs of the question's many merits.

The second focus of discontent was the Italian government, which found itself implacably and deliberately cut out of the entire process of decision. AFHQ and AMG hoped to freeze the state of affairs in Venezia Giulia so deeply that neither of the claimants in the dispute would appear favoured, therefore neither Carabinieri nor Tito's militia would patrol the streets, but a new force specially recruited and under Allied command. Even the AC was to be excluded, since it was seen as too closely bound up with the Rome government. Inevitably there were official protests, and the Council of Ministers complained of an 'unsatisfactory arrangement'. But AFHQ was not to be deterred, and while the legal system would be based on Italian law up to the surrender of 1943, no subsequent additions would be applied. AMG's rule, largely improvised on the spot beyond the basic guidelines, would be total. It was yet another confirmation that even after the full liberation of the country, the last word in Italy still rested with the 'rescuing powers' and their military representatives.[50]

'ITALY is at the parting of the ways,' wrote Admiral Stone in a comprehensive balance sheet on the liberation which appeared at the end of June 1945 and circulated extensively in the various levels of Anglo-American control. On the one hand there was her catalogue of miseries: political fragmentation, a million men in exile as slave labour or as prisoners-of-war, half a million refugees, financial and economic disruption, a total lack of productive tools and resources, the threat of several millions unemployed, the arms illegally held everywhere. On the other there lay the possible consequences: 'if present conditions long continue, Communism will triumph – possibly by force,' Stone pronounced.

Stone's analysis represented a further important milestone in the evolution of Anglo-American awareness of Italy's problems. It illustrated the ideological premises of policy in the new phase (rooted in anti-Communism), as well as an active and coherent programme of mediation for the reconstruction period. For Stone there could no longer be any question of harping on the theme of 'working her passage'; the Italians had actively supported the Allies with their armed forces[1] and with their Resistance movement, and they had demonstrated clearly that they were 'willing to abandon totalitarianism and work for the same freedoms as the Allies who liberated them.' But without a measure of 'help and guidance from the democracies', there was a real risk that fear would combine with lingering humiliation and the emptiness of deprivation to drive the country into the arms of 'the group of "police" states, united by Communism, which is extending westward from Russia.' Historical and moral considerations only added to the material interests at stake, in Stone's vision, and an 'expression of positive policy by the US and UK Governments' was now urgently needed so that the process of constructing a credible partner, 'however lowly', in the post-war structure of international security might begin.

To regain national self-respect and some strategic usefulness, Stone recommended that the armed services be returned to Italian control and strengthened (especially in their internal security capacity). To begin reconstruction, a new Allied economic organization was needed and an assured and immediate supply of raw materials and coal, with financing to be guaranteed by extensive credits. Last but not least there was to be 'the education of the minds of the Italians towards a democratic way of life.[2]

To most of those interested in Italy it was clear that only one power had the means to translate a programme such as that outlined by the chief commissioner into effective reality; the only question still open was whether American public opinion and the American administrative machine were prepared to assume such formidable, open-ended responsibilities. Harold Alexander, now supreme Allied commander, began a single-handed campaign of exhortation.

'SAC is deeply concerned re future of Italy,' Kirk reported in the middle of June; '[he] feels that if Americans are going to withdraw entirely from this country there is all the more reason why Britain must remain here longer and urge the U.S. to continue to give substantial economic assistance to Italy.' Alexander repeated the message in a visit to the Foreign Office two weeks later. 'He thought it most important to get the U.S. well embedded in Italy.' the minutes record, 'and he agreed that it did not matter from the British point of view allowing the U.S. to take the lead, more particularly in economic matters.'[3] Macmillan, who was leaving the theatre, took the same line: the only real hope of influence was through economic means and the Americans would have to be encouraged to take over the direction of affairs. But Churchill thought the chances of such a change less than even: 'Their desire to get out of Europe will lead to their taking the easiest course, whether towards Italy or towards Russia,' he commented gloomily on Macmillan's observations.[4] The overall ends of course remained much the same, and could be summed up by the Foreign Office without effort:

> Briefly we want to show that aggression does not pay but once Italy has made just amends we do not want to humiliate or weaken her unduly. We hope to restore her to the position of a second-class power incapable of further aggression but able, in case of need, to hold her own against her neighbours.[5]

But if American opinion was to realize the dangers and pick up its own share of the burden, a new level of persuasion was called for.

The results of such deliberations soon became clear. By the middle of June the British had shifted strategy towards the framing of choices on Italy in the starkest ideological terms. The Foreign Office, Macmillan and Churchill were all agreed: the real issue inside the country was no longer an 'institutional' one, monarchy versus republic, but was a battle between totalitarianism and democracy, between the threat of a Communist police state and the hope of liberal democracy on the Anglo-American model. The problem was that the means by which this struggle of values and ideals was to be fought were strictly secular, and it was Churchill himself who impressed on Lord Halifax in Washington the need to get raw materials and aid into Italy in order to underpin a series of manoeuvres he was planning around the institutional question and the problem of elections, each designed to 'encourage moderate elements' and deter the Communists. All this, said Churchill, so that Italy might become a strong Western-style democracy, 'uninfluenced in her internal affairs by the activities of any foreign power.'[6]

The leading Italian representative in America, the ambassador Tarchiani, began his own indefatigable campaign for support from the U.S. against the Left, even before the Bonomi government officially resigned on 12 June. Tarchiani's frame of reference was Europe as a whole, and in conversation with W. Phillips, a special assistant to the secretary of state (and ex-ambassador to Italy), he warned that if Italy should fall under Soviet domination, the Allies would be left without a single true friend in the entire Continent. Fear was spreading, said Tarchiani, particularly fear that the Anglo-Saxon powers were no longer greatly interested in the welfare of the Italian people. Europe was divided between the British and the Russians, and while Italy fell within the British sphere, she was aware that 'Britain could be of very little help to Italy at this time financially or otherwise and there was no-one else to whom Italy could turn except the United States.' Now, for instance, as crisis threatened the government and a Socialist-Communist regime appeared just round the corner, the attitude of the U.S. might have a considerable influence on the outcome of the political struggle, said the ambassador. As the historian Enzo Collotti has written, it was an open invitation to the Americans to intervene in the formation of the first post-liberation government.[7]

Certain sections of American opinion were indeed prepared to pick up the ball of freedom and independence for Italy, but they flung it first of all not at the Russians, but at the astonished British. 'In no part of Europe has our recent policy been more inept, and less calculated to advance the interests [of a nation], than in Italy,' boomed Sumner Welles from the columns of the *New York Herald Tribune*. 'We have acquiesced in the grotesque course pursued by the British Government. Affairs in Italy are involved in a vicious circle.' For Welles the only solutions could be economic ones, combined with the evacuation of troops to permit early elections. Walter Lippmann used this text as a basis for his own characteristically perceptive comments: British policy, he said, 'gives the impression of being an effort to maintain the control of Italy though Britain has not the means to make Italy a livable and workable national economy.' Urging a revision of the American official line, Lippmann asked why, 'the British with our support retain control of Italy and put off making peace.'[8]

But the inhabitants of the upper floors of the State Department were not yet in a position to carry out a plan of strategic, structural intervention in Italy, as demanded implicitly by these pressures. Truman responded positively to suggestions by his acting secretary of state Joseph Grew in the middle of June that a 'more vigorous and realistic treatment' of the problems of political and economic planning for Italy were required. According to Grew this should revolve round the civilianization of AC 'with a more dynamic American participation', the easing of the armistice terms and the preparation of local elections. The most concrete plan, however, came from the new secretary, James Byrnes, who submitted a plan at the beginning of

July for the continued presence of five Allied divisions, not including those in Venezia Giulia.[9]

But did the new administration possess the political force or will to fight the domestic battles which would inevitably ensue from any decision to leave troops in Italy? That was the key question of the moment raised by the Byrnes memorandum, and its real weight had been demonstrated in advance when another, similar commitment had come up for debate, namely whether or not Italy should participate in the United Nations conference of San Francisco. According to the Yalta agreements Italy was to be entirely excluded. But political factors inside Italy which had been latent in February now began to appear much more substantial and suggested a general shift in strategy on America's part. At the time Kirk had pressed for an invitation to Italy in order to enhance the government's prestige, and hence help to 'ensure continuity against the day when the North will be liberated' and this theme was taken up by a State Department committee at the end of April which decided to reopen the question of immediate participation, out of a desire to 'support the moderate and democratic elements represented in the Government at Rome at a time when the heavy responsibilities of the north's liberation will fall upon it.'[10] But the administration was not able to overcome the opposing pressures of the Italo-American groups on the one hand, anxious to see Italy a member of the United Nations, and the cold hostility of the British on the other.

The conference itself produced no surprises, but the State Department put the Federal Bureau of Investigation on the trail of the Russian delegation in order to discover what the Soviet attitude might be towards Italy, and finding by this and other means that the Russians might be favourable to a change in Italy's status, the Department now felt emboldened to plan a unilateral declaration of intent, prior to the planned meeting of the Big Three in Potsdam and regardless of British objections. Once again Italy, though not admitted to the U.N. deliberations, was furnishing the occasion for a significant shift in the relationship between the three principal members of the anti-Hitler coalition.[11]

If Italy was a passive object in these disputes and was unable to intervene practically in any substantial way, one reason was that her foreign policy was wholly uncoordinated and submissive in its essence. While Tarchiani was exalting the indispensable supremacy of America in Italy's future, his opposite number in London, Count Carandini, was courting the British in almost identical fashion. 'My people, as you know, are more sensitive to British opinion than any other,' Carandini wrote to Eden, pleading for some minimal constructive attention to Italy's sacrifices from Great Britain. It was Mussolini who had dragged Italy into war against England, said Carandini ('They didn't need much dragging,' Eden growled), but the contributions and changes which had come about since then were completely ignored: 'never has the reform of a nation been so little appreciated or encouraged,'

Carandini lamented, and the continuing opposition of public opinion was demonstrated 'by the systematic absence in the press of any information throwing light on any aspect of our collaboration and on Italy's rebirth.' With the definite exclusion of the country from San Francisco, Italian fighters were asking what the effort had been worth, said Carandini.[12]

What remained to be seen was whether pressures and arguments and analyses of this kind, which found an easy echo in many levels of Anglo-American decision-making, would produce results: a change in Italy's status, any even minimal abrogation of the armistice regime. For Americans there was the additional problem of deciding consciously whether, in the first place, the Parri government was an interim one consonant with their designs and worth supporting as such, and secondly, how to approach what might come after it. The British on the other hand had yet to become aware that circumstances had already settled what Alexander had presented as a free choice, namely the handing over of 'the lead' in Italy to the United States. The denizens of Whitehall continued to believe that they could, with effort, draw on American support to sustain their own national policies in Europe, and they continued to look at Italy's external and internal torments mainly in this light. As the last great tripartite conference of the war loomed up, starting-positions for the first phase of the post-war era were already being marked out.

Potsdam

THE AMERICAN PROPOSAL for Italian entry into the United Nations seemed a modest one when compared with the other weighty matters listed in the various agendas presented at Potsdam. Even after days of wrangling between the Big Three and their foreign ministers over it, it still seemed a minor problem to Secretary of State Byrnes, who wearily summed up what had happened during the course of the historic meeting:

the United States had offered its proposal originally in order to give some confidence to Italy. We had asked only for a declaration that the Three Powers support the entry of Italy into the United Nations Organization. The British Delegation had asked that we include neutrals and we had agreed. Then the Soviet Delegation expressed opinions with regard to the Franco Government of Spain and in the hope of getting an agreement we had added to the declaration that we would not support the entry of the Franco Government into the United Nations Organization. Then the Soviet Delegation had asked for the inclusion of the paragraph concerning Rumania, Hungary, Bulgaria and Finland and we had agreed to that. Then the Soviet Delegation had asked that the paragraph regarding Italy be modified to accord with the language used in reference to the other satellite states and we had agreed to that. Unfortunately, we found that if we agreed with the Soviet Delegation, the British Delegation did not agree; if we agreed with the British Delegation, the Soviet Delegation disagreed. It was now up to the Soviet and British Delegations to see if they could get together. If not, we would withdraw our modest request for the entry of Italy into the United Nations Organization.[13]

In reality the original American proposal had been considerably more complex than Byrnes suggested. Even before the opening formalities had been completed Truman had read out a position paper on Italy which outlined among other things, a plan for an interim agreement with Italy. Under this working arrangement, the short armistice and the 'obsolete' clauses of the long surrender document would have been abolished, to be replaced by certain undertakings of good conduct from Italy and a minimal form of Allied control related solely to military operations. The reaction of Truman's colleagues at Potsdam heralded a tough struggle. Stalin declared that the Italian problem was inseparable from that of the other ex-satellites; '[it] would be well,' said Stalin, 'in improving the position of Italy if they would also improve the position of the other satellite states and throw them all together.'[14]

Churchill set out on a daring path of oscillation. When the Americans threatened to treat Italy well, the Italians became in the prime minister's eyes 'dastardly' and 'lawless' people who had attacked Britain when she was alone and were therefore to be punished. When Stalin looked like carrying this line to the point of clubbing the Italians together with such marginal and undesirable races as the Bulgarians, the Finns, the Romanians and the Hungarians, then Italy became the first power to surrender, the country which had signed the harshest armistice and which had then done most to redeem herself in battle with the Germans.

The first of these tendencies appeared as soon as Truman presented his plan. The familiar indictment was read again and the verdict was clear: the Italian people were as guilty as the Germans under Hitler. 'Nevertheless,' said Churchill grudgingly, the British 'had endeavoured to keep alive the idea of the renewal of Italy as one of the important powers in Europe and the Mediterranean.' Churchill insisted that no peace treaty could be signed until a democratic government had been elected, but his concern for constitutionality, which had its own purposes, was subordinate to another much more fundamental objection to interim treatment, the essence of the British position *'If* [the British] *lost their existing rights under the surrender in the interval, they would not have the power to secure the peace to which they were entitled.'* Churchill declared himself entirely uninterested in Bulgaria, which he portrayed as having a political record quite as bad as Italy's.[15]

By the time of the Eighth Plenary Session, seven days after the conference had opened, deadlock on the separability of Italy from the other ex-satellites had become near-total, with the Russians insisting that Romania, Bulgaria, Hungary and Finland must not in any case be treated worse than Italy. The question of the extent of recognition necessary before treaties could be signed almost came down to an argument over percentages, when Churchill said that Italy had been 90 per cent recognized by Britain, and the Anglo-Americans had already introduced a new political element into the contest by claiming that because the Rome government contained representatives of the six principal political parties of the country, it was more democratic than that of any of the satellites except Finland (where elections had already taken place), and therefore deserving of better treatment. At this point Churchill's prejudices came down in favour of the Italian contribution to the war effort; Italian forces of all sorts had given 'a great measure of help', said the prime minister. But this tactic failed, and the exchanges soon deteriorated into a squabble over which powers had most rights of access in the territories liberated by the others.[16] Only when Churchill suggested that treaties be prepared 'for' the satellite countries rather than 'with' them, was a breakthrough achieved, though the question of Italy's precise position with respect to the other ex-satellites was no clearer than before, and had to be sent on in the end for consideration by the new Council of Foreign Ministers created by the Conference.[17]

The American line remained consistent throughout the conference and was not thrown off track by the question of concessions from Italy. For the U.S. no concessions were required, least of all concessions in the form of reparations as the Russians now demanded. In its planning the State Department had not even seriously considered the possibility that Italy might pay reparations, and as Byrnes now made clear, America was not pouring hundreds of millions of dollars into the country through one door to see them exit through another in the form of reparations to Russia. Since the Russians failed to clarify whether they wished to take their compensation from current production or from war surplus or how, the Americans were able to push home their economic advantage and block the Russian demand.[18] But they were not so fortunate on the political level. When the Soviet delegation attempted to link the Balkan satellites with Italy on the treaty question, the U.S. representatives replied by pressing for action to implement the Yalta Declaration on Liberated Territories in Bulgaria, Romania and elsewhere. Though Truman insisted that the overall aim was still to see democracy installed in the defeated countries of Europe, the ambitious plans for tripartite structures of control had, by this time, been almost entirely abandoned and had been replaced by more modest demands for the control of elections, access of the press and freedom for Control Commissions. Since these questions were subordinate in American minds to the far greater issues of Germany, Poland and the Pacific, there was no particular discontent over the lack of satisfaction obtained; no one believed that definitive solutions were being imposed. The Council of Foreign Ministers could perhaps be imagined as a safety-valve for undissolved tension on such issues. As the Potsdam meeting drew to a close, the Americans fell back on their original starting point – Italian admission to the U.N. – and with the new British Labour ministers falling in behind, agreed to postponement.[19]

If the Soviets had wished to maintain Italy as a power in a weak and humiliated position, they could almost consider the conference a success. Although they had failed to get any of the $600 million over six years which they suggested as a suitable reparations payment (ignoring the fact that under the armistice, the Italians were paying the Allies for their occupation), they had succeeded in blocking American moves in Italy's favour and had ruthlessly played on the uncertainties of the British caused by the change of government during the conference. At the opening of the meeting Stalin had instructed Churchill that in Italy's case 'it would be incorrect to be guided by the remembrance of injuries. The feeling of revenge, hatred or the desire for redress was a bad adviser in politics. He said it was not for him to teach, but he thought he should be guided in politics by the weighing of forces.'[20] Attlee received different advice: 'he should not forget what Italy had done to Britain', and the new prime minister promised not to forget.[21]

The old protests that Moscow was excluded from effective participation in the control of Italy were studiously renewed by Molotov in his meetings with Byrnes and Eden, but since they had not been heard for some considerable time, the British and American foreign ministers were able to pretend that they were a complete novelty. Molotov obtained some satisfaction in an apology from Eden and Byrnes for the lack of consultation at the time of Macmillan's new directive of February, but the Russian complaint was pressed no further. Similarly the Moscow Declaration of 1943 went without mention, and there was no reference as there had been at Yalta to the role of anti-Fascist forces in political reconstruction. Stalin, it seemed, had finally consigned Italy to the Western bloc, though he was not prepared to see her go without a determined rear-guard action of spoliation and entanglement.[22]

Because the Big Three 'took the world so unerringly into new hostilities,' says Charles Mee Jr. in a recent study on Potsdam, the conference has always been considered 'a "failure",' and therefore a minor episode in international diplomacy. Mee's own account refutes this reading and portrays three men 'who were intent upon increasing the power of their countries and of themselves and who perceived that they could enhance their power more certainly in a world of discord than of tranquillity.'[23] Mee supplements this classical balance-of-power interpretation by suggesting that the anti-Communism of the American executive offered the only 'saleable rationale' available to an interventionist ruling group confronted with a non-interventionist public opinion, and illustrates how Potsdam also marked the definitive eclipse of the Big Three in favour of face-to-face negotiations by the new Big Two.[24]

Although these observations are more clearly applicable to such issues as Poland, Germany and Japan, they also have relevance to Italy's treatment at the conference and afterwards. Mee depicts American intentions with respect to the Italian problem as being simply to 'neaten up [her] western sphere of influence and have it recognized.' Although such a purely formal interest might explain in part why the American executive was unable to translate is ambitious plans for reconstruction into deeds, it neglects certain factors in the complex network of constraints in which American relations with Italy moved by this time. Besides the opposing internal pressures from isolationists on the one hand and Italo-Americans on the other, there was the problematic relationship with the British. Resistance to British strategy in Europe was beginning to take more concrete form in Washington.

The State Department had already drawn up two long papers on the British decline and the British ideas for a Western European bloc under her own control, and came to conclusions which were not in Britain's favour in either case. As Joseph Davies, Truman's first emissary to London, told Churchill openly:

> there are many who believe that England, finding now no great rival power in Europe to offset the new rising power of Russia, would try to use American manpower and resources to support the classic British policy of 'leading' Europe.[25]

When Alexander returned to Caserta from Potsdam he was greeted by an unprecedented open challenge from the American representatives on exactly how the British intended to live up to their Italian responsibilities. On the one hand, said Kirk and his colleagues, the British

> wished to keep Italy from falling into Communism or Soviet influence and wished to win Italy's friendship but on the other were determined that Italy should be made to learn [the] price of war. We added that if Italy was to be a 'bulwark' against [the] police state (one of Churchill's expressions which SAC has used frequently) it should be decided here and now what the 'bulwark' was to be.

It was an unusual discussion, not least because the British side were forced to articulate what, in their views, the options in Italy might be.

> SAC said that to him there seemed to be three alternatives open to Allies: (one) a completely and permanently subjugated Italy (two) an Italy even though a second class power strong enough to give west time to mobilize itself against east and (three) a compromise, i.e. an Italy with small army, low armament potential and deliberately kept in suspense as to whether her place is in sun or shadow.

For Alexander the consequences of options one and three were much too serious for those lines to be pursued:

> He went on to say that even if we start now it will take many years to build up a second class Italy and it might be too late by 1950 to treat her in a kind-hearted manner. A compromise by which an attempt is made to combine punishment, threats, indecision and eventual hope of reward appeared to him too reminiscent of Hebrew theology. Today Europe thinks and acts quickly. No donkey allows prospect of amorphous carrot five years distant in space to influence its reactions to present. On what we do now will depend whether Italy goes left or right, and on how our ideology, which at moment is both incoherent and very badly propagated, is [organized] to permeate this country. In his opinion the short term measures which are now being proposed by us will only bring bewilderment, irritation and unemployment on a scale which will undoubtedly force country even more to left.

Alexander had always been in favour of returning to Italy the control of certain colonies and he repeated this view once again, 'even though he was fully aware of difficulties to handing back places in which British fomented revolts in desert in '40–'41.' As for economic problems, the supreme Allied commander was convinced that the real danger came not from poverty but from overcrowding. This was the special economic problem which in an intelligent peace treaty would be correlated – in SAC's eyes – 'with a clear perception of her place in [the] economic and strategic framework of the new Europe.'[26]

In a similar conversation prior to Potsdam (and the British elections), Alexander had offered a most unusual key to understanding why the British had always been so repressively hostile to Italy:

> 'the nigger in the woodpile' [sic] was Eden who apparently had not yet heard that Mussolini is dead and is no longer running Italy. He asserted that highest officials of [the Foreign Office] acknowledged that Eden was most unreasonable on subject of Italy and indeed almost psychopathic.[27]

Alexander felt that in the crucial decisions Churchill had always over-ridden Eden and supported the American position. But with Churchill gone the problems would be even greater: 'now that Winston is out there is no-one in Britain to take [the] lead in Italy', Alexander remarked gloomily. 'I hope your people will do it. They must be made to realize what a terribly important responsibility it is and that we cannot get away from it.' In particular SAC urged that the U.S. take the initiative immediately for a peace treaty.

The Potsdam conference left open the question of the Russians and their disturbing attempt to legitimize the arrangements they were setting up in central Europe by means of a shotgun marriage between the countries involved and the hapless Italian ex-enemy. In terms of its effect on the relationship of the wartime Allies with Italy, this was in many ways the most significant development of the entire conference. Because it linked Italy's future directly to the state of collaboration between the Big Three, the blight and hostility spreading at the general level inevitably conditioned the particular fate of the Italian peace treaty and consequently most other aspects of Italy's treatment. The potential for Russian and Communist advantage in this tactic had already been guessed in April when the reopening of the monarchy question by Togliatti in the spring had been interpreted by Admiral Stone as a Russian move to reacquire rights of consultation on Italy (as allowed in the Yalta agreements) in order to offset Anglo-American desires for consultation on Polish and Romanian questions. The important point is not that this view of Togliatti's move was correct – no available evidence supports it – but that the disruptive possibilities of such a Russian strategy with respect to Anglo-American freedom in Italy were clearly acknowledged. Most of Alexander's colleagues tended to agree with him when he said that the eventual treaty must not allow Russia equal rights in Italy with the U.S. and the U.K., 'even if that brings similar rights in the Balkans, as the bad effect in Italy would far outweigh any fleeting advantage we would get in the Balkans.[28]

When this approach was applied to the Venezia Giulia problem the result was deadlock. At Potsdam the issue, far from being resolved or even analysed on its merits, had simply become one of the lumps of mud the erstwhile allies flung at each other in their rounds of mutual recrimination. The general division of Europe into rigidly defined spheres of influence which Potsdam sanctioned was reproduced in miniature in Trieste, where over the following months the temporary military demarcation line would gradually turn into the southern terminus of the Iron Curtain.

Each side spent the summer consolidating its hold in its respective zones north and east of Trieste, and in accusing the other of maltreatment of the population under its control. The Yugoslavs accused the Allied military of frustrating the popular will by not holding local elections (refused by AFHQ on the grounds of the general instability); the British and the Americans put a great deal of effort into an only partially successful attempt to document the arrests, deportations and killings reportedly carried out by Yugoslav forces during their occupation in May and June. Above all AFHQ worried over the constant waves of anti-Allied propaganda, strikes and 'terrorist activity' which plagued their zone, and took precautions against a sudden Yugoslav onslaught west of the demarcation line. The Belgrade government for its part expressed astonishment that the Allies should go to such lengths to defend the territory and prerogatives of their own ex-enemy, and protested that in making lists of alleged Yugoslav war crimes they were simply playing into the hands of Italian ex-Fascists. By the end of the year the deadlock was almost total, with AMG dug in and governing its zone directly on a semi-permanent basis.[29]

Venezia Giulia and Potsdam's outcome were just two of the reasons why there could be no talk of a preliminary peace treaty in the second half of 1945. The result was that each of the major powers interested in the country found itself seeking space for independent unilateral or bilateral approaches on the major questions. The American plan for an interim settlement was not dropped altogether, instead it was transformed into a complex 'Civil Affairs Agreement', and it was the birth and development of this document which dominated Anglo-American discussions on Italy's formal status during the autumn and winter months of that year. The Italians groaned and protested at the delays and continuing humiliations, but theirs was now just one element in a much more dramatic confrontation.

AFTER THE INITIAL RELIEF tension began to mount again in the country throughout the summer and autumn. To rumours that Russian officers were infiltrating northern Italy and 'at times donning civilian clothes in order to enter into contacts with Italian partisans', as a military intelligence report claimed, were added the ever more desperate cries of certain Italian circles who continued to sound the tocsin against the day when the Allied troops would finally withdraw. The American consul in Genoa reported that throughout the North, 'all of the people who have property or extensive financial interests' were afraid of 'violent action by Communist groups' if the removal of Allied forces was in any way precipitate.

The fear and hysteria spreading in the weeks after the liberation even touched the Socialist leader Nenni, who at the beginning of July added his voice to those pleading with the Allied authorities for the troops to stay, at least until national elections had been held. As Washington noted, Nenni had been publicly demanding withdrawal as soon as possible up to that moment.[30]

Although the Allied intelligence community in Italy put a great deal of effort into studying what Communist strategy and intentions might be, the general conclusions were invariably ambiguous, not least because its various components steadfastly refused to consider Italian Communist ideas and analyses in their own terms and in their own historical and social context, a tendency naturally reinforced by the all-pervading orthodoxy which saw the PCI as a mere front organization for the world strategy of the Kremlin (although at Potsdam and over the question of Trieste the Russian line was anything but favourable to the interests of the Communist Party in Italy). In the last analysis, of course, military men were bound to weigh forces and consider all contingencies according to their own capabilities and the estimated interests of their employers, but the diplomats and political advisers made only occasional efforts to offer a more profound view of what was happening inside Italy. In a long appreciation of the general situation in August, for example, the intelligence staff of AFHQ (which had its own civilian political advisers), covered almost every important political and economic problem, analysing the major parties one by one (and suggesting that in terms of electoral strength the order was probably Christian Democrats, Socialists, Communists), and the specific political tendencies of each region. The dangers posed by serious food shortages were emphasized once again, with an unusual emphasis being placed on the need to restart the process of economic exchange between town and country. But the paper was oriented principally towards providing an estimate of security threats throughout the country, threats almost all connected in some way with the Communist Party.

Although the details had been fully provided in the infinite number of reports on the party drawn up by other Allied agencies, its history, structure, leadership and military potential were once again outlined. The essential element was, of course, the estimate of the party's likely line of action:

> There are no serious indications that the Communist Party intends or is capable of armed insurrection before the holding of elections. If, however, the elections should result in a narrow defeat for the Communists (and with them the Socialists and

perhaps the Action Party), a Communist coup d'état is possible but even so not likely unless by that time the Communists have achieved moral ascendancy over the Socialists. There is no sign of this at present. Communist policy appears to be long term rather than short term. In this it is likely to condone but not directly to promote local acts of lawlessness. It is likely also to encourage organised demonstrations and strikes when economic conditions afford the opportunity. If these should occur when neither the Communists nor Socialists were represented in the government, the general threat to security would be serious.

The corresponding measures of internal security proposed by AFHQ began with the recommendation that Anglo-American troops remain at least until elections had been held. The efficiency of the Italian army and police forces also required more urgent attention, it was noted, and AFHQ suggested that the five special combat groups of the Italian army which had accompanied the Allied advance should become 'an effective mobile force, purged of subversive elements and made capable of controlling local incidents as they occur.'[31]

THE IMMEDIATE PROBLEM arose of how to reconcile these demands – particularly the demand for a continued Anglo-American military presence – with the massive overall plans for demobilization, which to those involved seemed to be accumulating a momentum of their own in the late summer of 1945. For the Americans the correct line of action was indicated by what had happened to the British in Greece. The Chief of U.S. Naval Forces in Europe, Admiral Stark, on a tour of inspection in Italy in July, observed that 'had the British not gotten out of Greece, the bad situation which developed there might not have occurred and . . . it would have been cheaper in the long run to have kept troops there rather than taking them out and then having to come back to correct the bad situation which might have been prevented' (sic). The Americans well realized what the British meant when they referred to the 'solid Anglo-American front' in places like Greece and Italy, but as another American admiral pointed out, 'in the last analysis I believe that the British interests are so vital that they will see to it – with their own forces, if necessary, drawn from wherever they can get them – that any situation is controlled eventually to British satisfaction'.[32]

Just how accurate an estimation of British intentions this was the minutes of a high-level meeting in Whitehall at the end of August reveal. In the presence of the Chief of the Imperial General Staff (CIGS), Sir Alan Brooke, Ernest Bevin offered his own views on the Stone request for 5 divisions to remain in Italy, a request which Brooke saw as absolutely impossible. The new foreign secretary, who had already told a Labour Party conference that 'The British Empire cannot abandon its position in the Mediterranean. On the settlement of these countries much of the future peace of the world depends', now expressed very great concern 'lest our foreign policy should be hamstrung, as it had been in 1919 by the absence of sufficient British forces in the vital areas. Control of the Mediterranean [is] essential, and we must be in a position to be able to back our policy with force if trouble arose there.' Leaving aside for the moment the fact that those very elements of 'trouble' which Bevin feared were the Left parties which had greeted with mass demonstrations the election victory of the Labour Party in England,[33] the immediate problem was *how* the empire would make its dwindling weight felt in 'the vital areas'. The British chiefs of staff had already declared that the Stone proposal could not even be considered, such was its impracticability, and the CIGS now disclosed that at that moment there was available 'an overall strategic reserve of about two divisions,' which in any case were earmarked for trouble in the Middle East. However, the meeting chose to ignore the broader implications of this news, in particular that Bevin's strategy was quite without foundation, and fell back on another Stone suggestion, that of reinforcing the Italian police.[34]

In the State Department in contrast the conviction had become even more firmly rooted after Potsdam that the original American suggestion for a temporary 'civil affairs' working agreement constituted the only way to resolve the various conflicts and permit some form of continuous influence to be maintained. But there was much self-doubt. A member of the Southern European section of the State Department addressed a stern message to his colleagues at the beginning of August:

> In the face of his difficulties, we can only conclude that the Italian is an irrepressible optimist. But that optimism has been aided and abetted by encouraging statements from Allied capitals – particularly Washington – as well as by an appalling trust in Allied principles as purveyed to him by Allied propaganda. Italy, argues the Italian, is the one place in Europe where Anglo-American policy has had full play; therefore, it is the one place where Anglo-American policy towards Europe and the post-war world will prevail.

But beyond the abstract value of Italy as a testing area for the ideas of the peace, there were also certain concrete interests which could not be ignored. There was the conviction of the Italians that the nation had 'paid the price for her fascist sins' and was therefore entitled to full reinstatement – with her original colonies – in international politics. Then there were the 'permanently operating factors' of her 45 million population, and of her strategic situation in the Mediterranean which, in combination with the Italian character, had 'for some centuries now obtained for her an influence in world affairs wholly incommensurate with her meagre resources.'

Given such premises, a profoundly critical evaluation of American policy up to that moment could not be avoided:

> I fear that our thinking about Italy, now a primary peace theater, is still influenced by the fact that the Mediterranean was for so long a secondary war theater. American policy towards Italy has thus far been basically sound although it has never been put into effect. We have escaped the consequences of our failure to implement it only through a combination of circumstances which no longer exists. It is not now sufficient to continue our program of economic aid, and in fact to do so without a

definitive decision on political policy is to throw good money after bad. We must now decide if our policy is one which best serves the national interest and contributes to our future security and is therefore worthy of an all-out effort towards full implementation, or we must formulate a new policy adequate to meet the situation. These are not my views alone; they are shared by a majority of British and American officials in Italy, including Field Marshal Alexander, Mr. Harold Macmillan, Sir Noel Charles, Ambassador Kirk, and Admiral Stone.[35]

There is no evidence to suggest that the State Department functionaries would have acted any differently had they known that in worrying in this fashion, they were of course corresponding perfectly to the British design to get America 'embedded' in Italy.

BEFORE any further moves could be made for new initiatives or interim peace treaties, the Council of Foreign Ministers set up by the Potsdam conference had assembled in London and found the definitive peace treaty with Italy high on its agenda. The general background to the event could hardly have been less auspicious for an attempt to break the deadlock with the Russians which had emerged from Potsdam, and only a most exceptional diplomatic effort could by this time have bridged the gulf between the disposition of the Big Three and the daily situation as reported from much of northern Italy.

The breakdown of the Foreign Ministers' Conference after several weeks of increasingly bitter confrontation in London and Moscow therefore brought the American executive face to face with its own declarations of intent and its own prediction of disaster should the way remain blocked for political and economic succour. If the treaty itself could not provide a platform for a positive common approach to Italian problems, at least the removal of the armistice regime might allow unfettered unilateral action by the powers most interested in such an approach. Instead Bevin and Byrnes found Molotov more determined than ever to make no concessions on the position of Italy until the arrangements installed in Hungary, Bulgaria and Romania had received recognition and the promise of peace treaties, and from this nucleus of contention there spun off a long chain of exasperating difficulties.[36] Russian interest in the fate of the Italian colonies – reborn at Potsdam – was now interpreted as an attempt to reach uranium deposits in the Belgian Congo, and in addition there was a new claim for a share in the occupation and control of Japan, particularly embarrassing to the Americans in view of their own behaviour in Italy and their constant demands for representation in the Balkans.[37] When Byrnes finally reached an agreement with Stalin at the end of December, which saved face on both sides without providing any substantial changes in the principal countries under discussion, two and a half months had passed since the foreign ministers first met in conference; the Parri government had fallen and still there was no indication from Washington of what Italy's formal position in international relations was to be, nor even of when or how it might be decided.[38]

'With the opening of the London Conference, the Italian people had great hopes of an immediate settlement of Italy's status and that of her colonies,' a high-level British intelligence report declared. 'These hopes have now vanished, and it is generally felt here that the "Italian Question" [sic] has completely changed its complexion during the last few weeks and that it has been superseded by much vaster and farther reaching international political problems in which Italy is only a minor factor. . . . This has created bitter disappointment in all Italian circles.' The report added that the Communist Party was exploiting the general chaos, attacking the Western Allies and carrying out propaganda for Russia.[39] Stone too reported 'deep depression' in Italian government circles in his monthly report for September to the Advisory Council for Italy, and the reasons for the gloom were repeated to Noel Charles by Prunas, under-secretary at the Ministry of Foreign Affairs, who expressed open despair over the future of Italy's frontiers and colonies, as well as over the fact that the Americans had done little or nothing despite their many speeches and assurances.[40]

As these danger signals began to multiply, a crack appeared for the first time in the hard Whitehall face turned to Italy. To those who worried that 'our friends [might] be less and less inclined to continue the struggle' and who asserted that 'we must cease regarding Italy as a country outside the pale and try to treat her as any other friendly nation,' there came the timeworn refrain of the general contempt with which Italy was regarded by the British general public, of the efforts already made and, most telling of all, that Italy was not looked at with affection or appreciation as an ally, but was encouraged to turn to the West simply because it was in the West's interest so to do.[41] It was this line which had blocked an American suggestion in favour of Italy's participation in the foreign ministers' meeting, arguing that such a 'very dangerous' proposal would allow the Italians to leapfrog the Dominions and lesser allies such as Greece and Yugoslavia, as well as giving free rein to the Italian love of intrigue, which would most probably produce a 'free for all' at the very start of the meeting.[42] But by the beginning of November there was a marked change. The senior civil servants concerned discovered that:

> It seemed very undesirable for us to put ourselves in the position of wanting to treat the Italians more harshly than the Americans. Even if we subsequently withdrew from this position, once we let the Americans know that we had originally wanted to adopt it, this fact would certainly leak out and become known to the Italians and this would do us no good.

Hence they should be considered from this time on in the same light as the Belgians or the Dutch, for example, and it was now thought important that any working agreement covering the armistice regime should be negotiated and not imposed.[43]

The balancing of unilateral interests against the constraints and advantages of Two or Three Power collaboration now entered an unprecedented phase of delicacy and instability, a phase which was to cast long shadows over succeeding years. In Washington intense and momentous conflict dominated the treatment of every international issue, conflict inside the Truman administration, between the administration and Congress, and between the government and public opinion. With long-nurtured fervour, the protagonists of these struggles set about reducing the divers arguments to one simple, Manichean choice: collaboration or confrontation with the Soviet Union (hence *From Trust to Terror*, as Herbert Feis entitles his book on the years 1945–50). 'Much of the confusion which surrounded the formulation of American policy in the fall of 1945 stemmed from the fact that the Truman Administration had not yet committed itself to either point of view,' John Lewis Gaddis writes, adding that while the military and Congressional leaders had begun to press for 'a firmer approach to Moscow,' Truman and Byrnes had not yet abandoned all hope of reaching mutually convenient agreements with the Russians.[44]

Byrnes was disposed to recognize that American unilateralism in Japan was hard to differentiate from Russian operations in the Balkans, where, said Truman, legitimate Russian security interests did exist, but it was the president himself who in an important public pronouncement at the end of October reasserted the alternative, an outlook with far less accommodating implications: 'While in some cases it might not be possible to prevent forcible imposition of an unrepresentative regime on an unwilling people,' said Truman, 'the United States would never recognize any such agreement.'[45] An attitude based on these premises could only add to the difficulties of solving Italy's problems. There was no question of the Red Army's entering Italy – at least in the foreseeable future – but the very mechanism by which 'representativity' was to be tested, namely free national elections, might allow what the Foreign Office called 'the wrong side', the indigenous Communist forces, to come to power, and then where would the peace settlement be? Yet only when a United Nations peace settlement had been achieved could American action really get under way to check the advance of the Left. This was the dilemma, and no one underestimated the risks involved in its most obvious solution: a separate Western peace treaty *prior* to national elections.

'[It] would be a policy of despair for us to negotiate a separate peace with Italy,' Sir Orme Sargent commented on conversatons between the Washington embassy and the State Department on the proposal, which had originated in American executive circles. As the Foreign Office admitted, the United Nations Declaration forbade separate peace treaties, and sentiment at first had run in favour of an under-the-counter signal to the Rome government that they might simply consider themselves no longer bound by certain clauses of the armistice. Sargent's preference was for a public statement announcing the end of the state of war between the United States, the United Kingdom and Italy, supplemented by regulations on various immediate questions. But this would be meaningless, others objected, since the war could not be ended without the abolition of the armistice regime, a weighty formality which required Russian agreement. Those who conceded that a separate agreement might be needed in the end had no illusions about the consequences of such steps if generalized:

> of course it would split the world openly into camps. Russia's clients and semi-clients who are scared of her, would refuse to participate in the sponsored Anglo-American treaty. I imagine the Soviet Union would regard this grouping of states as tantamount to a new cordon sanitaire. It would certainly break the United Nations organisation.

The 'extraordinarily naif and rash' Americans could well precipitate a 'first-class crisis' by flirting with such ideas in Italy's case, the Foreign Office worried.[46]

By the end of October Bevin and his civil servants had decided that they were unwilling to restart the Foreign Ministers' Conference or in any way 'play into Soviet hands by rushing to them with "compromise" proposals,' but might instead contemplate the calling of a special conference – with American approval – for all those interested in an agreement with Italy. This was an attempt to seize the initiative from the Russians and at the same time test their disposition to collaborate, since a refusal to attend 'would imply the final breakdown of cooperation between the Big Three.' But brink-manship of this sort was, in reality, not something that Whitehall was eager to rush into.

ON THE GROUND the Alexander plan for ensuring a smooth American takeover was encountering temporary difficulties. The liberation had natur-ally placed question-marks against the continued existence of AFHQ and AC and formal decisions were required on what might replace them – if they were to be replaced – and who would run the new arrangements. AFHQ had already decided that a supreme Allied commander must remain as long as there was any possibility that force might be required to back the peace treaty, but Alexander wished for an American successor, and did not hide his intention to press the U.S. to take on greater responsibilities in Italy.[47] But the American candidate for Alexander's position, McNarney, balked at the thought of it, 'inasmuch as the British position here is predominant and he felt that if an American should succeed Alexander we would be "taking on the British baby"', Kirk reported.[48] Similarly pressure for civilianization of the AC to reduce its associations with wartime restrictions and put the emphasis on reconstruction ran into difficulties when the candidate for Stone's post, James Douglas, secretary of the Chicago Chamber of Com-merce (and former assistant secretary of the U.S. Treasury), tired of the wrangling over the nature and definition of his new job and withdrew his nomination.[49] The Allied Commission and its dwindling staff found them-selves in an invidious position. Lacking the moral authority either to encourage the Italian government or to substitute it, they hung on for month after month without instructions, purpose or positive effect. The leading figures had pressed from the end of June onwards for a full restoration of control to the Rome authorities in September, but found little response from higher quarters, where attention was exclusively directed to the political problems of the peace treaty and the holding of elections.

A diffuse sense of exasperation and unease began to pervade the Allied organs of control. With Allied Military Government rapidly demobilizing, its authority in the North was purely illusory, Stone's deputy, Brigadier Lush, reported from Milan in October: 'we are doing the Italians no good and ourselves much harm by continuing,' said Lush, and Kirk repeated this message to Washington with an implied rebuke for his employers: 'Department is of course aware of harmful political effect here resulting from failure even to announce date of AMG withdrawal from northern Italy.'[50] As Admiral Stone emphasized in October, the future of the Allied regime was far less important than the maintenance of the Allied promise to Italy to permit self-government when military interests and the development of the government allowed, and these conditions had been fulfilled at least since September. The State Department realized that the delayed restoration of the North was in fact a 'grave embarrassment to the Parri government and to AMG', and that 'sinister motives' were being attributed to the Allies, but explained that:

> Actually the hand-back problem has become entangled in CCS discussions with the questions of military supply responsibilities and the future organization of AC. We are endeavouring, so far without success, to disengage it. The situation is the more embarrassing in view of the rapid deployment of U.S. forces in Italy, which has stripped AMG to an ineffectual shadow of itself and has also reduced the U.S. voice in Allied councils by cutting down its representation at AFHQ and on AC to skeletal proportions.[51]

AFHQ asserted at approximately the same time: 'With the exception of public declarations of broad principles by Allied statesmen we remain in ignorance of Allied policy.'[52]

Kirk continued to battle almost single-handed until the end of the year for a document which would be 'neither an armistice nor a peace', dealing with the worry of a separate agreement leading to a breakdown in international cooperation with the defiant assertion that 'this argument leads from a sense of weakness which no United Nation can afford to admit.'[53] But this belief was shared by a minority, and while complex drafts of civil affairs' agreements continued to navigate between London and Washington well into 1946, Byrnes had made his compromise with Stalin without mentioning Italy, and the Combined Chiefs of Staff had gone so far as to end the formal occupation of most of Italy, but no further.

NONE OF THIS helped the government of Ferruccio Parri, which lasted only until the beginning of December 1945. As in May, the attack on the six-party coalition reminiscent of the CLNs was led off by the Liberal Party, which later explained in the following terms why Parri had to go:

> Parri was sacrificed for the same reason he was brought in . . . in June he appeared to be the man best suited to manage the reconciliation of the Partisan forces with the State. In November he seemed to be too closely connected with those forces to be able to integrate them completely in the system of law and order.[54]

Underlying this judgement was the feeling that Parri's well-known republicanism would not favour the aims of those forces most strongly identified with the traditional State and the monarchy, now that the time had come to restart the electoral process and arrive at a decision on how the 'institutional question' would finally be settled. The issue had rumbled on ever since the days of the first Bonomi government and had been brought decisively back to the centre of attention by Togliatti in April, who had declared that it must be the first priority for the new post-liberation cabinet. The Allies were closely involved with subsequent events, and hence with the fall of the government they themselves had most desired.

The first Bonomi government had quickly decided that the form of the constitution should be decided by a directly elected Constituent Assembly, thus apparently excluding the only alternative method, a decision by popular referendum. But in a direct letter to the Foreign Office in July, Bonomi hinted that the issue was not as closed as it appeared, that he favoured a referendum in the long term, while in the short term the best policy would be to avoid discussion of the question as far as possible. The Left and the anti-monarchist front in general held that 'the solution should be discussed and found in an elected chamber since the people were not educated enough to voice their opinions on such a question by plebiscite', which was precisely why people such as Admiral Stone declared (in private) their support of the referendum solution.[55] Macmillan declared that Kirk and himself 'hope that Bonomi holds the right view, that the least said about the matter now, the more chance there will be to arrange for [the] monarchical question to be settled by plebiscite.' The Vatican also pressed for a strategy most likely to preserve the monarchy 'as a symbol and element of stability'. A high Vatican official estimated that 25 per cent of the population was monarchist, 25 per cent Republican and 50 per cent undecided:

> It must be admitted [the British ambassador to the Holy See reported], that it was difficult to answer the argument that the Monarchy had done little to serve the interests of the country or the people during the past 30 years. In his opinion [that of the Vatican official] the only way in which the Monarchy could be saved was if it could be demonstrated that it had performed some conspicuous service to the country which neither the present Government nor a prospective Republic could have achieved, but he could not see how this was to be effected.

At the same time a Christian Democrat spokesman (thought by the Foreign Office to be De Gasperi) had told the British ambassador, Sir D'Arcy

Osborne, that majority public opinion demanded 'an efficiently functioning Republican regime, but at the same time he had no illusions at all about this being possible in Italy.'[56] For his part Churchill in Rome found even in the hapless Crown Prince Umberto a 'far more impressive figure than the politicians', individuals fit only for grandiloquent scorn:

> The Eternal City, rising on every side, majestic and apparently invulnerable with its monuments and palaces, and with its splendour of ruins not produced by bombing, seemed to contrast markedly with the tiny and transient beings who flitted within its bounds.

The monarchy could count on elevated supporters on the American side too:

> I believe that in an honest test of strength the nation would really rally round the House of Savoy as being traditional, definite and more dependable than any vague or untried group or system.

Myron Taylor told Roosevelt in January, 1945.[57]

The big question of course was who would decide what 'an honest test of strength might be'. The Allied controllers were agreed in their own circles that a referendum was the option to be aimed for, and their reasoning was stated with characteristic lucidity by the Foreign Office: '[The question] is not which procedure will benefit the Monarchy but which procedure will hamper the Communists.' Obviously, said the Foreign Office, the best solution was the plebiscite, since an Assembly would be made up of parties whose overall membership consisted of 5 per cent of the population, and among whom the PCI was the best organized. Only when the question of totalitarianism versus democracy was resolved (and consequently whether 'Italy is in foreign affairs to come within the British or Russian orbit') could the issue of monarchy versus republic be tackled, the Foreign Office asserted, and in the meantime it was 'unfortunate that the anti-Communists should have to fight under the banner of the Monarchy' ('I agree', Eden added).[58]

But how could a discredited if formally legitimate and securely conservative regime be buttressed against the challenges of 1945? How could such an institution be reconciled with the groundswell of demand for change coming from below? By now British opinions had begun to adapt to the new situation: Churchill said he was 'far from convinced' that the monarchy would be 'a source of strength', while Macmillan saw it as 'hopelessly compromised', the only possible tactic being to 'use our influence in favour of the moderate elements' in the case of an Assembly and insist on a plebiscite for certain parts of the constitution should it emerge.[59] The overall British strategy by the time Parri was installed was extremely finely balanced. As the Foreign Office saw things:

> By seeming to back the Right wing, we run the risk of increasing the opposition from the Left and of seeing the scales instead of remaining in the middle swinging from

side to side and finally coming to rest far to the left of centre . . . there is no certainty
that the survival of the Monarchy is in our interest, or that if it survives it can
guarantee a moderate stable regime. On the other hand, to attempt to guarantee that
survival might involve us in difficulties with the Americans and the Russians . . .
while exposing us to the charge of unwarranted interference in Italian internal
affairs.[60]

And for these reasons British policy kept up a tight-lipped neutrality during
the mid-1945 months.

In mid-summer the American attitude was still undefined; Admiral Stone
could not even 'hazard a guess at it' in private conversation, though the
State Department was known to have no sympathy for the House of
Savoy.[61] While Bonomi kept up his behind-the-scenes pressure on the Allies
for a referendum, De Gasperi told Kirk of his anxiety for the constituent
assembly, which he believed would pave the way for a dictatorship by
Nenni and Togliatti, and of his hopes in U.S. sympathies for local elections.
During the autumn and winter the State Department began to take up the
running on the institutional question by insisting on local elections before
the national ones for the assembly, in order 'to gauge the strength of the
parties section by section', the procedure favoured by the Right. Inevitably
this complicated relationships within the troubled Parri cabinet, and when
the American government sent Parri an expert legal opinion favouring the
Right's view of the powers of the Constituent Assembly, the stage was set
for a full-scale crisis.[62]

At every level of Allied control there was agreement that the immediate
cause of the government crisis had been an attempt made by the Liberal
Party to capitalize on the swing away from the Left in popular sentiment
which most observers noted (and some attributed to Russian behaviour at
the Foreign Ministers' Conference[63]), assisted by more or less active Christian Democrat acquiescence. There was also considerable suspicion that like
the Left, the Right intended to gain the Ministry of the Interior and
manipulate in its own way the preparations for the Constituent Assembly.[64]
The British, who had ample contacts with the main protagonists of the crisis,
made substantial efforts to block it but failed. Manlio Brosio, secretary of the
Liberal Party, was warned by Noel Charles that his party 'would be held
responsible for whatever economic and political troubles might ensue
during the coming winter,' and there was the additional risk that isolationists in Congress would be given an excellent excuse to withdraw their
support to UNRRA. The Italian mission in London received much the same
message from the Foreign Office, and promised that Carandini was going to
Rome to try to stop the Liberal manoeuvre. The Foreign Office even
contemplated intervention to end the crisis and restore Parri: 'we shall be
intervening in Italian internal affairs, but it is more than a mere question of
internal politics; we have the duty as well as the interest to encourage
democracy in Italy.'[65] Carandini himself met Bevin and leading Foreign

Office functionaries, and as one of the latter told the American embassy in London, had been 'more Liberal Party politician than Ambassador . . . [seeking] to justify Liberal Party positions and actions and . . . [hoping] to return to Italy with favourable British advice and even offers of financial assistance for Italy but . . . he got little satisfaction on any count.'[66]

The State Department took a generally negative line in the face of the crisis, ignoring the part its own heavy-handed interventions on the electoral issue had played in creating the confusion within the Rome cabinet which precipitated its downfall. The equivocal emotion it generated in American circles was discharged in one sharp attack on De Gasperi, who was obliged to listen to the American ambassador state

> in no uncertain terms my personal feeling of disgust that at time when foreigners were determining [the] measure of the sacrifice they would make in order to save the Italian people from starvation and anarchy, Italians themselves were thinking more of their personal and party ambitions than of the salvation of their country.[67]

But when the crisis was finally over and De Gasperi had formed a government in the manner he had predicted to Kirk several weeks before – with himself as prime minister and foreign minister and a moderate Socialist as minister of the interior – a situation believed by many to be close to civil war had to be faced:

> The Government crisis, together with open banditry, may be an explanation for the increased impetus given to the rumours that both the Communists and the neo-fascists are speeding up the organisation of their armed squads in order to carry out a coup d'état [a military intelligence report stated], each one accusing the other of being the offender.[68]

It was for these reasons that the British and the Americans worried as they did over the risks involved in embarking on the Byzantine intrigues of a change of government at such a moment. Admiral Stone felt that the significance of the solution was far from clear, even who had won, other than De Gasperi himself 'whose tact, skill and firmness at the crucial moment of the crisis have considerably enhanced his personal prestige,' he told the ACI.[69] The suspicion has inevitably persisted in Italian historiography that the crisis was deliberately manoeuvred by the Allies to obtain a more solidly Right-wing government,[70] but the transition from Parri to De Gasperi only served Allied conservatism in an objective sense, and was only securely realized to have done so some months later, when the threatened coups d'état from Right and Left failed to materialize, and the painful process of reconstruction under the still hesitant Christian Democrats got under way. In this context it might be more legitimate to measure the extent to which the presence and boasted favour of the Anglo-Americans was exploited as a form of guarantee or cover by those forces which brought Parri down, assuming – whether consciously or otherwise – that either the British or the Americans (or both) would have stepped in to save them if the manoeuvre had resulted in chaos and disorder. Suspicions of this kind are inevitably reinforced by the barrage of pleas for Allied – and particularly American – intervention which preceded the crisis and followed it, and by the grim picture of imminent insurrection painted by the conservative classes and their spokesmen. Parri himself said, in a message to the central CLN:

> One of the most insidious and fraudulent weapons used against the government was the diffidence towards it attributed to foreign business-men, the lack of confidence in it attributed to the Allied authorities in Italy and a desire presumed to be theirs to change the direction of the government: these are unfounded rumours, speculative manoeuvres, since the Allied representatives have personally denied to me any such intentions.

Parri went on to say that the problem of the restoration of the northern territories to the government's jurisdiction had been on the way to solution before the crisis, and that in the economic field, the government's requests had been met, while private enterprise had also expressed openly, in the week in which he spoke, a strong desire to resume commercial trading:

> Instead I insist that a real reason for lack of foreign confidence lies in the instability of the government, the ease with which a crisis can be started, the impression we give of a country which is ungovernable. In this sense the present crisis is gravely damaging.[71]

DE GASPERI'S reign did not begin auspiciously: almost immediately he had to face the set-back of the Moscow foreign ministers' meeting where, as the new prime minister pointed out to Charles, everything that had been gained at Potsdam regarding the importance of the Italian treaty seemed to have been lost. A wave of depression engulfed De Gasperi, who declared that Italy had apparently gained nothing as a result of 18 months of co-belligerency and combat. Even if the country now refused to sign a diktat the general wave of cynicism and disillusionment would inevitably be exploited by the far Right, who would sweep the country into a new Fascism, said De Gasperi.[72] In Moscow, Molotov – who according to a State Department source, 'clearly confessed Soviet assumption of "the white man's burden" in the Balkans' – told the Italian ambassador that while Italy should be granted a just peace as soon as possible, she could not possibly expect the same treatment as the Balkan countries in terms of Soviet support 'as long as [she] maintains [her] present orientation towards the Western powers,'[73] while in London Foreign Office mandarins brought their own special blend of ruthlessness and complacency to their end-of-year judgment on Italy's situation. De Gasperi was 'carried away', said Sir Noel Charles and his superiors; he should be warned against 'firing off at half-cock', and remember that Italy, 'thanks largely to the efforts of Great Britain and the United States, was possibly the happiest and most comfortable country on the continent of Europe.' 'I agree . . .', said Bevin.[74]

The Allied presence as an occupying force ended formally on 31 December for all of Italy with the exception of the contested areas in the region of Venezia Giulia. But the opening months of 1946 were a cardinal period in recent international history, which historians now call the opening of the Cold War. In such a context, when long-established American reform priorities confronted Soviet demands for a redistribution of international power in accordance with the strategic outcome of the war, there was little chance for a restoration of anything other than fragmentary sovereignty to a totally enfeebled country such as Italy. With the opening of the new year the decisions and commitments this situation implied for the United States began to coincide more rapidly and precisely with the strategic necessities of the conservative classes in Italy, relegating to the background the accusations of backwardness, egoism and lack of sense of national responsibility common up to that moment. The path to be followed in the future was indicated by the prime minister and the American ambassador in their discussions of the worrying electoral problem in February 1946.

> De Gasperi emphasized that not only was it his wish but that it was also the interest of Italy to find some solution of the problem which would be agreeable to the American Government

Kirk told the State Department. It was not difficult to draw conclusions from such a situation:

> In general, I might say that with full admission of the principle of non-interference in the internal politics of another country, it would seem that once we have assumed a responsibility for the establishment of a democratic form of government through the free expression of the popular will, we might find it possible to facilitate the efforts of elements tending to that end by some means more efficacious than the statement of generalities and the emission of pious wishes. . . . On that basis I hope that the Department will view with sympathy De Gasperi's appeal for guidance. . . . A reply is urgent.[75]

A new era was well under way.

12 The economics of liberation and the quest for stability

Every person that observes the conditions of the working classes in the North agrees on the absolute urgency to put them back to work at once, because it is feared that if this does not happen there will be a most serious agitation.[1]

THE CRY OF ALARM was Ivanoe Bonomi's a month after the liberation of the North, its recipient was Admiral Ellery Stone, guardian not only of the immediate political future of the country, but also of its economic plight. 'By stability is meant not prosperity but freedom from want and freedom from unemployment,' said Brigadier Lush, executive commissioner of AC in May 1945: 'the import of raw materials and coal is a prerequisite to that stability.' But Harold Macmillan, the skilled politician, was not inclined to agree: 'Prosperity like peace is indivisible . . .', said the British resident minister in his long policy paper implementing the Hyde Park Declaration.[2] To those in the British hierarchy who had offered furious resistance all along the line of American concessions these considerations were irrelevant, notwithstanding the tributes they themselves had paid to economic factors when framing their own counter-revolutionary strategies. In his paper Macmillan had taken pains to underline his trust that 'His Majesty's Government [would] contribute a percentage of whatever the sum may prove to be', though he can hardly have been unaware that from the top to the bottom of the Whitehall machine the order of the day was one supplied by Keynes: 'For heavens' sake, make no gestures [towards Italy]'.[3] As a Treasury official remarked in February 1945: 'The idea of creating a sterling balance in favour of Italy would be regarded by us individually as well as by the public as an outrage.' Consequently when the Italian government requested just such a concession from London in May 1945, it was indeed regarded as 'outrageous'. Two days after this judgment Macmillan was in London telling the Foreign Office that the only real hope for influence in Italy lay in economic means. This meant, Churchill and Macmillan agreed, that nothing could be done without the Americans.[4]

In Washington everyone who looked at the problems of liberated Europe in mid-1945 from former President Hoover on down was agreed on the order of priorities: ship food now to stop Communism. But the problems of who would pay and how, and with what public explanation, were formidable. The issue was even more complicated in Italy's case as a result of her formal status as an ex-enemy, which excluded her from anything other than

War Department supplies, the minimal 'hard tack' allowed under the old formula of preventing 'disease and unrest'. A variety of agencies were interested in the situation, the FEA, the Export-Import Bank, UNRRA, but the American executive branch felt that before any of them could be fully mobilized, Congress and public opinion would have to be persuaded that the inevitable large expense was likely to produce worthwhile results. The only certainties were that the British would be neither willing nor able to play any significant part in this operation, and that the dark question of reparations from Italy would have to be set aside once and for all.[5] In June the War Department declared that it would continue supplies on the original basis until the end of August, but not beyond, and then placed its weight behind an FEA request to Congress for $100 million to cover the period September to the end of December, when it was hoped that UNRRA would step in with the opening of the new year. Truman himself went on record in July as being 'deeply concerned' that substantial assistance should continue, to assure against 'a resurgence there of those forces we have fought in Europe', and then there was silence; the pronouncements stopped and no decisions were taken beyond that by the UNRRA Council, which in its August conference in London resolved to mount a full-scale operation in Italy in 1946. But not until the end of September was the improvisation proposed by the War Department and FEA finally approved.[6]

The Congressional hearings on the subject demonstrated the real extent of the neo-isolationist tendencies so often cited by members of the executive branch. The Congressmen were suspicious that the United States was becoming involved in operations similar to those of the British in Greece, or at least setting out on the path of unlimited liability towards Europe. The Director of the FEA, Leo Crowley, found himself obliged to swear that the FEA was not requesting funds for rehabilitation or reconstruction, that the Italians were in a much more desperate plight than the Greeks ('They have no work; they have no fuel, they are hungry, and there has been no stabilization of their government'), and that the presence of American troops in Italy since 1943 placed heavier responsibilities on the U.S. than in such recently taken countries as France.[7]

An FEA relief programme in Italy for the months of September to December 1945 was eventually undertaken, and was destined to represent the only unilateral American economic programme in Italy during the occupation period. Its objectives were, of course, far more limited than any of the FEA planners had foreseen in their pipedreams from 1942 onwards, the outcome of Congressional pressures which also demanded that the control of reconstruction operations be placed in the hands of the Export-Import Bank, when not carried out via direct credits from the legislative branch.[8] UNRRA too made great efforts to underline that its aid was not for reconstruction purposes. As a resolution passed at the August 1945 conference of UNRRA stated:

No work of construction or reconstruction is contemplated. . . . Problems such as that of unemployment are important but not determining factors. They are consequences and at the same time reasons for action. The administration cannot be asked to restore full employment in the world.[9]

Indeed it was only with considerable reluctance that Italy was admitted to the full benefits of UNRRA's aid, since in the UNRRA assembly the pall of British Empire resentment hung heavy, reinforcing the lingering suspicions of such countries as Yugoslavia and Greece. As in the earlier Montreal conference of 1944, it was explicitly felt that the U.S. was using the *force majeure* of its greater contribution, and the manoeuvrability of its client states in Latin America to force through support to a shiftless ex-enemy.[10] Whatever American expectations (and in spite of efforts by UNRRA's Italian staff to interpret their responsibilities as widely as possible), the ball of reconstruction aid was placed firmly back in the American court by the UNRRA deliberations. And there, as the UNRRA planners well knew, there had been very few attempts to live up to the expansive promises of Article VII of the Lend-Lease agreement on such problems as full employment, much less provide operational programmes for those excluded from Lend-Lease.[11]

Hence in the crucial months after liberation, when all seemed to depend on the instantaneous arrival of large quantities of coal and credit, the Italian government and the ACC found themselves with very little support from those numerous agencies – the Foreign Office, the State Department, FEA, UNRRA – which had warned of imminent collapse and political upheaval in northern Italy. Since the autumn of 1943 the Western Allies had of course poured in a vast amount of aid to the territory of liberated Italy, for a total of $490 million, according to UNRRA, of which two-thirds was given by the U.S. But we should need to know much more about the composition and eventual destination of this support before passing judgment on its social and political effects (UNRRA later sustained, for instance, that of the military imports of textiles, not one kilo remained in the country; all was re-exported clandestinely by profiteers).[12] Planners who had worked and preached thoughout the war on such problems as the occupation of Germany, the functions of UNRRA or the implementation of Article VII of Lend-Lease, saw the confusion of the post-hostilities months throughout Europe as confirming the dire forecasts they had made when their efforts had been contradicted or ignored. Their view that this period should be considered not as the laborious beginning of reconstruction but as initiating the long slide down to the conditions which made the European Recovery Programme necessary, deserves serious attention.

IN ITALY AC sent out a mission to assess the economic situation in the North within days of the liberation. On its return at the end of May it concluded:

The most important step is to dispel the false optimism which pervades Italian circles. Having seen one miracle, viz., the preservation of their plant, power and equipment from the deliberate destruction which ruined the center and south, they expect another, viz., the supply of coal and raw material on a scale which will enable them to resume full production.[13]

The discovery that only 10–15 per cent of northern industrial capacity had been destroyed produced critical reappraisal of the short- and long-term prospects in Italy in many Allied circles.[14]

On the ground, Ruini, the president of the Interministerial Committee for Reconstruction, suggested that the appropriate tactic for the government and the CLNAI's economic commission, the CCE, would be to deceive the Allies into believing that the damage was much more serious than in fact it was, but the Allied authorities got to know immediately what the real state of affairs was in the North.[15] The military were convinced that a broader outlook on their part was necessary if the new opportunities were to be seized and the great dangers deriving from unemployment avoided. In January 1945 General Robertson, the chief administrative officer of AFHQ, had drawn up a large-scale programme for industrial rehabilitation, and had pessimistically listed the obstacles to its realization:

(a) Lack of control. The Italian administration is incompetent, and Italian industrialists seek their own profit to the exclusion of their country's interests. . . .
(b) Lack of technical competence . . . [AC is] entirely lacking of men with technical competence and drive. . . .
(c) Lack of transport.
(d) Lack of priority of movements.
(e) Lack of policy. . . . There seems to be a complete lack of a coordinated policy for re-starting Italian industry. . . .[16]

From these premises came an elaborate post-liberation plan for centralized control of industrial rehabilitation to be carried out by AC, the CCE and a group of northern industrialists gathered in a special government board. Plant utilization, productivity surveys, restructuring projects, raw material and equipment allocation, distribution and price control were all in the plan, which was to be carried out by a network of 23 committees – divided by industry.[17]

The project brought an immediate howl of protest from the majority of northern industrialists, who had already made it clear that they wanted no controls on relief imports, or on production restarted by bartering supplies of raw material for quantities of finished product (a system which allowed the textile industry to restart work quickly and profitably). In one large and stormy assembly Allied controls in these areas were openly called Fascist ('the only thing missing is Mussolini', said one participant).[18] 'We don't want committees and certainly not in Milan', wrote the *Informazione industriale*, organ of the Union of Industrialists of Turin, and 244 small and medium-scale entrepreneurs signed a petition to the Allied military governor, to the regional CLN and the minister of industry protesting that such policies aimed at 'suppressing Turin'.[19]

The financial adviser of AFHQ nevertheless maintained that the attempt at planning the resumption of economic activity had been serious, and that there was in any case 'no prospect' that private enterprise could establish a rational set of priorities for reconstruction. Harlan Cleveland, head of AC's economic section, drew a solemn lesson from the experience:

> There should be no illusions: no plan of reconstruction can be successfully carried out by a Government which lacks the support of the principal economic groups of the country. We should not be frightened by words: planning does not mean totalitarian control, in fact it is that much more effective if based on a democratic consensus, and not on the secret police.[20]

BUT SUCH AN OUTLOOK appeared entirely utopian when matched against the profound social and geographical divisions which characterized the economic situation in Italy in mid-1945. The Parri government in Rome spent much of its energy – vainly in the end – struggling to persuade the middle classes of the necessity for a currency stabilization operation similar to those being carried out or planned in most European countries at that time. The spectre of increased State control of the economy and a more effective tax system (as long urged by AC) was sufficient to frighten the mass of small savers and rentiers prevalent in the conservative classes of the time, and played no small part in the Liberal Party's destruction of the Parri government.[21]

In the North there was inflation – up to 3000 per cent with respect to 1939 according to the Turin Chamber of Commerce – mass unemployment, forecast at 1.5 million by the end of 1945 by the CCE, and severe shortages of food and raw materials. Strikes, demonstrations and factory occupations were an everyday occurrence, inevitably raising the spectre of Communist organization and inspiration: in the case of Fiat itself, the largest industrial enterprise, 'the direction of the concern has been almost entirely Communist inspired', said a military intelligence report in July.[22] The economic responses of AC/AMG revolved round a ramshackle series of wage and price controls, including even a short-lived economic 'barrier' between North and South complete with road-blocks, in an attempt to construct a physical obstacle to the inflationary wave welling up from the South (inflation had been much lower under the German financial system).[23] There was also a rather more successful veto on redundancies, but with raw material and food supplies scarce and chaotic, AMG's authority dwindling and its powers of enforcement feeble, little real impact could be made in the short term by the Allied controllers.[24]

But watchfulness over the political dimensions of these troubles and their possible long-term implications was as intense as ever. In this perspective the key questions seemed to be: to what extent was the

disorder due to real material causes, to what extent produced or exacerbated by the PCI and the Left? What could be done immediately or soon to
neutralize the threats from the Left and their capacity to exploit this
situation to their own advantage?

FEA intelligence sources, referring to demonstrations involving up to
70,000 people, noted:

> an analysis of these demonstrations from various points of view leads to the
> conviction that they are not being instigated by the radical parties but they are
> rather spontaneous outbursts on the part of the working masses against their
> enforced idleness and against conditions in general. The dissatisfaction of the
> people finds its outlet in continuous attacks against the Fascist elements remaining
> in power. However it is evident that this is only a partial factor in the overall
> problem and that provisions should be made immediately to prevent a further and
> more serious deterioration of the situation.[25]

Much more sweeping in its range and sophisticated in its economics was
the paper produced by the resident minister's office in June 1945 entitled
'Food and Politics in Liberated Countries'. This paper took the cases of
Greece, Yugoslavia, Romania, Hungary, Austria and Italy, and isolated
one structural factor – the breakdown of economic relations between town
and country – from the range of causes of the prevalent disruption. The
document noted that most of the countries involved were largely agricultural in nature while possessing significant numbers of industrial
workers who depended on the surplus from the country for the basic
necessities of life. They in return supplied the farmers and peasants with
manufactured products such as agricultural machinery, textiles, shoes,
and so on. The breakdown of international trade – which had siphoned off
surpluses or made good deficiencies in normal times – when added to the
rupture of the town-country exchange caused by the standstill in industrial
activity, had produced a situation – said the resident minister's analysts –
in which money had lost most if not all of its purchasing power, while the
black market flourished. Consequently agricultural produce was no longer
brought to the towns – 'to [the farmers] it seems unreasonable that they
should be expected to produce food for people in the towns who are not
working and have nothing valuable to offer in return' – and the industrial
workers (particularly) faced starvation.

The representatives of the industrial workers were of course the
Socialists and the Communists:

> In fact the food situation in many European countries is one of the most important
> factors determining the present united, aggressive policy and influence of the parties
> of the Left in the internal politics of liberated countries. If Left-wing policies, actions
> and increased influence since liberation, are regarded solely as political
> phenomena, there is a temptation to explain them as due solely to Russian
> influence and direction, but in fact they cannot be exhaustively explained in such
> terms.

What was needed, the document concluded, was an approach which avoided 'Russophobia and too exclusive a distinction between economics and politics,' an approach capable of explaining the situation in broader terms.[26]

Not surprisingly, things were not seen in these terms at the base of the Communist Party. Referring to the immediate post-liberation moment, a Communist Party member of the Fiat Mirafiori labour-management committee recalled:

> One thing was clear: out with the bosses, power and leadership to the workers. Togliatti's line consisted simply in this: first detachment from the Americans, then considerations of that sort. We knew that [the workers] were pushing for a movement with revolutionary characteristics, but this would have been in the interests of America, a pretext for intervention. The Americans were very much on guard; they thought they were going to lose Italy. We hoped to detach the country from the influence of the Allies to gain freedom of manoeuvre. The Yalta agreements and the spheres of influence might not have counted at all in front of a situation which did not justify defensive, armed intervention.[27]

Italy, however, was not Yugoslavia, nor was the PCI leadership comparable in history, structure or temperament with Tito and his lieutenants. Looking back on the insurrection some three months later at a national economic conference of the PCI, a leading member of the party, E. Sereni, president of the Lombardy CLN, said:

> the situation of the big companies, especially in Lombardy and Piedmont, was dominated by the occupation of the factories by the workers, and although the northern insurrection took place under the flag of the national insurrection, the class content of this event was immediately apparent to all.[28]

As G. Quazza has pointed out, the importance of this observation was that it referred to past history.[29]

The extraordinarily rapid demobilization of the political organs of the Resistance was nowhere more thorough than in the industrial field, especially with respect to the spontaneous organs of the mass base, such as the factory CLNs, which in effect constituted the most representative expression of working-class participation in the Resistance.[30] Besides the direct intervention of the Allies in the demobilization process, a significant aspect of these events was the self-discipline or self-limitation of the Resistance leadership including the PCI which, acting ever more consciously under the long shadow projected by the Allies as they advanced up the peninsula, deliberately sought to limit the 'insurrectionary' aspect of developments in the factories in order – partially – to avoid Allied reprisals against 'revolutionary' tendencies.

The insistence of the Allied missions on the defence of the factories as a prime Resistance responsibility, the news that filtered through the lines of Allied policy in areas such as Tuscany, the explicit message brought by the under-secretary of the Ministry for Occupied Italy, Medici-Tornaquinci, that the CLNs at every level should merge with other organs to become consultative bodies at the disposition of AMG, all these indications left no doubt in the minds of the CLNAI that its agreement with the Allied command of December 1944 would in reality be applied rigorously in every sector where CLNs had come into being.[31]

In its clandestine economic planning, the CLNAI applied 'criteria of common sense and moderation', Parri recalled, and directives for the installation of non-Fascist managers in the factories emphasized that the key priority was minimum disturbance of the productive capacity of the companies. The industrialist Merzagora, Liberal Party president of the CLNAI's economic committee, the CCE, stated that while the military and political purge should be drastic, the economic and financial version should proceed with much greater caution. Impressed by a visit to the South in April and the scant preparation he found in Allied economic organs, Parri instructed the CCE to concentrate on providing liaison and technical cooperation when the Allies arrived, and this aspect of the CCE's activities was destined to prevail.[32]

On 17 and 25 April the CLNAI issued extensive decrees on relations inside the factories. These not only abolished the 'socialization' measures of the neo-Fascist regime, but provided also for elected labour-management committees, the installation of temporary CLN commissions according to technical qualifications, and made arrangements for the distribution of financial responsibilities, with the workers' share in profits going to a national reconstruction fund. According to the decree published on the day of the insurrection, the working class was assigned a 'new function of national responsibility in the direction of the factories.'[33]

Yet on 2 June the six parties meeting in Rome decided that 'the committees in factories and industries should be transformed into technical and trade union organisations according to the production needs or social requirements of the factory in question,' and by the middle of July the Milanese CLNs were being told that activity inside the factories should be directed *'at all costs* [sic] . . . towards the interest of the government and the nation, in the name of the supreme objective of reconstruction.'[34] The desire to avoid the continuity of the original factory CLNs was explicit, and in the middle of May the CLNAI had already moved to ensure the transfer of industrial epuration from the plant CLNs to the city or regional committees, and to hasten the election of technical management committees (the 'Consigli di Gestione'). The intention behind this strategy was 'to prevent the factory CLNs from going so far in the course of the insurrection as to expropriate the capitalists and establish cooperative management of the works,' writes the Communist historian, G. Manacorda. The principal motive for this caution was fear of 'the reaction of the Allies,' Manacorda explains, resulting in 'a concrete case – perhaps the most conspicuous – of the self-limitation of the revolution, a political intervention aimed at preventing the spontaneous movement of the working class from reaching towards socialist objectives.'[35]

For the most part the Allied authorities who arrived in the industrial cities of the North were indifferent to these sacrifices: agreements were after all agreements. Although the dangers reported by the OSS, the PWB and their informers were not taken with exaggerated seriousness, the absolute priority of enforcing constituted authority signified that the days were numbered for every form of CLN. By the end of May, AC labour representatives were urging immediate suspension of the labour-management committees, the substitution by AMG or the Italian government of the CLN-appointed factory commissions, 'and that orders should be issued that there should be no arbitrary replacement of existing managements.'[36]

There can be no doubt that in the first instance the factory CLNs were dominated by men acting in the name of the Left parties, that they were able in the first stages to impose their political will, and that a substantial wave of expulsions of management elements from the factories resulted.[37] But the alarm these developments provoked was not confined to the Allies or the entrepreneurs. The president of the CCE, Merzagora, complained bitterly of 'a carnival of personal resentment' in presenting his resignation, and the Communist leadership in the North hastened to repair the damage, seeking at the same time to incorporate the factory CLNs in those organs given consultative recognition by AMG.[38] Thus the substantial sections of the industrial working class in Milan, Turin and Genoa who looked to an effective removal of collaborationist management were destined to be disappointed, and when victims of the purge were allowed the right to appeal by the new AMG order, it was felt that the new and old authorities were combining to 'take on through the door the Fascists purged through the window.'[39]

In these circumstances attention began to be focused on the new trade unions emerging under the wing of the parties, particularly the Confederazione generale italiana del lavoro (CGIL), identified with the PCI and PSIUP, which now took up the running on defending the immediate interests of the working class. Here the Left could count on a figure of great authority and firmness in Giuseppe Di Vittorio, a member of the PCI, who saw as his prime responsibility the maintenance of trade-union unity in a fashion obviously parallel with Togliatti's strategy. Allied authorities frequently complimented the CGIL on its unity, efficiency, 'notable sense of equilibrium' and sympathy for their efforts, and there were increasingly frequent contacts between the CGIL and the trade unions of Britain and the U.S.[40] Moderation was also the distinguishing characteristic of the PCI's own behaviour at the highest levels when economic problems were under discussion. At its economic conference in August 1945, Togliatti had explicitly rejected the path of comprehensive nationalization and planning, and chose instead to emphasize structural reform (particularly in agriculture) with the aim of eliminating the worst features of autarky and monopoly privilege, and the resumption of production. In the short term the party even acknowledged the pressure of the industrialists for a freer hand in sacking surplus workers, its delegate Pesenti recommending a 'breathing-space' for companies in this direction in a September meeting of the CCE.[41]

In PCI propaganda the need to control prices, wages and production, to halt inflation and restart production, was portrayed as being in the interests of Allies and Italians alike, together with more autonomy for indigenous action: 'We are not asking for control to be removed altogether, rather that it should change form', said a pamphlet on 'The Allies and Us', by one of the party's economic experts.[42] At a special conference organized by the PCI at the end of December 1945 and conducted in English for Allied representatives, the party's economists expanded these themes and offered a picture of reconstruction based on 'agriculture and food production, textiles, light and precision industries'. As for investment, foreign capital would inevitably be needed and would be welcomed, as long as it did not harm national sovereignty: 'And we are sure that is not the intention of Anglo-Saxon investors', said a conference speaker. Political and economic guarantees would be given, and there would be safeguards in the event of 'structural and social reforms', or the extension of public control in the industrial sector, so that the investor benefited from the higher productivity and greater social peace which would result.[43]

Thus if the stabilization in prices, production and trade hoped for by the Allies did not materialize, little direct blame could be attached at this stage to the so-called 'extremist' parties or their representatives, though no attention seems to have been paid to the signals of the December conference. As supplies began to come into the country at the end of the year in a more encouraging fashion, the Left issued a successful call for the mobilization of productive energies on the part of the workers, a positive reaction against the stagnation and alienation of the previous months and years.[44]

ON THE GROUND the last months of 1945 saw the establishment of the UNRRA experts (many of whom had been American members of AC), the elaboration of a vast and detailed programme of imports for 1946, and most important of all, the clearing of decks by AC to permit unilateral action via national policies as soon as possible.[45] Although these processes were somewhat retarded by the failure of a much-discussed plan to 'civilianize' AC, by September the Commission had relinquished most of its control over trade, and by November had made plans for the transfer of the responsibilities of the economic subcommissions to the British and American embassies.[46] Kirk developed his old project for economic control in the regions, combined with an Allied economic mission, into a plan for a

'Tripartite Economic Advisory Council' (composed of the U.S., the U.K. and Italy). Cleveland demanded the establishment of an 'Industrial Projects Staff' in the American embassy to develop reconstruction projects, guide reconstruction financing authorities, advize the Italian government and induce the participation of American private enterprise in reconstruction. Planning, in other words, continued as energetically as ever.[47]

But it was the business community which proved most effective at the operational level, mobilizing trade delegations, the Italo-American Chamber of Commerce, the president of the Bank of America, Giannini, and the U.S. authorities in Italy. While the army, the FEA and the State Department proved unable to agree on a name to lead American economic operations in Italy or even to formulate an effective policy on a joint basis, all three moved to encourage a delegation of six New York businessmen who left for Italy at the beginning of November 1945, and as the *New York Herald Tribune* explained, this was done 'as part of foreign policy'.[48] A commercial agreement followed in December, a logical development from the attitudes of both American and Italian governments. As the Ministero degli Affari Esteri wrote:

> The Italian Government strongly desire to give the greatest growth to its economic relations with the United States of America, not only because such relations must constitute the basis of those sound and friendly political relations which Italy desires to maintain and develop, but also because the United States of America, in view of its financial and industrial power, is in a position more than any other country to assist in Italy's economic revival. The same is to be said as regards the future relations with Great Britain.[49]

Since this choice seemed so unashamedly linked to relationships of power, the addition that the same was true for Britain appeared purely diplomatic.

One of the first to point to the next step forward for America in Italy was John Chabot Smith, a feature writer for the *New York Herald Tribune*, whose premise – in a long article which appeared at the beginning of July – was a simple one: 'Everyone said win the war first. Now no one knows what to do.' Smith's article is important as a signal of an important shift in thinking on economic problems in liberated Europe taking place in certain sections of American official opinion at that moment. According to Smith, the objective circumstances were clear to all concerned: there was a general consensus that everything in Italy depended on U.S. aid, in economic and military terms. But the army had big plans to demobilize and/or send large contingents of its forces to the Pacific theatre. Those who had originally pressed for maintaining a strong U.S. presence in Italy had been conservatives fearing mob rule and civil war; but now many high-level Americans were coming round to the same opinion. They were concerned, said Smith, that the forces of the Left sought totalitarian rule and might well provoke civil war to get it. As for the conservatives who in the beginning had asked for nothing more than Allied charity, they were now more concerned with those conditions of poverty and disorder which fed Leftism: 'there is a growing disposition among some Italian and American officials and businessmen to look deeper into the problems of economic reconstruction,' Smith reported, 'and [into] the possibilities of developing a permanently higher standard of living in Italy.' In Smith's opinion, instead of merely asking for large public loans, Italy might have done better to interest U.S. businessmen in providing technical know-how and money, the essential resources necessary 'for re-building and developing Italy on a profit-making basis.' The essential political premises of course were stability and public order, so that the days of a 'hands-off' attitude on America's part were probably numbered. Many Italians and Americans, Smith concluded, 'would like to see the U.S. take a more direct hand in Italian politics.'[50]

In economics as in politics the way to the future – ignoring the chaos of the present, leaving aside the questions of 'how' and 'when' – was seen by some very early on indeed. It was a bold vision. As the Allied armies withdrew and their military government machines demobilized, this was how the OSS saw the situation in the country the British considered 'the most comfortably off in Europe':

> One thousand, seven hundred calories a head instead of the two thousand, one hundred which represent the minimum for healthy survival, worse general conditions than in any other European country except Germany, industries halted for lack of raw material and fuel, unemployment on the increase, possibly involving 40% of the work force by the end of winter with the only prospect massive emigration.[51]

But more than two unhappy years were to pass before the U.S. was able to combine this sort of knowledge with the alternative vision of men like Smith in a plan which was equipped with effective means of direct intervention on the ground. Nevertheless, in the economic sphere as in others, the line of descendancy from the days of the Allied Control Commission to those of the European Recovery Programme was a direct one.

Conclusions

IN ITALIAN HISTORY the liberation from Nazism and Fascism was a moment of exceptional drama. As in most occupied countries the weight of oppression and the demand for renewal had produced during the war a vigorous Left-wing movement which had proved itself politically and organizationally in armed resistance. More or less inspired by the feats of the Red Army, more or less directed by the indigenous Communist Party, this movement found itself at the end of the war confronted by two foreign powers *in occupation*, powers which not only held the trump cards of food and supplies, but expected that these would be accepted together with a particular idea of political and economic development and a particular strategic commitment.

For years afterwards it was to seem to all those parts of the Italian political spectrum left of centre that an unparalleled opportunity for radical change had been lost in 1945, and that this loss was somehow connected with the presence of the British and the Americans. As the Allies demobilized the Resistance and neutralized the political power which the northern working class had gained through it, so in 1948 were the Americans seen to move every political and economic muscle to stop the Left-bloc gaining power in the spring elections. After joining Nato, Italy's participation in the Marshall Plan was supervised by an American lady ambassador, Mrs Clare Booth Luce, of unusual anti-Communist conviction and energy even for those times. With her encouragement, we now know, Communists and ex-partisans were expelled from the factories and the Communist Party reduced to political isolation. Even the leader of the Socialist Party was considered *persona non grata* in the American embassy throughout the 1950s.

So for many years after the war Italy was a country of limited sovereignty and it became a truism to say that she had 'no foreign policy'. At the same time more and more sections of the population discovered that key institutions and structures of the Fascist and pre-Fascist periods had survived the war intact, that the victory of the republic over the monarchy was a superficial one, and that even the new Constitution was of strictly limited effectiveness in regulating political life either ethically or democratically. Under the Christian Democrats, who first came to government in 1944 attained a majority in 1946 and still hold sway, a power-bloc was patiently

constructed which eventually gained control of almost all the key levers of
state, at almost all levels.

For the Left opposition, both Communist and non-Communist, this
Italian post-war situation has always been connected in some way with
American intervention and American patronage of various forms of conservatism. Yet the eagerness of many sections of Italian political life to attribute
part of their condition to American influence was not matched by consistent
political or historical analysis of Italy's position in the international context,
still less of her relationship with the United States. Even the era of the
Second World War tended to be treated overwhelmingly from an internal
and not an international point of view. Once it became clear that the
continuity of the State, and certain basic social structures, was the
phenomenon to be explained, that the fall of Fascism did not represent a
dramatic rupture with the past, then it could be assumed that the Allied
intervention had 'conditioned' events and prejudiced them in certain directions. To test this assumption was an important part of the present project
from the beginning.

THE EVIDENCE of these chapters suggests that the most decisive Allied
contribution to the evolution of Italian political life in the years after Fascism
lay in the restoration of the apparatus and authority of the Italian State. The
consequences of the 'continuity of the State' have provoked a wide debate in
Italian political and historical writing; less attention has been paid to the
causes of this continuity, to the mechanisms and guarantees which allowed
it to come about.

In the midst of a bitter and intractable military campaign there was little
chance that the Allies would carry out a revolution in the State such as they
carried out in Germany and Japan when the war was over. Co-belligerency
muddied the waters even further in this area with its equivocal recognition
that the king and Badoglio were indispensable in the circumstances of the
Italian surrender. At that moment the State effectively collapsed, and a vast
Control Commission was needed to fill the void, with its legitimacy guaranteed by the two ancient figures who had survived the fall of Fascism. It was
the Control Commission which did whatever was done to help the State to
its feet again, filling in, protecting, urging and chastising it back to life. In
reality the ministries, the agencies and the forces of law and order showed
little gratitude and accepted none of the modernizing suggestions ACC, the
State Department and others thrust upon them. Then as now, reform of the
State seemed almost impossibly difficult and as the Allied managers soon
came to realize, tampering with such a construction threatened its very
collapse. Confronted by such a risk they had little choice: de-Fascistization
was the prime example of this form of surrender by the Allies, with
consequences – just as the Foreign Office predicted – to this day.

What the Allies took no heed of was the necessity of building an active popular consensus for the institutions of the State – this, they felt, was the job of the Italian political forces who would make the decisions necessary when conditions allowed. But the reborn Italian political forces were agreed on one thing if nothing else: that politics could not be postponed to the future, least of all to a moment decided as favourable by the Allies. The development of positions, the regrouping of interests, the emergence of alternatives and other political processes were already under way in North and South when the Allies and the Germans came into the country and were accelerated, not frozen, by the war passing through their midst. Yet Allied control did everything it could to isolate itself and its cherished Rome governments from the impact of these processes, and to neutralize and dissolve them wherever possible.

This was above all the case with respect to the CLNs, where from the first moment of contact with the relatively moderate example of Florence, the Committees were regarded with undisguised hostility and diffidence (by the Rome authorities themselves of course even more than by the Allies). Not wishing to use the full weight of their authority, the Allies employed a range of psychological and political tactics to counter the 'threat' of break-away, alternative governments in the North, tactics which distinguished 'administration' from 'politics' and which aimed to balance out Left and Right, North and South, centre and periphery, old and new.

'The whole attitude after liberation was one of dreary discouragement,' said a thoughtful observer in the *Manchester Guardian* in August 1945;

> In Southern Italy under Allied occupation there was . . . a demoralisation which penetrated into every walk of life and left the people more listless even than before. In the north there was still a chance. . . . [Yet] the monarchy was bolstered up by the transparent pretext of permitting no change until constitutionally demanded; and men who had risked their lives in trying to redeem Italy from Fascism were obliged to go cap in hand to a prince they, almost to the last man, condemned.

As for the Resistance:

> The Allies could have made of the movement a means of national regeneration, another Risorgimento. . . . Instead of that, the Allies preferred to reduce the movement to a mere accessory, and rather a disreputable one at that.[1]

Parri's disappointment, expressed twenty years later, also concerned the lack of effective support to the Resistance: 'they did not want a really effective co-belligerent force which might claim the same rights as De Gaulle had claimed.'[2]

MUCH of this behaviour (though by no means all) can be explained by the great dangers seen in the rise of the Communist Party from the spring of 1944 onwards. Though not necessarily the largest party – in the 1946 elections it would in fact come third behind the Christian Democrats and the Socialists – it was the best organized and by the end of the war appeared in many forms; as party, trade union, network of group representation, and movement, and of course it was backed to some degree by the resources and prestige of the U.S.S.R. As William Reitzel wrote, its tactical position after the formation of the all-party Badoglio government in April 1944 was extremely strong and at any moment it could 'force a crisis whose repercussions would run far beyond the borders of Italy'. In reality Togliatti was far too cautious a political operator to cause such a crisis, whose consequences would be entirely unpredictable.

Togliatti's problem was that no one could quite believe the seriousness with which he seemed determined to play both ends against the middle. On the one hand respect for legality, mass party politics and the vision of 'progressive', non-revolutionary democracy; on the other militant participation in the Resistance, the retention of a leninist party organization (with potential for a return to armed secrecy), exaltation of working-class identity and the Soviet Union; in the middle anti-Fascist unity, the search for agreements with rival and even opposing parties, breathing space for entrepreneurs, and a seat in the Rome governments. Inside the party and outside it too, the belief was widespread that such a position would not be kept up, that sooner or later the insurrectionary break-out would come: the problem was to be prepared for it, either in its promotion or its neutralization according to one's own position. But the signal never came; Togliatti was serious, and as the years after were to show, would consolidate and rationalize his position until it became the central tradition of the contemporary PCI.

At this point Italian history becomes international history, since it is generally assumed that Togliatti's guide and mentor, Giuseppe Stalin, had issued orders to the effect that spheres of influence and unity of action were to be respected, and that Togliatti should recognize the predominance of Anglo-American power in his country. Greek events, which weighed heavily in the Italian balance from the end of 1944 on, could only confirm Soviet attitudes, which on the question of Trieste chose Tito rather than Togliatti at Potsdam, and were not in the least helpful to the PCI in their attempts to equate Italy with Romania or Bulgaria. For the U.S.S.R national interests, whether short- or long-term, always came first: if Togliatti could get himself into a position which might sooner or later be helpful, so much the better, otherwise it was up to the PCI to fight its own battles and develop its own line according to local circumstances. As hostility grew between the two great conceptions of post-war reconstruction – reform under capitalism versus revolution under the destroyers of Nazi-Fascism – the pressure on the PCI to choose one or the other became almost intolerable, and would surely have broken a party which had not planted substantial roots in Italian reality (just as it did break the Socialist Party in 1947).

It was of course the danger from the Left which brought the Americans to define their interests in the country and finally reconcile their stakes in arms and money with their declared political objectives:

> Slowly but surely, and at times almost in contradiction of its other policy statements [writes William Reitzel], the U.S. developed in Italy a course of action whose objective came to be more and more definable as the shoring up of a bulwark against ideological and strategic encroachments on the part of communism and Soviet Russia.

The building bricks of such a policy were to be encouragement of reform plans and above all economic aid, since there was considered to be a simple deterministic link between material chaos and political underdevelopment on the one hand and the surge of the Left on the other. That this vision pointed to the construction of a complete model of political and economic modernization emerged only later in the years of the Marshall Plan. In Italy there was greater need to recognize the sovereignty of a liberated, friendly country and at the same time it was by no means clear to all those concerned that a commitment was being made or what the overall trend of events meant. Above all there was a general American reluctance to recognize that the ambitious plans for a new world order of economic growth and collective security were under challenge: from the British empire, which had its own interests to defend, from the Soviet Union, with its own definition of power and its strategic victory in the European war, and above all from the unhappy realities of wartorn countries such as Italy. The Americans had the plans, the political will and the power to offer a future to the country, but they were neither organized nor had they yet decided to apply these assets in a coherent way on the ground.

The Americans had the means but no organized strategy, the British had the strategy but no longer had the power to bring it to bear. It would be wrong, I believe, to treat the British domination of the occupation of Italy as a mere historical curiosity, quite marginal in interest in comparison with those activities of the Americans which foreshadowed their eventual assumption of leadership in the West. Such notions as the desire to have Italian political life evolve on British lines, to inculcate British ideas in Italian trade-unionism, to seek a Lord Cromer figure to run the country,[3] to 'attach' Italy, to make her 'a member of the European family under British direction'; none of this has anything to do with the often-told tale of British participation in the Second World War as we know it.

Not the least curious aspect of British approaches to Italy is that among all the expressions of imperial impulse, none can be described as a *plan of future development*. Compared to the State Department's 'The Treatment of Italy', the Foreign Office Research Department's 'The Future of Italy' is a poor exercise indeed, not even taken seriously by the Foreign Office managers. Yet it appears to be the only document indicating a possible general path and purpose for British influence in Italy after the war. This contradiction confirms once again that British interest was overwhelmingly concerned with the past, specifically with Mussolini's unprecedented violation of the highways and equilibrium of empire. Defeated and humiliated, Italy as a power paid the full price and more of this offence of the totalitarian minority. Yet it was against the entire Italian people that the British vented their vindictiveness and their prejudices, injecting into Allied action in the country a kind of malevolent inertia which set the tone of the occupation. The essence of British strategy was explained with typical frankness by Churchill at Potsdam:

> If [the British] lost their existing rights under the surrender . . . they would not have the power to secure the peace to which they were entitled.

For this reason the British had no political interest in seeing co-belligerency, active Italian participation in the war, a substantial Resistance movement, a vigorous anti-Fascist government in Rome or any other manifestation of the difference between a Fascist and an anti-Fascist Italy. For this reason a government such as Badoglio's represented the perfect interlocutor, guaranteeing the continuity not only of the State and constitutional authority, but also of Fascism's responsibilities. To entrust the government of the country to the signers of the armistice meant enforcing the conception that the nation as a whole had lost the war: little wonder that the Allies as occupiers insisted on each government's pledging anew its commitment to the armistice (even when in ignorance of its terms). With this legal sanction, liberation and occupation became synonymous in Italy. The British on the spot, particularly Harold Macmillan, were often embarrassed and critical of their government's attitudes, which remained unchanged no matter how long the war dragged on or how hard the Resistance fought. But their pleas that the difference between a Fascist and an anti-Fascist Italy was real and should be recognized went unheeded; and it was the British who set the tone of the punitive peace treaty of 1947, a cause of great dismay in the country at the time.

THE ALLIED OCCUPATION ended in a situation of limited political, economic and military sovereignty for Italy, the outcome of an application of superior force on all these levels which removed from the Italian ruling class the last trace of any autonomous strategic impulse *vis à vis* the leading powers of the West. As it ended, stability and prosperity were offered – from outside – as the beacons of the future, but the delicate, self-regulating equilibrium required by the workings of power in the West in the second half of the twentieth century, between international commitments and internal development, was far from guaranteed. The last word may be left to a perceptive writer of *The Times* of London, who began an account of the atmosphere in Rome in July 1945, with a quotation from Proudhon: '"Until the Italians have had their revolution they will be at the mercy of the foreigner, the priest and the praetorian"'. The war was over, but the familiar figures lingered:

> The Praetorians have been disposed of for the moment, but they may rise again. The

influence of the priest extends further into politics than in almost any other country. The foreigner is much in evidence.[4]

Abbreviations

AAI	Allied Armies in Italy
AC	Allied Commission
ACC	Allied Control Commission
ACI	Advisory Council for Italy
AFHQ	Allied Force Headquarters
AMG	Allied Military Government
AMGOT	Allied Military Govt. of Occupied Territories
AT(E)	Administration of Territories (Europe) Committee
BOT	Board of Trade
CAD	Civil Affairs Division
CAO	Civil Affairs Officer
CCAC	Combined Civil Affairs Committee
CCE	Comitato Centrale Economico
CCS	Combined Chiefs of Staff
CERP	Comitato economice regionale piemontese
CIAI	Comitato industriale alt'Italia
CIGS	Chief of the Imperial General Staff
CG/CVL	General Command of the Corps of Volunteers of Freedom
CGIL	Confederazione generale italiana del lavoro
CLN	Committee of National Liberation
CLNRP	CLN of Piedmont
CTLN	CLN of Tuscany
CLNAI	CLN of Upper Italy
FEA	Foreign Economic Administration
FO	Foreign Office
FOGC	Foreign Office General Correspondence
FORD	Foreign Office Research Department
FRUS	Foreign Relations of the United States
GAP	Urban Guerrilla Unit
INML	Istituto nazionale per la Storia del Movimento di Liberazione in Italia
ISRT	Istituto storica della Resistenza in Toscana
JCS	Joint Chiefs of Staff
MGS	Military Government Section (of AFHQ)
NA	National Archives
OEW	Office of Economic Warfare
OFEC	Office of Foreign Economic Coordination
ORI	Organizzazione per la Resistenza italiana
OSS	Office of Strategic Services

PCI	Partita comunista italiano
PRO	Public Record Office (London)
PSI	Partito socialista italiano
PSIUP	Partito socialista italiano di unità proletaria
PWB	Psychological Warfare Board
RG	Record Group
SAC	Supreme Allied Commander
SACMED	Supreme Allied Commander Mediterranean
SF	Special Force
SOE	Special Operations Executive
UNRRA	United Nations Relief and Rehabilitation Administration
WD	War Department
WO	War Office

Churchill, *Closing the Ring* — Churchill, Winston S., *The Second World War. Closing the Ring* (1951)

Coles and Weinberg, *Civil Affairs* — H.L. Coles and A.K. Weinberg, *Civil Affairs: Soldiers Become Governors* (Special Studies series of the official history *The U.S. Army in World War II*; Washington D.C., 1964)

Delzell, *Mussolini's Enemies* — Delzell, C.F., *Mussolini's Enemies. The Italian Anti-Fascist Resistance* (Princeton, 1961)

Gaddis, *The United States and the Cold War* — Gaddis, J.L., *The United States and the Origins of the Cold War 1941–1947* (New York, 1972)

Garland and Smyth, *Sicily* — Garland, A.N. and Smyth, H.McG., *Sicily and the Surrender of Italy* (*The U.S. Army in World War II* series, Washington D.C., 1965)

Harris, *Allied Administration* — Harris, C.R.S., *Allied Military Administration of Italy, 1943–1945* (1957)

Howard, *Mediterranean Strategy* — Howard, M., *The Mediterranean Strategy in World War II* (1968)

Macmillan, *Blast of War* — Macmillan, H., *The Blast of War* (1967)

Reitzel, *The Mediterranean* — Reitzel, W., *The Mediterranean. Its Role in American Foreign Policy* (New York, 1948)

Woodward, *British Foreign Policy* — Woodward, Sir Llewellyn, *British Foreign Policy in the Second World War* (1 vol. edn 1962; 5 vols, 1962, 1971, 1976). In general the single-volume study has been used for this analysis; reference is made to specific volumes of the five-volume series wherever more detail is required.

Notes

1   The Italian surrender and the wartime Alliance

1. R.Murphy, *Diplomat Among the Warriors* (New York, 1964), 166–7.
2. M.Howard, *The Continental Commitment* (1972), Ch.5; Keith Middlemas, *Diplomacy of Illusion, The British Government and Germany 1937–1939* (1972), 153. See also 'Appeasement Revisited', a lecture by Norman Gibbs, King's College, London, 1 June 1975. British attempts to reach an accord which might produce Italian neutrality by means of a wide variety of concessions continued until the last moment: see S.J.Woolf, 'Inghilterra, Francia e Italia: settembre 1939–giugno 1940', *Rivista di storia contemporanea*, 4 (1972), 477–95. These issues have now been comprehensively analysed by L.R.Pratt in *East of Malta, West of Suez: Britain's Mediterranean Crisis 1936–1939* (1975).
3. E.H.Carr, 'Great Britain as a Mediterranean Power', Cust Foundation Lecture, University College, Nottingham (1937), 3.
4. *Ibid.*, 3–4.
5. *Ibid.*, 20.
6. *Ibid.*, 24–5; Gibbs, *op.cit.*
7. Howard, *op.cit.*, 102–3.
8. Middlemas, *op.cit.*, 210–11, 240.
9. Howard, *op.cit.*, 140–1; Pratt, *op.cit.*, 150 ff.
10. Howard, *ibid.*
11. Howard, *Mediterranean Strategy*, 10.
12. *Statistical Abstract of the United States*, Washington D.C.(1942), table 613, 564–5.
13. Reitzel, *The Mediterranean*, 116.
14. *Ibid.*, 117. Reitzel notes here that the State Dept had consistently refused pre-war attempts to involve the government in the activities of the oil companies to balance similar British operations. The Office of Economic Warfare drew up a balance of American investments in Italy which demonstrated that, at $75.5 million in 1940, they ranked fourth in importance among American investments in Europe; 'almost half of the investments in Italy were in petroleum companies while the remainder was distributed largely among electrical and other machine manufacturing concerns and distributing firms.' Report in 'Italian International Banking Connections' (Aug. 1943) in RG 169, FEA files. For the background of American relations with Italy up to 1940, see J.P.Diggins, *Mussolini and Fascism : the View from America* (Princeton, 1972).
15. G.Kolko, *The Politics of War* (New York, 1968), 21.
16. NA,RG 218, JCS/CCS Records; Decimal File, JCS 81st Meeting, 14 June 1943; cf.F.P.King, *The New Internationalism Allied Policy and the European Peace* (1973), 16–24.
17. PRO, 'Churchill Papers', PREM 3, 434/2; meeting of 9 Oct. 1944.
18. A.Quinlan, 'The Italian Armistice', in *American Civil-Military Decisions*, ed. Harold Stein (Birmingham, Alabama, 1962), 206.

19. Howard, *Mediterranean Strategy*, 37.
20. Cf. the 'Foreign Letter' of the Whaley–Eaton news service, issue dated 17 Aug. 1943. A copy of this confidential, high-level newsletter is to be found in PRO, WO 204, file 2161.
21. Quinlan, *op.cit.*, 204.
22. Cited in *ibid.*, 208.
23. *Ibid.*, 208.
24. *Ibid.*, 208; the background to this position is analysed in A.Varsori, 'Italy, Britain and the problem of a separate peace in the Second World War, 1940–1943', *J. Italian History* (winter 1978), 455–91.
25. Quinlan, *op.cit.*, 208.
26. On 'senior partner' issue see Coles and Weinberg, *Civil Affairs*, 165; also A.Varsori, '"Senior" o "Equal" Partner', *Rivista di studi politici internazionali*, 2 (1978), 229–38; message Attlee to Churchill, 25 Aug.1943, cited in King, *op.cit.*, 47.
27. Woodward, *British Foreign Policy*, p. 376; cf. G.Ross, 'Foreign Office attitudes to the Soviet Union 1941–1945', *J. Contemporary History* (July 1981), 521–40. The general area of British post-war foreign policy planning for Europe still awaits detailed research.
28. Woodward, *British Foreign Policy*, 439–43; Gaddis, *United States and the Cold War*, 23–7.
29. Report from British Delegation in Washington on conversation with Under-Secretary of State Sumner Welles, 23 Mar.1945, in PRO,Foreign Office General Correspondence (FO 371), file W/5317/99/49.
30. E.May, *'Lessons' of the Past. The Use and Misuse of History in American Foreign Policy* (New York,1973), 22–3; cf.Coles and Weinberg, *Civil Affairs*, 14–29, 325.
31. Gaddis, *The United States and the Cold War*, 108–9; comment by FO on letter from the Cabinet Office to the Min. of Production and the FO, 13 July 1945, in PRO, FO 371, U/3751/3646/74.
32. Report on conversation with Sumner Welles, cited in n.29 above.
33. Conv. and FO comments in PRO,FO 371,W/5317/99/49; cf.Varsori, "Senior", *op.cit.*, 229–60.
34. Woodward, *British Foreign Policy*, 443–4; FRUS (1943),I, 709–10.
35. Woodward, *British Foreign Policy*, 444.
36. FRUS (1943),I, 600.
37. NA,RG 59, Records of Harley A.Notter (henceforth Notter File), Policy Summary H3007, 22 July 1943.
38. Tel. Sir.A. Cadogan (in Washington) to the Foreign Office, 4 Sept.1943, FO comment and reply, in PRO, FO 371, file U/4132/3646/74.
39. FRUS (1943),I, 782–3.
40. Record of conversation dated 29 July 1943 in PRO, FO 371, file U/3401/324/70.
41. Message and background in Coles and Weinberg, *Civil Affairs*, 224–5.
42. Tel. Sir A.Clark Kerr to FO, 31 July 1943, in PRO, FO 371, file U/3404/324/70.
43. Note, Russian chargé d'affaires, London, to FO, 1 Aug. 1943, in PRO, FO 371, file U/3444/324/70.
44. Tel. British embassy, Washington, to FO, 9 Aug. 1943, in PRO, FO 371 file U/3550/324/70.
45. War Cabinet, Post-Hostilities Planning Sub-Committee, paper on Control Commission and Allied Military Government of Occupied Territory (AMGOT), 7 Aug. 1943; in PRO, FO 371 file U/3555/324/70.
46. Coles and Weinberg, *Civil Affairs*, 222–6.
47. Post-Hostilities Planning Sub-Committee, Paper on American draft surrender terms, 10 Aug. 1943; in PRO, FO 371, file U/3736/324/70.

48. Gaddis, *The United States and the Cold War*, 106. For the effects of Eisenhower's and War Dept's suspicions of the British, see Coles and Weinberg, *Civil Affairs*, 159–60, 165–70.
49. G.Warner, 'Italy and the Powers, 1943–9', in *The Rebirth of Italy 1943–50*, ed. S.J. Woolf (1972), 32.
50. FO Paper on 'Functions of the Political-Military Commission' in PRO, FO 371, file U 4678/324/70; excerpt in King, *op.cit.*, 48.
51. This was the famous occasion when Petain's deputy in North Africa, Admiral Darlan, after first resisting the Allied landings in the area (November 1942), was subsequently granted political control of the area by Generals Clark and Eisenhower in the name of military expediency. Public opinion in America was much disturbed: cf. H.G.Nicholas (ed.), *Washington Despatches, 1941–1945* (Chicago, 1981).
52. FRUS (1943), I, 518; Coles and Weinberg, *Civil Affairs*, 256.
53. Churchill, cited in Gaddis, *The United States and the Cold War*, 90; Eden, cited in Coles and Weinberg, *Civil Affairs*, 256 (message of 1 Oct. 1943).
54. See comments of War Dept Civil Affairs Divn cited in letter of Lt Col.Chester Hammond (War Dept General Staff) to Aml Leahy, JCS, in F.D. Roosevelt Library, Map Room Files, Box 32.
55. Churchill and Roosevelt had apparently decided they had no use for the Political-Military Commission by the beginning of October; cf. King, *op.cit.*, 48.

2   The armistice struggle

1. Letter, Dunn to Carmel Offie, Office of U.S. Political Adviser, 14 Feb. 1945; in NA,RG 59, State Decimal File 865.00. Official versions of the events leading up to the armistice are to be found in Garland and Smyth, *Sicily*, Woodward, *British Foreign Policy*, II, Ch.XXXII, in Coles and Weinberg, *Civil Affairs*, Ch.IX, and in the memoirs of protagonists such as Churchill and Macmillan. N.Kogan, *Italy and the Allies*, (Cambridge, Mass., 1956), remains a useful historical narrative stitching together Italian internal and inter-Allied events. Italian historiography, after establishing the sequence of events and commenting critically on the collapse of the country's leadership [e.g. M.Toscano, *Dal 25 luglio al 8 settembre* (Florence, 1966), R.Zangrandi, *L'Italia tradita: 8 settembre, 1943* (Rome, 1971)], has concentrated almost entirely on the development of Allied positions on the Italian internal situation; see bibliography (articles by Aga-Rossi, DiNolfo, Leonardis, Pinzani, Varsori).
2. The development of American policy has been thoroughly researched; see in particular, E.Di Nolfo, 'Stati uniti e Italia tra la seconda guerra mondiale e il sorgere della guerra fredda', in *Italia e Stati uniti dall'indipendenza americana ad oggi (1776/1976)* (Genoa, 1978); E.Aga-Rossi, 'La politica degli alleati verso l'Italia nel 1943', *Storia contemporanea*, 4 (1972); on Italian-American politics, J.E.Miller, 'The politics of relief: The Roosevelt administration and the reconstruction of Italy, 1943–44', *Prologue* (autumn 1981), 193–208.
3. British lack of information was reported by Sir A.Cadogan to John G.Winant, U.S. ambassador to London; tel. U.S. embassy, London to State Dept, 25 May 1943, in NA,RG 59, State Dec. File 865. Italian anti-Fascist groups in London were small and, besides Radio Londra of the BBC, poorly connected to official channels: see M.De Leonardis, 'La Gran Bretagna e la monarchia italiana (1943–1946)', in *Storia contemporanea* (Feb. 1981), 60; A.Varsori, *Gli alleati e l'emigrazione democratica antifascista (1940–1943)* (Florence, 1982).

4.   The result, according to the head of the British Political Warfare Executive, R.Bruce Lockhart, was to leave the propaganda initiative in the hands of the military on the spot, interested in any means of achieving quick results; R.Bruce Lockhart, *Comes the Reckoning* (1947), 251.

5.   Tel.FO to State Dept, 30 Nov. 1942, in NA, RG 59, State Dec.File 740.0011 European War. Cf.De Leonardis, *op.cit.*, 59–61.

6.   Comments to FO tel. of 30 Nov. 1942 cited in n.5 above; cf.J.E.Miller, 'The search for stability: an interpretation of American policy in Italy: 1943–46', *J. of Italian History* (autumn 1978), 267–9.

7.   Letter Rockefeller, Coordinator of Inter-American Affairs, to secretary, JCS, 14 Jan.1943, in NA,RG 218, Combined Civil Affairs Committee (CCAC) Dec.File, Geographical Series.

8.   Cited in D.A.T.Stafford, 'The detonator concept: British strategy, SOE and European Resistance after the Fall of France', *J. of Contemporary History* (Apr. 1975), 207.

9.   Salvemini and G.La Piana, *What To Do with Italy* (New York, 1943), 5.

10.   *Ibid.*, 7; see also J.E.Miller, 'A question of loyalty: American liberals, propaganda and the Italian-American community, 1939–43', *Maryland Historian* (spring 1978), 49–72.

11.   Salvemini and La Piana, *op.cit.*, xiv, 4–10.

12.   *Ibid.*, 15–19.

13.   Churchill, *Closing the Ring*, 51; see also Aga-Rossi, *op.cit.*, De Leonardis, *op.cit.*, Varsori, 'Italy, Britain and the problem of a separate peace. . .' *J.Italian History* (winter 1978), Grandi, originally a lawyer and Fascist agitator, had been ambassador to Gt Britain from 1932 to 1939 and had made efforts to keep in touch with Churchill: cf. Deakin, *The Brutal Friendship. Mussolini, Hitler and the Fall of Italian Fascism* (New York, 1962), 522–27.

14.   FRUS (1943) II, 322. In a joint broadcast on 16 July Churchill and Roosevelt broadcast to the Italians urging them to eliminate the Fascist regime and holding out the possibility of honourable treatment if this was done; text in Churchill, *Closing the Ring*, 43–4.

15.   The British even prepared a propaganda leaflet with the two formulae on the two different sides of the paper; the incident and Eden's reaction to it are jokingly described in Bruce-Lockhart, *op.cit.*, 252–3.

16.   Churchill, *Closing the Ring*, 52–60; Macmillan's account is in Macmillan, *Blast of War* Ch.15, Eisenhower's in *Crusade in Europe* (New York, 1948), 201–5. The memoirs of Marshal Badoglio and General Castellano, the chief Italian negotiator, are also relevant (see bibliography).

17.   *House of Commons Debates*, 5th ser., vol.391, cols.1399–1400; Churchill had drawn up a long memorandum on the situation the day before and sent it to Roosevelt who endorsed it almost as written: Churchill, *Closing the Ring*, 52–4; see also Aga-Rossi, *op.cit.*, 208–9; De Leonardis, *op.cit.*, 65.

18.   Churchill, *Closing the Ring*, 40.

19.   Not only were there differences between the British and the Americans on the 'blame' to be apportioned between the people and the regime, but also within the respective governments. Churchill shifted his opinion on more than one occasion, but the Foreign Office had no doubts: [The Italians] would forget the accumulated grievances which the democratic peoples had against them, and would assume that in getting rid of the fascist regime they had freed themselves from responsibility for its acts'; Woodward, *British Foreign Policy*, 227,n.3.

20.   Churchill to Roosevelt, 5 Aug. 1943, cited in Churchill, *Closing the Ring*, 89; cf. B.Lanza d'Ajeta, 'Relazione sulla missione a Lisbona (Aug. 1943)', *Rivista di studi politici internazionali* (1947), 581–8.

21. Sir D'A.Osborne to FO, 5 Aug. 1943, in PRO, FO 371, R/7417/5880/22; FO comment on this suggested that Osborne was over-influenced by the Vatican atmosphere.
22. Tel.U.S.embassy, Madrid to State Dept, 16 July 1943; in NA.RG 59, State Dec.File 865.00. It was reported here also that 'Ciano's presence in the Vatican is of course embarrassing. He is the principal black market operator in Italy. He is on excellent terms with the British Ambassador in the Vatican.'
23. Discussion in PRO,FO 371, R/7162/5880/22, R/7111/5880/22.
24. Rt Hon.Lord Hankey, *Politics, Trials and Errors* (1949), 38–45.
25. Churchill, *Closing the Ring*, 59; FRUS (1943), The Conferences at Washington and Quebec, 521.
26. Aga-Rossi, *op.cit.*, 210–11.
27. *Ibid.*, 212–13; details and commentary in H.G.Nicholas (ed.), *Washington Despatches 1941–1945* (Chicago, 1981), 228–9.
28. Tel. FO to Macmillan, 29 July 1943, in PRO, FO 371, R/6973/6447/22; on the American view Garland and Smyth, *Sicily*, 268–80.
29. Memo. by Eden, 'Administration of Italy after Defeat and Question of Instruments of Surrender', 12 July 1943, in PRO, 'Churchill Papers', PREM 3,241/1; 16 June document mentioned in Garland and Smyth, *Sicily*, 25–6.
30. Cf. docs in Coles and Weinberg, *Civil Affairs*, 169, 170–3, 222–3; on the attitude of the Joint Intelligence Committee, H.Cliadakis, 'Implications politiques du plan américain pour l'invasion de l'Italie (1943)', *Rev. d'histoire de la deuxième guerre mondiale* (Apr. 1981), 41–2.
31. Cited in tel. Washington embassy to FO, 28 July 1943, in PRO,FO 371, U/3358/324/70.
32. Churchill, *Closing the Ring*, 102.
33. Garland and Smyth, *Sicily*, 275–6; Woodward, *British Foreign Policy*, 229.
34. Woodward, *British Foreign Policy*, 230; Churchill, *Closing the Ring*, 104–9; Garland and Smyth, *Sicily*, 446–8.
35. Woodward, *British Foreign Policy*, 230; Garland and Smyth, *Sicily*, 448–50.
36. Woodward, *British Foreign Policy*, 230–1; Garland and Smyth, *Sicily*, 482–5.
37. Garland and Smyth, *Sicily*, 489–521; Woodward, *British Foreign Policy*, 230–1; Badoglio's account is to be found in his *Italy in the Second World War. Memories and Documents* (Milan, 1946); his attempts to bluff the Germans are also recounted in F.K. von Plehwe, *The End of an Alliance* (1972), together with Hitler's plan to overthrow Badoglio by force (von Plehwe was German military attaché in Rome at the time). Cf. also, Kogan, *op.cit.* For Italian revisions, cf. C.Pinzani, '8 settembre 1943, elementi e ipotesi per un giudizio storico', *Studi storici*, n.2 (1972), and Aga-Rossi, *op.cit.*, 207–14.
38. Woodward, *British Foreign Policy*, 232; Garland and Smyth, *Sicily*, 543–52; FRUS (1943), II, 369; for Eisenhower's doubts, Coles and Weinberg, *Civil Affairs*, 231–2; for Roosevelt's, Churchill, *Closing the Ring*, 190,194.
39. Royal Institute of International Affairs, *The Realignment of Europe*, Part IV, *Italy* (1955), 416–17.
40. Harris, *Allied Administration*, 105.
41. *Ibid.*, 106–7. The 'Long Terms' armistice is published in the British official paper Cmnd.6693; the 'civil affairs' provisions of this armistice (Clauses 18–24,29–37,42) are to be found in Coles and Weinberg, *Civil Affairs*, 234–6.
42. R.Murphy, *Diplomat Among the Warriors* (New York, 1964), 190–1; the king reportedly considered the terms 'monstrous', De Leonardis, *op.cit.*, 66.
43. Cited in FO comment on tel. Joint Staff Mission, Washington to War Office, 8 Oct. 1943, reporting American desires to publish Sicily directives, and complaints of American press that they had been let into the 'civil affairs picture' far less than

into the operational one; in PRO, FO 317, R/9943/6447/22.

44. The only exception to this rule appears to have been the Communist leader Togliatti, who became part of the government in Apr.1944, and would in any case have had his own sources; cf. P.Spriano, 'I riferimenti internazionali della svolta', *Rinascita*, 29 Mar.1974.

45. H.Nicholson, *Diaries.1939–45* (1973), 324.

46. Mussolini's puppet republic was set up at Salo on 15 Sept.

47. Churchill, *Closing the Ring*, 158–61.

48. For Don Sturzo's protest, *New York Times*, 11 Sept.1943; for De Gasperi's reaction, O.Lizzadri, *Il regno di Badoglio* (Rome, 1963), 99–100; on the general harm to the anti-Fascist forces, L.Valiani, *Dall 'antifascismo alla Resistenza* (Milan, 1960), 19.

49. Delzell, *Mussolini's Enemies*, 324; Churchill, *Closing the Ring*, 188.

50. Churchill, *Closing the Ring*, 133–5.

51. FRUS (1943),II; Kogan, *op.cit.*

52. Eisenhower to CCS, 18 Sept. 1943, in Coles and Weinberg, *Civil Affairs*, 231.

53. *Ibid.*, 231–2; cf. Garland and Smyth, *Sicily*, 540–4.

54. Coles and Weinberg, *Civil Affairs*, 229; Churchill, *Closing the Ring*, 189; Coles and Weinberg, *Civil Affairs*, 233 (for directive of 23 Sept.).

55. 'Italian Policy', memorandum of 20 Sept. 1943, in PRO,FO 371, R/8935/5880/22.

56. Woodward, *British Foreign Policy*, 233; Churchill, *Closing the Ring*, 190–1; Coles and Weinberg, *Civil Affairs*, 245; Macmillan, *Blast of War*.

57. The declaration is published in Coles and Weinberg, *Civil Affairs*, 245; legal experts quoted in Harris, *Allied Administration*, 130, n.3; an extraordinary incident occurred when Macmillan and Murphy stole back from Badoglio a document handed to him by Mason-MacFarlane which apparently guaranteed his position until the end of the war; they immediately destroyed the paper, Macmillan, *Blast of War*, 464–5.

58. King, *op.cit.*, 50.

59. *Ibid.*, 50–1; cf. Robert E.Sherwood, *Roosevelt and Hopkins: An Intimate History* (New York, 1950), 744.

60. Tel. Murphy to State Dept, 4 Oct. 1943; in NA,RG 59, State Dec. File 865.00.

61. Churchill, *Closing the Ring*, 284.

62. FRUS (1943), I, 588–9. Cf. also tels British Joint Staff Mission (Washington) to War Office, 1 Oct.1943 in PRO, FO 371, R/9512/6447/22.

63. FRUS, *ibid.*; cf. also Warner, 'Italy and the Powers, 1943–44', in *The Rebirth of Italy 1943–50*, ed. S.J.Woolf (1972), 33–5. A draft tel. from the FO to Macmillan, (presumably of early September) explained that: 'our machinery for bringing in the Dominions and the [British] Allies depends on having an advisory council, on the side-lines, which would be run by you', in PRO, Treasury Papers, T.160.1278/18640/02/1.

64. FRUS, *ibid.*, 609; reports were coming in from Eisenhower and Alexander at this time that the battle in Italy was not progressing speedily; see Churchill, *Closing the Ring*, 243–7.

65. FRUS, *ibid.*, 610, 714.

66. For Hull's comment, FRUS, *ibid.*, 617 (the *New York Times* later claimed that the principles had been written by the American delegation; see *New York Times*, 19 Apr. 1944); Eden's comments are in a tel. Eden (in Moscow) to FO, 25 Oct. 1943, in PRO,FO 371 R/10707/6447/22, and a tel. Eden to prime minister, 24 Oct. 1943 in PRO, Private Secretary's Papers FO 800, file 409. The Moscow Declaration is reproduced in Harris, *Allied Administration*, 131.

67. FRUS (1943) I, 619–20: the London body became known as the European Advisory Commission.

68. V.Mastny, *Russia's Road to the Cold War* (New York, 1979), 122.

69. Tel. Murphy to State Dept, 30 Nov.1943, in Coles and Weinberg, *Civil Affairs*, 259.

70. The Moscow Resolution on the Advisory Council for Italy is printed in Harris, *Allied Administration*, 126.

71. Tel. Murphy, 30 Nov., cited in 69 above; on the incident as a whole see Warner, *op.cit.*, 35; FO reaction in PRO,FO 371, R/11394/6447/22.

72. Harris, *Allied Administration*, 117. Of all the Allies, none were more bitterly determined to punish Italy for the imperial adventures of Fascism than the French, who refused to recognize co-belligerency. De Gaulle's directives ordered that measures should be taken 'to ensure that militarily an Italian war will never again be possible, neither in Tunisia, nor in the Mediterranean, nor in the Alps nor in Corsica.' The French determined to reserve the right to 'intervene offensively by land against Turin, Milan and Genoa', and designed a peace treaty to destroy every element of Italian military, naval and political power in international politics and to place the country under a constant menace of French invasion with Austrian, Yugoslav and Greek support; see P.Guillen, 'I rapporti franco-italiani dall'armistizio alla firma del Patto atlantico', in *L'Italia dalla liberazione alle Repubblica*, Proceedings of the Florence Conference, (March, 1976); and below, Ch.9 n.53.

73. FRUS (1943), I, 612–13; Churchill, *Closing the Ring*, 294–6.

74. Mastny, *op.cit.*, 114: Gaddis, *The United States and the Cold War*, 90; the Soviet historiographical point of view, sticking close to Molotov's original positions, is to be found in G.Filatov, 'La politica del l'Unione sovietica nei confronti dell'Italia alla fine della Seconda guerra mondiale', in *L'Italia dalla liberazione alla Repubblica*, *op.cit.*.

75. Cited in Gaddis, *The United States and the Cold War*, 91; other writers on the Italian analogy with central European problems include W.McNeill, *America, Britain and Russia. Their Cooperation and Conflict* (Royal Inst. International Affairs, 1953), 310; G.Kolko, *The Politics of War* (New York, 1968), 50–2, 130–1; G.Warner, *op.cit.*, 37.

76. J.Harvey (ed.), *The War Diaries of Oliver Harvey* (1978), 325,317.

77. J.E.Miller, 'The Search for Stability . . .', *op.cit.*, 268–9; E.Di Nolfo, 'Stati uniti e l'Italia tra la Seconda guerra mondiale e il sorgere della Guerra fredda', *op.cit.*, 128–9.

3 Liberators or occupiers? The Allies in Southern Italy, autumn–winter 1943

1. A.Moorehead, *Eclipse* (1945), 62–3. But the Neapolitans were victims of a no less striking and historic moral collapse by some of the new invaders, the Americans, a crisis described with great force in the novel of John Horn Burns, *The Gallery*, which includes the following passage: 'They figured it this way: these Ginsoes have made war on us; so it doesn't matter what we do to them, boost their prices, shatter their economy, and shack up with their women.' This novel (considered the best novel of the Second World War by Gore Vidal [preface to *Williwaw*, 1970 edn, 9] is analysed in relation with others produced by the Italian campaign in J.P.Diggins, 'The American writer, Fascism and the liberation of Italy', *American Q.* (winter 1966), 599–614.

2. T.R.Fisher, 'Allied Military Government in Italy', *Annals of the American Academy of Political and Social Sciences* (Jan. 1950), 122.

3. Harris, *Allied Administration*, 89, n.1.

4. Reitzel, *The Mediterranean*, 14, 17.

5. Cf. the title of Coles and Weinberg, *Civil Affairs*, Ch.IX.

6. Coles and Weinberg, *Civil Affairs*, Ch.VI, Sect. 6.; M.Neufeld, 'The failure of Allied Military Government in Italy', *Public Administration Rev.*, VI (spring 1946), 138;

Mason-MacFarlane referred to ACC's 'Cinderella' status in his monthly conference as deputy president of the commission, 14 Apr. 1944, adding, 'A fitting end to the Cinderella story would be in the glass factory at Venice,'; minutes in NA.RG 331, ACC files, 10000/132/6. AMGOT was shortened to AMG in Jan. 1944.

7. Macmillan, *Blast of War*, 453.

8. Memo. by S.K.Padover, 8 Jan. 1943, cited in Coles and Weinberg, *Civil Affairs*, 26.

9. Note of 10 June 1943 cited in *ibid.*, 173.

10. 'Occupation Problems: Organization of Occupation Forces in Italy', memo. by International Security Divn, State Dept, 22 July 1943; doc. cited in Ch.1, n.37 above.

11. *New York Herald Tribune*, 20 June 1943.

12. Meeting of Official Committee on Control Commission for Italy, 31 Aug. 1943, with representatives of the Foreign Office (Sir Orme Sargent in the chair), Admiralty, War Office, Dominions Office, Ministries of War Transport, Air, Economic Warfare, Aircraft Production, Production, Supply, Treasury. The purpose of the meeting was indicated at the beginning by Sargent, who declared that a British scheme for control was necessary if the Americans were to be forestalled; minutes in PRO, Treasury Papers, T.160.1278/186640/02/1. (No other trace of this committee has been found so far; most problems of this type were discussed by the Ministerial Committee on Armistice Terms and Civil Affairs).

13. Coles and Weinberg, *Civil Affairs*, 177.

14. *Ibid.*, 185.

15. *Ibid.*, 221–2.

16. *Ibid.*, 288.

17. *Ibid.*, Ch.IX, esp. 237–8, 245–6; quotation from minutes of meeting of Allied officials at home of British resident minister, 13 Oct. 1943, in *ibid.*, 245–6.

18. Harris, *Allied Administration*, 109; the original design of ACC and the reorganization of Feb.1944 are explained in diagrammatic form in Coles and Weinberg, *Civil Affairs*, 126.

19. Harris, *Allied Administration*, 110.

20. FO memo. on 'Control Commission and Existing Arrangements in Italy', 29 Oct. 1943, in PRO, FO 371, R//9356/6447/22.

21. Harris, *Allied Administration*, 108.

22. Comment on FO memo. 'Relations with the Italian Government and Control Commission in Italy', 4 Oct. 1943, in PRO,FO 371, R/10069/6447/22.

23. Macmillan, *Blast of War*, 469–70.

24. Tel. to FO, 5 Sept. 1943, in PRO, Treasury Papers, T.160,1278/18640/02/1.

25. Coles and Weinberg, *Civil Affairs*, 230.

26. Harris, *Allied Administration*, 132.

27. *Ibid.*, 134–5; cf. Ch.4, below.

28. On the first point, see Churchill's message to the House of Commons, 27 July 1943, cited in Ch. 2 above; on second see comments by Coles and Weinberg, *Civil Affairs*, 275.

29. Minutes of the conference between the Italian under-secretary for education and the education advisers of ACC, 25 Nov. 1943; in Coles and Weinberg, *Civil Affairs*, 290.

30. R.W.Komer, *Civil Affairs and Military Government in the Mediterranean Theater* (Washington, p.c., n.d.), 14–17; cf. Coles and Weinberg, *Civil Affairs*, Ch.IV, Sec. 3.

31. Memo. of 18 Apr. 1943, cited in Coles and Weinberg, *Civil Affairs*, 171–2.

32. C.J.Friedrich (ed.), *American Experiences in Military Government in World War II* (Washington D.C.,1948), 17.

33. Report by Spofford, head, G-5, AFHQ (Oct. 1945); cited in Coles and Weinberg, *Civil Affairs*, 280.

34. The control of appointments and communications (even telephonic) was a constant complaint of the Badoglio governments; cf. letter from the prefect of Matera to all the public offices of the province, 8 Jan.1944, in ACS, Presidenza del Consiglio, Salerno-Brindisi, Cat.2, Busta 6, f.1; Sicilian report in Coles and Weinberg, *Civil Affairs*, 279; the condition of the govt is described in N.Gallerano, 'La disgregazione delle basi di massa del facismo Nel Mezzogiorno e il ruolo della masse contadine', in *Operai e contadini nella crisi italiana del 1943–1944* (Milan, 1974), 471–81.

35. Directive of 6 Sept. 1943 cited in Coles and Weinberg, *Civil Affairs*, 284.

36. *Ibid.*, 208. These attitudes are confirmed by Harris, *Allied Administration*, 61, who adds however that the bishops 'refused to take any part in denouncing either *mafiosi* or prominent Fascists. The influence of Cardinal Lavitrano in Palermo and two other important prelates was rather engaged in endeavouring to persuade the Allied authorities to release interned Fascists and let bygones be bygones.'

37. Tel. Berne embassy to State Dept, 2 Jan. 1943, in NA,RG 59,S.D.864.911.

38. Cited in Harris, *Allied Administration*, 63.

39. N.Lewis, *The Honoured Society* (1964), 11–16, 19–20, 79–92, 106–14 (quotation from p.16); on links with U.S Naval Intelligence, L.Mercuri, 'La Sicilia e gli Alleati', *Storia contemporanea, 4* (1972), 954–5.

40. L.Mercuri, *ibid.*, 961–5; M.Ganci, 'Appunti per la storia dei Comitati di liberazione nazionale in Sicilia', in *Regioni e Stato dalla Resistenza alla Costituzione*, M.Legnani, ed. (Bologna, 1975), 117, 132.

41. Coles and Weinberg, *Civil Affairs*, 209; Harris, *Allied Administration*, 243.

42. Coles and Weinberg, *Civil Affairs*, 286.

43. Harris remark in *Allied Administration*, 147–8; Letter from naval officer in charge, Brindisi, to C-in-C Allied Forces, 23 Dec. 1943, in PRO,WO 204/2162.

44. *Chicago Daily News*, 13 Dec. 1943; *News Chronicle*, 1 Oct. 1943; *Saturday Evening Post*, 23 Sept. 1944.

45. Letter to Sir B.Robertson, chief administrative officer, AFHQ, 10 May 1945, in NA,RG 331, AFHQ files, R-316A.

46. Coles and Weinberg, *Civil Affairs*, 341–2.

47. On Roosevelt's views cf. letter to Stimson, 3 June 1943 (and discussion by interested departments) in Coles and Weinberg, *Civil Affairs*, 100–1; on Palermo incidents, Coles and Weinberg, *Civil Affairs*, 346–7.

48. *Chicago Daily News*, 13 Dec. 1943; *New York Herald Tribune*, 11 Sept. 1943 (two days previously the same paper had reported Hull as saying that Italy would require few supplies).

49. Cf. Harris, *Allied Administration*, 87–9; below Ch.6, n.2, below.

50. Stimson criticized the agreements produced by the Moscow conference for their lack of economic content: 'while these political arrangements are good, they haven't any grasp apparently of the underlying need of proper economic arrangements to make the peace stick.' Cited in G.Kolko, *The Politics of War* (New York, 1968), 251.

51. Newsletter of 17 Aug. 1943, in PRO,WO 204, file 2161.

52. Letter Gueterbock, planning staff for ACC, Tizi Ouzou (North Africa), to War Office, 10 Oct. 1943, in FOGC,R/10951/6447/22.

53. Cited in J.Norman, *Adlai Stevenson's Wartime Mission to Italy* (New York,[n.d.]), 2–3. Stevenson also emphasized that supply was not an altruistic problem, *ibid.*, 4.

54. ACC report (8 May 1944) and FEA reply (19 May 1944) in NA, RG 169 (FEA records): cf. E.Aga-Rossi, *Il Rapporto Stevenson. Documenti sull'economia italiana e sulle direttive della politica americana in Italia nel 1943–44* (Rome, 1979).

55. Coles and Weinberg, *Civil Affairs*, 340.

56. V.Petrov, *Money and Conquest: Allied Occupation Currencies in World War II* (Baltimore, 1967), 91–2; B.Foa, *Monetary Reconstruction in Italy* (New York, 1949), 19–20.
57. On the advantage offered to the British by American bureaucratic confusion, see internal State Dept memo, 2 May 1944, in NA,RG 59, State Dec.File 865.01; quotation from memo. Office of Foreign Economic Coordination to Dean Acheson (asst. secretary of state), 11 Oct. 1943, in NA,RG 59, State Dec.File 740.0019 Control (Italy).
58. Internal Treasury memo., 27 Oct. 1944, in PRO, Treasury Papers, T.160,1278/18640/02/3.
59. 'Supplemental Guide to Labor Directive for "Husky"', 24 Aug. 1943, in NA, RG 218, JCS/CCAC files.
60. M.Neufeld, 'The Failure of AMG in Italy', *Public Administration Rev.*, 6 (spring 1946), 142.
61. *New York Times*, 6 Sept. 1943.
62. Coles and Weinberg, *Civil Affairs*, 348–9.
63. Letter Caccia to res.min., 27 Dec. 1943, in PRO, FO 371, 691/691/22.
64. Doc. cited in n.43 above.
65. Mins of meeting of Ministerial Committee on Armistice Terms and Civil Affairs, 21 Dec. 1943, in PRO, FO 371, U/6634/3646/74.
66. Harris, *Allied Administration*, 114.
67. Rennell comment in *ibid.*, 113; Caccia comment in *ibid.*, 113, n.1.
68. H.Stuart Hughes, *The United States and Italy* (Cambridge, Mass., 1953), 127–8; Hughes was a member of the Research and Analysis Branch of the OSS at the time.

4 The politics of the Italian problem from Monte Cassino to the liberation of Rome, January–June 1944

1. Reported in a letter Caccia to res.min's Office, 26 Jan. 1944, in PRO,FO 371, R/2338/15/22.
2. Comments of 7 Jan.1944 accompanying letter in *ibid.*
3. JCS meeting, 19 Nov. 1943, mins in NA,RG 218, JCS/CCS Decimal File.
4. Memo. pres to P.M., 31 Dec. 1943, in PRO, 'Churchill Papers', PREM 3, 241/7.
5. Cf.Howard, *Mediterranean Strategy*, 48; R.Murphy, *Diplomat Among the Warriors* (New York, 1964), 211; To Churchill's stalwart defence of the Italian campaign at Teheran, Stalin replied that 'he had never regarded the operations in the Mediterranean as being of a secondary character. They were of the first importance, but not from the point of view of invading Germany'; mins of 1st Plenary Meeting, 28 Nov. 1943, in PRO, private secy's Papers, 800, 409.
6. FRUS (1944), III, 1007.
7. Conv. J.Wesley Jones,S.Eur.Divn and Herbert Matthews, 22 Jan. 1944; memo. in NA, RG 59, S.D.865.01, Box 5036.
8. FRUS (1944), III, 1018.
9. Churchill, *Closing the Ring*, 201; Churchill's desire to postpone political discussion was seconded at this point by the new British supreme commander, Wilson: cf. message Wilson to CCS, 9 Feb. 1944, in PRO,WO 204, f.2162.
10. M.De Leonardis, 'La Gran Bretagna e la monarchia italiana (1943–1946)', *Storia contemporanea* (Feb. 1981), 75–81; Macmillan, *Blast of War*, 462–4.
11. *Chicago Daily News*, 11 Oct. 1943.
12. On the Naples Committee, Delzell, *Mussolini's Enemies*, 324–5; B.Croce, *Quando l'Italia era tagliata in due* (Rome, 1947); on Sforza much has been written: cf. in particular, E.Di Nolfo, 'Problemi della politica estera italiana, 1943–1950', *Storia e*

politica (Jan.–June 1975), 300; J.E.Miller, 'Carlo Sforza e l'evoluzione della politica americana verso l'Italia. 1940–1943', *Storia contemporanea*, 4 (1976), 825–53; for the official British view, Woodward, *British Foreign Policy*, 234; quotation from memo. 'Questions Relating to Political, Economic and Social Forces in Southern Italy', 10 Dec. 1943, by HQ, AMG Security Intelligence (Palermo), in PRO, WO204, f.2161.

13. Report Murphy to State Dept, on visit to Italy 25–30 Oct. 1943, in PRO, WO 204, f.2317.

14. Delzell, *Mussolini's Enemies*, 273.

15. L.Valiani, *Dall'antifascismo alla Resistenza* (Milan, 1960), 98; C.L.Ragghianti, *Il disegno della liberazione italiana* (Pisa, 1954), 43–55.

16.ᐧ Delzell, *Mussolini's Enemies*, 273–4; F.Chabod, *L'Italia contemporanea (1918–1948)*, (Turin, 1961), 124–5 emphasizes the role of the Holy See in filling the vacuum of authority in this situation and providing a rallying point for the people of Rome.

17. P.Nenni, *Tempo di guerra fredda. Diari 1943–1956* (Milan, 1981), 37–8, 41; the Rome CLN briefly attempted to improvise a military organization under Luigi Longo of the Communist Party, Sandro Pertini for the Socialists and Riccardo Bauer of the Action Party, Delzell, *Mussolini's Enemies*, 274.

18. Ragghianti, *op.cit.*, 55; Delzell, *Mussolini's Enemies*, 327; message Eisenhower to CCS, 16 Nov. 1943, in PRO,WO 204, f.2317.

19. This story is eloquently told by survivors from the Piedmontese experience in the documentary film, *Le prime bande*, Archivio nazionale cinematografico della Resistenza (Turin, 1980).

20. Beside the work of Delzell, which includes comprehensive information as well as a political overview, the best presentation of the political problems of the Resistance in English is G.Quazza, 'The politics of the Italian Resistance', in S.J.Woolf (ed.), *The Rebirth of Italy, 1943–50*, 1–29; for a recent treatment of the Resistance in the overall context of Italian contemporary history, G.Carocci, *Storia d'Italia dall'unità ad oggi* (Milan, 1982), ch.34.

21. G.Grassi and M.Legnani, 'Il governo dei CLN' in M.Legnani (ed.) *Regioni e Stato dalla Resistenza alla Costituzione* (Bologna, 1971), 69–85.

22. Among the best accounts from English survivors of this experience are Stuart Hood, *Pebbles from my Skull* (1963) and Eric Newby, *Love and War in the Apennines* (1978).

23. Chabod, *op.cit.*, 128; some statistical work has been carried out on the social composition of the Resistance in certain areas; cf.Delzell, *Mussolini's Enemies*, 295–6; R.Battaglia, *Storia della Resistenza italiana* (Turin, 1964), chs.V, VII.

24. Carocci, *op.cit.*, Ch.33; cf. F.Catalano, 'The rebirth of the party system, 1944–48', in Woolf (ed.), *op.cit.*, Ch.3.

25. R.Battaglia, *La seconda guerra mondiale. problemi e nodi cruciali* (Rome, 1966), 288–92, indicates that the question of unity was in many ways the key political problem facing the Resistance and its political organizations; cf.Valiani, *op.cit*, chapter on 'La Resistenza e la questione istituzionale'.

26. Delzell, *Mussolini's Enemies*, 306–14; key testimony from survivors is to be found in M.Salvadori, *The Labour and the Wounds* (1958), from the SF side, and from R.Craveri, an Italian officer who worked with the OSS: *La campagna d'Italia e i servizi segreti. La storia dell'ORI* (Milan, 1981), a highly critical review by Salvadori of this book is to be found in *Storia contemporanea*, 1 (1981), 190–8; the memoirs of a former head of SF in Italy are published in J.G.Beevor, *S.O.E.Recollections and Reflections* (1981), cf. also D.A.T.Stafford, *Britain and European Resistance, 1940–1945. A Survey of the Special Operations Executive with Documents* (1980), 192–202, which however adds little new material; the key Italian source is P.Secchia and F.Frassati, *La*

Resistenza e gli alleati (Milan, 1962), an account with documents by a historian and a protagonist, both members of the Communist Party.

27.   Cf. D.W.Ellwood, 'Al tramonto dell'impero britannico: Italia e balcani nella strategia inglese, 1942–1946', in *Italia contemporanea, 134* (1979), 77–84.
28.   Delzell, *Mussolini's Enemies*, 312; Quazza, *op.cit.*, 21–2.
29.   B.Sweet-Escott, 'S.O.E. in the Balkans', in P.Auty and R.Clogg (eds), *British Policy Towards Wartime Resistance in Yugoslavia and Greece* (1975), 15–16.
30.   Delzell, *Mussolini's Enemies*, 313.
31.   *Ibid.*, 310–11.
32.   A number of detailed reports from SF mission leaders, written on completion of their activities, are conserved in War Office files, in particular (PRO), WO 204, files 7293–98; cf. G.Lett, *Rossano. An Adventure of the Italian Resistance* (1955), Chs. V–X; Lett was a British officer who experienced the Resistance from the first days to his appointment as local AMG officer; for a very different account of a similar experience, B.Davidson, *Special Operations Europe. Scenes from the Anti-Nazi War* (1980), Ch.V.
33.   Churchill, *Closing the Ring*, Bk Two, Ch.10.
34.   The most detailed account in English is in Delzell, *Mussolini's Enemies*, 331–6; cf. Quazza, *op.cit.*, 16; the proceedings were published in C.Buonanno and O. Valentini, *Gli atti del Congresso di Bari* (Bari, 1944).
35.   Delzell, *Mussolini's Enemies*, 331.
36.   Macmillan, *Blast of War*, 479–80.
37.   *Ibid.*
38.   Minute by Churchill, 19 Feb. 1944, in PRO,FO 371, R/2662/691/22.
39.   Message MacFarlane to AFHQ, 17 Feb. 1944, reporting meeting with king, in PRO,WO 204, f.2162.
40.   Letter PWB, Bari to Military Government Section (MGS) AFHQ in *ibid*; Badoglio's complaint reported in Letter MacFarlane to MGS, 13 Feb. 1944, in *ibid*.
41.   MacFarlane's opinion in letter to MGS, 24 Feb.1944, in *ibid*; that of Wilson in messages to CCS of 18 Feb. and 20 Feb. 1944, in *ibid*.
42.   On Wilson's change of heart cf. docs in Coles and Weinberg, *Civil Affairs*, 442–3; quote from Harris, *Allied Administration*, 139; cf.Delzell, *Mussolini's Enemies*, 335; full text of Junta's proposal in FRUS (1944), III, 104–7.
43.   Harris, *Allied Administration*, 138–9.
44.   Churchill, *Closing the Ring*, 497–8 (message of 13 Feb.).
45.   In fact Roosevelt immediately distanced himself from the prime minister's position, protesting about the use of force against anti-Fascism: message to Churchill of 7 March 1944 in Coles and Weinberg, *Civil Affairs*, 444; excerpts from the Commons speech in Churchill, *Closing the Ring*, 498–9; Naples strike and official reaction in Harris, *Allied Administration*, 140.
46.   Cited in P.Spriano, *Storia del partito comunista italiano*, (Turin, 1975), V, 300; Croce and Sforza protested in a direct, joint letter to Churchill, reproduced in Coles and Weinberg, *Civil Affairs*, 444; in the U.S. leading Italian liberals Salvemini, La Piana, Borgese, Toscanini, Pacciardi, Venturi wrote an 'impassioned protest' to the *Herald Tribune*, H.G.Nicholas (ed), *Washington Despatches 1941–45* (Chicago, 1981), 327.
47.   FO comments on a tel. res. min. to FO, 21 Mar. 1944, in PRO,FO 371, R/4484/51/22.
48.   Tel.FO to res. min., 21 Jan. 1944, in PRO, 'Churchill Papers', PREM 3,243/8; an accompanying note by Churchill said: 'I entirely agree that Italian Government should be warned off Atlantic Charter for a good long time yet.' (23 Jan. 1944).
49.   Comments by Eden in PRO,FO 371, R/8236/15/22.
50.   Tel. res.min. to FO, 24 Jan. 1944, in PRO, 'Churchill Papers', PREM 3, 243/8.
51.   Quazza, *op.cit.*, p.51.

52. The strikes and their background are described in Quazza, *op.cit.*, 17; Delzell, *Mussolini's Enemies*, 360–2, 370–2; Spriano, *op.cit.*, Ch.X; *New York Times* editorial of 9 Mar. 1944; (the reference to the fate of the Italian fleet concerns a largely misinterpreted Roosevelt statement at a press conference; in fact the Soviets, who had reiterated their demand for a share in the fleet at Teheran, were just beginning to get some small British and American merchant ships in substitute for a share of the Italian fleets; cf. docs in *Roosevelt and Churchill. Their Secret Wartime Correspondence*, F.L.Loewenheim, H.D.Langley, M.Jonas (eds) (New York, 1975), 458–9).

53. Spriano, *op.cit.*, V., 301.

54. Harris, *Allied Administration*, 141; MacFarlane's version of events as told to the supreme Allied commander is in a personal message of 19 Mar.1944, in PRO, WO 204, f.2318; cf. docs in Coles and Weinberg, *Civil Affairs*, 445–9.

55. Tels res.min. to FO, 9, 10, 12 Mar. 1944 and FO comments in PRO,FO 371, R/3823/51/22; tel. Eden to Clark Kerr, 13 Mar. 1944 in *ibid*; cf. also FRUS (1944) III, 1040–2 for similar American views.

56. Tel. P.M. to Clark Kerr, 11 Mar. 1944, in PRO, 'Churchill Papers', PREM 3,243/8; also P.M.'s Personal Minute, 7 May 1944, in PRO,FO 371, R/7202/691/22; cf. Woodward, *British Foreign Policy*, 240.

57. Full text in FRUS (1944) III, 1062–5; the statement should be compared with the comments made by Russian ambassador Maisky on the future governments of liberated countries, comments made in a conversation with Anthony Eden before Fascism fell. Did the British in Italy, Maisky asked, propose to set up Badoglio and a few of his friends?

    'His government did not want communist regimes set up in Europe and they did not intend to interfere in the internal affairs of other states, but they did hope that we would join with them in trying to make sure that in the countries of Europe as they were freed there were administrations that broadly represented the national will. This meant that they must contain representatives of the Left, the Centre and the Right, and not only the Right. The Secretary of State said the Ambassador seemed to be describing exactly the kind of national government that we had here',
    conversation of 22 June 1943 recorded in PRO,FO 371, R/6793/5880/22.

58. Harris, *Allied Administration*, 143; for the Foreign Office position see memo of 4 Oct. 1943 in PRO,FO 371, R/10069/6447/22; draft minute Eden to P.M. 7 Feb. 1944, in *ibid.*, R/2003/48/22.

59. Coles and Weinberg, *Civil Affairs*, 447–8; cf. 'The resumption of diplomatic relations between Italy and the Soviet Union during World War II', in M.Toscano, *Designs in Diplomacy. Pages from European Diplomatic History in the Twentieth Century* (Milan, 1953), Ch.IV.

60. FO comments on tels res.min. to FO, 13, 21 Mar. 1944, in PRO,FO 371, R/3983/51/22, 4484/51/22.

61. Chiefs of Staff report of 30 Mar.1944 in PRO,FO 371, R/5290/51/22; cf. FRUS (1944), III, 1040–1.

62. Macmillan, 'Note on the Italian Situation', 22 Mar. 1944, in PRO,FO 371, R/4999/51/22.

63. *New York Times*, 15 Mar., 18 Mar. 1944.

64. *Ibid.*, 18 Mar. 1944; cf. the comments of Isaiah Berlin in the British embassy in Washington, in Nicholas, *op.cit.*, 327.

65. *New York Times*, 10 Apr. 1944; full text in *Documents in American Foreign Relations*, ed. Goodrich and Carroll (1943–44), VI, 25–35.

66. For American rejection of the 'coffee-pot' speech, tel. Macmillan to FO, 19 Mar. 1944, in PRO, FO 371, R/4579/51/22; for American CCAC views, memo. from the Director on the 'Political Situation in Italy', 23 Feb.1944, in F.D.Roosevelt Library,

Map Room Files, Box 30; cf. Woodward, *British Foreign Policy*, 236.

67. Tels Roosevelt to Churchill, 13 Mar. 1944, in FRUS (1944), II, 1053, 1055; for Murphy's view, Murphy, *op.cit.*, 215.

68. Reported in tel. Macmillan to FO, cited in n.66 above; Wilson and Churchill were in direct contact at all times; on 21 Feb. for instance the prime minister told the supreme commander of the cabinet's judgment of events: 'as I expected, there was firm resolve not to be intimidated by threats from people who have already surrendered unconditionally'; in PRO,'Churchill Papers', PREM 3, 243/8.

69. Harris, *Allied Administration*, 143; Murphy's report on this dramatic meeting is reproduced in Coles and Weinberg, *Civil Affairs*, 450–1.

70. Note of State Dept to British government, 25 Mar. 1944, in FRUS (1944), III, 1075.

71. Report, 'Problems Related to a Government of Italy Based on the House of Savoy', 7 Jan. 1943, in NA,RG 59, 'Notter File'. Macmillan arrived at the same kind of conclusion by more flippant methods:
   'Our experience with the French since the collapse shows the importance which the Latin mind attaches to respect for (existing) form. Should we not turn this to our purpose in the case of Italy? The fact that even Mussolini maintained the House of Savoy illustrates the point and shows the particular value of being able to operate under Royal cover.' tel. to FO of 21 July 1943, in PRO, 'Churchill Papers', PREM 3., 241/1.

72. Report, 'Italy: Political Reconstruction: Nature of a Permanent National Government', 4 Aug. 1943, in NA,RG 59, 'Notter File'.

73. Report, 'Italy: Political Reconstruction: National Government During the Transition Period', 9 June 1943, in *ibid.*

74. Message Taylor to Macmillan, Murphy, 18 Oct. 1943, in PRO,WO 204, f.2317.

75. Tel.Murphy to State Dept, on visit to Italy with Macmillan, 25–30 Oct. 1943, in *ibid.*

76. Memo. 'Note on the Italian Situation', 22 Mar. 1944, cited in n.62 above; British and American attitudes to the monarchy have been amply investigated in recent historiography: see articles by Cliadakis, Di Nolfo, 'Stati uniti e Italia . . .', Miller, 'The search for stability . . .', De Leonardis, listed in bibliography.

77. Harris, *Allied Administration*, 142–4.

78. Tel. Charles to FO, 22 Apr. 1944, in PRO,FO 371, R36449/15/22.

79. Cf.Delzell, *Mussolini's Enemies*, 341–6.

80. A.Eden, *The Eden Memoirs, The Reckoning* (1965), 439; De Leonardis, *op.cit.*, 91.

81. Conversation with Togliatti reported in tel.Charles to FO, 24 May 1944; reply Churchill to Charles, 26 May 1944; both in PRO,FO 371, R/8237/15/22.

82. FO comments in *ibid.*

83. P.Spriano, 'I riferimenti internazionali della svolta', *Rinascita*, 29 Mar. 1974.

84. Harris, *Allied Administration*, 142; personal messages MacFarlane to AFHQ, 20 Apri., 21 Apri. 1944, in PRO,WO 204, f.2162.

85. Sir Noel Charles's account (dated 19 Apr. 1944) is in PRO,FO 371, R/6443/691/22; Kirk's estimate accompanied an ACC report on the growth of the PCI of 16 Apr. 1944; in NA,RG 59, State Decimal File 865.00. A useful statement of PCI positions at that period is to be found in an unsigned editorial 'L'Italia e il mondo', in *Rinascita*, 1.1, 1 June 1944.

86. Comments by FO and Eden on tel. Charles to FO, 19 Apr. 1944, cited in n. 85 above.

87. Sargent minute in PRO.FO 371, R/7308/691/22; partial discussion in Woodward, *British Foreign Policy*, II, 538–9.

88. V.Mastny, *Russia's Road to the Cold War* (New York, 1979), 144.

89. G.Quazza, *Resistenza e storia d'Italia* (Milan, 1976), ca.4⁰; G.Garocci, 'Togliatti e la Resistenza', *Nuovi Argomenti*, n.53–4 (1961–2), 137–45; E.Santarelli, 'Quadro e transformazione dei partiti', in *L'Italia dalla liberazione alla Republica*, Proceedings of

the Florence Conference (Mar.1976), 231–40.
90. cf.A.Gambino, *Storia del dopoguerra dalla liberazione al potere DC* (Bari, 1975), 35–50; G.Warner, 'Italy and the Powers 1945–49' in *The Rebirth of Italy 1943–50*, ed. S.Woolf (1972), 40–2.
91. E.Di Nolfo, 'The United States and Italian Communism 1942–1946: World War II to the Cold War', *J. of Italian History*, I (spring 1978), 86–7. Samuel Reber, American joint head of ACC's political section, told the State Dept at the end of March: 'We were handed the ball nearly two months ago and through our apparent failure to adopt a constructive policy have let it drop. The Russians have picked it up and are running down the field with it.'; cited in Coles and Weinberg, *Civil Affairs*, 449.
92. Tel.Murphy to State Dept, 22 Apr. 1944, in NA,RG 59, State Dec.File, 865.00; cited in part in FRUS (1944), III, 1103.
93. Report Tittmann to Dunn, Director, European Office, State Dept, 16 Apr. 1944 (with enclosure); in NA,RG 59, State Decimal File 865.00.
94. OSS Intelligence Report 95645, 'Italian Political Aspirations', 13 Sept. 1944, by Counter Intelligence Corps, Vth Army; in NA,RG 226.
95. Minutes of JCS meeting of 30 May 1944 in NA,RG 218, JCS/CCS Decimal File. On the leading role ascribed by Roosevelt to the Vatican cf. E.Aga-Rossi, 'La Politica degli Alleati verso l'Italia nel 1943', *Storia Contemporanea*, 4 (1972), 877–8.
96. Tel. Kirk and Murphy to State, 5 May 1944, and reply, 11 May 1944 in NA,RG 59, State Decimal File 865.01.
97. Murphy, *op.cit.*, 219.
98. Churchill, *Closing the Ring*, Bk. Two, Ch.17; cf.R.Trevelyan, *Rome 'Forty-Four: The Battle for the Eternal City* (New York, 1982).
99. Cited in Coles and Weinberg, *Civil Affairs*, 459.
100. AFHQ political directive, 3 June 1944, in *ibid.*, 458; Charles's analysis in tels to FO, 31 May, 2 June 1944, in R/8617, R/8967/15/22.
101. Detailed chronology in Delzell, *Mussolini's Enemies*, 389–91; MacFarlane's message in Coles and Weinberg, *Civil Affairs*, 465.
102. Harris, *Allied Administration*, 203.
103. Notes Churchill to Eden, 14 June, 20 June 1944 in PRO, 'Churchill Papers', PREM 3, 241/6 (related material also in 243/12). Cf. also Harris, *Allied Administration*, 201–4; Woodward, *British Foreign Policy*, II, 541–5.
104. State Dept reactions are to be found in NA,RG 59, State Decimal File, 865.01, Cf. also Hull, *The Memoirs of Cordell Hull* (New York, 1948), II, 1563–4; Hull's public reaction is reported in the *New York Herald Tribune*, 21 June 1944. Asked by a journalist on the 20th who the Italian prime minister was, Hull said he was unable to reply as he did not know all the claims (although the Bonomi government had been sworn in on 18 June): *NYHT, ibid.*
105. Woodward, *British Foreign Policy*, II, 544–5; Hull, *op.cit.*, II, 1564–5.
106. *Chicago Daily News*, 10 June 1944; *Christian Science Monitor*, 20 June 1944.
107. *Saturday Evening Post*, 17 June 1944.
108. Minutes of meeting of 20 June 1944 recorded verbatim in F.D.Roosevelt Library, Morgenthau Diaries, vol.745, 195–7; cf.Di Nolfo, 'The U.S. and Italian Communism', *op.cit.*, 87.

5 Staking claims and making plans: British and American approaches to the Italian question, June–December 1944

1. Harris, *Allied Administration*, 230; on intention not to conclude treaty, FO minute in

PRO,FO 371, R/10755/691/22.

2. Possible concessions are listed in a memo. by Macmillan, 20 June 1944 in *ibid.*, R/9600/48/22; the necessity to consolidate the penal clauses of the settlement and deter American generosity are in FO comments and reactions to a tel. British embassy, Washington, to FO 5 Aug. 1944 conveying U.S. views on the preliminary peace plan.

3. FO memo., 'Note on the Political Situation in Italy', 10 Aug. 1944, in *ibid.* R/13015/53/22. The official British view of the peace proposal is in Woodward, *British Foreign Policy*, II, 540–2, III, 440–2. The CCS increased the presence of Italian armed forces to 45,000 men (equivalent of 3 Allied divisions) at this time, divided into 5 combat groups known as CIL: Delzell, *Mussolini's Enemies*, 406.

4. FO comment on a tel. resident minister's office to FO, 23 June 1944; in PRO.FO 371, R/9957/691/22.

5. *Ibid.* Also FO comment on a tel. Charles to FO, 10 July 1944; in *ibid*, R/11177/15/22.

6. Cf. M.Howard, 'Strategy and Politics in World War II: the British Case', paper delivered at the XIV International Congress of Historical Sciences, San Francisco (Aug., 1975).

7. Churchill, *Triumph and Tragedy* (1953), 72–9.

8. Eden comments on a letter res.min's. office to FO, 18 June 1944, in PRO,FO 371, R/10071/15/22, and on a tel. res.min's. office to FO, 23 June 1944, in *ibid.*, R/9957/691/22.

9. Churchill, *Triumph and Tragedy*, Bk 2, Chs 4,6; Howard, *Mediterranean Strategy*, 63.

10. Tel.Wilson to SHAEF (Supreme HQ of Allied Expeditionary Force), British chiefs of staff, American JCS, ca.18 June 1944; in PRO,WO 204, f.84.

11. P.J.Dixon, *Double Diploma: The Life of Sir Pierson Dixon* (1968), 98.

12. Tel. P.M. (at AFHQ) to Eden, 22 Aug.1944; in PRO, Private Secretary's Papers, 800/409; cf. Woodward, *British Foreign Policy*, III, 444.

13. Tel. Dixon (at AFHQ) to FO, 16 Aug.1944; in PRO, Private Secretary's Papers, 800/409. Dixon was Eden's private secretary.

14. Letter Dixon to FO, 17 Aug. 1944; in PRO,FO 371, R/13772/15/22.

15. Dixon, *op.cit.*, 107; for Churchill's comments, *The Times*, 29 Aug. 1944. Michael Howard claims that although Eden had been warning of the emergence of rival East–West spheres of influence since the beginning of May, no one thought of using anti-Russian arguments in the summer of 1944 to justify the ambitious strategic plans being promoted by the Allied command in Italy; Howard, *Mediterranean Strategy*, 63–5.

16. *The Times*, 29 Aug. 1944.

17. Tels.P.M. (at AFHQ) to FO,22 Aug. 1944, as n.12 above.

18. Attlee's visit is recorded in a tel. Charles to FO, 7 Sept. 1944, which describes a long conversation with Nenni and Togliatti, 'who showed a bland ignorance of the advanced social laws existing in the British Isles' in PRO.FO 371, R/14671/15/22; that of Hall in minutes of a conversation with Togliatti, 30 Aug. 1944, in *ibid.*, R/15263/15/22; that of Amery in minutes of a conversation with Bonomi in *ibid.*,R/15264/15/22 (dated 8 Sept. 1944). The FO design for propaganda policy is in comments on a tel.Charles to FO. 7 July, 1944; in *ibid.*, R/10939/15/22.

19. 'The Future of Italy' by FO Research Dept, 12 Aug. 1944; in *ibid.*, R/12735/481/22. A brief FO comment noted that it seemed unlikely that the 'Russians and the Americans will be ready to leave us as the Chief Mentors [sic] whatever happens', (7 Sept. 1944); in *ibid.*

20. War Cabinet minute on finance of supplies to Italy, 19 Aug. 1944, in *ibid.*; Eden's opposition to UNRRA aid is recorded in comments on a FO minute of 1 Sept. 1944; in *ibid.*, R/14030/691/22; cf. also Woodward, *British Foreign Policy*, III, 445–7.

21. Note to Eden, 10 Sept. 1944, accompanying letter Macmillan to FO, in PRO,FO 371, R/14893/691/22.
22. Tels. Charles to FO, 2 July and 7 July 1944 in R/10361, 10939/15/22 (with FO comments).
23. *Ibid.*; also tel. Charles to FO, 10 July 1944, with FO and Eden's comments, in *ibid.*, R/11177/15/22. The American view of this time, looking favourably on the 'demo-cratic and anti-Fascist character' of Bonomi's government, is recorded in a message Hull to Roosevelt, 13 June 1944, published in E.Aga-Rossi, 'La situazione politica ed economica del-l'Italia nel periodo 1944–45: governi Bonomi', in *Quaderni dell'Isti-tuto romano per la Storia d'Italia dal Fascismo alla Resistenza* (1971), 11–12.
24. Tel. Charles to FO, 23 July 1944, in PRO,FO 371, R/11780/15/22.
25. Manoeuvre and Stone's reaction reported in tel. Charles to FO, 10 Aug. 1944, in *ibid.*, R/12525/15/22.
26. FO comments on letter Caccia, ACC, to MGS, res.min., 15 Aug. 1944, in *ibid.*, R/13248/15/22.
27. Letter Dixon to FO, 17 Aug. 1944, with FO comments in *ibid.*, R/13772/15/22.
28. One of the rare political archives of the time outside that of the PCI, belonging to Lelio Basso, appears to contain almost nothing on the activities of the Allies as seen by the PSIUP socialists: see Mariuccia Salvati, 'Il PSIUP nelle carte dell'archivio Basso', in *Il Movimento di Liberazione in Italia, 110* (1972), 61–88; Pietro Nenni's diary, *Tempo di guerra fredda. Diari 1943–56* (Milan, 1981), likewise has few refer-ences in spite of his public concern at the time with their activities (see below Ch.7); on the northern CLN tendency to ignore the Allies, H.C.Coles and A.K.Weinberg, *Civil Affairs*, 565, n.7.
29. Cf. E.Santarelli, 'Quadro e trasformazione dei partiti', in *L'Italia dalla liberazione alla Repubblica*. Proceedings of the Florence Conference (March 1976), 222–49; A.Gam-bino, *Storia del dopoguerra dalla liberazione al potere DC* (Bari, 1975), Ch.I; Aga-Rossi, *op.cit.*, 49.
30. Counterweight concept mentioned in letter to FO, 16 June 1944 (accompanying a letter from Nenni to the Labour Party), in PRO,FO 371, R/9912/15/22; comments on unity pact in tel. Charles to FO, 11 Aug. 1944, in *ibid.* R/12493/15/22.
31. Tel. Charles to FO including text of Nenni's speech, 6 Sept. 1944, and FO com-ments, in *ibid.* R/14132/15/22.
32. PWB, 'D' Section, 'Supplement to Report on Conditions in Liberated Italy', 11 Sept. 1944, in NA,RG 59 State Dec.File 865.00. The dinner is not mentioned in Nenni's diary, although its tone in these months reflects considerable suspicion of Togliatti's behaviour.
33. Nenni's public pronouncements in the Socialist paper *Avanti!*, 21 Sept., 14 Oct., 12 Nov. 1944; Charles's suspicion of the CLNs ('what are these soviets?') reported in Nenni, *op.cit.*, 102; Nenni's impressions as reported to a member of ACC, and Macmillan's remarks in PRO 'Churchill Papers', PREM 4,19/5; FO comment (on original Labour Party invitation, 16 Nov. 1944), in PRO,FO 371, R/18756/15/22.
34. Text of Bonomi's message and Hull's reply in FRUS (1944) III, 1142–7; the message was preceded by a fulsome message of personal tribute to Roosevelt, reproduced in *ibid.* 1139–40.
35. British official comments are to be found in Harris, *Allied Administration*, 210–11 ('This move on the part of Signor Bonomi . . . looked uncommonly like an attempt to drive the thin end of a wedge into what he fancied was a split in Allied policy towards Italy.'); Woodward, *British Foreign Policy*, III, 441, n.1; PRO,FO 371, R/13134, 14133/48/22.
36. Murphy citation in R.Murphy, *Diplomat Among the Warriors* (New York, 1964), 219; Dunn is quoted in Coles and Weinberg, *Civil Affairs*, 497.

37. State Dept Policy Committee, Survey of Principal Problems in Europe, 15 July 1944; in NA,RG 59, (Notter File).
38. FEA aspirations are outlined in a memo. Hunt, Chief, Italian Divn., FEA to deputy administrator, 4 July 1944, in NA,RG 169, Records of the FEA; American trade union activity is reported in the *New York Herald Tribune*, 3 June 1944, *New York Times*, 17 Sept. 1944.
39. Taylor's report to Roosevelt of 17 July 1944 is in F.D.Roosevelt Library, President's Secretary's File, Box 69 Vatican; *New York Herald Tribune* report is dated 16 June 1944; Cerabona interview, 12 July 1944, in NA,RG 59, State Decimal File 865.01.
40. Tel. Kirk to James C.Dunn, State Dept, 21 July 1944; in NA,RG 59, State Decimal File, 740.0019 Control (Italy), (hereafter S.D.740).
41. Tel. Kirk to State Dept, 8 Sept. 1944; in NA,RG 59, S.D.740.
42. CAC Document 248, 'The Treatment of Italy', 31 Aug. 1944; in NA,RG 59, (Notter File).
43. *News Chronicle*, 27 Sept. 1944.
44. Spellman's words reported in the *New York Times*, 1 June 1944; those of General Hume, Head of Vth Army AMG in Tuscany, in Harris, *Allied Administration*, 192.
45. *New York Times*, 7 Sept. 1944.
46. La Guardia's remarks reported in the *New York Herald Tribune*, 9 Aug. 1944; those of Baldanzi in the *New York Times*, 24 Sept. 1944; Anne McCormick's warning in the *New York Times*, 23 Sept. 1944.
47. Reitzel, *The Mediterranean*, 30; Harris, *Allied Administration*, 231–2. Full text of the Hyde Park Declaration is published in Harris, *ibid.*, 251–2; cf. also Woodward, *British Foreign Policy*, III, 446–53. Kirk and Charles became full ambassadors; the Italian government appointed as its 'Representatives' the Liberal Carandini to London and the Actionist Tarchiani to Washington.
48. Harris, *Allied Administration*, 252.
49. Cited in Reitzel, *The Mediterranean*, 33. The French authorities under de Gaulle took the Hyde Park Declaration as a sign that any continuation of their ultra-rigid line on Franco-Italian detente might leave them isolated with respect to the Western Allies, and negotiations were subsequently opened for the re-establishment of diplomatic relations between the two countries; these proved extremely difficult; Guillen,P., 'I rapporti franco-italiani dall'armistizio alla firma del Patto atlantico', in *L'Italia dalla Liberazione alla Repubblica*, 10.
50. State Dept comments from *Bulletin of the State Department*, 6 Aug. 1944, 15 Oct. 1944; *Newsweek* comment in issue of 9 Oct. 1944; cited in Reitzel, *The Mediterranean*, 32–3.
51. E.g. State Dept Policy Committee, memo by A.A.Berle Jr, 26 Sept. 1944; in NA,RG 59, (Notter File) (this includes intelligence estimates on the latest probable date for a German collapse).
52. On the Polish-American campaign, Gaddis, *The United States and the Cold War*, 140–9.
53. Minutes of conversation in FRUS (1944), III, 1149–51.
54. Recent comment on the electoral factor in the Hyde Park Declaration in Aga-Rossi, *op.cit.*, 10; Gallup Poll results reported in letter Washington embassy to FO, 19 Oct. 1944, in PRO,FO 371, R/17571/691/22; use of the troop pay concession for electoral propaganda purposes is discussed in a telephone conversation between Roosevelt's adviser Judge Sam Rosenmen and Treasury Secretary Henry Morgenthau, 30 Oct. 1944, in F.D.Roosevelt Library, Morgenthau Diaries, vol.788 (30 Oct. 1944; verbatim record); *New York Times* report is of 13 Oct. 1944; Dewey's speech is reported in the *New York Herald Tribune*, 11 Oct. 1944.
55. Comments by FO on letter Washington embassy to FO, 19 Oct. 1944, cited in n.54

above, and by Sir N.Charles in letter to FO, 19 Oct. 1944; in PRO,FO 371, R/17157/22.

56. Note Churchill to Roosevelt, 12 Sept. 1944; in PRO, 'Churchill Papers', PREM 3, 241/6; cf. Woodward, *British Foreign Policy* III, 447. The discussion 'seems only to have been a short one', notes Woodward, confirming the impression that it left no trace in the records.
57. Tel. P.M. (in Quebec) to Charles, 18 Sept. 1944; in PRO,FO 371, R/14901/691/22.
58. Macmillan had told Churchill in Rome that the ACC needed 'a high-ranking civilian with Cabinet rank who would be really effective, really run Italy, and be able to play such a role as Cromer played in Egypt'; cited in tel.Kirk to State Dept, 10 Sept. 1944, NA,RG 59, S.D. 740, (Evelyn Baring, Lord Cromer, was consul general and plenipotentiary in Egypt from 1883 to 1907); FO comments in PRO,FO 371, R/14989/48/22; on armistice revision tel. FO to Washington embassy, 21 Sept. 1944, in *ibid.*, R/15028/691/22.
59. Nenni comment in *Avanti!*, 28 Sept. 1944; Harris, *Allied Administration*, 232; see also Coles and Weinberg, *Civil Affairs*, 506.
60. Croce's words and Matthews' comments in *New York Times*, 14 Oct. 1944.
61. Harris, *Allied Administration*, 234, 247; for the conditions of the campaign in this period, Douglas Orgill, *The Gothic Line. The Autumn Campaign in Italy 1944* (1967), Chs 10 ff.
62. Record of a meeting at the Kremlin, 9 Oct. 1944; in PRO 'Churchill Papers', PREM 3, 434/2. The outcome of Churchill's worries was 'Operation Cinders'; see below Ch.8, n.53. Churchill spent 4 hours in conversation with Wilson and Alexander in Naples on his way to Moscow; *Triumph and Tragedy*, 192; records of their meeting have not yet been found.
63. Record of after-dinner conversation at the British embassy, Oct.11–12 1944; in PRO, Private Secretary's Papers, FO 800/414.
64. Gaddis, *The United States and the Cold War*, 154–7; Gabriel Kolko, *The Politics of War* (New York,1968), 146–7.
65. Letter Charles to FO, 19 Oct. 1944; in PRO,FO 371, R/17157/691/22.
66. 'British long-term interests in Italy', memo. by Harold Caccia, 26 Oct. 1944, together with accompanying letter by Charles, 16 Nov. 1944, and FO comments in *ibid.*, R/19126/691/22.
67. Reitzel, *The Mediterranean*, 51.
68. 'Memorandum concerning Anglo-American relations in Italy', n.d. (presumed Oct. 1944), in F.D.Roosevelt Library, President's Secretary's File, Box 70; cf. E.Di Nolfo, *Vaticano e Stati uniti 1939–1952: dalle carte di Myron C.Taylor* (Milan, 1978), 377–83.
69. Reitzel, *The Mediterranean*, 50; *New York Times*, 26 Nov. 1944.
70. *Christian Science Monitor*, 27 Nov. 1944.
71. *Chicago Daily News*, 4 Dec. 1944.
72. On the origins of the crisis see Aga-Rossi, *op.cit.*, 56–60; for Bonomi's views as expressed to Sir N.Charles, tels. Charles to FO, 19 Nov, 24 Nov. 1944, in PRO,FO 371, R/18661/15/22, 19337/15/22; for Socialist suspicions of Bonomi's intentions cf. *Avanti!*, 10 Aug., 11 Aug. 1944.
73. Macmillan comments in memo. of 4 Dec. 1944, in FOGC, R/20304/15/22; Bonomi–Stone conversation reported in tel. Kirk to State Dept, 17 Nov. 1944, in NA,RG 59, State Decimal File 865.01, Box 5041; rumours of Communist pressure on certain ministers reported in tel. Charles to FO, 22 Nov. 1944, with reply, 25 Nov. 1944, containing FO recommendations, in FOGC, R/19153/15/22. Interpretation of the crisis as a struggle by the extreme left parties to seize power in order to carry through their political aims without regard to the rights and interests of other

sections of the community, is contained in FO comments on a tel. Charles to FO, 27 Nov. 1944, in FOGC, R/19413/15/22. The official British interpretation is in Woodward, *British Foreign Policy*, III, 453–66.

74. Stettinius statement in *New York Times*, 6 Dec. 1944; Connally's approval reported in *New York Times*, 8 Dec. 1944 (and Woodward, *British Foreign Policy*, III, 464, n.1).

75. *Christian Science Monitor*, 5 Dec. 1944.

76. *New York Times*, 3 Dec. 1944; *New York Tribune*, 7 Dec. 1944. The Greek civil war began in the first week of December.

77. *Daily Telegraph*, 7 Dec. 1944; *Manchester Guardian*, 1 Dec. 1944, *Daily Herald*, 1 Dec. 1944.

78. Tels. FO to Washington embassy and vice versa in FOGC, R/20027/15/22; cf. also Woodward, *British Foreign Policy*, III, 461–3, which contains Roosevelt–Churchill correspondence on the incident.

79. *Avanti!*, 26 Nov., 28 Nov., 2 Dec. 1944.

80. *La Nazione del popolo*, 29 Nov., 4 Dec. 1944.

81. Tel. Charles to FO and FO comments in PRO,FO 371, R/19555/15/22.

82. Aga-Rossi, *op.cit.*, 52–3, 56–68, (inc. Hopkins' quote). Togliatti's view of the crisis was summed up in a letter to the Milan secretariat of 9 Dec. 1944, which included the following instruction: 'Try to influence our Actionist friends so that their irritation over the Sforza case doesn't provoke them into making undesirable anti-English propaganda, which would be playing the game of the Fascists, objectively. Our international policy consists of unity among the Great Powers, and no other'.; cited in P.Secchia, 'Il Partito comunista italiano e la guerra di liberazione, 1943–45', *Annali dell'Istituto Giangiacomo Feltrinelli* (Milan 1971), 791–2. Nenni's view in Nenni, *op.cit*, 100–7.

83. A very good example of the type and level of discussion around this issue is to be found in 'Town Meeting: Bulletin of America's Town Meeting of the Air,' (sponsored by *Reader's Digest*), 21 Dec. 1944; debate entitled 'Should the Allies Maintain a Hands-Off Policy in Liberated Countries?', with Sir Norman Angell, Jay Allen (foreign correspondent), Congressman John M.Coffee (House,Democrat), Dr Frank Kingdon (author and commentator).

84. Memo. by Carmel Offie, Office of the U.S. Political Adviser, 177 Jan. 1945 (on British reactions to the Stettinius statement and related events), in NA,RG 59, S.D., 865.01.

85. The British continued to insist officially on the right to veto particular individuals, as in SAC's Political Conference of 16 Dec. 1944 (excerpt from minutes in Coles and Weinberg, *Civil Affairs*, 507–8); the general justification which Churchill cited was the *carte blanche* he believed he had been given by the other Allies in the previous months: 'We felt ourselves fully entitled to make the Italian Government aware of our view upon this matter because we have been accorded command in the Mediterranean, as the Americans have command in France, and therefore we have a certain special position and responsibility'; tel. P.M. to Halifax, 4 Dec. 1944, in FRUS (1945), 'The Conferences at Malta and Yalta', 267.

86. Reply of 14 Feb. 1945 to Offie memo, cited in n.84 above, same location.

87. Hopkins's Rome experiences are reported in E.R.Stettinius, *Roosevelt and the Russians. The Yalta Conference* (New York, 1949), 52–3, in tels. Office of the Resident Minister, Rome to Macmillan (in Athens), 4 Feb., 5 Feb. 1945, in PRO, 'Churchill Papers', PREM 3, 241/7, and, from the FO point of view, in Woodward, *British Foreign Policy*, III, 470–2.

88. FEA, 'Program for Italy', 8 Dec. 1944, in NA,RG 169, Records of the FEA.

89. Minutes of CCAC meetings of 15 Dec. 1944, 22 Jan. 1945, together with report of the American members of the subcommittee in NA,RG 218, JCS/CCS Decimal File,

1942–5. cf. Coles and Weinberg, *Civil Affairs*, 514–15.

90. Tel. Washingtom embassy to FO, 20 Dec.1944, and FO comments in PRO,FO 371, R/21516/691/22; cf. Woodward, *British Foreign Policy*, III, 469–70.
91. *New York Times*, 3 Dec. 1944.
92. For American perceptions of imperial decline in the Mediterranean, J.Latrides, *Revolt in Athens* (Princeton, 1972), 125, and in general, Kolko, *op.cit.*, Chs 11–12; the American JCS were already predicting in Aug. 1944 that: 'both in an absolute sense and relative to the United States and Russia, the British Empire will emerge from the war having lost ground both economically and militarily', *ibid.*, 275.
93. Reitzel,*The Mediterranean*, 34.

6   Material conditions and the rise of the Left: the economics of the war in Italy in 1944

1. As illustrated by many of the films made during or shortly after the war, e.g. Roberto Rossellini's 'Paisa' (1946), openly dedicated to the liberation process and its human consequences.
2. FEA Intelligence memo., Italian Division, No.1, 12 May 1944, n.4, 6/6/44, in NA,RG 169.
3. FO comments on a letter Charles to FO, 28 Apr. 1944, in PRO,FO 371, R/5878/53/22; details of post-war food planning are to be found in E.F.Penrose, *Economic Planning for the Peace* (Princeton, 1953), esp. 136. According to Frank A.Southard Jr, a former financial adviser to AFHQ, by the second half of 1944 90 per cent of the money spent on food was spent on the black market, while from December 1943 to January 1945 'the official ration did not exceed a daily average of 850 calories'; Frank A.Southard Jr, *The Finances of European Liberation* (New York, 1946), 181.
4. Comments on letter Charles to FO, 28 Apr. 1944, cited in n.3 above.
5. FEA memo., 'Economic Problems in Italy', 15 Dec. 1943, in NA,RG 169.
6. G.Kolko, *The Politics of War* (New York, 1968), 259–65; cf. Penrose, *op.cit.*, Chs I–III, esp. 37–57 on the scope of American post-war planning.
7. British reaction to Grady's presence is indicated in an internal Treasury memo, of 25 Jan. 1944, in PRO, Treasury Papers, (T.160), 1278/18640/02/3; Grady's report (28 Mar. 1944) is located in NA,RG 169.
8. Letter Murphy to James C.Dunn, State Dept, 13 June 1944, and comments by Eden and FO officials in PRO,FO 371, R/11074/48/22.
9. On the unreliability of American economic nominees, Harris, *Allied Administration*, 255; MacFarlane's remarks cited in tel. Chapin, asst.U.S.political adviser, to State Dept, 4 June 1944, in NA,RG 59, S.D. 740.
10. Tels. Kirk to James C.Dunn, State Dept, 23 June, 25 June 1944, in NA,RG 59, SD 740.
11. Harris, *Allied Administration*, 255; UNRRA, *Venti mesi con l'UNRRA per la ripresa industriale italiana* (Rome, 1948), 46–7.
12. 'Memorandum on Wage Rates in Italy', 28 Oct 1944, in PRO,FO 371, R/17661/15/22.
13. *Ibid.*
14. *Ibid.*
15. 'The Treatment of Italy', CAC Document 248, 31 Aug. 1944, in NA,RG 59, 'Notter File'.
16. *Ibid.*
17. *Ibid.*

18. Cf. docs in Coles and Weinberg, *Civil Affairs*, 353–8; Harris, *Allied Administration*, 216–20.
19. On the legal basis of army's relief programme as justifying Lend-Lease, letter George W.Ball to Deputy Administrator, FEA, 5 July 1944, in NA,RG 169; quotation from Morgenthau Diaries, Bk. 745 (19–20 June 1944), meeting of 2 June 1944; F.D.Roosevelt Library.
20. On Lend-Lease effects in 'backward' countries, internal memo, office of Lend-Lease Administrator, 11 Nov. 1942, in NA,RG 169. Views of commercial circles reported in *New York Herald Tribune*, 12 Sept. 1943.
21. Harris, *Allied Administration*, 249–51.
22. Harris, *Allied Administration*, 11; Coles and Weinberg, *Civil Affairs*, 176–7 (an internal War Dept, Civil Affairs Division memo of 10 May 1943 is quoted which gives the official dollar exchange rate as L.1=$05.26, and in protest against the British rate says that the occupiers should make it clear to the world that 'the United Nations do not intend to destroy property values'). British Treasury documentation on this problem has not so far been located.
23. British protests reported in the *Financial News*, 19 July, 24 July, 26 July 1943; Eisenhower's protest recorded in 'Memo for Files', 1 Oct. 1943, U.S. Treasury Papers, Monetary Research Division, Papers Relating to Italian Exchange Rate (in comment on this the Treasury experts rejected Eisenhower's suggestion, arguing that more settled conditions must be established before any reconsideration was given); White's remarks cited in V.Petrov, *Money and Conquest: Allied Occupation Currencies in World War II* (Baltimore, 1967), 78. Petrov attributes to White the view that AM Lire 'would be the responsibility of some future government of the country, [and so] its introduction (via the armistice) offered a seemingly simple way to make Italy pay for the Allied occupation', *ibid.*, 77.
24. U.S. Treasury views expressed in memo., 'Dollar Lira Rate of Exchange', n.d. (presumed autumn 1943), in U.S. Treasury Papers, Divn of Monetary Research, Papers Relating to Italian Exchange; FEA arguments were listed in a memo 'Currency and Banking Problems of Occupation in Italy', Apr. 1943, in NA,RG 169. (FEA experts favoured a rate of L.30–50 = $1); Grady's view reported in Coles and Weinberg, *Civil Affairs*, 355, n.11; Macmillan's in tel. to FO, 2 May 1944, in PRO, Board of Trade Papers, BT 11/2243.
25. On Italian govt views, memo., Finance Subcommission, ACC, 29 May 1944, cited in Coles and Weinberg, *Civil Affairs*, 355; (Badoglio told Reuter's correspondent Cecil Sprigge that the rate was 'disastrous', cited in letter Caccia to Makins, 26 Jan. 1944, in FOGC, R/2338/15/22); Treasury views cited in tel. FO to Washington embassy, 29 Sept. 1943, in FOGC, R/9464/242/22; discussion of economic concessions above.
26. 'Notes on a Visit to Italy', n.d., (but visit made in March 1944), in PRO, FOGC, ZM/3600/3/22.
27. For British Treasury complaints of U.S. economic policy in Italy, letter Treasury to U.K. Treasury Delegation, Washington, 12 Feb. 1945 in FOGC, ZM/983/1/22; for further discussion of these problems, Southard, *op.cit.*, 86; B.Foa, *Monetary Reconstruction in Italy* (New York, 1949), 17–19; Harris, *Allied Administration*, 381–2; personal experience described in N.Lewis, *Naples '44* (1978), 119–20.
28. J.E.Miller, 'The Politics of Relief: The Roosevelt Administration and the Reconstruction of Italy, 1943–44', *Prologue* (autumn 1981), 205–7.
29. Letter Eden to Sir P.J.Grigg, n.d. (reply to letter Grigg to Eden, 26 Sept. 1944) in PRO, 'Churchill Papers, PREM 3, 241/6.
30. Washington embassy minute, 7 Dec. 1944, in PRO,FO 371, ZM/257/18/22.
31. Remarks of May by Labour subcommission at chief commissioner's monthly conference, 30 May 1944, in NA, RG 331, 10000/136/163.

32. Southard, *op.cit.*, 41–4; figures (calculated by Bank of Greece) in W.O.Candilis, *The Economy of Greece, 1944–66. Efforts for Stability and Development* (New York, 1968) 16–19.

33. Candilis, *op.cit.*, 15; Penrose, *op.cit.*, 44–5. For AFHQ worries of the economic parallels between Greece and Italy, Coles and Weinberg, *Civil Affairs*, 366; Macmillan's warning cited in AC meeting of 2 March 1945, mins in NA,RG 331, ACC files, 10000/136/258.

34. On ACC Anti-Inflation Committee, Harris, *Allied Administration*, 217–19; views of U.S. Treasury expert in 'Report on Assignment to Italy, April and May, 1944', n.d., in U.S. Treasury Papers, Division of Monetary Research, Italy Country File.

7 Military necessities and political purposes: the evolution of Allied control

1. Cited in A.Sampson, *Macmillan. A Study in Ambiguity* (1967), 70.

2. For Macmillan's approach, see above, Ch.4, n.50; Churchill's views in tel. to Eden, 22 Aug. 1944, in PRO, Private Secretary's Papers, FO 800/409.

3. OSS, Research and Analysis Branch, Report n.2781, 'An Analysis of the Second Bonomi Cabinet', 30 Dec. 1944, in NA,RG 226.

4. Reorganization described in Harris, *Allied Administration*, 118–20 and Ch.IV, Annexes II, III; in general the archival documentation offers no clues on the choice of names for these various posts.

5. *Ibid.*, 120.

6. *New York Times*, 2 Apr. 1944.

7. Memo 'Future Organization – ACC', to AFHQ, G-5, 29/7/44, in NA,RG 331, ACC files, 10000/136/256.

8. Calculation relating to a third of ACC officers based on figures in Harris, *Allied Administration*, 253–5, 259–61; excerpts from Macmillan note of December 1944 in Coles and Weinberg, *Civil Affairs*, 510–11; in the Palermo riot (19 October) Italian troops opened fire on a crowd demonstrating against food shortages and rising prices when it seemed that a bomb had been thrown; no less than 26 civilians were killed and 150 wounded; Harris, *Allied Administration*, 213.

9. Advertisement in the *New York Times*, 1 Apr. 1944; for the impact and significance of this book see Diggins, 'The American Writer, Fascism and the liberation of Italy', *American Quarterly* (winter 1966), 599–614.

10. W.A.Swanberg, *Luce and His Empire* (New York, 1972), 226, which includes information on Hersey's career in this period.

11. J.Hersey, *A Bell for Adano* (New York, 1944), Foreword and 45.

12. Memo. for the president from the Executive Office of the president, 20 Nov. 1942, in F.D.Roosevelt Library, Official File, file 5136.

13. Cited in G.R.Gayre, *Italy in Transition* (1946), 115–16.

14. Tel. res.min. to FO, 22 July 1943, and FO comments, in PRO,FO 371, R/7138/5880/22, and FO minute, 'Personnel for Employment in Italy after Capitulation', 4 Aug. 1943, in R/7345/5880/22; on usefulness of colonial administrators, see Rennell in Gayre, *op.cit.*, 11.

15. V.Peniakoff, *Popski's Private Army* (1950), 360–1.

16. 'The lands which they helped to administer retain the memories of men who did their best in all honesty and disinterestedness for the populations committed to their charge and even instituted some reforms, which is not a primary duty of any military government,' Lord Rennell records (Gayre, *op.cit.*, 15); there were even those who took the job too seriously, such as Commander Michael A.Musmanno,

whose curious memoir, *La guerra non l'ho voluta io* (Florence, 1947), contains the
following:

'That night [of arrival] I never slept for a moment in my bed in the Jesuits'
College where the Father Superior of the Missionaries had prepared a room for
me. I thought of my good fortune in being given the task of administering and
governing with almost absolute powers a town of 15000 inhabitants. I looked at the
Cross on the wall, at the American flag on a bedside table in a corner of the room,
at the heap of posters proclaiming the liberation and salvation of a beaten and
oppressed people. It was a dream, a utopia, Christianity in action! With the United
States of America behind me I was one of the elect, chosen to turn the dream of
brotherly love into reality. What greater field of service could there be? Here was
the means to end war and bring understanding between the peoples of all nations.' (pp.43–4)

However, Musmanno's fervour was frowned upon in ACC, where he was
thought to have 'gone native' and was recommended for return to the U.S. as soon
as possible. (Correspondence in NA, RG/331, 10000/136/178.)

17.   On the variety of local experiences, cf. Istituto storico della Resistenza in Toscana,
      La Resistenza e Gli Alleati in Toscana (Florence, 1964), and below, Ch.7, pp.00–00; on
      the general situation of AMG officers, R.T.Holt and R.W.van de Welde, *Strategic
      Psychological Operations and American Foreign Policy* (New York, 1960), 127–9; on the
      case of Naples, Coles and Weinberg, *Civil Affairs*, 281. cf. P.De Marco, 'Il difficile
      esordio del governo militare e la politica sindacale degli Alleati a Napoli. 1943–
      1944, *Italia contemporanea, 136* (1979), 39–66.
18.   Though the AMG men were often honoured by eloquent tributes in local news-
      papers (e.g. that on Hannibal M.Fiore in *La Nuova Stampa*, Turin, 10 Jan. 1946:
      'There isn't a Torinese who doesn't know him or hasn't heard his characteristic
      Monday radio programme.'), when not by honorary citizenship of the towns they
      ran, e.g. Gordon Lett in Pontremoli, *Rossano. An Adventure of the Italian Resistance*
      (1955), 218; Thomas and Carter in Bologna, *G.Dozza e L'Amministrazione Comunale
      della Liberazione*, 74–6; Murchie in Novara, *Stella Alpina*, 5 Aug. 1945.
19.   Letter Salvadori to L.Mercuri, 7 Mar. 1971, in Istituto storico della Resistenza in
      Toscana (ISRT), Fondo Mercuri.
20.   Letter Murphy to Dunn, 13 June 1944, in PRO,FO 371, R/11074/48/22.
21.   Order on separation of ranks mentioned in Gayre, *op.cit.*, 187; Taylor's comments
      in memo. 'Concerning Anglo-American Relations in Italy', Oct. 1944; doc. cited in
      Ch.5, n.68.
22.   *New York Times*, 7 Sept. 1944; cf.M.Neufeld, 'The failure of Allied Military Govern-
      ment in Italy', *Public Administration Rev.* (April 1946), 139–40.
23.   Doc. cited in, n.21; in May 1944 Assistant Secretary of War McCloy was already
      telling the British in Washington of reports that 'a Cairo atmosphere' was develop-
      ing in Italy, and that the Americans felt themselves treated as junior partners;
      observations in tel. Dill, Joint Staff Mission, Washington, to FO, 24 May 1944, in
      PRO,FO 371, R/8869/48/22.
24.   Archivio centrale dello Stato, Roma (ACS), Presidenza del Consiglio, Salerno-
      Brindisi, Cat.2, busta 6 (excerpts published in Ellwood, 'L'occupazione alleata e la
      restaurazione istituzionale: il problema delle Regioni', *Italia contemporanea*, 115
      (1974), 25; cf. N.Gallerano, 'La disgregazione delle base di massa del fascismo nel
      Mezzogiorno e il ruolo delle masse contadine', in G.Bertolo *et al.*, *Operai e contadini
      nella crisi italiana del 1943–1944* (Milan, 1974).
25.   Minutes in NA,RG 331, 10000/132/6.
26.   Harris, *Allied Administration*, 144–5, 148.
27.   Coles and Weinberg,*Civil Affairs*, 292 (letter of 14 Mar. 1944).
28.   Observations of Gayre, education officer, AMGOT, in Gayre, *op.cit.*, 176; exam-

ples of hesitation cited in Coles and Weinberg, *Civil Affairs*, Ch.XIV, Sec.2; interview with AMG 5th Army head, Hume, and assistant Boetigger reported in tel. Murphy to State Dept, late Oct. 1943, in PRO, WO 204, file 2317.

29. Internal CAD memo, 21 Dec. 1943, cited in Coles and Weinberg, *Civil Affairs*, 392.
30. FO comment on letter Charles to FO, 29 Apr. 1944, reporting epuration law of 15 Apr. 1944; in PRO, FO 371, R/7390/15/22.
31. 'under the influence of M.Scoccimarro [said the FO] vendettas will more than probably be carried out in the name of the salutary purging of Fascists, which will result in considerable confusion and dislocation.'; comment on tel. Charles to FO, 13 Nov. 1944, in *ibid*, R/19127/15/22.
32. Comments on tel. Charles to FO, reviewing purge progress, 16 June 1944, in PRO,FO 371, R/10050/15/22.
33. Comment on tel. Charles to FO, 26 June 1944 relaying declaration by Rome cabinet, in *ibid.*, R/10446/15/22.
34. Poletti told the chief commissioner's conference of Aug. 1944 that under his direction, and that of the CLN, AMG in Rome had ensured that '[T]housands of leading Fascists were turned out of office; hundreds arrested and interned. . . . Without a thorough and rugged clearance of leading Fascists from positions of public trust and influence, a new Italy of liberty can never arise.'; mins of conference of 22 Aug. 1944 in NA,RG 331, 10000/125/42; Charles's remark based on allegations by Sforza that all Poletti's activities were 'done with an eye on the governorship of New York and with a view to ousting La Guardia.', in tel. Charles to Sargent, PRO,FO 371, R/11996/15/22, on Poletti's alleged Mafia connections, N.Lewis, *Naples '44* (1978), 120.
35. Badoglio protest in letter to MacFarlane, 17 Mar. 1944, and memo. Corbino (Min. dell'Industria, Commercio e Lavoro), n.d.; Poletti's reactions in letter to chief commissioner, 13 Apr. 1944; all in PRO,WO 204, file 9834.
36. Orlando remarks reported by Charles in tel. to FO, 23 July 1944; in PRO,FO 371, R/11780/15/22.
37. Veto in prefectural nominee cited by Neufeld, *op.cit.*, 145.
38. AMG's relief described in Coles and Weinberg, *Civil Affairs*, 374; problem of decrees mentioned in address Upjohn, vice-president, Civil Affairs Section, AC, to Advisory Council for Italy, 6 Apr. 1945, on progress of epuration; copy in NA,RG 331, 10000/136/329; quotation from internal memo Civil Affairs Section, AC, 27 July 1945, cited in Coles and Weinberg, *Civil Affairs*, 477; cf. M.Flores, 'L'epurazione', in G.Quazza *et al.*, *L'Italia dalla liberazione alla Repubblica* (Florence, 1976).
39. Details published in D.W.Ellwood, 'Nuovi documenti sulla politica istituzionale degli Alleati in Italia', *Italia contemporanea, 119* (1975).
40. Gayre, *op.cit.*, 88, 109.
41. Coles and Weinberg, *Civil Affairs*, 403; cf.ACC, 'La politica e la legislazione scolastica in Italia, 1922–1943' (Milan, 1947).
42. *Ibid.*, 404 (Director, Education subcommission, Final Report on Education Mission to Mideast, Nov. 1944). Emphasis in text.
43. *Ibid.*, 206; on the State Dept's view of the judiciary under Fascism, cf. 'Italy: Political Reconstruction: Nature of a Permanent National Government', 4 Aug. 1943, in NA,RG 59, (Notter File). cf. Harris, *Allied Administration*, 55, 166, 358–9.
44. Cf. Ch. 11 below.
45. On Badoglio's purge, 'Il Movimento dei Prefetti', in INML, L'Italia dei Quarantacinque Giorni'; purge of Sicilian prefects cited in Coles and Weinberg, *Civil Affairs*, 202; reliance on Badoglio's purge mentioned in Harris, *Allied Administration*, 72.
46. Catanzaro episode cited in N.Gallerano, 'L'Influenza dell'amministrazione militare alleata sulla riorganizzazione dello Stato italiano, 1943–45', *Italia contemporanea*, 115

(1974), 8; on the purge of Podestas, cf. Harris, *Allied Administration*, 73; on attitude towards Carabinieri, *ibid.*, 37, 52–3 (cf.Coles and Weinberg, *Civil Affairs*, 283).

47.   Harris, *Allied Administration*, 53.
48.   Coles and Weinberg, *Civil Affairs*, 281.
49.   After a particularly discouraging episode Norman Lewis, a 'Field Security Officer', wrote in his diary, 'Once again it's evident that nobody knows what we're really supposed to be doing here. This time we seem to be seen as a sort of watered down version of the SS. Yet over and over again we've been told it is not our job to take over the duties of the Italian police'; *op.cit.*, 192.
50.   The discussion was summed up in C.J.Friedrich (ed.), *American Experiences in Military Government in World War II* (Washington D.C., 1948); quotes from Merle Fainsod, 'Military Government in Germany', *Public Administration Rev. 5*, (1945), 398; E.F.Penrose, *Economic Planning for the Peace* (Princeton, 1953), 308–9.

8   The road to the North: Italian politics and the Resistance Question after summer 1944

1.   Treasury visitor's report, n.d. (but Mar. 1944), in PRO,FO 371, ZM/3600/3/22. *New York Times*, 2 Apr. 1944.
2.   See above, Ch.5, n.33; Pietro Nenni's diary, *Tempo di guerra fredda* (Milan, 1981), 97–8, contains his account of an interview with Adml Stone (14 Oct. 1944) airing his various grievances.
3.   *Avanti!*, 4 July, 9 July 1944.
4.   *Ibid.*, 12 July, 5 Sept., 7 Sept.1944.
5.   Interview of 31 July 1944; summary in NA,RG 331, 10000/132/316.
6.   Interview of 8 Aug. 1944; summary in *ibid.*
7.   Interview of 8 Aug. 1944; summary in *ibid.* A PWB interview with V.E.Orlando of the same period (9 Aug. 1944) recorded that 'Orlando began by saying that everything was effectively in the hands of the Allies. It was rather absurd to speak of any constitutional authority in the land, since constitutional authority must rest on power, and the only power in the country was the might of the Allied armies'; in *ibid.*
8.   See above, Ch.5, n.34.
9.   Stone's remarks in note to SAC, 9 Oct. 1944 (accompanying documents submitted by under-secretary for foreign affairs, Visconti Venosta, 16 Nov. 1944, on demobilization of AC), in NA,RG 331, 10000/136/285; subcommission doubts in Coles and Weinberg, *Civil Affairs*, 507.
10.   On necessity for outside stimulus, Wkly Rept, Patriots Branch, to Civil Affairs Section, 17 Oct. 1944, in NA,RG 331, 10000/125/353; denunciation of inactivity in memo. Lush to Stone, 7 Dec. 1944, in Coles and Weinberg, *Civil Affairs*, 478.
11.   *Ibid.*, 479.
12.   In Nov. 1943, Badoglio attempted to install a 'civil affairs' representative at AFHQ, but was told that ACC was sovereign; message Eisenhower to Joyce, deputy president, ACC, 30 Nov. 1943, in PRO,WO 204, file 2317; the subject was raised by Bonomi in his letter to Hull of August, and again in the govt's memos after Hyde Park. In a meeting of SAC's Political Committee in Dec. 1944, membership of Italians in the important technical committee, the Local Resources Board, was rejected since 'points would inevitably arise the discussion of which in the presence of Italian representatives would be undesirable and embarrassment would therefore result'; Stone's assertion that only regular membership of such boards

was 'consistent with cobelligerency', and that Italian understanding of Allied difficulties would be increased, was to no avail. (Minutes in NA,RG 331, ACC files, 10000/136/257.)

13. Reitzel, *The Mediterranean*, 46–9 (emphasis added).
14. OSS, R & A Branch, Report n.2620S, 'The Political Role of the Tuscan Committees of Liberation', 20 Oct. 1944, in NA,RG 226.
15. *The Times*, 25 Oct. 1944; C.Pavone comments that this article constitutes 'a fine example of how something which to an enlightened Englishman (without responsibilities of power) might appear simple and realistic, is turned in Italy into something ultra-complicated and practically utopian'; in 'Sulla continuità dello Stato 1943–45', *Rivista di storia contemporanea*, 2 (1974), 197.
16. Harris, *Allied Administration*, 187–90; OSS, *op.cit.*, n.14 above.
17. *Corriere del Mattino*, Florence, 6–7 May 1945, cited in Pavone, *op.cit.* (n.15 above), 197.
18. Istituto storico della Resistenza in Toscana (ISRT), Fondo Berti, minutes of the meeting of the CTLN of 30 Dec. 1944.
19. On importance of Florence post, letter director, Local Government subcommission, to regional commissioner, Region V, 4 Sept. 1944, in NA,RG 331, 10000/141/212; regional commissioner's comments at meeting with AMG and local government subcommission representatives, Florence, 25 Aug. 1944, minutes in *ibid.*
20. Local Govt subcomm. head's remarks in meeting of 25 Aug. 1944, cited above; in meeting with Bonomi (who reaffirmed his support for the career official), 2 Sept. 1944, minutes in *ibid.*, and in interview with Ministry of Interior representative, 10 Oct. 1944, minutes in *ibid.*, cf. now R.Absalom, 'Il ruolo politico ed economico degli Alleati a Firenze, (1944–1945)', in E.Rotelli (ed.) *La ricostruzione un Toscana dal CLN ai partiti* (Bologna, 1980).
21. Views of regional commissioner expressed in interview with Local Govt subcomm. representative, 6 Jan. 1945; minutes in *ibid.*; remarks by Calasso in n.17.
22. Minutes of chief commissioner's conference (and supplement), 22–23 Aug. 1944, in NA,RG 331, 10000/125/42.
23. The word 'Patriot' was preferred to 'Partisan' because of the latter's 'communistic tinge', Sir Noel Charles explained to the FO in a letter of 2 July 1944; in PRO,FO 371, R/10361/15/22.
24. On Resistance as organization, C.L.Ragghianti, in *La Resistenza e Gli Alleati in Toscana* (Florence, 1964), 49; on AMG's initial choices, E.E.Agnoletti in *ibid.*, 65–6.
25. On the fate of the political appointees in the various provinces, see in *ibid.*, F.Chioccon (on Grosseto), 80–7; V.Nardi (on Pistoia), 159–67; A.De Vita (on Lucca), 179–87; G.Mariani (on Massa Carrara), 191–9.
26. *Ibid.*, 84–7 (Grosseto); 145–8 (Livorno).
27. *Ibid.*, 119–33, (Arezzo), 101–3 (Siena), 186 (Viareggio); the Arezzo case was also discussed in a letter from the CCLN in Rome to the under-secretary at the Ministry of the Interior and Admiral Stone, 27 Jan. 1945, copy in NA,RG 331, 10000/132/311; the Siena case was also mentioned in the OSS report cited in n.14 above, and in C.Grove Haines, 'Italy's struggle for recovery' in *Foreign Policy Reports*, 1 Dec. 1944; Pisa situation indicated in Harris, *Allied Administration*, 191; for conditions on the East Coast, in the Marche in particular, see report 'Informazioni da Ancona dopo la Liberazione', 15 Aug. 1944, in P.Secchia, 'Il partito comunista italiano e la guerra di liberazione 1943–1945', *Annali dell Istituto Giangiacomo Feltrinelli* (Milan, 1971), 489–93.
28. E.Rotelli, *L'avvento della Regione in Italia* (Milan, 1967), 40.
29. Harris, *Allied Administration*, 172.
30. *Ibid.*, 175.

31.   ISRT, Fondo Berti, minutes of mtng of 30 Dec.1944.
32.   The Gothic Line was a chain of deeply fortified positions stretching from Massa Carrara in the west to Pesaro on the east coast; details in D.Orgill, *The Gothic Line. The Autumn Campaign in Italy, 1944* (1967).
33.   *The Times*, 23 May 1944; proclamation published in P.Secchia and F.Frassati, *La Resistenza e gli Alleati* (Milan, 1962), 111–13.
34.   R.Battaglia, *Storia della Resistenza italiana* (Turin, 1964), 338–40.
35.   P.Spriano, *Storia del Partito comunista italiano. V. La Resistenza, Togliatti e il Partito nuovo* (Turin, 1975), 339–40; Delzell, *Mussolini's Enemies*, 415–16.
36.   Macmillan's comment in tel. to FO, 20 Aug. 1944; in PRO,FO 371, R/14714/155/22. Charles's in letter to FO, 11 Aug. 1944, forwarding report by Mott-Radycliffe, military liaison officer of High Commissioner's Office; Selborne's comments in minute dated 24 Oct. 1944 from the minister of economic warfare to the prime minister on 'Italian Maquis', in PRO,FO 371, R/17772/53/22.
37.   Churchill's comment in War Cabinet, Chiefs of Staff Committee, 29 Oct. 1944, minute from Churchill to COS; weather conditions and chronic shortage of planes were additional problems complicating supply; however, from Selborne's minute it appeared that while Yugoslavian partisans had been sent a total of 10,000 tons, only 550 had gone to northern Italy.
38.   Cadorna's appointment described in Delzell, *Mussolini's Enemies*, 413–14; Cadorna's report cited in Coles and Weinberg, *Civil Affairs*, 544.
39.   Paper by Roseberry, War Office, 'The Communist Party in Italy', 30 Aug. 1944, in FO 371, R/14156/15/22.
40.   Report by Mott-Radycliffe and comments, cited in n.36 above.
41.   Cited in Spriano, *op.cit.* (n.35 above), 373.
42.   Cited in Secchia, *op.cit.* (n.27 above), 739.
43.   cf. E.Piscitelli, *Da Parri a De Gasperi. Storia del dopuguerra, 1945–1948* (Milan, 1975), Guido Quazza, *Resistenza e storia d'Italia* (Milan, 1976), 328–9.
44.   Cf.G.Perona, 'Torino tra Atene e Varsavia', *Mezzosecolo*, n.1 (1976), 365, n.41.
45.   Minute cited in n.36 above.
46.   G.Quazza, *The Politics of the Italian Resistance* in S.J.Woolf (ed.), *The Rebirth of Italy 1943–1952* (1972), 21–2.
47.   cf. Delzell, *Mussolini's Enemies*, 367–9; Sogno's role cited in SF Situation Report, 2 Sept. 1944, in PRO,WO 204, file 7295; R.Craveri of ORI has been the most outspoken critic of the links between the right and the Allies, cf. 'La campagna d'Italia . . .', and the critical review by former SF officer Salvadori, cited in Ch.4, n.26 above.
48.   Berne representative cited in letter Roseberry, SF, to Dew, FO, 9 Aug. 1944, in PRO,FO 371, R/12472/155/22; Salvadori's remarks to report of 29 Aug. 1944, in *ibid.*, R/14847/15/22; Raffaele Cadorna's view in his memoirs, *La Riscossa* (Milan, 1948), 116.
49.   Macmillan's instruction in letter to AFHQ, G-5 and Stone, 16 Sept. 1944, in NA,RG 331, 10000/136/286 (cf.Coles and Weinberg, *Civil Affairs*, 538).
50.   Stone's message in letter to AFHQ, 17 Sept. 1944, in NA,RG 331, 10000/136/286; instruction to SF missions in PRO,WO 204, f.7293; the instruction mentioned that 'In provincial capitals the principal local official to whom matters relating to local expenditure as well as other civic affairs in doubt, should be referred, is the Prefect', though no mention was made of de-Fascistization; cf. Perona, *op.cit.*, 370–1.
51.   J.M.Stevens, G.Vaccarino and F.Venturi, 'L'Inghilterra e la Resistenza italiana', *Il Movimento di Liberazione in Italia*, *80* (1965), 82; for an example of the working of this approach on the ground, P.Secchia, *op.cit.*, 972 (doc. of the Lombardy CLN of Mar. 1945).

52. Cf. observations in No.1 Special Force, 'Supplement to Operation Order to Rankin Missions', 10 Oct. 1944, in PRO, WO 204, f.7293.

53. Alexander's comments in message to SACMED, 11 Sept. 1944, in Coles and Weinberg, *Civil Affairs*, 538; the parachute landing operation code-named 'Cinders' has been examined for the first time by G.Perona, *op.cit.*, 348–423. Perona emphasizes that like the 'Rankin' operations for Germany, studied by G.Kolko, like 'Manna' in Greece, and 'Freeborn' in Austria, the intentions were to:
   'guarantee the control of zones not yet assigned to specific areas of influence or politically unstable. Such operations were all based on the same principle: to establish a friendly governing authority or military government using the presence of a body of troops with political, not strategic weight, capable of imposing law and order as conceived by the Allies, and without depending in any way on the autonomous local political forces.' (p.365)

54. PWB instruction, 13 Oct.1944, in Coles and Weinberg, *Civil Affairs*, 531.

55. Cited indirectly in Patriots Branch report, 25 Oct. 1944, in Coles and Weinberg, *Civil Affairs*, 530.

56. Macmillan's warnings that the military importance of the movement made the political risks necessary were expressed, for example in SACMED's Political Committee meeting of 22 Nov. 1944; excerpt from minutes in Coles and Weinberg, *Civil Affairs*, 540, exec. commissioner's message, 23 Sept. 1944, in NA, RG 331, 10000/ 2136/286.

57. G.Perona, *op.cit.*, 375; cf. Macmillan, *Blast of War*, 670ff.

58. The key Italian sources are Secchia and Frassati, *op.cit.*, Pt III; F.Catalano, *La Storia del CLNAI* (Bari, 1956), Ch. XIII. Massimo Salvadori of SF was present during these discussions and has given an account in his memoir *The Labour and the Wounds* (1958), 201–5.

59. Special Force view in report of 31 Oct. 1944, in PRO,FO 371, 18569/1555/22; FO opinion in comment on same.

60. AC political section's view in 'Draft Statement for Chief Commissioner', 18 Dec. 1944, in NA,RG 331, 10000/132/311; FO view in comments on tel. resident minister to FO, 4 Dec. 1944, in PRO,FO 371, R/19995/155/22. Here Macmillan urged that the probability of a German withdrawal was so great that urgency alone imposed an immediate military agreement, with a political one later, but the separation of military and political approaches was a fundamental aspect of Macmillan's strategy from the beginning.

61. Macmillan's reference to 'legal pedantry' in *Blast of War*, 671; Kirk's support recorded in 'Problem Sheets – Italy', 30 Dec. 1944, in NA,RG 59, Records of the Office of W. Eur. Affairs Relating to Italy, Box 3; citations from 'Memo of Agreement Between SACMED and the CLNAI', 7 Dec. 1944, in Coles and Weinberg, *Civil Affairs*, 541–2.

62. Bonomi's observation in letter to Stone, 23 Dec. 1944, in Coles and Weinberg, *Civil Affairs*, 542–3; the disgruntled reaction of the CLNAI to this turn of events is recorded in Secchia and Frassati, *op.cit.*, 169–242; F.Catalano, 'La missione del CLNAI nel Sud', *Il Movimento di Liberazione in Italia*, 36 (1955), 3–25; F.Parri, 'Il movimento di liberazione e gli alleati', *ibid.*, 1 (1949), 7–26; E.Sogno, *Guerra senza bandiera* (Milan, 1950), 320–4; Secchia, 'Il Partito . . .', *op.cit.*, 793–5; letters of Pajetta to the North of 27 Dec. 1944, 10 Jan. 1945. Pajetta said that the entire thrust of the accords was to avoid 'any further (Allied) commitment of any kind to the Resistance movement'.

63. Cf.Perona, *op.cit.*, 376; Spriano, *op.cit.*, 443–50.

64. Cited in Coles and Weinberg, *Civil Affairs*, 544.

65. Facts and context in Delzell, *Mussolini's Enemies*, 451–4.

66. B.Davidson, *Special Operations Europe. Scenes from the Anti-Nazi War* (1980), 239–40;

Perona, *op.cit.*, 378–9; Delzell, *Mussolini's Enemies*, 451; Spriano, *op.cit.*, 439–43;
Luigi Longo later called the message 'a stab in the back' (cited in Spriano, *op.cit.*,
441); Perona notes that the message was broadcast the day before the arrival of the
CLNAI mission to Caserta and suggests that it may have been a move partly aimed
to appease those opposed to the negotiations inside the Allied camp.No new
documentation on this subject has been found in the course of the present
research.

9 The end of the wartime Alliance and the approach of liberation

1. Reitzel, *The Mediterranean*, 48–9.
2. V.Mastny, 'The Cassandra in the foreign commissariat. Maxim Litvinov and the Cold War', *Foreign Affairs* (Jan. 1976), 371–2.
3. Winston S.Churchill, *Triumph and Tragedy* (1953), 311.
4. Letter Charles to Sir Orme Sargent, FO, 19 July 1944, in PRO,FO 371, R/11996/15/22.
5. Cf. C.S.Maier, 'The politics of productivity; the foundations of American international foreign economic policy after World War II', *International Organization* (autumn 1977); D.W.Ellwood, 'Egemonia americana in Europa', in B.Bongiovanni, C.Jocteau and N.Tranfaglia (eds), *Storia d'Europa* (Florence, 1980), 1.
6. Comments by Mrs Luce in *New York Times*, 4 Jan. 1945; administration remarks and press comments in *ibid.*, 5 Jan. 1945.
7. *New York Times*, 28 Jan. 1945, cf. J.E.Miller, 'The politics of relief: The Roosevelt administration and the reconstruction of Italy, 1943–1944', *Prologue* (autumn 1981), 193–208.
8. *New York Times* and *New York Herald Tribune*, 31 Jan. 1945.
9. *New York Herald Tribune*, 31 Jan. 1945.
10. *The Times*, 19 Jan. 1945.
11. *Italia Libera*, 20 Jan. 1945; *New York Times*, 20 Jan. 1945. Italian feeling was slightly less aggrieved when Churchill corrected his statement to soften the blow; *Italia Libera*, 24 Jan. 1945.
12. Tel. Charles to FO, 5 Feb. 1945; in PRO,FO 371, ZM/980/1/22.
13. Tel. Eden to State Dept, 19 Jan. 1945; in NA,RG 59, State Decimal File 740.00119 Eur. War.
14. Comments on tel. Charles to FO, 1 Feb. 1945 conveying remarks made by Hopkins; in FOGC, ZM 758/1/22.
15. Memo.Southern European Dept, 10 Jan. 1945, Problem Sheet – Italy, 17 Feb. 1945, Problem Sheet – Italy, 22 Jan. 1945; in NA,RG 59, Records of the Office of W. Eur. Affairs, Box 3.
16. Reports of Meetings, 22 Feb., 24 Feb., 5 Mar. 1945, between U.S. Treasury, State Dept and British embassy representatives; in NA,RG 59, S.D. 740; the row also surfaced in the press, see *Newsweek*, 12 Mar. 1945.
17. On American inability to document charges, State Dept report of meeting of State Dept–British embassy representatives, 24 Feb. 1945, as n.16 above; Macmillan's denial is reported in a letter U.K.Treasury Delegation to Morgenthau, 28 Mar. 1945, in NA,RG 59, S.D. 740; Foreign Office comments in PRO, FO 371, ZM/1225/1/22.
18. Letter Treasury to U.K. Treasury Delegation, Washington, 12 Feb. 1945, in *ibid.*, ZM 983/1/22.
19. Comments on tel. Washington embassy to FO; in *ibid.*, ZM/826/1/22.

20. Under the directive the political section of AC was abolished and the obligation to submit all Italian government to the Commission lifted; the AC presence in the regions and at various levels of Italian State administration was also removed (though with all rights reserved to return if necessary); the first moves were made to restart the local election process; details in Harris, *Allied Administration*, 237–40, text in Coles and Weinberg, *Civil Affairs*, 515–17; Stettinius's opposition is recorded in a tel. Athens embassy to FO, 15 Feb. 1945, recording conversations between Macmillan, Stettinius and members of the Anglo-American delegations at the Yalta and Malta conferences, in PRO,FO 371, ZM/1055/1/22; the perceptions of American officials on British policy are reported in a tel. FO to Eden (in Yalta), 4 Feb. 1945, in PRO, 'Churchill Papers', PREM 3, 241/7.

21. Tel. FO to Eden, 4 Feb. 1945, as n.17 above. The sentiments in certain conservative sections of British opinion were reflected by the *Daily Mail*, which said that '[If] Italy has been humiliated it is because she shared in the insensate ambitions of Nazi Germany. Italy, we must stress, is a conquered nation which has been treated not ungenerously, and is expected to "work her passage home",' (5 Feb. 1945). This statement provoked vigorous protest in the Rome press, most newspapers pointing out (e.g. *Unità*, 6 Feb. 1945) that the *Daily Mail* had been among the most enthusiastic admirers of Fascism, presenting it as the saviour of the European order. The clash was reported in the *New York Times* without significant comment (7 Feb. 1945).

22. Letter Roosevelt to Churchill, 11 Feb. 1945; in FRUS (1945), I, 963–4.

23. *Italia Libera*, 31 Jan. 1945.

24. FRUS, *The Conferences at Malta and Yalta* (Washington D.C., 1955), 93.

25. Briefing Book Paper, Liberated Countries, *ibid.*, 102.

26. FRUS, *The Conferences*, cited n.24 above, 102–3.

27. Briefing Book Paper, U.S. Policy Towards Italy, in FRUS, *The Conferences*, 280. This document was based on State Dept analyses of the preceding July; see above, Ch.5 nn.37, 42.

28. Roosevelt's opposition to the control plan is recorded in Edward R.Stettinius, *Roosevelt and the Russians. The Yalta Conference* (New York, 1949), 36; on Stalin's concern over unconditional surrender, cf. D.S.Clemens, *Yalta* (New York, 1970), 141 (based on Stalin's remarks recorded in FRUS, *The Conferences*, 611, 613); for Molotov's proposal, FRUS, *The Conferences*, 868, for Stalin's exception, *ibid.*, 878; for British and American Reaction, *ibid*, 264.

29. Stalin cited in M.Djilas, *Conversations with Stalin* (1969 edn), 90; Djilas in *Wartime* (1977), 424; commenting on the clandestine Radio Milano Libera's transmission of a Soviet message supporting the CLNs, and on the attitude of the Soviet press to the disarming of the resistance in France and Belgium, the FO said: 'Soviet support for the recognition of the local resistance movements as representative of public opinion implies that all constitutional forms are ignored, that all links with the past are broken and that what amounts to a revolution is carried out in each liberated country' (however, the same commentators also acknowledged that the Soviets were maintaining 'officially a correct attitude' in the context of formal Italian politics); memo. by Southern Dept, FO, 5 Dec. 1944, in PRO,FO 371, R/21909/51/22.

30. Cf.Clemens, *op.cit.*, 264; Stettinius, *op.cit.*, 248–9; Gaddis, *The United States and the Cold War*, 163–4; G.Kolko, *The Politics of War* (New York, 1968), 343–8, 366–9; H.Feis, *From Trust to Terror. The Onset of the Cold War, 1945–1950* (New York, 1970), 50–1.

31. *Italia Libera*, 14 Feb. 1945, 18 Feb. 1945; *Unità* (clandestine edition), 15 Feb. 1945; *Avanti!*, 17 Feb. 1945.

32. *New York Times*, 28 Feb. 1945.

33. State Dept pressure is reported in a tel. Washington embassy to FO, 5 Mar. 1945; in PRO,FO 371, ZM/1401/1/22; armistice discussions were the subject of a minute Eden to Churchill, 12 March. 1945; in *ibid*, ZM/1572/1/22.

34. Post-Hostilities Planning Staff, 'Peace Treaty with Italy', 6 May 1945; in *ibid*., U/3554/50/70; FO draft of 'Political Clauses for Peace Treaty', 13 May 1945, in U/3986/50/70; Colonial Office views in letter Colonial Office to FO, 27 Feb. 1945, in U/1511/50/70; Dominions Office views in Letter Dominions Office to Board of Trade, 5 July 1945, in U/5308/50/70; Board of Trade advice discussed in letter FO to Board of Trade, 18 June 1945 (in which the FO pressed for a less harsh view and a 'reasonable' commercial treaty), in U/3569/50/70: cf Woodward, *British Foreign Policy*, III, 477 ff.

35. Tel. Charles to FO, 28 Apr. 1945, in *ibid*., U/3265/50/70.

36. Discussion and notes of conversation Cadogan–Carandini (ca. 22 Feb. 1945), in *ibid*., ZM/1642/1/22.

37. Kirk's views reported in tel. Charles to FO 30 Apr. 1945 (the Foreign Office condemned them as 'hopelessly unrealistic'), in *ibid*., U/3557/50/70. Macmillan comment accompanies tel. Charles to FO, 16 Apr. 1945, in ZM/2266/1/22.

38. Tel. Kirk to State Dept, 4 Apr. 1945, in NA,RG 59, S.D.740 . . . Italy, Box C-198.

39. 'Policy Governing Support to Italian Partizans', report with accompanying letter from No.1 Special Force to 15th Army Gp, G-3 Special Operations, 15 Jan. 1945; in PRO,WO 204, f.7301.

40. Macmillan, *Blast of War*, 685–6.

41. *Ibid.*; on incorporation of certain brigades in Italian army, Harris, *Allied Administration*, 198–9; Coles and Weinberg, *Civil Affairs*, 535–7; on anti-scorch policy, P.Secchia and F.Frassati, *La Resistenza e gli Alleati* (Milan, 1962), 351–2, 408–15, 436–68 (includes detailed Special Force reports in English); in October the SF commander Roseberry had tackled a Communist leader in the CLNAI, Concetto Marchesi, directly on the subject of disarmament and the authority of the CLNAI in this area. While Marchesi reassured the British officer that that all would go according to plan, Roseberry strongly suggested that the Allies would use force if disarmament were resisted and disorder ensued; minutes of conversation, 17 Oct. 1944 (in Lugano) in Secchia and Frassati, *op.cit.*, 101–2.

42. Draft minute, Macmillan to SACMED, 23 Jan. 1945, and letter Stone to British and American ambassadors, 2 Feb. 1945, in NA,RG 331, 10000/136/339; CCS warning, 28 Feb. 1945, in Coles and Weinberg, *Civil Affairs*, 546.

43. The background to Medici-Tornaquinci's mission is given in Rosalia Manna (ed.), *L'Archivio di A.Medici-Tornaquinci* (Florence, 1975), xxii–xxv; report by M-T., 'Situazione politica nel Nord Italia' (March 1945) in ISRT, Fondo Medici-Tornaquinci, Busta 4, Fasc.3, Sottofasc.4. (The Ministry of Occupied Territory, with at its head the Communist Scoccimarro, was established under the second Bonomi government with the aims of assisting the Resistance movement materially, with propaganda, and in seeking greater recognition from the Allies. They, however, saw it as an attempt to 'gain control' of the movement and firmly restricted its ambitions, gradually whittling them down until not even radio broadcasts to the North were permitted; details in Harris, *Allied Administration*, 226–7; documentation in ISRT, Fondo Medici-Tornaquinci, b.3, fasc.5, 6.)

44. There is no evidence that these commitments, which would have contradicted a great deal of what the CLNAI stood for, were ever carried out: cf. D.W. Ellwood, 'L'occupazione e le reforme istituzionali . . .', in M.Legnani (ed), *Regioni e Stato dalla Resistenza alla Costituzione* (Bologna 1975).

45. Minutes of meeting Bonomi–Upjohn, vice-president, Civil Affairs Section, AC, 26 Apr. 1945, in NA,RG 331, 10000/136/110; cf. directive Stone to AMG Officers, 27

Apr. 1945, in Coles and Weinberg, *Civil Affairs*, 548–9.
46. Minutes of acting president's conference, 8–9 Mar. 1945, in NA,RG 331, 10000/136/ 155.
47. *Ibid.*
48. Tel. Kirk to State Dept, 19 Apr. 1945, in NA,RG 59, SD 865.00.
49. Churchill, *Triumph and Tragedy*, 90–3.
50. P.Spriano, *Storia del Partito communista italiano* (Turin, 1975), 432–9 (includes documents of Togliatti's talks with Yugoslav and northern PCI representatives).
51. This intense minor controversy is treated in E.Di Nolfo, 'L'Operazione "Sunrise": Spunti de Documenti', *Storia e politica*, fasc.3, 4 (1975); E.Aga-Rossi and B.F.Smith, *Operation Sunrise. The Secret Surrender* (New York, 1979); Churchill, *Triumph and Tragedy*, Bk Two, Ch.7.
52. This account is largely based on articles by G.Valdevit, using unpublished British and some Yugoslav secondary sources: 'Resistenza e Alleati fra Italia e Jugoslavia', *Qualestoria* (Mar. 1980), 3–12; 'Gli Alleati e la Venezia Giulia 1941–1945', *Italia contemporanea, 142* (1981), 55–88; also Harris, *Allied Administration*, 328–34; Coles and Weinberg, *Civil Affairs*, Ch.XX; Churchill, *Triumph and Tragedy*, 551–3; memoir of an Allied officer in G.Cox, *The Road to Trieste* (1947, 1977); cf. also D.W.Ellwood, 'Al tramonto dell'Impero britannico: Italia e Balcani nella strategia inglese 1943–45' *op. cit.*; Macmillan, *Blast of War*, 526–37, 691–4.
53. The official histories of this dispute are to be found in Harris, *Allied Administration*, 317–28, Coles and Weinberg, *Civil Affairs*, 551–2, 568–71; a new and significant contribution, based on unpublished French documentation is P.Guillen, 'I rapporti franco-italiani dall'armistizio alla firma del Patto atlantico', in *'L'Italia dalla Liberazione alla Repubblica* (Florence, 1976), 145–80; for a detailed examination of Allied action, Ellwood, 'Il comando alleato e la questione delle Alpi occidentali', in E.Passerin d'Entrèves (ed.), *Guerra e resistenza nelle regioni alpine occidentali: 1940–1945* (Milan, 1980), Ch.2.
54. Guillen, cited n.53 above, 145–51.
55. *Ibid.*, 159.
56. *Ibid.*, 159–60; for Alexander's fears of immediate and larger consequences, docs in Coles and Weinberg, *Civil Affairs*, 568–70; Truman's message to de Gaulle (6 June 1945) is reproduced in *ibid.*, 570.

10   The liberation and its aftermath

1. Coles and Weinberg, *Civil Affairs*, 561.
2. Tel. State Dept to Rome embassy, 16 May 1945, in NA,RG 59, S.D.865.00.
3. Tel. Kirk to State Dept, 25 May 1945, in NA,RG 59, S.D.865.00.
4. Tel. Kirk to State Dept, 27 Apr. 1945, in NA,RG 59, S.D.865.00.
5. F.Catalano, *Storia del CLNAI* (Bari, 1956), 411–25; cf. A.Giobbio, 'Milano all'Indomani della liberazione', *Il Movimento di Liberazione in Italia, 69* (Oct.–Dec. 1962), 3–5, which also records Bonomi's action.
6. CLNL discussion in minutes of meeting of 26 Apr. 1945, INML, Fondo CLN Lombardo, Scat.17; on CLNAI and surrender of Fascists, Giobbio, *op.cit.*, 10–11; CLNAI decree cited by G.Grassi and M.Legnani, 'Il governo dei CLN', in *Regioni e Stato dalla Resistenza alla Costituzione* (Bologna, 1975), 77.
7. Talk of dissolution of army cited by Giobbio, *op.cit.*, 19; on development of committees after liberation, cf. B.Soggia, 'Sistema politico e CLN', *Sociologia, 7.1* (1973), 109–37; Grassi and Legnani, *op.cit.*, 70, 78–85; L.Casali, 'Le giunte popolari

nel Ravennate dalla liberazione alla crisis dell'unita anti-fascista', in L.Bergonzini (ed.), *La Resistenza in Emilia-Romagna*, (Bologna, 1976), 267–99.

8.   Estimate of deaths cited in Giobbio, *op.cit.*, 10; situation in Genoa reported in *Corriere Ligure*, 4–29 May 1945.

9.   Cited in Casali, 'Le giunte popolari nel Ravennate . . .' n.7 above, 271; the author takes pains to assert that this description was exceptionally dramatic with respect to the province and the region as a whole.

10. Report in tel. Kirk to State Dept, 28 May 1945, in NA,RG 59, S.D.740.

11. Valerio report 22 Aug. 1945, forwarded by Military Intelligence Dept, War Office, in PRO,FO 371, ZM/5539/3/22.

12. On Valletta's near-execution, L.Lanzardo, *Classe operaia e Partito comunista alla FIAT 1945–1948* (Turin, 1971), 51; on Valletta's epuration case, R.Gobbi, 'Note sulla Commissione d'epurazione del CLNRP e sul caso Valletta,' *Il Movimento di Liberazione in Italia*, 89 (1967), 57–73; Amendola's testimony in *La Resistenza in Lombardia* (Milan, 1965), 242–3.

13. Cited in report, American consul general, Genoa, to State Dept, 31 May 1945, in NA,RG 59, S.D.865.00.

14. PWB interview with Piaggio included in report, American consul general, Genoa, to State Dept, 29 June 1945, in *ibid*.

15. Intelligence summary, AFHQ G-3 to War Dept, 28 July 1945, in NA,RG 331, AFHQ files, R-99-F.

16. Camerana remarks cited in report ISLD (Intelligence Services Liaison Dept) to British embassy, Rome, 11 Aug.1945, in NA,RG 331, AFHQ files (G-2), R-485-C; AFHQ visitor was Spofford, asst chief of staff, AFHQ (G-5), report to deputy theatre commander, 9 July 1945, in NA,RG 331 AFHQ files (G-3), R-395-D; wool manufacturer's views cited in report, American consul general, Genoa, to State Dept, 16 June 1945, in NA,RG 59, S.D.865.00.

17. Tel. Kirk to State Dept, 28 June 1945, in NA,RG 59, S.D.865.00, Box C-761; (now published in R.Faenza and M.Fini, *Gli Americani in Italia* (Milan, 1978), 147–8.) The availability of such sums contrasts strikingly with the public pleas of bankruptcy, current in wage negotiations: see below Ch.12.

18. Charles's view and those of FO, in discussion Charles–Harvey (FO official), 8 July 1945 (in Rome), in PRO,FO 371, ZM/3802/3/22; AFHQ's views stated in report G-2 to G-3, 9 Oct. 1945, in NA,RG 331, AFHQ files (G-2), R-485-C.

19. Coles and Weinberg, *Civil Affairs*, 561.

20. On ignorance of Resistance forces on what to expect, cf. G.Franzini, 'La Resistenza reggiana e gli Alleati', in *La Resistenza in Emilia Romagna* (n.d.), 134–5; citation from *ibid.*, 140–1.

21. Giobbio, *op.cit.*, 6–9, 13, 25–6.

22. Cited in Patriots Branch, monthly report for Apr.1945, 21 June 1945; in NA, RG 331, 10000/125/257; this should be compared with the account in Bologna, Documenti del Comune, 'G.Dozza e l'amministrazione comunale della liberazione', esp. 40–1, 74–6. The Bolognesi, who were well aware that the division of powers between the CLN, the government and AMG was a political, not an administrative or juridical problem, preferred the Allied authority to be termed 'Allied military command', not 'Allied military government'; *ibid.*, 41.

23. VIIIth Army comment in Patriots Branch, monthly report, Apr. 1945, cited n.22 above; Veneto comments in *ibid.*, monthly report, June 1945, 13 Aug. 1945.

24. Cited in Patriots Branch, monthly report, May 1945, 11 July 1945, in *ibid*.

25. On prefect's problems, 'Aide-Memoire on Supply of Prefects and Prefectural Officials', 20 Apr. 1945, by AC, Civil Affairs section, in NA,RG 331, ACC files (Local Government subcommission), 10000/141/423; Bonomi's suggestion in letter

to Local Govt subcomm., 3 Jan. 1945; negative reply, 3 Mar. 1945 and note from Subcomm. to vice-president, Civil Affairs Section, n.d., suggesting that successive governments had often attempted to re-employ dismissed officials, all in *ibid*.

26. Instruction to RCs in letter Local Govt subcomm., 8 June 1945, comments also in subcomm. notes for conference with vice-president, Civil Affairs Section, 8 June 1945; both in *ibid*.

27. Apennine provincial governor cited is G.Lett, author of *Rossano. An Adventure of the Italian Resistance* (1955) (where the experience of provincial governorship is described in 203–17).

28. Prefects' conference cited in Giobbio, *op.cit.*, 6; party leaders' meeting discussed in E.Piscitelli, *Da Parri a De Gasperi. Storia del dopoguerra, 1945–1948* (Milan, 1975), 53–4.

29. Two cases of AMG's sternness to the CLNs after the first weeks may be cited: a newspaper article insisting on the consultative role of the Committees earned the following rebuke for the president of the Piedmont CLN, Antonicelli:

    'I [must] direct your attention to the fact that no CLN has the slightest degree of executive or administrative authority . . . .. Any attempt at usurpation or other violation is contrary to Italian Law and orders and other instruments of AMG. It would be most unfortunate . . . if it should become necessary to take action against any persons for offences of the type described above.'

    (Letter Marshall, regional governor, to Antonicelli, 25 July 1945, in INML, Fondo CLNAI, Scat.49, f.1, sf.7.)

    In Genoa the Liguria CLN was told at the end of October that: 'In this region the CLN has been more influential than in any other. All your activity is intended for the public good but it is better that things pass completely now to the normal organs, the Prefettura, etc. [sic], without your advice or interference.' ACS Genoa, Fondo CLN Ligure, document attached to minutes of meeting 24 Oct. 1945; published in D.W.Ellwood, 'L'occupazione alleata e la restaurazione istituzionale: il problema delle Regioni', in M.Legnani (ed.), *Regioni e stato dalla Resistenza alla costituzione*, 30. Epitaph by writer in *Corriere d'informazione*, 5 June 1945, cited in Giobbio, *op.cit.*, 26.

30. Harris, *Allied Administration*, 352, 357.

31. Coles and Weinberg, *Civil Affairs*, 585.

32. P.Secchia, 'Il Partito comunista italiano e la guerra di liberazione', *Annali dell'Istituto Giangiacomo Feltrinelli* (Milan, 1971), xxxii. It is worth noting that G.Quazza, a prominent Resistance figure familiar with the same experiences, areas and problems as Secchia, argues in a recent survey that the Resistance organs did possess a significant measure of power (*Resistenza e storia d'Italia* (Milan, 1976), 331), though it seems clear that the experiences referred to were those of autonomous sections of the population, in diverse areas, not that of the CLN structure exclusively and as a whole. The exceptional tension between possibilities and circumstances which characterized this moment has been brought out by F.Claudin, *La crisi del movimento comunista dal Comintern al Cominform* (Milan, 1974), 274–95, 349–50, and by E.J.Hobsbawm, 'Revolution', paper delivered at the XIV International Congress of Historical Sciences (San Francisco, 1975), 18.

33. Tel. AC to VIIIth Army HQ, 5 May 1945, in NA,RG 331, 10000/136/120.

34. This account based on F.Catalano, 'The rebirth of the party system', in S.J.Woolf (ed.), *The Rebirth of Italy, 1945–50* (1972), 57–68; cf. E.Piscitelli, *op.cit.*, n.28 above, 15–60; E.Santarelli, 'Quadro e trasformazione dei partiti', in *L'Italia dalla liberazione alla Repubblica* (Florence, Mar. 1976), 240–9; Quazza, *op.cit.*, 299–316.

35. Catalano, *op.cit.*, 63; M.Djilas, *Wartime* (1977), 409; De Gasperi described in L.Valiani, *L'avvento de De Gasperi* (Turin, 1949), 23–4; on the evolution of the crisis,

E.Piscitelli, *op.cit.*, 31–40; for Togliatti's position, G.Carocci, *Storia d'Italia dall'unità ad oggi* (Milan, 1982), 326–9.

36. Giobbio, *op.cit.*, 21.
37. Discussion of 2 June meeting in Piscitelli, *op.cit.*, 53; report by Central 'D' Section, PWB, 5 July 1945, in NA,RG 59, S.D.865.00.
38. Giobbio's comments in article cited n.5 above, 31; on the economic aspect of the identification between sections of the traditional political class and the State, see C.Daneo, *La politica economica della ricostruzione 1945–49* (Turin,1975), 65–6; FO views in comments on tel. Charles to FO, 24 May 1945, in PRO,FO 371, ZM/2984/3/22, and comments on tel. Charles to FO, 1 Oct. 1945, in ZM/5051/1/22; in the local context AMG's attitude to the CLNs had obvious political implications; a Genoa observer noted that AMG's 'firm policy' to the CLN was 'quite obviously causing the Communists considerable inconvenience, to the open delight of right-wing Christian Democrats and Liberals', report of 9 Nov. 1945 in ZM/5892/3/22; the Communists were hardly surprised, having repeatedly noted and complained of the preference of the Allied missions for the 'autononous' forces which looked to the army or to Badoglio's image, cf. Amendola, 'La lezione dei CLN', *Rinascita*, 24 Apr. 1965.
39. There were constant reports of imminent Communist insurrection in the months before and after the liberation, most directed from official or semi-official Italian sources to the Allied authorities; e.g. 'Communist Activities Report' by Information Office of Joint Committee of Anti-Fascist and Anti-Communist Parties, 7 Jan. 1945, in NA,RG 331, AFHQ G-2 files, R-485-C; letter AFHQ liaison officer, Italian army intelligence to AFHQ, G-2, 16 Sept. 1945, in *ibid.*, (quoting It. Army source); letter Questore of Rome to (Rome area Allied Command presumed) liaison officer, 27 Nov. 1945, in *ibid.* While Special Force felt that the PCI's takeover would happen in the long term, rather than by an immediate insurrection ('Communism in Italy', pre-liberation, in *ibid.*), leading AC figures believed it would occur on Allied withdrawal, probably with violence (memo. Lush *et al.* to Stone, 30 May 1945, in NA,RG 331, 10000/136/256). A classic discussion of Communist strategy in this period, emphasizing the lack of hegemony of any one force over the others in the political struggle is contained in G.Carocci, 'Togliatti e la Resistenza', *Nuovi Argomenti*, n.53–4 (Nov. 1961–Feb. 1962), 123–51.
40. Cf. E.Ragionieri, in *Regioni e Stato dalla Resistenza alla Costituzione* (Bologna, 1975), 279–89; C.Pavone, 'Sulla continuità dello Stato, *Rivista di storea contemporanea*, 2 (1974), 189–92; G.Carocci, *op.cit.*, 145.
41. Relative importance of parties reported by Kirk to State Dept, tel. of 9 Jan. 1946, in NA,RG 59, S.D.865.00; state of Action Party described by Pavone, *op.cit.*, 186–7.
42. It was Macmillan's desire that the Actionists and Socialists should be in the government, instead of criticizing it from outside as under Bonomi's Second cabinet; *Blast of War*, 686.
43. Orlando's remarks recorded in tel. Kirk to State Dept, 18 June 1945, on formation of Parri government; FO observations in tel. FO to Washington embassy, 6 July 1945, in PRO,FO 371, ZM/3830/1/22; for discussions on local government reform, see above, Ch.7 n.39.
44. Tel. State Dept to Rome embassy, repeating message from Dulles in Bern, 20 June 1945; in NA,RG 59, S.D. 865.00.
45. *Christian Science Monitor*, 18 June 1945; *New York Times*, 18 June 1945.
46. *Manchester Guardian*, 19 June 1945.
47. Sereni cited in Giobbio, *op.cit.*, 21; Amendola, 'La lezione dei CLN', *Rinascita* 24 Apr. 1965; Foa's comment in 'La ricostruzione capitalistica nel secondo dopoguerra', *Rivista di storia contemporanea*, 4 (1973), 452; information on Consulta in

Giobbio, *op.cit.*, 23, n.49; Piscitelli comment in *op.cit.*, 65.
48. Memo. to Stone, 30 May 1945, cited in n.39 above.
49. Letter Alexander to Stone, 21 Aug. 1945, in NA,RG 331, AFHQ G-3 files, R-346–F.
50. This simplified account based on G. Valdevit, 'Gli Alleati e la Venezia Giulia, 1941–1945', *Italia contemporanea*, n.142 (1981), 76–88; G.Valdevit, 'Politici e militari alleati di fronte alla questione della Venezia Giulia (giugno 1945–luglio 1946)', *Qualestoria*, 3 (1981), 83–92; also Harris, *Allied Administration*(1977), 334–46; Coles and Weinberg, *Civil Affairs*, 592–607; M.Djilas's account in *Wartime* (1977), is not helpful on the question, saying simply, 'We were rather afraid of a conflict with the West', *op.cit.*, 442.

11   The end of Allied authority and the politics of stalemate, July–December 1945

1. Details of army, navy and air force contributions in Delzell, *Mussolini's Enemies*, 318–22, 360.
2. Report, 'Future Policy Towards Italy', 23 June 1945; in PRO,WO 204, file 86; excerpts also in Coles and Weinberg, *Civil Affairs*, 622–3.
3. Tel. Kirk to State Dept, 15 June 1945, in NA,RG 59, S.D.740; record of conversation Alexander–Sir O.Sargent, 2 July 1945; in PRO,FO 371, ZM/3710/1/22.
4. Notes on FO meeting with Macmillan (30 May 1945), and comments by Churchill (10 June 1945), in *ibid.*, ZM/3140/1/22 (also Woodward, *British Foreign Policy* III, 484).
5. FO draft minute, 'Policy Towards Italy', for Eden, 18 May 1945; in PRO,FO 371, ZM/2838/22.
6. Tel. Churchill to Halifax, 13 June 1945; in *ibid.*, ZM/3140/1/22. Macmillan's opinions are cited in notes on meeting FO–Macmillan, cited in n.4 above.
7. Memo on conversation Tarchiani–Phillips 30 May 1945 in FRUS (1945) IV, 1260–1. Observations by Collotti in 'Collocazione internazionale dell'Italia dall'armistizio alla premesse dell'alleanza atlantica (1943–1947)', in *L'Italia dalla Liberazione alla Republica* (Florence, Mar. 1976), 72.
8. Welles' comments in *New York Herald Tribune*, 6 June 1945; Lippmann and La Follette remarks cited in tels Washington embassy to FO, 4 June, 8 June 1945, in PRO,FO 371, ZM/3146/1/22.
9. Grew's memo. 18 June 1945 in FRUS (1945), *Potsdam*, i, 686–8; Byrnes plan in memo. for the president, 4 July 1945; in NA,RG 59, S.D.740.
10. Agreement to exclude Italy from San Francisco was expressed at a tripartite meeting at Yalta, 8 Feb. 1945, in FRUS, *The Conferences at Malta and Yalta* (Washington D.C., 1955), 774; this was confirmed in a letter Stettinius to Tarchiani, 7 Apr. 1945, in FRUS (1945), I, 206–7. Kirk's comments were expressed in a tel. Kirk to State Dept, 24 Feb. 1945; in FRUS (1945), I, 207, fn 37; State Dept intentions at end of April are recorded in a tel. acting secy of state to chairman, U.S. delegation, San Francisco, 30 Apr. 1945, in *ibid.*, 499.
11. Russian views (and their discovery) are discussed in an internal memo., W. European Office to Southern European Divn (State Dept), 25 July 1945; in NA,RG 59, Records of the Office of W.Eur.Affairs Relating to Italy; State Dept intentions to over-ride British protests are discussed in a note of 16 July 1945 in NA,RG 59, 'Top Secret Daily Staff Summary'.
12. Letter Carandini–Eden (with comments), 25 Apr. 1945, in PRO,FO 371, ZM/2400/1/22.
13. FRUS, *Conference of Berlin (Potsdam)*, II, 462.

14. Truman's statement in FRUS (*Potsdam*), II, 54 (full copy of document *ibid.*, 1080–1); cf. 'Proposal to Modify the Status of Italy', 14 June 1945, in NA,RG 59, S.D.740 . . . European War; first discussion of statement at 4th Plenary Session, 20 July 1945, in FRUS (*Potsdam*), II, 168–75 (Stalin's remarks cited p.169).

15. FRUS (*Potsdam*), 169–71 (emphasis added).

16. For Russian insistence on Romania, Bulgaria etc., FRUS (*Potsdam*), 327; for the question of percentages, FRUS (*Potsdam*), 361, 463; on the greater representativeness of the Rome government, FRUS (*Potsdam*), 326; Churchill's statement and the subsequent argument on rights of access in FRUS (*Potsdam*), 361–2.

17. FRUS (*Potsdam*), 364, 463–4.

18. *Ibid.*, 148–9, 155, 433, 464–5. Cf. memo., Pauley, head of the American delegation to the Allied Reparations Commission, to Truman, 18 July 1945, which emphasized that with estimates of Italy's needs in aid for winter 1945 ranging from $500m to $1 bn, there could be no question of adding to this bill by paying reparations. In FRUS (*Potsdam*), 1087–8.

19. FRUS (*Potsdam*), 228, 359, 462–4. The American delegation noted that the new representatives from Britain gave 'no very clear indication' of their attitude to Italy, FRUS (*Potsdam*), 1087.

20. The Soviet reparations proposal is recorded in FRUS (*Potsdam*), 1092; Stalin's remark to Churchill is on p.172.

21. FRUS (*Potsdam*), 465.

22. Molotov's complaints and replies of Byrnes and Eden in FRUS (*Potsdam*), 228–30, 245 fn 6.

23. Cf. L.Mee Jr, 'Meeting at Potsdam', xii–xiii; cf. the remark of Dulles: 'we are not negotiating peace with Italy, or Rumania or Germany. We are negotiating peace with the Soviet Union, Great Britain, France and the other United Nations.' cited in R.Opie, *The Search for Peace Settlements* (Washington D.C., 1951), 75–6.

24. Mee, *op.cit.*, 291, 296–7; 230 (for eclipse of British).

25. *Ibid.*, 129 (American desire for recognition of sphere of influence); for American views on British capabilities and intentions, FRUS, *The Conferences, op.cit.*, Briefing Book Paper, 'American Policy Toward Spheres of Influence', 103 ff.; FRUS (*Potsdam*), I, Briefing Book Paper, 'British Plan for a West European Bloc', 256–64; Davies quote in Mee, *op.cit.*, 36. Cf. G.Kolko, *The Politics of War* (New York, 1968), Ch.12; Woodward, *British Foreign Policy*, V, 181–98.

26. Tel. Kirk to State Dept, 31 July 1945, in NA,RG 59, S.D.740 . . . European War.

27. Tel. Kirk to State Dept, 15 July 1945; in NA,RG 59, S.D.740 . . . European War.

28. Stone's view reported in note of 13 Apr. 1945, in 'Top Secret Daily Staff Summary', NA,RG 59; Alexander's in note of 9 Aug. 1945, in *ibid.*

29. G.Valdevit, 'Politici e militari alleati di fronte alla questione della Venezia Giulia' (giugo 1945–luglio 1946)', *Qualestoria, 3* (1981), 92–108.

30. Notes of 4 July 1945 in 'Top Secret Daily Staff Summary', in NA,RG 59.

31. Memo. 'Political Situation in Italy', AFHQ G-2, 26 Aug. 1945, in NA,RG 218, JCS Files, CCAC Decimal File.

32. Reports of conversations with American and Italian officials, July 1945, in NA, RG 218, JCS Files, CCAC Decimal File.

33. Cf. D.W.Ellwood, 'La vittoria laburista inglese del 1945: l'impatto in Italia, visto da Torino', *Mezzsecolo, 2* (1976–7), 229–60.

34. Overseas Reconstruction Committee, meeting of 30 Aug. 1945, notes in PRO,FO 371, ZM/4588/1/22; Bevin's remarks to the Labour Party Conference of Oct. 1944 reported in P.Addison, *The Road to 1945* (1975), 254–5; chiefs of staff conclusions (28 Aug. 1945), in PRO,FO 371, ZM/4746/1/22.

35. Memo of 8 Aug. 1945, in NA,RG 59, SD 740 . . . It.

36. Gaddis, *The United States and the Cold War*, 265; FRUS (1945), II, 194–201.
37. Gaddis, *The United States and the Cold War*, 267; Opie, *op.cit.*, 79–80.
38. Gaddis, *The United States and the Cold War*, 280–1; cf.Mee, *op.cit.*, 291–4. For the central priorityof the re-establishment of Italy's formal status in De Gasperi's foreign policy of this period, cf. E.Di Nolfo, 'Problemi dela politica estera Italiana, 1943–50', *Storia e Politica*, XIV (Jan.–June 1975), 297–8.
39. 'General Staff Intelligence, Weekly Intelligence Summary', 28 Sept. 1945; in PRO-,FO 371, ZM/5212/3/22; PCI view in 'L'Italia a Londra', *Rinascita* (Sept.–Oct. 1945).
40. Notes of 43rd Meeting of ACI, 12 Oct. 1945, in PRO, WO 204, file 2164; Prunas remarks reported in tel.Charles to FO, 26 Sept. 1945, with FO comments, in PRO,FO 371, ZM/5565/1/22.
41. FO discussion of Charles tel. of 26 Sept. 1945, *ibid.*
42. FO comment, 12 Sept. 1945, on an American paper on procedure for Italian treaty at foreign ministers' meeting; in *ibid.*, U/7173/50/70.
43. FO discussion of draft civil affairs agreement, 8 Nov. 1945; in *ibid.* U/9098/50/70.
44. Gaddis, *The United States and the Cold War*, 273–6.
45. *Ibid.*, 274; cf. Mee, *op.cit.*, 294–7.
46. Sargent comments in minute on conversation Dunn (State Dept)–Campbell (Washington embassy), 5 Oct. 1945, in PRO,FO 371, U/8106/50/70; informal approach suggested in comments by FO on breakdown of foreign ministers' meeting, 29 Sept. 1945, in *ibid.*, ZM/5006/1/22; fear of American action on inter-Allied collaboration expressed in further comments on Dunn–Campbell conversation, as cited above.
47. The necessity for a supreme commander in relation to the enforcement of the peace treaty was discussed in a meeting of the Mediterranean Joint Planning Staff (AFHQ), 8 June 1945; in NA,RG 331, AFHQ,G-3, reel R-342-F; Alexander's view reported in a tel. Kirk to State Dept, 31 July 1945, in NA,RG 59, S.D.740.
48. Tel. Kirk to State Dept, 6 Aug. 1945, in NA,RG 59, S.D.740.
49. Tels between Kirk, Offie and State Dept, June 1945, in *ibid.*; cf. FRUS (*Potsdam*), II., 1100–3.
50. Tel. Kirk to State Dept, 5 Oct. 1945; in NA,RG 59, S.D.740.
51. Stone's remarks reported in tel. Kirk to State Dept, 20 Oct. 1945, in NA,RG 59, S.D.740 . . . It. State Dept's explanations in memo. of 30 Oct. 1945, in NA,RG 59, Records of the Office of W. Eur. Affairs Relating to Italy.
52. AFHQ/AC complaint (probably originating with the executive commissioner, Lush), in Coles and Weinberg, *Civil Affairs*, 624; Alexander's action described in tel. Kirk to State Dept, 22 Sept. 1945, in NA,RG 59, S.D.740.
53. Tel. Kirk to State Dept, 1 Nov. 1945, in NA,RG 59, S.D.740.
54. P.Gentile, cited in C.Daneo, *La politica economica della ricostruzione 1945–49* (Turin, 1975), 71–72.
55. Background in Harris, *Allied Administration*, 205; letter Bonomi to FO, 24 July 1944, in PRO,FO 371, R/12308/15/22 (which also contains Stone's viewpoint).
56. Macmillan–Kirk views reported in tel. to FO, 5 Aug. 1944, *ibid.*, Vatican and De Gasperi's observations in tel. Osborne to FO, 5 Oct. 1944, in FOGC,R/16051/691/22; the American chargé d'affaires in the Vatican, Tittman, reported shortly afterwards that in its alarm over the spread of Catholic republicanism, the Vatican was even disposed to instruct the faithful to vote for pro-Monarchist Liberals rather than republican Christian Democrats wherever possible (tel. to State Dept, 14 Dec. 1945 in NA,RG 59, S.D.865.00).
57. Churchill's remarks in *Closing the Ring* (1951), 115–16; Taylor's in memo. to president, 22 Jan. 1945, in NA,RG 59, S.D.865.00; cf. F.Di Nolfo, *Vaticano e Stati Uniti 1939–1952: dalle carte di Myron C.Taylor* (Milan, 1978), 411–14.

58. FO memo., 'Italy: The Institutional Question', 16 May 1945, with comments by Sir O.Sargent, in PRO,FO 371, ZM/2845/3/22.
59. Churchill's comments in tel. to Halifax, Washington, 13 June 1945, those of Macmillan in record of conversation in FO of 30 May 1945; both in PRO,FO 371, ZM/3140/1/22.
60. FO memo. cited in n.58 above; cf.Woodward, *British Foreign Policy*, III, 480–4; M.De Leonardis, 'La Gran Bretagna e la monarchia italiana (1945–1946)', *Storia contemporanea* (Feb. 1981), 109–29.
61. Stone's remark in conversation with De Gasperi, 11 Apr. 1945; summary in NA,RG 331, 10000/136/576.
62. Memos of 2 Sept, 30 Oct. 1945, in NA,RG 59, Records of the Office of W.European Affairs Relating to Italy, Box 3; cf. Coles and Weinberg, *Civil Affairs*, 632; Harris, *Allied Administration*, 383; J.E.Miller, 'The search for stability: An interpretation of American Policy in Italy, 1943–46', *Journal of Italian History*, n.3 (1978), 272–3.
63. Memo by American consul general Genoa, 10 Oct. 1945; in PRO,FO 371, ZM/5534/3/22.
64. For representative view of action of right in the crisis cf. State Dept memo. of 7 Dec. 1945, in NA,RG 59, Records of the Office of W. Eur. Affairs Relating to Italy, Box 3; on suspicions of Right-wing intentions with respect to the Constituent Assembly, tel. Charles to FO, 17 Nov. 1945, in PRO,FO 371, ZM/5720/3/22; also observations by Stone at meeting of ACI, 23 Nov. 1945, in PRO,WO 204, file 2164.
65. Conversation with Brosio reported in tel. Charles to FO, 10 Nov. 1945, in PRO,FO 371, ZM/5642/3/22; meeting 21 Nov. 1945 Italian embassy representative–Foreign Office mentioning Carandini's action in Rome in *ibid.*, ZM/5838/1/22; intervention discussed in FO minute in *ibid.*, ZM/5777/3/2. In the light of this evidence it is difficult to understand the assertion of H.Stuart Hughes that the Allied authorities encouraged the forces of the Right in their onslaught on the Parri administration, *The United States and Italy* (Cambridge, Mass., 1953), 139–40.
66. Tel. Winant to State Dept, 27 Nov. 1945, in NA,RG 59, S.D.865.00.
67. For effect of intervention on electoral issue, A.Gambino, *Storia del dopoguerra dalla Liberazione al potere DC* (Bari, 1975), 69–71, 132–8, for State Dept view and Kirk's comment, tel. Kirk to State Dept, 30 Nov. 1945; in NA,RG 59, S.D.865.00; cf. Miller, 'The Search . . .' *op.cit.*, 273.
68. On De Gasperi's views on composition of government, tel. Kirk to State Dept, 30 Nov. 1945, cited n.67 above; on situation in North according to military intelligence, tel. Kirk to State Dept, 19 Dec. 1945, in NA,RG 59, S.D.865.00 (an earlier military intelligence report forwarded by Kirk, 7 Dec. 1945, led the ambassador to note that information on underground neo-Fascism in the centre and South was 'of such nature as to prove beyond doubt that such organizations do actually exist'; in *ibid.*).
69. Report to meeting of 21 Dec. 1945, in PRO,WO 204, file 2164.
70. E.g. L.Valiani, *L'avvento di De Gasperi* (Turin, 1949), 33; Gambino, *op.cit.*, 80–6, 102–3.
71. Cited in F.Parri, *Scritti, 1915–75* (Milan, 1976), 199.
72. Conversation with De Gasperi reported in tel. Charles to FO, 28 Dec. 1945, in PRO,FO 371, 1052/50/70; this threat was embodied in the 'Uomo Qualunque' movements cf. S.Setta, *L'Uomo Qualunque. 1944–1948* (Bari, 1975).
73. Note of 4 Jan. 1946 in 'Top Secret Daily Staff Summary', in NA, RG 59.
74. Tel. Charles to FO, 28 Dec. 1945 and FO comments in PRO, FO 371, U/10451/50/70.
75. Tels Kirk to State Dept, 22 Feb. 1946, in NA,RG 59, S.D.865.00; the result of this appeal was continuing support for De Gasperi's efforts on behalf of the referendum, a successful effort which produced the popular decision for a republic in June 1946; cf. Miller, 'The Search . . .' *op.cit.*, 273–4.

12   The economics of liberation and the quest for stability

1. Letter Bonomi to Stone, 30 May 1945, in Coles and Weinberg, *Civil Affairs*, 525.
2. Memo. Lush *et al*. to Stone, 30 May 1945, in NA,RG 331, 10000/136/256; Macmillan's remark cited in Coles and Weinberg, *Civil Affairs*, 509.
3. Note by Keynes, 22 Mar. 1945, in PRO, Treasury Papers (T160)1380/18640/066/5.
4. Treasury remarks in letter to U.K.Treasury Delegation, Washington, 12 Feb. 1945, cited in Ch.6, n.26; reaction to request for credit expressed in FO comments on letter Treasury to FO, 28 May 1945, in PRO,FO 371, ZM/2998/7/22; meeting FO–Macmillan with comment by Churchill cited in Ch.11, n.4.
5. Hoover's advice cited in Gaddis, *The United States and the Cold War*, 237; discussion of economic policy in memo. for the president (by Joseph Grew), 18 June 1945, cited in Ch.11, n.9.
6. Cf. docs in Coles and Weinberg, *Civil Affairs*, 627–9 (Truman message of 2 July 1945 cited on p.628); John Harper emphasizes the bureaucratic confusion prevailing in Washington at this time of transition and its direct impact on Italian problems: Harper, 'The United States and the Italian Economy, 1945–1948'(PhD.thesis, John Hopkins University, Baltimore,Md., 1981), Ch.3.
7. Statement of McCloy to Subcommission of the Committee on Appropriations, House of Representatives, 15 June 1945, in Coles and Weinberg, *Civil Affairs*, 627–8; statement of Crowley before same committee 13–15 June in NA,RG 169, Box 1023.
8. Cited in memo. Grew for Truman, 18 June 1945, cited in n.5 above.
9. UNRRA, *Venti mesi con l'UNRRA per la ripresa industriale italiana* (Rome,1948), 29.
10. E.F.Penrose, *Economic Planning for the Peace* (Princeton, 1953), 161–2, 209–10; the position was further complicated by the fact that the U.S. supported UNRRA aid to Italy but not to the USSR in the 1945 conference, *ibid.*, 210 ff.
11. Penrose, *op.cit.*, Chs II, V, X–XII.
12. UNRRA, *op.cit.*, 156.
13. Coles and Weinberg, *Civil Affairs*, 575–6.
14. On the extent of destruction, De Cecco, 'Economic Policy in the Reconstruction Period', in S.J.Woolf (ed) *The Rebirth of Italy, 1943–50* (1972), 158; A.Graziani (ed), *L'economia italiana, 1945–1970* (Bologna, 1972), 15.
15. Meeting of CCE with Ruini, 21 May 1945; minutes in INML, Fondo Merzagora, Box 13, f.6.
16. Memo. Robertson to Macmillan, 12 Jan. 1945, in NA,RG 331, AFHQ files, R-316 A, Italian Industries; the Americans were intensely suspicious of this plan, Kirk seeing in it a British attempt to 'emasculate' Italian industry and eliminate a competitor; tel.Kirk to State Dept, 18 May 1945; in NA,RG 59, S.D.740.
17. Plan reproduced in Coles and Weinberg, *Civil Affairs*, 577.
18. Minutes of Milan assembly of 28 May 1945, in INML,Fondo Merzagora, Box 6, f.3; on the industrial situation in Piedmont, D.W.Ellwood, 'Ricostruzione, classe operaia e occupazione alleata in Piemonte 1943–1946', *Rivista di storia contemporanea*, 3 (1974), 289–325.
19. *Informazione industriale*, 22 Sept. 1945; the industrialists' petition is conserved in Istituto storico della Resistenza in Piemonte (ISRP), CLNRP papers, H 58 a.
20. A.Frank Southard, Jr, *The Finances of European Liberation* (New York, 1946), 187; Cleveland's conclusions in UNRRA, *op.cit.*, 65.
21. De Cecco, cited in n.14 above, 162–3; E.Piscitelli, *op.cit.*, pr.II, Ch.2; Harper, *op.cit.*, 142–60; A.Gambino, *Storia del dopoguerra dalla Liberazione al potere DC* (Bari, 1975), 129–39.

22. Inflation figure published in *L'Opinione*, Turin, 19 Dec. 1945; unemployment figure in CCE, mins of meeting of 24 Aug. 1945, in INML, Fondo Merzagora, Box 13, f.1; military intelligence report in memo. from G-2, AFHQ to G-2 Counter-Intelligence, 11 July 1945, in NA,RG 331, AFHQ files, R-485–C.

23. Harris, *Allied Administration*, 291–313; Coles and Weinberg, *Civil Affairs*, 575–8; D.W.Ellwood, 'Allied Occupation Policy in Italy, 1943–45' (PhD. thesis, University of Reading, 1977).

24. Ellwood, 'Ricostruzione, classe operaia . . .', *op.cit.*, 311–16.

25. FEA Intelligence Memo. (Italian Divn), n.63, 24 July 1945, in NA,RG 169.

26. 'Food and Politics in Liberated Countries', 19 June 1945, in PRO,WO 204, f.2164.

27. Cited in L.Lanzardo, *Classe operaia e Partito comunista alla FIAT, 1945–48* (Turin, 1971), 53, n.1.

28. Cf. Guido Quazza, *Resistenza e storia d'Italia* (Milan, 1976), 332–8.

29. Sereni, cited in *Ricostruire. Resoconto del Convegno economico del PCI, Roma 21–23 agosto, 1945*, 120; Quazza observation in Quazza, *op.cit.*, 360.

30. Cf.B.Salvati, 'The rebirth of Italian trade unionism 1943–1954', in Woolf, *op.cit.*, 342–6; P.Spriano, *Storia del Partito communista italiano* V *La Resistenza, Togliatti e il partito nuovo* (Turin,1975), 535–56.

31. Cf. L.Ganapini, 'Alle origini della normalizzazione: l'operato della Commissione centrale economica del Comitato di liberazione nazionale Alta Italia (primavera– autunno 1945)', in Ganapini (ed.) *La ricostruzione nella grande industria* (Bari, 1978), 17–81.

32. F.Parri, 'La politica economica del CLNAI, *Il Movimento di Liberazione in Italia*, 48 (July–Sept. 1957), 42–51; M.Legnani, 'Documenti sull'opera di governo del CLNAI: la nomina dei commissari', *Il Movimento di Liberazione in Italia,* n.74 (Jan.–Mar. 1964), 47–77; A.P. (A.Pizzoni), 'Documenti della Commissione economica del CLNAI', *Il Movimento di Liberazione in Italia*, n.49 (Oct.–Dec. 1957), 56–9. On results of visit to South, P.Secchia and F.Frassati, *La Resistenza e gli Alleati* (Milan, 1962), 356–7.

33. V.Castronovo, 'La storia economica', in *Storia d'Italia* IV (Turin, 1975), 349.

34. Summary of meeting in Coles and Weinberg, *Civil Affairs*, 567; Milanese instruction cited in F.Levi, P.Rugafiori and S.Vento, *Il triangolo industriale* (Milan, 1975), 131.

35. Quazza, *op.cit.*, 356–9; citation from G.Manacorda, *Il Socialismo nella storia d'Italia* (Bari, 1966), 787.

36. Memo. Braine to ACHQ, 21 May 1945, in Coles and Weinberg, *Civil Affairs*, 564–5; a CLNAI attempt to raise its own funds via a levy on industrial wages was quickly blocked under the decree suspending all CLNAI action; fears were of a separate tax system: minutes of meeting of SACMED's Economic Committee, 22 May 1945, in *ibid.*, 565.

37. G.Grassi and M.Legnani, 'Il governo dei CLN', in *Regioni e stato dalla Resistenza alla Costituzione* (ed. M.Legnani) (Bologna, 1975), 74–5, 80.

38. Merzagora quoted by M.Legnani in 'Documenti sull'opera . . . cited in n.32 above, 51; Communist reaction in Grassi and Legnani, 'Il Governo dei CLN', *op.cit.*, 80–1.

39. Levi, Rugafiori and Vento, *op.cit.*, 68.

40. For positive comments on CGIL, Labour subcommission final report, Mar. 1946, cited in Coles and Weinberg, *Civil Affairs*, 399; article by Piedmont Regional Labour officer, 'L'Informazione industriale', 24 Feb. 1946; FO observations in PRO,FO 371, ZM/4889/66/22. Space does not permit discussion here of British and American actions at various levels for the reconstruction of Italian trade unionism; these had in common their anti-Communism and the belief that trade unions should be strictly economic organizations separate from political parties, but otherwise were

competitive, the British in particular energetically attempting to 'persuade Italian labour to think and act along British lines' via the Labour subcommission of AC; detailed discussion in Ellwood, 'Allied Occupation Policy . . .', *op.cit.*, Ch.10.

41. PCI, 'Ricostruire . . .', cited in n.29; Pesenti's observation in mins of meeting of CCE of 10 Sept. 1945, in INML, Fondo Merzagora, Box 13, f.1; cf. C.Daneo, *La politica economica della ricostruzione, 1945–49* (Turin, 1975), 104; L.Barca, F.Botta, A.Zevi, *I comunisti e l'economia italiana 1944–1974, Antologia di scritti e documenti* (Bari, 1975), pt.1.
42. A.Pesenti, *Noi e gli Alleati* (Rome, 1944), 9.
43. 'Problemi della ricostruzione. Note introduttive al dibattito tenuto in lingua inglese per gli alleati a Palazzo Venezia il 19 dicembre, 1945', in A.Pesenti, *Ricostruire dalle rovine* (Rome, 1945), 138–49.
44. V.Foa, 'La ricostruzione capitalistica nel secondo dopoguerra', *Rivista di storia contemporanea 4* (1973), 445–6.
45. UNRRA, *op.cit.* in n.9 above, Chs 1,2.
46. Memo., Civil Affairs Division, War Dept on policy for Italy and AC (n.d., presumed Sept. 1945), and study by Stone on same, in NA,RG 331, 10000/136/69.
47. Kirk's plan in memo. of 5 Dec. 1945, and that of Cleveland (in letter to Kirk of 5 Nov. 1945) in NA,RG 331, 10000/136/69.
48. *New York Herald Tribune*, 4 Nov. 1945; Giannini's well-publicized visit had considerable political impact in favour of the right, cf.Harper, *op.cit.*, n.6 above, 140–1; in this area too there was considerable Anglo-American rivalry and suspicion, details in Ellwood, 'Allied Occupation Policy . . .' *op.cit.*, Ch.8.
49. Memo. for political Section, AC, from minister degli affari esteri, 8 Dec. 1944, in NA,RG 331, 10000/132/184.
50. *New York Herald Tribune*, 8 July 1945.
51. OSS Research and Analysis Branch, rept of 2 Feb. 1946, cited in R.Faenza and M.Fini, *Gli Americani in Italia* (Milan, 1978), 158.

Conclusions

1. *Manchester Guardian*, 2 Aug. 1945.
2. Cited in F.Parri, in *La Resistenza in Lombardia* (Milan, 1965), 227.
3. For British trade union strategy, Ch.12, n.40; for Cromer figure Ch.5, n.58.
4. *The Times*, 14 July 1945.

Bibliography

Archives and Manuscript Collections

BRITAIN

Public Record Office
  Board of Trade Papers
  Cabinet Papers (War Cabinet conclusions)
  'Churchill Papers'
  Foreign Office General Correspondence (FO 371)
  Private Secretary's Papers
  Treasury Papers
  War Office Papers (WO 204)
Imperial War Museum
  Papers of Lt Gen.Sir Noel Mason-Macfarlane

UNITED STATES

Dept of the Treasury
  Selected Papers, 1943–6
F. D. Roosevelt Library
  Map Room Files
  Official File
  President's Personal File
  President's Secretary's File
National Archives
  ACC Files (RG 331)
  AFHQ Files (RG 331)
  Commerce Dept Files (RG/285)
  Papers of the Foreign Economic Administration (RG 169)
  Office of Strategic Services Records (RG 226)
  State Department Records (RG 59)
  War Department Records (RG 165,RG 218)
  Records of the Office of War Information (RG 208)

ITALY

Archivio centrale dello Stato, Rome
  Presidenza del Consiglio Salerno – Brindisi
  Presidenza del Consiglio 1944–1945
  Comitato centrale della Liberazione nazionale
Archivio dello Stato, Genoa
  Fondo CLN Ligure

Istituto nazionale per la Storia del Movimento di Liberazione in Italia, Milan
  Fondo CLNAI
  Fondo CLN Lombardo
  Fondo Corpo Volontari della Libertà
  Fondo Merzagora
  Fondo a Prato
Istituto storico della Resistenza in Piemonte, Turin
  Fondo CLN Regionale Piemontese
  Fondo Comitato economico regionale piemontese
  Fondo 'Franchi'
  Fondo 'Glass e Cross'
Istituto storico della Resistenza in Toscana, Florence
  Fondo Berti
  Fondo Boniforti
  Fondo Comitato toscano di Liberazione nazionale
  Fondo Medici-Tornaquinci
  Fondo Mercuri
Unione industriale, Torino, Turin
  Archivio (selected papers)

Official Documents, Reports and Histories

Alexander, Field Marshal Sir Harold, 'The Allied armies in Italy from 3 September 1943 to 12 September 1944', Supplement to the *London Gazette* (12 June 1950), 2889

Allied Control Commission, *Review of the Allied Military Government and the Allied Control Commission in Italy* (Rome, 1945)

Allied Control Commission, *La politica e la legislazione scolastica in Italia, 1922–1943* (Milan, 1947)

Allied Control Commission, Presidenza del Consiglio and Istituto centrale di Statistica, *Censuses and Surveys for the National Reconstruction* (Rome, 1945)

American Federation of Labour, *Italian Labour Today* (Washington D.C., 1944)

Bologna, Ufficio stampa del Comune, *G.Dozza e l'amministrazione comunale della Liberazione* (Bologna, 1972)

Camera di Commercio, Sezione internazionale, *La Camera di commercio e l'attività della Sezione internazionale* (Rome, 1946)

Coles, H.L. and Weinberg, A.K., *Civil Affairs: Soldiers Become Governors*, a volume in the 'Special Studies' series of the official history, *The U.S. Army in World War II* (Washington D.C., 1964)

Comitato interministeriale per la Ricostruzione, *Lo sviluppo dell'economia italiana nel quadro della ricostruzione e della cooperazione europea* (Rome, 1952)

Comitato di Liberazione nazionale Alt Italia, *Unire per Costruire: Atti del 1° Congress del CLNAI, 31/8–1/9/1945* (Milan, 1945)

Confederazione generale italiana del Lavoro, *Un anno di trattative sindacali. Noti e documenti* (Rome, 1946)

——, *I Congressi della CGIL* (Rome, 1949)

——, *La CGIL dal Patto di Roma al congresso di Genova* (Rome, 1949, 1952)

Donnison, F.S.V., *Civil Affairs and Military Government: North-West Europe, 1944–1946* (1961)

——, *Civil Affairs and Military Government: Central Organisation and Planning* (1966)

Garland, A.N. and Smyth, H. McG., *Sicily and the Surrender of Italy*, a volume in the series, *The U.S. Army in World War II* (Washington D.C., 1965)

Goodrich, L. and Carroll, M.J. (eds), *Documents on American Foreign Policy*, V (Boston, 1944); VI (Boston, 1945); VII (Princeton, 1947)

Harris, C.R.S., *Allied Military Administration of Italy, 1943–1945* (1957)

Hilldring, John H., *American Policy in Occupied Areas* (Washington D.C., 1948)

Holborn, Hajo, *American Military Government, its Organization and Policies* (Washington D.C., 1947)

House of Commons Debates, 5th Series, Vols 392, 397

Istituto centrale di Statistica, *Annuario statistico italiano* (Rome, 1949)

——, *Compendo statistico italiano* (Rome, 1946)

Istituto storico della Resistenza in Toscana, *L'archivio di A. Medici-Tornaquinci*, ed. R. Manna (Florence, 1975)

Labour Party, *Annual Conference Reports, 1943–1946* (1946)

Medlicott, W.N., *The Economic Blockade* (1952, 1959)

Ministero degli Affari esteri, *Il Contributo italiano nella guerra contro la Germania* (Rome, 1946)

——, *Governo e diplomazia al servizio del popolo italiano* (Rome, 1948)

Ministero per la Costituente, Commissione per Studi attinenti alla Riorganizzazione dello Stato, *Relazione all'Assemblea costituente* (Rome, 1946)

——, Commissione economica dell'Assemblea constituente, *Rapporto della Commissione economica presentato all'Assemblea costituente* (Rome, 1946)

Ministry of Foreign Affairs of the U.S.S.R., *Correspondence Between the Chairman of the Council of Ministers of the U.S.S.R. and the Presidents of the U.S.A. and the Prime Ministers of Great Britain . . . 1941–1945* (Moscow, 1957)

Notter, Harley A., *Post-War Foreign Policy Preparations, 1939–1945* (Washington D.C., 1949)

Partito Comunista Italiano, *Trent'anni di vita e di lotte del PCI* (Rome, 1952)

——, *Problemi di Storia del PCI* (Rome, 1971)

——, *Politica comunista* (Rome, 1945)

Partito della Democrazia Cristiana, *Idee ricostrutive, 1943–67* (Naples, n.d.)

——, *Atti e documenti della Democrazia cristiana, 1943–59* (Rome, 1959)

Pogue, Forrest C., *The Supreme Command*, a volume in the series, *The U.S. Army in World War II* (Washington D.C., 1954)

Presidenza del Consiglio, Ufficio storico per la Guerra di Liberazione, *Atti del Comando generale Corpo Volontari della Libertà dalla sua costituzione all'Insurrezione nazionale, giugno 1944–aprile 1945* (Rome, 1946)

——, *Costituzione ed attività degli organi di potere democratico nelle zone liberate* (Rome, 1946)

Royal Institute of International Affairs, *The Realignment of Europe*, a volume in the series *Survey of International Affairs, 1939–1946* (1955)

——, *America, Britain and Russia: their Cooperation and Conflict*, ed. W.H. McNeill (1953)

UNRRA, *Venti mesi con l'UNRRA per la ripresa industriale italiana* (Rome, 1948)

——, *Survey of Italy's Economy* (Rome, 1947)

——, *Economic Recovery in the Countries Assisted by UNRRA* (Washington D.C., 1946)

U.S. Army, *Joint Army–Navy Manual of Military Government and Civil Affairs* (Washington D.C., 1942)

——, Office of the Chief of Military History, *Civil Affairs and Military Government in the Mediterranean Theater*, ed. R.W. Komer (Washington D.C., n.d.)

U.S. Embassy, Rome, *Economic Conditions in Italy, 1946* (Rome, 1947)

U.S. Information Service/FOA Mission in Italy, *Cooperazione economica Italia–Stati Uniti, 1944–54* (Rome, 1954)

U.S. Senate, Foreign Relations Committee, *A Decade of American Foreign Policy, Basic Documents 1941–1949* (Washington D.C., 1950)

U.S. State Department, *Bulletin of the State Department* (1943–6)

——, *Foreign Relations of the United States. 1945. The Conference at Berlin (Potsdam)* (Washington D.C., 1960)
——, *F.R.U.S. 1943. The Conferences at Cairo and Teheran* (Washington D.C., 1961)
——, *F.R.U.S. 1945. The Conferences at Malta and Yalta* (Washington D.C., 1955)
——, *F.R.U.S. The Conferences at Washington 1941–42 and Casablanca 1943* (Washington D.C., 1968)
——, *F.R.U.S. The Conferences at Washington and Quebec 1943* (Washington D.C., 1970)
——, *Making the Peace Treaties, 1941–47* (Washington D.C., 1947)
——, *The U.S. and Italy, 1936–46* (Washington D.C., 1946)
——, *The Axis in Defeat* (Washington D.C., 1945)
U.S. War Department, *Background of Our War* (Washington D.C., 1942)
The Vatican, *Actes et Documents du Saint Siège relatifs à la Deuxième guerre mondiale*, 7 (City of the Vatican, 1973)
Woodward, Sir Llewellyn, *British Foreign Policy in the Second World War* (1-vol. edn 1962; 5 vols, 1962, 1971, 1976)

Memoirs, Biographies, Diaries

NOTE: This section is arranged alphabetically under the names of persons who are the *subjects* of biographies, etc.

Acheson, Dean, *Present at the Creation. My Years in the State Department* (New York, 1969)
Alexander, Field Marshal Sir Harold, *The Alexander Memoirs*, ed. John North (1962)
Nicolson, Nigel, *The Life of Alexander of Tunis* (1973)
Badoglio, Maresciallo Pietro, *Italy in the Second World War* (Westport, Conn.1976; original edition, Milan 1946)
De Luna, Giovanni, *Badoglio. Un militare al potere* (Milan, 1974)
Beevor, J.G., *SOE. Recollections and Reflections* (1981)
Berio, A., *Missione segreta. Tangeri, agosto 1943* (Milan, 1947)
Bonomi, Ivanoe, *Diario di un anno* (Milan, 1947)
Bruce Lockhart, R.H. *Comes the Reckoning* (1947)
Butcher, Harry C., *My Three Years with Eisenhower* (1946)
Byrnes, James F., *Speaking Frankly* (New York, 1947)
Dilks, D. (ed.), *The Diaries of Sir Alexander Cadogan* (1971)
Castellano, G., *Come firmai l'armistizio di Cassabile* (Milan, 1945)
Churchill, Winston S., *The Second World War. Closing the Ring* (1951); *The Grand Alliance* (1950); *The Hinge of Fate* (1950); *Triumph and Tragedy* (1953)
Clark, Mark, *Calculated Risk* (New York, 1950)
Cox, Geoffrey, *The Road to Trieste* (1977; original edition 1947)
Croce, Benedetto, *Croce, the King and the Allies. Extracts from a Diary* (1950)
Davidson, Basil, *Special Operations Europe. Scenes from the Anti-Nazi War* (1980)
De Gasperi, Maria Romana, *De Gasperi scrive* (Brescia, 1974)
Dixon, Piers (ed.), *Double Diploma. The Life of Sir Pierson Dixon* (1968)
Djilas, Milovan, *Conversations with Stalin* (1962; Penguin edn. 1969); *Wartime* (1977)
Eden, Anthony (Earl of Avon), *The Eden Memoirs. The Reckoning* (1965)
Carlton, David, *Anthony Eden: a Biography* (1981)
Eisenhower, Dwight D., *Crusade in Europe* (New York, 1948)
Chandler, Albert D. et.al. (eds), *The Papers of Dwight David Eisenhower. The War Years* (Baltimore, 1970)
Farran, Roy, *Winged Dagger. Adventures on Special Service* (1948)
Grigg, P.J., *Prejudice and Judgment* (1948)
Hankey, the Right Hon.Lord, *Politics, Trials and Errors* (1949)

Harriman, W.A. and Abel, E., *Special Envoy to Churchill and Stalin, 1941–46* (New York, 1975)

Harvey, John (ed.), *The War Diaries of Oliver Harvey* (1978)

Hood, Stuart, *Pebbles from my Skull* (1963)

Hull, Cordell, *The Memoirs of Cordell Hull* (New York, 1948)

Pratt, Julius W., *The American Secretaries of State and their Diplomacy* XII, XIII, *Cordell Hull* (New York, 1964)

Lett, Gordon, *Rossano. An Adventure of the Italian Resistance* (1955)

Lewis, Norman, *Naples '44* (1978)

Macintosh, C. *From Cloak to Dagger. An SOE Agent in Italy* (1982)

Macmillan, Harold, *The Blast of War* (1967)

Sampson, Anthony, *Macmillan. A Study in Ambiguity* (1967)

Fisher, Nigel, *Harold Macmillan: a Biography* (New York, 1982)

Moorehead, Alan, *Eclipse* (1945); *The Villa Diana* (1951)

Butler, Ewan *'Mason-Mac': the Life of Lt Gen.Sir Noel Mason-Macfarlane* (1973)

Murphy, Robert, *Diplomat among the Warriors* (Garden City, N.Y., 1964)

Musmanno, Michael, *La guerra non l'ho voluta io* (Florence, 1947)

Nenni, Pietro, *Una battaglia vinta* (Rome, 1946); *Tempo di guerra fredda. Diari 1943–56* (Milan, 1981)

Newby, Eric, *Love and War in the Apennines* (1978; original edition 1971)

Nicolson, Harold, *Diaries, 1939–45* (1973)

Peniakoff, Vladimir, *Popski's Private Army* (1950)

Pesenti, Antonio, *La cattedra e il bugliolo* (Milan, 1972)

von Plehwe, F.K., *The End of an Alliance* (1972)

Salvadori, Massimo, *The Labour and the Wounds* (1958)

Sforza, Carlo, *L'Italia dal 1924 al 1944 quale io la vidi* (Rome, 1945)

Soleri, Marcello, *Memorie* (Turin, 1949)

Stimson, Henry L. and Bundy, McGeorge, *On Active Service in Peace and War* (New York, 1947)

Strong, Sir Kenneth, *Intelligence at the Top* (1968)

Swanberg, W.A., *Luce and his Empire* (New York, 1972)

Tarchiani, Alberto, *Dieci anni fra Roma e Washington* (Milan, 1955)

Di Nolfo, E., *Vaticano e Stati Uniti, 1939–1952: dalle carte di Myron C. Taylor* (Milan, 1978)

Tilman, H.W., *When Men and Mountains Meet* (1946)

Wilson, Henry Maitland, *Eight Years Overseas 1939–1947* (1950)

British Politics and Foreign Policy

NOTE: This and the following bibliographical sections contain indications of secondary sources used for the text. Headings do not therefore imply a complete survey of their respective fields.

Addison, Paul, *The Road to 1945* (1975)

Auty, Phyllis and Clogg, Richard, *British Policy Towards Wartime Resistance in Yugoslavia and Greece* (1975)

Barker, Elisabeth, *British Foreign Policy in South-East Europe in the Second World War* (1976)

Carr, E.H., 'Britain as a Mediterranean Power', Cust Foundation Lecture, University College, Nottingham (1937); *Conditions of Peace* (New York, 1943); *Nationalism and After* (1946)

Ellwood, D.W., 'Al tramonto dell'impero britannico: Italia e Balcani nella strategia inglese, 1942–1946', *Italia contemporanea*, 134 (1979) 73–91

Gibbs, Norman, 'Appeasement Revisited', Annual War Studies Lecture, Kings College,

University of London (1 May 1975)

Howard, Michael, *The Continental Commitment* (1972); 'Strategy and Politics in World War II: the British Case', paper delivered at the XIV International Congress of Historical Sciences, San Francisco (August 1975)

Iatrides, John O., *Revolt in Athens* (Princeton, 1972)

'L'Inghilterra e l'Italia nel "900"; Atti del convegno di Bagni di Lucca (Florence, 1972)

Middlemas, Keith, *The Diplomacy of Illusion. The British Government and Germany, 1937–1939* (1972)

Pelling, Henry, *Britain and the Second World War* (1970)

Pratt, Lawrence E., *East of Malta, West of Suez. Britain's Mediterranean Crisis, 1936–39* (1975)

Ross, Graham, 'Foreign Office attitudes to the Soviet Union, 1941–45', in W.Laqueur (ed.), *The Second World War. Essays in Military and Political History* (London and Beverley Hills, 1982)

Rothwell, V.H., *Britain and the Cold War, 1941–1947* (1982)

Stafford, David, *Britain and European Resistance, 1940–1945: A Survey of the Special Operations Executive with Documents* (1980)

Varsori, Antonio, 'Italy, Britain and the problem of a separate peace during the Second World War: 1940–1943', *J. Italian History*, 3 (1978), 455–91; 'Aspetti della politica inglese verso l'Italia (1940–1941)', *Nuova antologia*, 2147 (1983), 271–98

Woodhouse, C.M., *The Struggle for Greece 1941–1949* (1976)

Woolf, S.J., 'Inghilterra, Francia e Italia, settembre 1939–giugno 1940', *Rivista di storia contemporanea*, 4 (1972), 477–95

American Politics and Foreign Policy

Alperovitz, Gar, 'The United States, the Revolutions and the Cold War', in *Cold War Essays* (New York, 1970), 75–121

Aron, R., *The Imperial Republic* (1973)

Bean, L.H., 'Nationalities and 1944', *Public Opinion Q.* (1944), 368–75

Bogart, Leo, *Premises for Propaganda: the USIA's Operating Assumptions in the Cold War* (New York, 1976)

Bullitt, William C., 'The World from Rome', *Life* (4 Sept. 1944); cf. G. Salvemini, 'Mr. Bullitt's Romans', *New Republic* (2 Oct. 1944)

Diggins, J.P., *Mussolini and Fascism: the View from America* (Princeton, 1972)

Di Nolfo, E., 'The United States and Italian Communism 1942–1946: World War II to the Cold War', *J. Italian History*, 1 (1978) 74–94

Divine, Robert A., *Second Chance. The Triumph of Internationalism in America during World War II* (New York, 1967)

R. Faenza and M. Fini, *Gli americani in Italia* (Milan, 1978)

Gaddis, J.L., *The United States and the Origins of the Cold War, 1941–47* (New York, 1972)

Gardner, Lloyd C., *Architects of Illusion. Men and Ideas in American Foreign Policy, 1941–49* (Chicago, 1970)

Gerson, L.L. *The Hyphenate in Recent American Politics and Diplomacy* (Lawrence, Ka., 1964)

Harris Smith, R., *OSS: the Secret History of America's First Central Intelligence Agency* (New York, 1973)

Kolko, Gabriel, *The Politics of War* (New York, 1968)

Kolko G. and Kolko, J., *The Limits of American Power* (New York, 1972)

Kolodziej, E., *The Uncommon Defence and Congress* (Columbia, Ohio, 1966)

Krippendorff, E. (ed.) *The Role of the United States in the Reconstruction of Italy and West Germany, 1943–1949* (Berlin, 1981)

La Feber, Walter, *America, Russia and the Cold War* (New York, 1967)

Lippmann, Walter, *U.S. Foreign Policy: Shield of the Republic* (Boston, 1943); *U.S. War Aims* (Boston 1944)

May, Ernest, *'Lessons' of the Past. The Use and Misuse of History in American Foreign Policy* (New York, 1973)

Miller, J.E. 'The search for stability: an interpretation of American policy in Italy: 1943–46', *J. Italian History*, 3 (1978), 264–86

Morison, Samuel Eliot, *American Contributions to the Strategy of World War II* (1958) *Prefaces to Peace. A Symposium* (New York, 1943)

Range, Willard, *FDR's World Order* (Athens, Ga. 1959)

Reitzel, William *The Mediterranean. Its Role in American Foreign Policy* (New York, 1948)

Sherwood, Robert E., *The White House Papers of Harry L.Hopkins* (1949); *Roosevelt and Hopkins: an Intimate History* (New York, 1950)

Stettinius, Edward R., *Roosevelt and the Russians. The Yalta Conference* (New York, 1949)

Stuart, Graham H., *The Department of State: A History of its Organization, Procedure and Personnel* (New York, 1949)

Warner, Geoffrey, 'From Teheran to Yalta. Reflections on FDR's foreign policy', *International Affairs*, n.3 (1967), 530–6

Welles, Sumner, *The Time for Decision* (New York, 1944); *Where are we heading?* (New York, 1946)

Yergin, Daniel, *Shattered Peace* (Boston, 1977)

Italian Foreign Policy

'Adstans', *Alcide De Gasperi nella politica estera italiana, 1944–53* (Milan, 1953)

Bononate, L., 'L'Italia nel nuovo sistema internazionale, 1943–1948', *Comunità*, 170 (1973), 13–75

Collotti, E., 'Collocazione internazionale dell'Italia dall'armistizio alle premesse dell'alleanza atlantica (1943–1947)', in 'L'Italia dalla liberazione alla repubblica', Atti del convegno di Firenze, 1976.

Di Nolfo, E., 'Problemi della politica estera italiana, 1943–1950', *Storia e politica*, (Jan.–June 1975), 295–317; 'Stati Uniti e Italia tra la seconda guerra mondiale e il sorgere della guerra fredda', in *Atti del I Congresso Internazionale di Storia Americana* (Genoa, 1976), 123–35

Lanza D'Ajeta, B., 'Relazione sulla missione a Lisbona, agosto 1943', *Rivista di Studi Politici Internazionali* (July 1946–Oct. 1947), 581–8

Luciolli, M., *Palazzo Chigi: anni roventi* (Milan, 1976)

Merlini, C., 'Italy in the European Community and the Atlantic Alliance', *The World Today* (April 1975), 160–6

Migone, G.G., *Problemi di storia nei rapporti tra l'Italia e Stati Uniti* (Turin, 1971)

Mondolfo, Ugo Guido, 'L'Italia e le potenze vincitrici', *Critica Sociale*, 2 (1945), 17–23

Parri, Ferruccio, 'L'armistizio, gli Alleati e il governo Badoglio', *Il Movimento di Liberazione in Italia*, 54 (1959), 64–75; 55 (1959), 41–57; 56 (1959), 22–51; 58 (1960), 24–41

Pinzani, Carlo, 'L'8 settembre 1943: elementi e ipotesti per un giudizio storico', *Studi Storici*, 2 (1972), 289–337

Salvemini, Gaetano, 'P. Badoglio's role in the Second World War', *J. Modern History*, 4 (1949), 326–32.

Treves, Paolo, *Sul fronte e dietro il fronte italiano* (Rome, 1945)

Visconti-Venosta, G., 'La politica estera della liberazione nel 1944–1945', *Il Movimento di Liberazione in Italia*, 48 (1957), 52–7.

Wollenberg, L.J., *Tra Washington e Roma. Sguardi e giudizi americani sull'Italia* (Rome, 1959)

Zangrandi, Ruggero, *L'Italia tradita: 8 settembre, 1943* (Rome, 1971)
Zanussi, Giacomo, *Guerra e catastrofe d'Italia, II* (Rome, 1945)

Inter-Allied Politics and Diplomacy

Aga-Rossi, Elena, 'La politica degli Alleati verso l'Italia nel 1943', *Storia contemporanea, 4* (1972), 847–95
Aga-Rossi, Elena and Smith, Bradley F., *Operation Sunrise. The Secret Surrender* (New York, 1979)
Anderson, T.H., *The United States, Great Britain and the Cold War, 1944–1947* (Columbia, Mo., 1981)
Armstrong, A., *Unconditional Surrender. The Impact of the Casablanca Policy upon World War II* (New Brunswick, 1961)
Baldwin, Hanson W., *Great Mistakes of the War* (1950)
Balfour, M., 'Another look at unconditional surrender', *International Affairs* (October 1970), 719–36
Battaglia, Robert, *La Seconda guerra mondiale; problemi e nodi cruciali* (Rome, 1966)
Buchan, Alastair, *The End of the Postwar Era* (1974)
Calvocoressi, P. and Wint, G., *Total War. Causes and Courses of the Second World War* (1972)
Cianfarra, Camilla, *The Vatican and the War* (New York, 1945)
Clemens, D.S., *Yalta* (New York, 1970)
Comité internationale de l'Histoire de la Deuxième guerre mondiale, *La guerre en Méditerranée: actes du colloque internationale tenue à Paris du 8 au 11 avril, 1969* (Paris, CNRS, 1971)
Danan, Y-M., *La vie politique à Alger de 1940 à 1944* (Paris, 1963)
Deborin, G., *The Second World War* (Moscow, n.d.)
De Santis, H., 'In search of Yugoslavia: Anglo-American policy and policy-making 1943–45', in W.Laqueur (ed.), *The Second World War. Essays in Military and Political History* (1982)
Di Nolfo, E., 'L'Operazione "Sunrise", spunti de documenti', *Storia e politica, 3* (1975), 345–76; 4 (1975), 501–22
Dulles, Allen, *The Secret Surrender* (1967)
Feis, Herbert, *Churchill, Roosevelt, Stalin: the War they Fought and the Peace they Sought* (Princeton, 1957); *Between War and Peace: the Potsdam Conference* (Princeton, 1960); *From Trust to Terror: the Onset of the Cold War, 1945–1950* (New York, 1970)
Higgins, Trumbull, *Soft Underbelly* (1968)
Holborn, Louise (ed.) *War and Peace Aims of the United Nations* (Washington D.C., 1948)
Howard, Michael, *The Mediterranean Strategy in World War II* (1968)
Hughes, H.Stuart, *The United States and Italy* (Cambridge, Mass., 1953)
Israelian, V., *Die antihitler koalition* (Frankfurt-am-Main, 1975)
Kecskemeti, P., *Strategic Surrender: The Politics of Victory and Defeat* (Stanford, 1958)
King, F.P., *The New Internationalism. Allied Policy and the European Peace* (1973)
Kogan, Norman, *Italy and the Allies* (Cambridge, Mass., 1956)
Kucklick, B., 'The genesis of the European Advisory Commission', *J. Contemporary History, 4* (1969), 189–201
Leigh, Michael, 'Is there a revisionist thesis on the Cold War?' *Political Science Q.* (March 1974), 101–16
Loewenheim, F.L., Langley, H.D. and Jonas, M. (eds), *Roosevelt and Churchill: their Secret Wartime Correspondence* (New York, 1975)
Mastny, Vojtech, 'The Cassandra in the Foreign Commissariat: Maxim Litvinov and the

Cold War', *Foreign Affairs*, **2** (1976), 366–76; *Russia's Road to the Cold War* (New York, 1979)

Matthews, Herbert L., *The Education of a Correspondent* (New York, 1946)

Mee, Charles L.Jr, *Meeting at Potsdam* (1975)

Nicholas H.G. (ed.), *Washington Despatches 1941–45* (Chicago, 1981)

Novak, Bogdan C., *Trieste 1941–54: the Ethnic, Political and Ideological Struggle* (Chicago, 1970)

O'Connor, R.G., *Diplomacy for Victory: FDR and Unconditional Surrender* (New York, 1971)

O'Neill, C.H. ('Strategicus'), *Foothold in Europe: the Campaigns in Sicily, Italy, the Far East and Russia between June 1943 and May 1944* (1945)

Opie, Redvers, *The Search for Peace Settlements* (Washington D.C., 1951)

Passerin d'Entrèves, E. (ed.), *Guerra e Resistenza nelle regioni alpine occidentali: 1940–1945* (Milan, 1980)

Pinzani, C., 'Yalta: la forza del mito', *Rinascita* (25 Apr. 1975)

Quinlan, A., 'The Italian armistice', in H. Stein (ed.), *American Civil-Military Decisions* (Birmingham, Ala, 1962)

Ragionieri, E., *Da Teheran a Yalta* (Rome, 1965); 'Il Mediterraneo nella Seconda guerra mondiale', *Studi storici*, **3** (1969), 653–9

Rhodes, A., *The Vatican in the Age of the Dictators 1922–45* (1973)

Spriano, P., 'I riferimenti internazionali della svolta'(di Salerno), *Rinascita* (29 Mar. 1974)

Toscano, Mario, 'Gli archivi militari americani e gli armistizi italiani del 1943' *Nuova antologia* (Jan. 1966), 28; 'Altre rivelazioni sull 'armistizio "lungo" di Malta e sulle dichiarazioni di cobelligeranza delle Nazioni Unite con l'Italia', *Nuova antologia* (Nov. 1964), 311; *Pagine di storia diplomatica contemporanea* (Milan, 1953); *Dal 25 luglio al 8 settembre* (Florence, 1966)

Varsori, A., '"Senior" o "Equal" Partner?', *Rivista di Studi Political Internazionali*, **2** (1978), 229–60

Warner, Geoffrey, 'Italy and the Powers 1943–49', in S.J.Woolf (ed.), *The Rebirth of Italy 1943–50* (1972)

Wheeler-Bennett, Sir J. and Nicholls, A., *The Semblance of Peace: the Political Settlement after the Second World War* (1972)

Wilmot, Chester, *The Struggle for Europe* (New York, 1952)

Military and Strategic History

Battaglia, R., 'Esame della condotta di guerra degli anglo-americani in Italia', *Rinascita* (Sept. 1952), 496–502

Berradi, P., 'Il contributo dell'Esercito italiano alla guerra delle Nazioni Unite', *Rivista militare*, 7 (1947), 741–55; 'Le conseguenze strategiche della diffidenza alleata verso l'Italia', *Rivista militare*, 8–9 (1947), 898–903

Chambre, R., *L'epopée français de l'Italie, 1944* (Paris, 1953)

Hammond, P., *Organising for Defence: the American Military Establishment in the Twentieth Century* (Princeton, 1961)

Hlen, L., 'Sicily, 1943. Post-invasion', *Army Quarterly and Defence Journal* (Oct.1979), 486–90

Jackson, W.G.F.,*The Battle for Italy* (New York, 1967)

Lyautey, P., *La campagne d'Italie, 1944* (Paris, 1945)

Macdonald, Charles B., *The Mighty Endeavour* (New York, 1969)

Matloff, M., *Strategic Planning for Coalition Warfare* (Washington D.C., 1959)

Orgill,Douglas, *The Gothic Line. The Autumn Campaign in Italy 1944* (1967)

Sheppard, G.A., *The Italian Campaign 1943–45* (New York, 1968)

Starr, C.G., *From Salerno to the Alps* (Washington D.C., 1948)

Trevelyan, Raleigh, *Rome 'Forty-Four: the Battle for the Eternal City* (New York, 1982)

Military Government – General

Collotti, Enzo, *L'amministrazione tedesca dell'Italia occupata* (Milan, 1963)

Dallin, Alex, *Deutsche Herrschaft in Russland, 1941–45: eine studie der Besatzungspolitik* (Dusseldorf, 1958)

Davis, Franklin, M.Jr, *Come as a Conqueror: the U.S. Army's Occupation of Germany, 1945–49* (New York, 1967)

Debasch, Odile, *L'occupation militaire: contribution à l'étude des pouvoirs reconnus aux forces armées hors de leur territoire nationale* (Aix-en-Provence, 1960)

Fainsod, Merle, 'Military government in Germany', *Public Administration Rev.* (1945), 397–9

Foulon, Charles, *Le pouvoir en province à la Liberation* (Paris, 1975)

Fraenkel, Ernst, *Military Government and the Rule of Law: Occupation Government in the Rhineland, 1918–23* (1944)

Friedmann, W., *Allied Military Government of Germany* (1947)

Friedrich, C.J. (ed.), *American Experiences in Military Government in World War II* (Washington D.C., 1948)

Gimbel, John, *The American Occupation of Germany* (Stanford, 1969)

Harris, J.P., 'The selection and training of civil affairs officers', *Public Opinion Q.* (winter 1943), 700

Holt, R.T. and van de Welde, R.W., *Strategic Psychological Operations and American Foreign Policy* (New York, 1960)

Huntington, Samuel P., *The Soldier and the State: the Theory and Politics of Civil-Military Relations* (Cambridge, Mass., 1957)

John Hopkins University, Research and Operations Office, *A Survey of the Experiences and Opinions of U.S. Military Government Officers in World War II* (Chevy Chase, Md, 1956)

Lewis,H.O., *New Constitutions in Occupied Germany* (Washington D.C., 1948)

Montgomery, John D., *Forced to be Free: the Artificial Revolution in Germany and Japan* (Chicago, 1957)

Motherwell, Hiram, 'Military occupation and then what?', *Harper's Mag.* (20 Oct. 1943)

Rennell, Lord, *British Military Administration in Africa, 1941–1947* (1948)

Military Government in Italy

Absalom, Roger, 'Il ruolo politico ed economico degli Alleati a Firenze (1944–1945)', in E. Rotelli (ed.), *La ricostruzione in Toscana dal CLN ai partiti* (Bologna, 1980); 'Contadini italiani ed ex-prigionieri alleati, 1943–45', *Italia contemporanea, 140* (1980), 105–22

Campbell, Ian, 'Some legal problems arising out of the establishment of Allied military courts in Italy', *International Law Q.* (Summer 1947), 192–206

Fisher, Thomas R., 'Allied Military Government in Italy', *Annals of the American Academy of Political and Social Sciences* (January 1950), 114–22

Galbreath, J., 'Allied policy in Italy, 1943–45', (Ph.D. thesis, Fletcher School of Law and Diplomacy, 1970)

Gayre, G.R., *Italy in Transition* (1946)

Greenlees, Ian, 'Radio Bari, 1943–44', in *Inghilterra e Italia nel '900. Atti del convegno di Bagni di Lucca, ottobre 1972* (Florence, 1973)

Haines, C.Grove, 'Italy's struggle for recovery', *Foreign Policy Reports* (1 Jan. 1944)

Hearst, J.A. Jr, 'The evolution of Allied Military Government policy in Italy' (Ph.D. thesis, Columbia University, 1960)

Kromer, R.W., 'The establishment of Allied control in Italy', *Military Affairs* (spring 1949), 20–8

Mercuri, Lamberto, 'La Sicilia e gli Alleati', *Storia contemporanea, 4* (1972), 897–968; 'Amministrazione alleata e vita politica nel "Regno del Sud"', *Rivisita trimestrale di Scienza Politica e dell'Amministrazione, 3* (1972), 49–88; *1943–45: gli Alleati e l'Italia* (Naples, 1975)

Neufeld, Maurice F., 'The failure of Allied Military Government in Italy', *Public Administration Rev.* (Apr. 1946), 137–47

Piccialuti Caprioli, M., *Radio Londra 1940–1945* (Rome, 1976)

'I rapporti con gli Alleati nel 1945 in un promemoria di Harold Macmillan', *Il Movimento di Liberazione in Italia, 50* (1958), 52–6

Italian Politics, The State and the Allies

Aga-Rossi, Elena, 'La situazione politica ed economica dell'Italia nel periodo 1944–45: i governi Bonomi', *Quaderni dell'Istituto romano per la Storia d'Italia dal Fascismo alla Resistenza, 2* (1971), 5–151

Amendola, Giorgio, *Il comunismo italiano nella seconda guerra mondiale* (Rome, 1963)

Andreotti, Giulio, *De Gasperi e il suo tempo* (Milan, 1964); *Concerto a sei voci* (Rome, 1945)

Bartlett, Vernon, 'After Darlan and Badoglio what now?', *News Chronicle* (27 Sept. 1943)

Bartoli, D. *La fine della monarchia* (Milan, 1956)

Bertoldi, S., *Vittorio Emanuele III* (Turin, 1970)

Bocca, Giorgio, *Palmiro Togliatti* (Bari, 1973)

Buonanno, C. and Valentini, O., *Gli atti del Congresso di Bari* (Bari, 1944)

Caracciolo, F. 'Il governo di Salerno', *Il Movimento di Liberazione, 7* (1950), 3–18

Chabod, Federico, *L'Italia contemporanea (1918–1948)* (Turin, 1961)

Claudin, Ferdinando, *La crisi del movimento comunista dal Comintern al Cominform* (Milan, 1974)

Cortesi, L., 'Lotta politica e continuità dello Stato nel 1943', *Movimento operaio e socialista, 4* (1969), 335–68

Deakin, F.W., *The Brutal Friendship. Mussolini, Hitler and the Fall of Italian Fascism* (New York, 1962)

De Leonardis, M., 'La Gran Bretagna e la monarchia italiana (1943–1946)', *Storia contemporanea* (Feb. 1981), 57–134

De Luna, Giovanni, *Storia del Partito d'Azione* (Milan, 1982)

Dieci anni dopo: 1945–55 (Bari, 1955)

Degli Espinosa, A, *Il Regno del Sud* (Rome, 1946)

Ellwood, David W., 'L'occupazione alleata e la restaurazione istituzionale: il problema delle Regioni', in M. Legnani (ed.), *Regioni e Stato dalla Resistenza alla Costituzione* (Bologna, 1975); 'La politica anglo-americana verso l'Italia, 1945: l'anno del trapasso del potere', in *L'Italia dalla Liberazione alla Repubblica*, atti del convegno di Firenze (1976); 'Washington 1943–45: Conflitti di potere e evoluzione dell'intervento americano in Italia', *Quaderni dell'Istituto storico della Resistenza in Modena e provincia, 10* (1976); 'Nuove fonte americane sull'Italia nella Seconda guerra mondiale', *Rassegna degli Archivi di Stato, 1* (1976), 115–30; 'Nuovi documenti sulla politica istituzionale degli Alleati in Italia', *Italia contemporanea, 119* (1975), 79–104; *L'alleato nemico. La politica dell'occupazione anglo-americano in Italia 1943–1946* (Milan, 1977); 'Allied occupation policy in Italy, 1943–45', Ph.D. thesis, University of Reading (1977)

Fried, Robert C., *Il Prefetto in Italia* (Milan, 1967)

Gallerano, N., 'L'influenza dell'amministrazione militare alleata sulla riorganizzazione dello Stato italiano (1943–45)', *Italia contemporanea*, **115** (1974), 4–22

Gambino, A., *Storia del dopoguerra dalla Liberazione al potere DC* (Bari, 1975)

Giarizzo, G., 'Sicilia politica 1943–45', *Archivio storico per la Sicilia orientale, 1–2* (1970), 9–136

Istituto nazionale per la Storia del Movimento di Liberazione in Italia, *L'Italia dei 45 giorni. Studi e documenti* (Milan, 1969); *Operai e contadini nella crisi italiana del 1943–44* (Milan, 1974)

La Torre, M., 'Prefetti e prefetture', *L'Amministrazione italiana*, **3** (1948), 311–17; *Cento anni di vita politica e amministrativa italiana*, **III** *1943–1948* (Florence, 1954)

Lizzadri, O., *Il regno di Badoglio* (Rome, 1963)

Lussu, Emilio, *Diplomazia clandestina* (Florence, 1956); *Sul Partito d'Azione e gli altri* (Milan, 1968); *La ricostruzione dello Stato* (Rome, 1944)

Lussu, Joyce, *Freedom Has No Frontier* (1969)

Manacorda, Gastone, *Il socialismo nella storia d'Italia* (Bari, 1966)

Matthews, H.L., 'Can Italy slay the Fascist dragon?' *New York Times Mag.* (1 Oct. 1944)

Miller, J.E. 'Carlo Sforza e l'evoluzione della politica americana verso l'Italia. 1940–1943', *Storia contemporanea, 4* (1976), 825–53

Murialdi, P., *La stampa italiana del dopoguerra* (Bari, 1973)

Nenni, P., 'The rebirth of Italy', *The Nation* (23 Sept. 1944)

Pallotta, G., *Il qualunquismo e l'avventura di Giuglielmo Giannini* (Milan, 1972)

Panzieri, R., 'L'alternativa socialista. Scritti scelti 1944–45', ed. S. Merli (Turin, 1982)

Parri, Ferruccio, 'Il congresso di Bari e il governo di Salerno', *Il Movimento di Liberazione in Italia, 67* (1962), 39–57; *Scritti 1915–1975* (Milan 1976)

Pavone, Claudio, 'Sulla continuità dello Stato', *Rivista di storia contemporanea*, **2** (1974), 172–205

Perona, Gianni, 'Ricerche archivistiche e studi sulle relazioni tra gli Alleati e l'Italia', *Italia contemporanea*, **142** (1981), 89–101

Piscitelli, E., *Da Parri a De Gasperi. Storia del dopoguerra, 1945–1948* (Milan, 1975)

Ragghianti, C.L., 'Croce contro Roosevelt', *Il Mondo* (2 June 1945)

Romita, G., *Dalla Monarchia alla Repubblica* (Pisa, 1959)

Rotelli, E., *L'avvento della Regione in Italia* (Milan, 1967)

Sala, T., 'I rapporti italo-jugoslavi dalla liberazione al trattato di pace. Una verifica locale: la situazione della provincia di Udine', in *L'Italia dalla Liberazione alla Repubblica*, atti del convegno di Firenze (1976)

Salvemini, Gaetano, 'L'Italia vista dall'America', ed. E.Tagliacozzo (Milan, 1969)

Scirocco,A., 'Napoli, 1943–45', *Nord e Sud, 146* (1972), 91–110

Scoppola,P., 'L'avvento di Gasperi', in *L'Italia dalla Liberazione alla Repubblica*, atti del convegno di Firenze (1976)

Setta, Sandro, *L'Uomo qualunque 1944–1948* (Bari, 1975)

Settembrini,D., *La Chiesa nella politica italiana* (Pisa, 1964)

Spriano,P., *Storia del Partito comunista italiano, V, La Resistenza, Togliatti e il partito nuovo* (Turin, 1975)

Sturzo, Don Luigi, *La mia battaglia da New York* (Milan, 1949); *L'Italia e l'ordine internazionale* (Rome, 1944)

Togliatti, Palmiro, *La politica di Salerno, aprile–dicembre, 1944* (Rome, 1969); *Per la salvezza del paese. Scritti e discorsi, 1941–45* (Turin, 1946)

Tupini, G., *Democratici cristiani. Cronache di dieci anni* (Milan, 1954)

Valiani, Leo, *L'avvento di De Gasperi* (Turin, 1949); *Tutte le strade conducono a Roma* (Florence, 1947); *Dall'antifascismo alla Resistenza* (Milan, 1960); 'The Italian crisis', *The Nation* (15 Dec. 1945)

Valdevit, Giampaolo, 'Gli alleati e la Venezia Giulia, 1941–1945', *Italia contemporanea, 142*

(1981), 55–88; 'Politici e militari alleati di fronte alla questione della Venezia Giulia (giugno 1945–luglio 1946), *Qualestoria, 3* (1981), 83–119

Varsori, A., *Gli alleati e l'emigrazione democratica antifascista (1940–1943)* (Florence, 1982)

Vlahovic, C., 'A Mosca nel 1943: prima formulazione del policentrismo', *Rinascita* (28 Aug. 1965)

Wiskemann,Elisabeth, 'Socialism and Communism in Italy', *Foreign Affairs, 24* (1946), 487–8

The Resistance and the Allies

Agnoletti, Enzo Enriques, 'La politica del CTLN', *Il Ponte, 1* (1945), 424–9

Amendola, Giorgio, 'La lezione dei CLN', *Rinascita* (24 Apr. 1965); 'L'avvento della Rupubblica', *Critica marxista, 2* (1966), 3–32; *Lettere a Milano* (Rome, 1974); Aspetti della Resistenza in Piemonte (Turin, 1977)

Basso, L. and Conti, L., 'Sul carattere nazionale e internazionale della Resistenza in Italia', *Il Movimento di Liberazione, 70* (1963), 27–50

Baudot, M., 'La Resistenza francese e gli Alleati', *Il Movimento di Liberazione in Italia, 64* (1961), 3–32

Bergonzini, L. (ed.), *La Resistenza in Emilia Romagna* (Bologna, 1976); 'Missioni OSS in Emilia Romagna' (unpublished MS, 1976)

Bolis, L., 'Resistenza italiana e Resistenza europea', *Il Movimento di Liberazione in Italia, 9* (1950), 32–9

Boltri, E., 'L'Unione sovietica e la Resistenza in Europa', *Il Movimento di Liberazione in Italia, 68* (1962), 5–41

Cadorna, Raffaele, *La Riscossa* (Milan, 1948)

Calamandrei, Piero 'La funzione rivoluzionaria dei CLN', *Il Ponte, 1* (1945), 138–40; *Uomini e città della Resistenza* (Bari, 1965)

Carocci,Giampiero, 'Togliatti e la Resistenza', *Nuovi argomenti, 53–4* (1961–2), 123–51

Catalano,F., 'La politica estera dei CLN', *La politica estera della Repubblica italiana* (Milan, 1967); 'Resistenza e Alleati nei primi mesi di vita del CLNAI', *Il Movimento di Liberazione in Italia, 33* (1954), 32–50; 'La missione del CLNAI al Sud', *Il Movimento di Liberazione in Italia, 36* (1955), 3–43; 'La situazione internazionale e l'antifascismo italiano fra il 1944 e l'inizio del 1945', *Il Movimento di Liberazione in Italia, 96* (1969), 3–52; *La storia del CLNAI* (Bari, 1956)

Codignola, C., *Lotta per la libertà* (1951)

Collotti, E., 'Solidarietà europea e prospettive di un nuovo ordine internazionale nel pensiero della Resistenza italiana', in *Annali della Facolta di Lettere e Filosofia dell'Università di Trieste*, II (1965–6), 15–51

'Il contributo della Resistenza italiana in un documento alleato: relazione sull'attività del No.1 Special Force', *Il Movimento di Liberazione in Italia, 3* (1949), 3–23; n.4 (1950), 3–24

'La crisi italiana del 1943 e gli inizii della Resistenza', Atti del convegno di studi sulla storia del movimento di Liberazione, *Il Movimento di Liberazione in Italia, 34–5* (1955)

Curiel, Eugenio, *Scritti 1935–45*, ed. F.Frassati (Rome, 1973)

Deakin, F.W., 'La Gran Bretagna e la Resistenza europea' *Il Movimento di Liberazione in Italia, 65* (1961)

Delle Piane, M., *Significato storico dei CLN* (Florence, 1946)

De Luna, G., 'Lotte operaie e Resistenza', *Rivista di storia contemporanea*, n.4 (1974), 504–34

Delzell, Charles F., *Mussolini's Enemies. The Italian Anti-Fascist Resistance* (Princeton, 1961)

'Documenti relativi all'attività politica e militare del rappresentante del Partito d'Azione nei suoi rapporti con gli Alleati', *Il Movimento di Liberazione in Italia*, 27 (1953), 3–26

Fascismo e antifascismo. Lezioni e testimonianze (1936–1948) (Milan, 1962)

Francovich, C., *La Resistenza a Firenze* (Florence, 1962)

Franzini, G., 'La Resistenza reggiana e gli Alleati', in *Aspetti e momenti della Resistenza reggiana*, Amministrazione provinciale di Reggio Emilia (eds), n.d.

Gallante Garrone, Carlo, 'Vita, morte e miracoli di un Prefetto politico', *Il Ponte*, 2 (1946), 861–76

Giobbio, A., 'Milano all'indomani della Liberazione', *Il Movimento di Liberazione in Italia*, 69 (1962), 14–26

Italia e Gran Bretagna nella Lotta di Liberazione, atti del convegno di Bagni di Lucca, 1975 (Florence, 1977)

Longo, Luigi, *Sulla via dell'insurrezione nazionale* (Rome, 1971)

Lussu, Emilio, *Diplomazia clandestina* (Florence, 1956)

Lussu, Joyce, *Fronti e frontiere* (Bergamo, 1945)

Michel, Henri, *The Shadow War. Resistance in Europe 1939–1945* (1972)

'Maurizio' (Ferruccio Parri), 'Il movimento di liberazione e gli Alleati', *Il Movimento di Liberazione in Italia*, 1 (1949), 7–26

Momenti cruciali della politica della Resistenza nel 1944, atti del III° convegno di studi sulla storia del movimento di liberazione, 1958, *Il Movimento di Liberazione in Italia*, 52–3 (1958)

Pajetta, Giancarlo, *Lezioni sull'antifascismo* (Bari, 1962)

Parri, Ferruccio, 'La mancata resistenza nel sud (da Pescara alla Guerra fredda)', *Astrolabio* (1 Jan. 1973)

Perona, Gianni, 'Torino fra Atene e Varsavi', *Mezzosecolo*, 1 (1976), 349–424; 'Le forze economiche e sociali della Resistenza e l'intervento alleato: la preparazione del dopoguerra', unpublished paper read to conference on *L'Italia dalla Liberazione alla Repubblica* (Florence, 1976)

Il Ponte, special number (Sept. 1954), on 'La battaglia di Firenze'

'Il proclama Alexander e l'atteggiamento della Resistenza all'inizio dell'inverno, 1944–45', *Il Movimento di Liberazione in Italia*, 26 (1953), 25–50

Quazza, Guido, *La Resistenza italiana. Appunti e documenti* (Turin, 1966); *Resistenza e storia d'Italia* (Milan, 1976); (ed.), *Fascismo e società italiana* (Turin, 1973)

Quazza, G., Valiani, L. and Volterra, E., *Il governo dei CLN* (Turin, 1966)

Ragghianti, C.L., *Il disegno della liberazione italiana* (Pisa, 1954)

Ragionieri, E., 'Il PCI nella Resistenza: la nascita del partito nuovo', *Studi storici*, n.1 (1969), 83–113; 'Le condizioni della vittoria', *Rinascita* (29 Mar. 1974)

La Resistenza europea e gli Alleati (Milan, 1962)

La Resistance européenne, 1939–45 (Paris, 1960)

Istituto storico della Resistenza in Toscana, *La Resistenza e gli Alleati in Toscana* (Florence, 1964)

'Resistenza e Governo italiano nella Missione Medici-Tornaquinci', *Il Movimento di Liberazione in Italia*, 24 (1953), 3–38

La Resistenza in Lombardia (Milan, 1965)

Salvati, Mariuccia, 'Il PSIUP nelle carte dell'archivio Basso', *Il Movimento di Liberazione in Italia*, 109 (1972), 61–88

Secchia, Pietro, *I comunisti e l'insurrezione 1943–45* (Rome, 1954); 'Il Partito comunista italiano e la guerra di liberazione', *Annali dell'Istituto Giangiacomo Feltrinelli* (Milan, 1971); *La Resistenza accusa, 1945–73* (Milan, 1973)

Secchia, P. and Frassati, F., *La Resistenza e gli Alleati* (Milan, 1962)

Sogno, Edgardo, *Guerra senza bandiera* (Milan, 1950)

Stafford, D.A.T., 'The detonator concept: British strategy, SOE and European Resistance after the fall of France', *J. of Contemporary History*, 2 (1975), 185–217

Stevens, John M., Vaccarino, Giorgio and Venturi, Franco, 'L'Inghilterra e la Resistenza italiana', *Il Movimento di Liberazione in Italia 80* (1965), 74–100; based on *Proceedings of a Conference on Britain and European Resistance, 1939–45*, St Antony's College, Oxford, 1962

Trabucchi, A., *I vinti hanno sempre torto* (Turin, 1947)

Treves, P., *Italy's Struggle for Liberation* (1944)

Valiani, L., Bianchi, G. and Ragionieri, E., *Azionisti, cattolici e comunisti nella Resistenza* (Milan, 1971)

Italian Economic History

'Alcuni documenti delle gerarchie di Salò sull'industria italiana e sulla classe industriale del Nord', *Il Movimento di Liberazione in Italia*, 11 (1951), 38–54

Amato, Giuliano, *Il governo dell'industria in Italia* (Milan, 1973)

Baffi, P., 'L'evoluzione monetaria in Italia', in *Studi sulla moneta* (Milan, 1965)

Bairati, P., *Vittorio Valletta* (Turin, 1983)

Barca, L., Botta, F. and Zevi, A., *I comunisti e l'economia italiana 1944–74. Antologia di scritti e documenti* (Bari, 1975)

Barucci, P., *et al.*, 'Saraceno e la politica economica del dopoguerra', *Nord e Sud* (Aug.– Sept. 1970), 43–74; 'La politica economica internazionale e le scelte di politica economica dell'Italia 1945–67', *Rassegna economica* (May–June 1973)

Battaglia, R., 'Un'aspetto inedito della crisi del 1943: l'atteggiamento di alcuni gruppi del capitale finanziario', *Il Movimento di Liberazione in Italia, 34–5* (1955), 29–36

Bertolino, A., *Economia di guerra* (Florence, 1946)

Cafagna, L., 'Note in margine alla "Ricostruzione"', *Giovane critica, 37* (1973), 1–12

Candeloro, G., *Il movimento sindacale in Italia* (Rome, 1950)

Castronovo, Valerio, 'La storia economica', in *Storia d'Italia, IV* (Turin, 1975); *Giovanni Agnelli* (Turin, 1971)

Catalano, F., *L'economia italiana di guerra, 1935–43* (Florence, 1969)

Corbino, Epicarmo, *Limiti e scelta nella ricostruzione economica* (Rome, 1946)

Daneo, C., *La politica economica della ricostruzione 1945–49* (Turin, 1975)

De Maria, G., *Problemi economici e sociali, del dopoguerra 1945–1950*, ed. T. Bagiotti (Milan, 1951)

D'Attorre, P.P. (ed.), *La ricostruzione in Emilia Romagna* (Parma, 1980)

Foa, Vittorio, 'La ricostruzione capitalistica nel secondo dopoguerra', *Rivista di storia contemporanea, 4* (1973), 433–55

Fossati, A., *Lavoro e produzione in Italia* (Turin, 1951)

Ganapini, L., 'I documenti della Commissione economica centrale del CLNAI. Per una ricostruzione della situazione industriale settembre 1943–aprile 1945', *Il Movimento di Liberazione in Italia, 101* (1970), 195–215; (ed.), *La ricostruzione nella grande industria* (Bari, 1978)

Gardini, T.L., *Towards the New Italy* (1943)

Gobbi, R., 'Note sulla Commissione di epurazione del CLNRP e sul caso Valletta', *Il Movimento di Liberazione in Italia*, n.89 (1967), 57–73

Graziani, A. (ed.), *L'economia italiana 1945–70* (Bologna, 1972)

Horowitz, Daniel L., *Storia del movimento sindacale in Italia* (Bologna, 1966)

Ilardi, M., 'Nuovi documenti sugli interventi tedeschi nell'industria italiana tra il 1943 e il 1945', *Il Movimento di Liberazione in Italia, 106* (1972), 77–92

Lanzardo, Liliana, *Classe operaia e partito comunista alla FIAT 1945–48* (Turin, 1971); 'I Consigli di gestione nella strategia della collaborazione' *Annali della Fondazione Giangiacomo Feltrinelli* (Milan, 1975), 325–65

Levi, F., 'Organizzazione del lavoro e classe operaia alla FIAT, 1945–1948', *Rivista di storia contemporanea*, 3 (1972), 324–40

Levi, R., 'L'azione economica e sociale del CLNAI', *Il Ponte*, 3 (1947), 994–1000

Manzocchi, Bruno, *Lineamenti di politica economica italiana 1945–1949* (Rome, 1960)

Merzagora, C., *I pavidi* (Milan, 1946)

Morandi, Rodolfo, *Democrazia diretta e ricostruzione capitalistica, 1946–1948* (Turin, 1960)

Mori, Giorgio, 'La storia dell'industria italiana contemporanea', in *Annali della Fondazione Giangiacomo Feltrinelli* (Milan, 1959)

Parri, Ferruccio, 'La politica economica del CLNAI', *Il Movimento di Liberazione in Italia, 48* (1957), 42–51

Salvati, Mariuccia, 'Stato e industria nella ricostruzione. Alle origini del potere democristiano (1944–1949) (Milan, 1982)

Saraceno, Pasquale, *Ricostruzione e pianificazione, 1943–48* (Bari, 1969)

Sarti, R., *Fascism and the Industrial Leadership in Italy 1919–1940* (Berkeley,1971)

Scoccimarro, M., *Il secondo dopoguerra* (Rome, 1956)

Tortoreto, E., 'Le condizioni economiche di Milano e la politica dei prezzi del CLNAI', *Rivista storica del socialismo, 3* (1958), 310–28

Tremelloni, R., 'Per una politica industriale dell'Italia', *Critica sociale, 3* (1945), 41; *Storia recente dell'industria italiana* (Milan, 1956)

Turone, S., *Storia del sindacato in Italia (1943–69)* (Bari, 1973)

Allied Industrial, Trade Union and Economic Policy

Aga-Rossi, E., *Il rapporto Stevenson. Documenti sull'economia italiana e sulle direttive della politica americana in Italia nel 1943–44* (Rome, 1979)

Allason, Barbara, *UNRRA–CASAS* (Rome, 1950)

Candilis, Wray O., *The Economy of Greece, 1944–1966* (New York, 1968)

Clarke, R., *Anglo-American Economic Collaboration in War and Peace 1942–1949* (1982)

De Marco, P., 'Il difficile esordio del governo militare e la politica sindacale degli Alleati a Napoli, 1943–1944', *Italia contemporanea, 136* (1979), 39–66

Di Paola, M.T., 'La politica del lavoro dell'amministrazione alleata in Sicilia', *Italia contemporanea, 127* (1977), 31–51

Einaudi, Luigi, *La guerra e l'unità europea* (Milan, 1953)

Ellwood, D.W., 'Ricostruzione, classe operaia e occupazione alleata in Piemonte 1943–1946', *Rivista di storia contemporanea, 3* (1974), 289–325

Foa, Bruno, *Monetary Reconstruction in Italy* (New York, 1949)

Grindrod, Muriel, *The Rebuilding of Italy: Politics and Economics 1945–55* (1955); *The New Italy: the Transition from War to Peace* (1947)

Harper, John L., 'American economic policy in Italy, 1945–49' (Ph.D. thesis, John Hopkins University, School of Advanced International Studies, Washington D.C., 1980)

Hickman, Warren L., *Genesis of the European Recovery Program: A Study on the Trend of American Economic Policies* (Geneva, 1949)

Kamarck, A.M., 'Allied financial policy in Italy' (Ph.D. thesis, Harvard University, 1951)

Kemmerer, D.L. and Beatty, T.E., *Allied Military Currency in Italy* (Washington D.C., 1944)

Lawther, Will, 'What I saw of Italy in process of liberation', *Daily Telegraph* (28 Sept. 1944)

Macartney, M.H.H., *The Rebuilding of Italy* (1945)

Maier, Charles S., 'The politics of productivity: foundations of American international economic policy after World War II', in Peter J. Katzenstein (ed.), *Between Power and Plenty: Foreign Economic Policies of Advanced Industrial States* (Madison, Wi., 1978)

Miller, J.E., 'The politics of relief: the Roosevelt administration and the reconstruction of Italy, 1943–44', *Prologue* (autumn 1981), 193–208

Milward, Alan S., *War, Economy and Society 1939–1945* (Berkeley, 1977)

Mowyer, J.E., 'An analysis of U.S. economic aid to Italy from 1943 to 1949' (Ph.D. thesis, University of Illinois at Urbana-Champaigne, 1951)

Norman, J., *Adlai Stevenson's Wartime Mission to Italy*, Pace University, New York (n.d.)

Penrose, E.F., *Economic Planning for the Peace* (Princeton, 1953)

Pesenti, A., *Noi e gli Alleati* (Rome, 1944); *Ricostruire dalle rovine* (Rome, 1945)

Petrov, Vladimir, *Money and Conquest: Allied Occupation Currencies in World War II* (Baltimore, 1967)

Radosh, Ronald, *American Labour and U.S. Foreign Policy* (New York, 1969)

Rugafiori, P., Levi, F., Vento, S., *Il triangolo industriale* (Milan, 1975)

Sampson, Anthony, *The Sovereign State: The Secret History of ITT* (1973)

Southard, Frank A. Jr, *The Finances of European Liberation* (New York, 1946)

Thomas Ivor Bulmer, *The Problem of Italy: An Economic Survey* (1946)

Wallace, Henry A. 'America's part in world reconstruction', *Public Administration Rev.* (winter 1943), 1–7

Woodbridge, G., *History of UNRRA* (New York, 1950)

Literary Sources

Brown, Harry, *A Walk in the Sun* (New York, 1944)

Burns, John Horn, *The Gallery* (New York, 1947)

De Filippo, Eduardo, *Napoli miliardario* (Naples, 1947)

Diggins, John P., 'The American writer, Fascism and the liberation of Italy', *American Q.* (winter 1966), 599–614

Fenoglio, Beppe, *Il partigiano Johnny* (Turin, 1968); *I venti-tre giorni della Città di Alba* (Turin, 1963)

Hayes, Alfred, *All Thy Conquests* (New York, 1946); *A Girl on the Via Flaminia* (New York, 1949)

Heller, Joseph, *Catch-22* (New York, 1961)

Hersey, John, *A Bell for Adano* (New York, 1944)

Levi, Carlo, *L'orologio* (Turin, 1963)

Linklater, Eric, *Private Angelo* (1946)

Malaparte, Curzio, *La pelle* (Milan, 1949)

Morante, Elsa, *History: a novel* (1980)

Paoluzzi, A., *La letteratura della Resistenza* (Rome, 1956)

Fig. 2 A.C. regional boundaries, after the Allied Commission Desk Diary of January 1945.

306

Fig. 3 The return of territory to the Italian Government, after C.R.S. Harris, *Allied Military Administration of Italy 1943–1945* (*History of the Second World War series*, HMSO, 1957).

YUGOSLAVIA

July 44
Ancona
Oct. 44
Feb. 44
ramo
Pescara
Aug. 44
July 44
Feb. 44
Bari
Brindisi
Otranto
Foggia
Taranto
Avezzano
Isernia
Benevento
Cassino
Potenza
ROME
Naples
Salerno
Castrovillari
July 44
Crotone
Nettuno
Dec. 45
Cosenza
Feb. 44
Catanzaro

N

Messina
Reggio

TYRRHENIAN SEA

Catania
Syracuse
Palermo
Enna
SICILY
Ragusa
Trapani
Agrigento

MEDITERRANEAN SEA

Dec. 45
PANTELLARIA
C. Bon

Fig. 4   Zones as of 16 January 1945, after the Allied Commission Desk Diary of January 1945.

Index